Homo Exploratoris

Is Humanity an Apprentice God?

Alex Shenderov

Copyright © 2022 by Alex Shenderov

All rights reserved.

No part of this book may be reproduced in any form or by any electronic or mechanical means, including information storage and retrieval systems, without written permission from the author, except for the use of brief quotations in a book review.

Nothing is perfect.
Stephen Hawking

No one can make you feel inferior without your consent.
Eleanor Roosevelt

All generalizations are false, including this one.
Mark Twain

…the human race has no future if it doesn't go to space.
Stephen Hawking

To us

Table of Contents

Acknowledgements vii
1 Introduction 1
2 Lay of the Land 19
    2.1 The most successful species on the planet...........................19
    2.2 What did Adam do for a living? 29
    2.3 Us and them 35
    2.4 The shrine of Buridan's ass 40
    2.5 Free will denial as an act of free will....................................48
    2.6 The Causality Delusion 56
    2.7 What else could it possibly have been? 83
    2.8 Our interconnected world 101
    2.9 Holistic science for a holistic world?..................................120
    2.10 Humanist hypothesis 144
3 Quo Vadis?..163
    3.1 Which way's tomorrow? 168
    3.2 Where is my time machine? 182
    3.3 Between a rock and a hard place 212
    3.4 Power to the people 228
4 Humanism: The Last Monotheistic Religion of *H. Sapiens*? 277
5 Afterword (and Preview of What's to Come).................................313
6 Bibliography...323

Acknowledgements

I am grateful for the many discussions with the friends, colleagues, and correspondents who shaped the views reflected in this book: Keith Lofstrom, Alexander Bolonkin, John Knapman, Anatoly Mayburd, Brian Hayes, Max Fomitchev-Zamilov, Paul Chefurka, Alexander Belousov, Eric Garza, and founders and members of the Facebook group Exploring the World of Yuval Harari: Heiner Bodden, Frank Rothkamm, Teodora Kamenova, Ane Galardi, Ida Tong, Rocio Navarro, Olga Sapunova, Joe Kingi, Hadiqa Sohail, Louis Mortimer, Antonio Dias, Anette Flm, Ma Al, Gerson Pinho, Stefano Muzi, Wisam Saleem, Mabvuto Zulu, Hussain Rumi, Per Ekström, and Tamas Simon, among many others.

I am indebted for the generous encouragement and practical advice of David Shenderov, Robert Zubrin, Larisa Rudelson, Steven Pinker, Olga Shenderova, David Ross, Marina Zhadovich, Isaac Arthur, and Eugene Shenderov.

This book owes much to the professional contributions of its editor, Jeremy Elvis Herman, as well as to artists Briana Tran and Sergio Botero. When appropriate, I have acknowledged image contributors in the image captions.

1 Introduction

In a Hollywood shootout, the good guys never miss. That's how you know they're the good guys.

In WWII, it took an average of 45,000 rounds of small-arms ammo to kill one enemy soldier. If we weren't such lousy shots, we'd have gone extinct many times over.

There's a very big difference between what you see and what you actually get. And most of that difference isn't fabricated in Hollywood. Most of it is fabricated by our own minds. Figure 1 below is a diagram called the "Cognitive Bias Codex" [1], a compilation of the 175+ ways we routinely get things wrong (and these are just the most common ones). If looking at that fails to teach one some humility, nothing ever will.

This book is the most important book you'll ever read, and it'll teach you The Ultimate Truth, which will guide you on the Right Path for the rest of your life and beyond. Just kidding. Someone ignorant and biased wrote this book: a human. At least half of this book is wrong, and it's up to you to figure out which half. No Almighty commanded me to tell you The Ultimate Truth. No Almighty told me what The Ultimate Truth was. There's no Ultimate Truth here (in my humble opinion, the whole concept of Ultimate Truth is the ultimate BS – no, not Bachelor of Science – but that's by the by). Instead, you'll find questionable suppositions and falsifiable hypotheses and poetic myths and majestic worldviews. We humans worked all of these out. Imperfect and biased and ignorant and awed and curious and proud and hopeful humans. It's a sign of hope more than anything else that we chose to call ourselves *Homo sapiens*, despite ample evidence to the contrary.

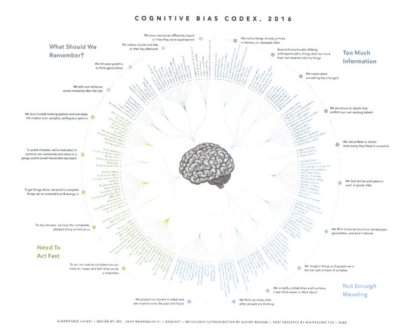

Figure 1 – *Cognitive biases. Image courtesy of Buster Benson.*

This, by the way, is as good a place as any to thank Yuval Noah Harari, the author of *Sapiens: A Brief History of Humankind*, for inspiring me to write this book. Harari once said, "Humans think in stories, and we try to make sense of the world by telling stories." This book is my attempt to do just that.

So, what's in a name? According to the ethereal embodiment of our collective wisdom (a.k.a. Google), our species' name, "*Homo sapiens*," means wise, or rational, or perceptive humans. The equivocation is significant. Modern Latin is an artificial construct, so no one knows what "sapiens" really means. It means different things to different people.

Come to think of it, most everything means different things to different people. Take the shortest word in English: "I." It has 7.9 billion meanings, and new ones are born every day. The connection between humans and meaning will be explored throughout this book.

Let's first try "wise humans." Yep, I hear your exasperated sigh, and I'm with you all the way. There are very few things science and religion agree on. One of them is that if you turn to humans for wisdom, you're looking in the wrong place. Religions place The Source of All Wisdom in the heavens, and the telescopes and antennae searching for intelligence are just as pointedly looking up and away from Earth and us earthlings. Our own media portray us as greedy locusts, driven by some brain-eating virus to destroy our home planet. No space alien unfortunate enough to catch our evening news broadcast would risk contracting such a horrible infection. When Italian-American physicist Enrico Fermi famously asked where the heck everyone (meaning aliens) was, he should have recalled a hint from the first-ever TV broadcast from planet Earth: the opening ceremony of the 1936 Berlin Olympics, with Adolf Hitler all over the screen.

That broadcast has been whooshing through the cosmos for eighty-five years, and there's nothing we can do to stop the damn thing from ruining our galactic reputation at the speed of light. The little green folks' first image of us was of Hitler, whose low opinion of most humans is by now known across 170 light-years of space. Anyone with a radio telescope and a computer within eighty-five light-years of Earth has seen one of the biggest monsters humanity ever produced. Fermi himself was an alien who wisely put as much distance between himself and fascists as he could. He might have expected any advanced civilization to be at least as sensible. The Fermi paradox isn't about alien civilizations. It's about our own civilization.

"Wise humans" would presumably know better than to mess up the only chance we'll ever get to make a good first impression. And the follow-up messages, chasing our first TV announcement across the Universe, would get you instantly fired from any advertising agency, too. Sir David Attenborough believes that we humans are a plague on Earth, and his message to that effect was broadcast far and wide. The venerable Club of Rome chimes in, saying that we aren't plague. We're a cancer. And in case somebody out there didn't get the message, Hollywood emphasized the point with the post-apocalyptic genre. The Church of Euthanasia joined the chorus, telling humans to "Save the Planet, Kill Yourself." And just so you don't think that such thoughts are the exclusive domain of marginalized extremists, here's Nobel Peace Prize winner Desmond Tutu: "As human beings we have the most extraordinary capacity for evil. We can perpetrate some of the most horrendous atrocities." And it's not just older folks either. A prominent youth movement sends the message that, "We are in the midst of a mass extinction of our own making."

They're talking about the only species we know that can understand a word of what they're saying, the only species we know that has developed a means to broadcast their message far and wide, the only species we know that has some concept of how far and wide "far and wide" really is. They're talking about their mothers, and they're talking about your mother, too.

No, these messages aren't addressed to little green men. They may be listening in by accident, but the folks certainly hearing that humans are bad-bad-bad are, like you and me, humans. And we hear it loud and clear. When asked to draw how they see the world fifty years from now, most kids in a test group aged six to twelve drew apocalyptic pictures [2]. Our parents grew up learning that they may be one of the last generations of humans to be restricted to just one planet; our children are growing up learning that they may be one of the last generations of humans, period. As young adults, they're understandably disinterested in having children of their own. Mass media keeps publishing materials that "scientifically prove" that having children is an environmental crime [3], and with click-o-meters measuring readers' responses every millisecond, they know very precisely what to publish to conform to their audience's views. So that one-of-the-last-generations thing may become a self-fulfilling prophecy.

Expectations—both high and low—are among the oldest self-fulfilling prophecies known to humanity. Just name identical twins Albert and Butthead, and see how their lives turn out. Amazon founder Jeff Bezos once remarked that the Solar system can support a trillion humans, which means that we'd have a thousand Mozarts and a thousand Einsteins. Investing in a thousand Mozarts and a thousand Einsteins is a decision wise humans might choose to make one day. If this book helps to move that day up, then writing it was worth the candle.

Let's try "rational humans" on for size. According to omniscient Google, such humans would behave "based on or in accordance with reason or logic." The trouble is that no one knows what the heck others base their actions on (often we don't quite know that even about our own actions). Sure, sometimes we can imagine reason or logic behind human behavior, but there's nothing rational about the belief that what we imagined was what someone else actually thought.

And I submit that it's not the rational that makes us what we are anyways. Anybody, or anything, can act in accordance with some reason or logic we the observers tend to ascribe to everything we see. And we're very good at noticing patterns (that we then use as proxies for "reasons" and "causes"). In fact, we're so good at finding patterns that we sometimes see them where there aren't any. The behavioral patterns of chimps, wolves, and ants are rich and complex and fun to watch. Slugs fight for food, defend themselves from predators, and have sex. Bacteria move toward food and away from poison. Viruses inject their genes into cells that make copies of viruses. Planets go about their business, sweeping around their stars, in accordance with some "reason" that they may be completely unaware of. So do slugs and wolves and even humans. There is, by definition, a reason for rational behavior, but you don't have to know that reason to behave according to it, and neither do bacteria or planets. Everyone and his brother can do rational. Rational ones are a dime a dozen.

But have you ever met a chimp that dreamed of building the Great Sphinx of Giza? Have you ever seen a wolf paint the *Mona Lisa*? Have you ever heard of an ant that, while gainfully employed by the Swiss Patent Bureau, conducted groundbreaking research on time and space, matter and energy in its spare time? Can you imagine a group of city-dwelling, water-drinking bacteria being persuaded by a particularly charismatic microbe to go into a deadly scorched desert for forty years in pursuit of some abstract concept he calls "freedom"? Or a bunch of viruses praying to an Almighty that none of them has seen? Or planets trading their valuables for pieces of green paper?

It's we the humans who do all these odd, irrational things. And most of the odd, irrational things that we do don't work out anywhere nearly as well as inventing money or the theory of relativity. When we act irrationally, we screw up most of the time. Yet, irrationally again, we keep trying.

All we have to guide us rationally is our past experience, which reliably fails us in any unfamiliar situation; yet it does teach us a very valuable lesson.

The lesson is, you can't succeed unless you try. To, say, a very successful ape some millions of years back, whose life in the jungle was damn near perfect, it may have seemed at the first glance that the rational thing to do was to keep things the way they were. So he hung where he was and didn't climb down that tree and didn't try to walk upright on his hind legs or grow an oversized brain, and he sneered at the oddballs that did. They would feed their energy-hungry brains for many generations without getting much evolutionary advantage in return, and their bipedal females would have a hard time giving birth, and a lot of them would fall prey to the big cats of the savanna. But oddballs' descendants—you and me—now visit the rational ape's descendants at a zoo. Then we leave to do some more oddball things, most of which turn out to be a complete waste of time. But a few are spectacularly successful. And the apes whose great-grandparents chose to go nowhere keep going nowhere. They stay behind. At the zoo.

It appears that the ability to occasionally make irrational, sometimes counterintuitive choices—outside of our experience, tradition, dogma, and shortsighted self-interest—is part of a distinctly human heritage. An important part. An endangered part. Our oddball, winning strategy may be becoming a victim of its own success.

Success gives you options. The trouble is that the more options you have, the harder it is to make a choice. The price you pay for choosing to do something is not doing everything else. It's called opportunity cost. The more options you have, the steeper the price of any choice. And the menu of really good, safe, easy-to-justify choices has grown so massive that it's ridiculous. Barry Schwartz, who did some serious research on the matter, reported that his local supermarket had 175 kinds of salad dressing[1] [4] Why bother painting the *Mona Lisa* or crossing an ocean or discovering DNA—and very possibly failing—when you can have a new salad dressing every day for half a year without leaving the block?

I hope that by the time you're done reading this book, you'll have your own answer to this question. I wouldn't have written it if I didn't have mine. And now I'll share with you the first secret of this book, which is how I found my answer: The Exercise.

The Exercise is really easy. All you have to do is to go out on a clear night and look up. I don't know what you'll see, but what I see when I look up is—literally—a universe of challenges and experiences and resources and opportunities.

And then close your eyes and imagine 175 kinds of salad dressing. Delivered to your door, preferably by a drone.

What you see with your eyes closed is the cost of known opportunities; what you see when you open your eyes is the cost of ignoring the whole universe of unknown opportunities. That's the cost of hubris.

The cost of hubris is incalculable. You don't know what you're missing, so you can't put a price on it. It can't be known in advance, not without a time machine. We can choose to take a leap of faith, or not. We can choose to believe that the unknown opportunities are better than the known ones, and then—if we and our entire lineage are lucky—folks settling the Milky Way galaxy in a distant future may be our descendants. Or we can make the easily justifiable, commonsense, rational choice of the bird in hand over two in the bush. Then—if we and our entire lineage are lucky—folks settling the Milky Way galaxy in a distant future may be visiting our descendants in some cosmic zoo. They may even bring 175 kinds of salad dressing.

---

[1] As far as I can tell, 175 salad dressings and 175 biases are just a coincidence. But if somebody can see a deeper pattern, please let me know.

What about "perceptive humans"? According to Google, those would be humans "having or showing sensitive insight." How the heck can I tell if somebody has or shows sensitive "insight"? Which, again according to omniscient Google, means "the capacity to gain an accurate and deep intuitive understanding of a person or thing?"

A reckless ape on the savanna with a wrong intuitive understanding of surrounding predators and resources gets eaten and leaves no offspring. A cowardly ape on the savanna with a wrong intuitive understanding of surrounding predators and resources doesn't forage enough, dies of hunger, and leaves no offspring. We're descendants of the ones who got it just right.

So are all living chimps, wolves, ants, slugs, bugs, and viruses. In evolutionary terms, surviving long enough to reproduce means understanding of everything and everyone that matters that is, for all intents and purposes that matter, deep enough and accurate enough. So chimps and wolves and ants and slugs and bacteria and even viruses qualify. Even computer viruses qualify. As for "intuitive," that means "using or based on what one feels to be true even without conscious reasoning; instinctive." Despite unrelenting efforts to misinterpret cute animal behavior as "conscious reasoning," chimps and wolves and ants and slugs and bugs and viruses don't appear to rely on conscious reasoning most of the time. Neither do we. Are we any different then?

I think we are. And it's not just because some humans occasionally paint a *Mona Lisa* or discover the theory of relativity. I think it's all of humanity—not just the geniuses—that's very different from chimps and wolves and ants and slugs and bugs. I submit that our collective perception of the world percolates through humanity and distills into such seemingly solitary achievements as the *Mona Lisa* and the theory of relativity. I think a strong argument can be made that without the folks who never get to paint a *Mona Lisa*, Da Vinci wouldn't have either. I actually make that argument later in the book, and you can judge for yourself if my version of this argument is convincing enough for you.

When it comes to perception, the difference between humans and chimps—and wolves and ants and slugs and bugs—is that we're a storytelling species, and they aren't. They all exchange information (yes, even viruses do), but our stories are much more than that. Ant colonies send out scouts, and the U.S. military has recently tested a swarm of reconnaissance drones to gather information from different points of view, but location is the only unique feature of a particular scout ant or drone. Replace one with another at the same point, and you'll get the same report. But two identical essays on *Romeo and Juliet* from two human students would land both students—and their parents—in the principal's office for a serious chewing-out. Ant, bee, or drone reports are efficient, precise, flat and lifeless. No military drone delivering a report on *War and Peace* would spend two whole pages describing an oak tree (unless that particular tree concealed an especially nasty military installation). Leo Tolstoy did.

Like all humans—but unlike ants or drones—Tolstoy had 175 cognitive biases, and probably many more. The biases are filters through which we see the world, and we all watch through different filter sets. We make value judgments about things that matter to us, and we make value judgments about their importance. Each individual human's perception of reality comes through those filters (a.k.a. biases). Anything I see is an interpretation, and it's almost guaranteed to be different from yours, even if we're watching the same sunset from the same beach. Sure, each of us has the whole filter set, but some biases are more pronounced in you than in me, and vice versa. And with hundreds of filters, you can get a lot of unique combinations when you look at the same oak tree. There are 7.9 billion unique sets of cognitive biases on planet Earth right now. Those filters are what make each of us a unique perceptive human.

But if each filter/bias is yet another way to get things wrong, then one has to wonder: How do we ever get anything "right" in some sense? And the answer apparently is that we do that together. We trade pieces of our worldviews as stories. We then vote on stories by giving them our attention, our money, or our actual votes (namely, elections). Or we vote by letting some stories influence our decisions and actions more than others. We give the champion of a story feedback, and the story evolves in his/her mind and in ours. In the process, we integrate our unique perceptions, and from perceptive humans evolves a wise(r) humanity. We reason together, and we're much better at it than even the smartest of us are at reasoning alone. Reasoning together is as close to being rational humans as we're ever likely to get.

And here's another uniquely human thing: we get the Human Itch, which is a completely irrational dissatisfaction with the status quo. Sure, a hungry, thirsty parasite-infested animal may be very dissatisfied (I would be too), but there's nothing irrational about it. Any robot programmed for self-diagnostics would also assess such a situation as unsatisfactory. Humans, on the other hand, get dissatisfied with a world without the Sphinx, the *Mona Lisa*, the theory of relativity, or Moon expeditions. These are imaginary deficiencies that any rational ant or ape would laugh at, if they knew what the heck we were talking about. But a world without the Sphinx, the *Mona Lisa*, the theory of relativity, or Moon expeditions doesn't make sense to us. The Human Itch is the powerful hunger for the world to make sense—and when it doesn't, we make sense of it ourselves. We change it.

Like bubbles on crests of waves, the Human Itch keeps popping up here and there in our minds. Like bubbles on the crests of waves, most are very short lived. The only way some of them survive is by interaction with the outside world that transforms them into something else, something that lasts. If they fail to click with the world in the fleeting moment of their emergence, they go right back into non-being. This cycle of creation and selection is everywhere you look, from virtual particles in a quantum field to biological evolution to human societies and civilizations. Bubbles lucky enough to stick together make foam. Mutations lucky enough to happen in the right body give it abilities it didn't have before. Shared itches in humans prompt the construction of a Sphinx or a Moon rocket or the World Wide Web.

Nothing is perfect. Any meditation practitioner can tell you that to imagine perfection, you must learn to think of nothing. Nothing has no properties. You can't find any flaws in nothing.

But nothing is pregnant with everything. Everything in our reality, that is. Sometimes the birth it gives is a Big Bang and the newborn turns out to be hard to miss, like our Universe. Sometimes it's a virtual particle so shy you get a Nobel Prize for detecting vague hints of its existence.

Reality is imperfect: it has properties, lots of them. We—often quite arbitrarily—declare those properties to be good or bad. Advantages or flaws. Features or bugs. If your girlfriend tells you the stinking lilies you brought her are perfect, she either suffers from olfactory paralysis, or she likes you a lot more than you deserve. Or both.

The florist stand at your local grocery has mums, carnations, roses, and those damn lilies. White mums look fresh, but they remind you of a funeral. Carnations are stylish, and the color selection is okay, but aren't they for Mother's Day? Roses—sure they send a nice message, but they have thorns. Lilies look regal and out of the ordinary, but the smell... Are any flowers here good enough? Would they send the right message? What the heck *is* the right message anyway? Maybe you should go to the florist shop instead? Is it worth the trouble? If you go, should you call her to say you'll be late? Or should you ask if it's okay to be late? Should you tell her the reason or not?

There's no end to it. That's life, man. You can always find an argument against anything. So if you want a date tonight, stop staring at the damn flowers. Remember Buridan's ass, staring at the two haystacks and starving himself to death? Don't be an ass. Just make a choice. For real. It won't be perfect because only nothing is perfect. But reality is better than nothing.

Our reality (a.k.a. life) is the process of getting from yesterday to tomorrow. And the Human Itch is the drive to make tomorrow better than yesterday, in some irrational sense that can't be rigorously proven but can be shared and debated and cultivated and cherished. I submit that choosing what "better" means is a choice we can make. I submit that we'll be proud if we do.

Somewhere between the swarms of robots too primitive to have any individuality and lone wolves too full of themselves to unite around anything other than a really big walking steak is a sweet spot, where we just get it. We're remote descendants of the oddball apes that got it just right. We tell stories that go far beyond utilitarian information to immediately benefit you and your small pack. We have myths that unite and inspire us to do things together that no chimp or wolf or ant or slug or bug can conceivably conceive of. Ants aren't flexible enough to imagine a Taj Mahal. Wolves aren't cooperative enough to build it. We humans are both.

Figure 2 – Cooperating flexibly in large numbers: striped eel catfish, starling murmuration, Penicillum fungi, fairy rings.

As Harari puts it, we're the only animals that can cooperate flexibly in very large numbers (it turns out that we aren't—see picture above—but we *are* good at it). And I submit that without this flexible cooperation of large numbers of humans, we wouldn't have the individual geniuses either. I personally perceive reality through a set of filters that, while being uniquely mine, nevertheless depends on you and billions of other fellow humans in the noosphere, the sphere of information we create and populate. We communicate our understanding of persons and things—intuitive or otherwise, deep or shallow, accurate or way off, sensitive or numb—to each other. We tell stories, and most of our stories gain no traction at all. Most of those that do gain traction eventually get clobbered. A lot of experts tell us in detail why this or that proposition is sheer lunacy, then we bicker and get personal and use words and arguments that make us blush when we stumble upon them decades later. Miraculously, this very untidy process somehow yields a worldview that makes sense, meaning that it has some predictive power, meaning that it both accurately describes patterns and correlations with what we have seen, and it makes some non-trivial predictions about what we haven't seen yet. If these predictions are falsifiable by experiments or observations that we mere mortals can do in our finite lifetimes—and write home about it so other mere mortals can exercise their inalienable right to enumerate the ways that we screwed up—then that's science. If not, it's religion. Chimps, wolves, ants, slugs, bugs, or viruses have neither. Only civilization-building species do.

The mid-twentieth century was a heady time in the history of the only civilization-building species we know so far. Computers doubled in power every couple of years. Cars doubled in number every decade. Earthlings started crisscrossing the globe in jet airliners. Earthlings reached the lowest and highest points on the surface of the planet—and we orbited it and took the first pictures of Earth from space. Satellites became commonplace, and a launch got less press coverage than the Beatles coming to town. It took just over a decade from the theoretical prediction of black holes to experimental confirmation of their existence. Magazines were full of images of cities floating in the skies of Earth and other planets of the Solar system. Between the images ran ads advertising do-it-yourself, ultralight aircraft kits, amphibious cars, and cars that could, more-or-less, fly. People put on jetpacks, flipped switches, and went flying, usually to the nearest hospital. People dreamed up jet-powered trains, and some actually built them. Scientific, engineering, and popular publications seriously discussed cities in orbit, connected to the planet's surface by space elevators. Our robots landed on other planets. Engineering studies on nuclear propulsion in space got to working prototypes. It looked like we were going places. Fermi's question of where the heck all aliens were—and what they looked like and how we can deal with them when they show up—was looking less and less academic to a lot of folks.

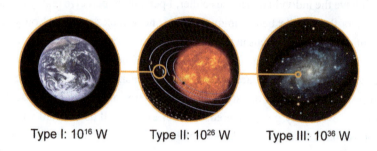

Type I: 10^{16} W   Type II: 10^{26} W   Type III: 10^{36} W

Figure 3 – The original Kardashev scale.

One of those folks was Russian astrophysicist Nikolai Kardashev. In 1963, the year that President Kennedy used a UN podium to offer Soviets a joint Moon-landing program, Kardashev was in Moscow, investigating the source of a signal from the heavens suspected to be an alien message. The signal was later attributed to a quasar, which was supposed to exclude any intelligent control of the source (come to think of it, it doesn't, but that's by the by). Thinking about space aliens is a hard habit to quit though, so Kardashev developed and published the Kardashev scale, a measure of a civilization's advancement, based on how much energy it controls. Originally, it included three types. Type I controls the energy of its mother planet. Type II controls the energy of its home star. Type III controls the energy of its entire galaxy. Paraphrasing Richard Feinman's famous "there's plenty of room at the bottom" (he meant particle physics), there is indeed plenty of room on top as well. And we were doing something about it. We humans learned to hop off our home planet, and within a few years, we were confident enough in space to cross it and land on a celestial body other than Earth. Humans walked and drove and joked and took pictures and collected rock samples on the Moon, and safely got back to talk about it. Neil Armstrong's "small step for a man, giant leap for mankind" was a step down a little flimsy ladder, but it led up the Kardashev scale.

And then the excitement of the first Moon landing passed, Kennedy died, the Vietnam War costs mounted, and rational pragmatists made the worst decision in the history of *Homo* (occasionally) *sapiens*: they decided not to continue on to Mars. The mighty Saturn V's went nowhere, and the people who knew how to build them went on to build other things that didn't take us all that far. The long-range exploration of space by human astronauts was put on the back burner until further notice. We have heard quite a few of those notices since, and so far all of them have turned out to be duds, each harder to believe than the one that came before.

Figure 4 – Cybertruck ancestry research results.

And now we celebrate as a major achievement a propulsive landing of a rocket stage, almost half a century after the little Apollo lander did that with two people aboard. On the Moon. With less computing power than you have in your wristwatch. From scratch in under a decade. And me make a big to-do of a hybrid of an electric utility cart with a stovetop coffeemaker (yes, I'm talking about the Cybertruck). We were going to make printers that could build Mars habitats from local materials; instead, we got printers that can make icing on a birthday cake look like anything you want, including Mars habitats.

Bored half to death while stationed at Sakhalin Island in the USSR, Sergeant Oleg Lavrentiev wrote a letter in 1950 to none other than the Central Committee of Communist Party of the Soviet Union. He suggested the use of a nuke to produce a magnetically stabilized thermonuclear energy source. The letter inspired the development of TOKAMAK technology that continues to this day at ITER, among other places.

Our world was getting smaller. We used to make jumbo jets for a lot of people who wanted to travel around their planet. We used to make supersonic passenger planes for those who were in a particular hurry to get to their destinations. Now the supersonic Tu-144 and Concorde are a distant memory, and jumbo Boeing 747s and A-380s are on their way out.

Figure 5 – Our reflection in trains: rusting hulk of a turbojet-powered bullet train built 1970s (left); icing on a cake in the 2010s (righ).

We were going to control weather. With all the computing power available sixty years later, we still can't even get a reliable forecast more than a few days out. We were going to have Moon bases by 2001 and send a manned expedition to Jupiter no less that same year. We were going to have cities in orbit by 2018 and send solar energy down to Earth. As of this writing, we haven't sent any human beyond low Earth orbit (LEO) for half a century.

A patent clerk could get nonconformist papers published in prestigious scientific journals and revolutionize human understanding of the Universe. An army sergeant could prompt development of thermonuclear reactor. The Empire State Building could open 410 days after construction started. How likely is any of this to happen today?

Figure 6 – Building a civilization.

We used to give our dreamers some leeway. Have we lost our touch? Have we lost some spark that made it possible—amid the devastation after WWII; the onset of the Cold War, Korea, Angola, Vietnam; and the growth of environmental concerns—to believe in ourselves? Has that invisible hand that pushed us from the caves to the Moon grown tired? Did we lose the fire Prometheus supposedly stole from the gods to give us? Have we become what space visionary Robert Zubrin (sadly) calls *Homo mundanis*?

I submit that Prometheus' fire is still there, but it's starved for fuel and flickering alarmingly. I believe that we still have a choice between two paths: forth to the stars or back to the caves. I believe that most of the humans responsible for making this choice are alive today, as I write these words. I don't think the people living today have the luxury of not making a choice because—as usual—not making a choice is very much a choice. I don't think the people making these choices have the luxury of making them completely rationally because that would require knowing all outcomes of all your choices—and last I checked, there was no time machine in my basement to tell us those outcomes.

And I submit that our ability to make irrational choices has been the fuel in the engine of our progress, stoking Prometheus' fire. Our irrationality, our ability to take a chance and risk being wrong, and our belief that we can't afford the incalculable losses of going nowhere are a big part of what got us here. Our irrationality is to be cherished and celebrated. Of course, we need our rational half to help us reach our goals, but we need our irrational half to choose those goals. Misanthropes refuse to give our irrational side this much credit—it's up to us to prove them wrong.[2]

---

[2] It has become fashionable to treat humanity with cynicism and contempt. Some people attract a lot of publicity by discounting humans as hackable, obsolescent bio-robots, incapable of free will and free thought.

If some crafty little green men wanted our beautiful planet for themselves, they couldn't do better than to infect humans with cynicism and contempt for humanity. The misanthropes claim that the best tool humanity has for conquering the Universe (a.k.a. science) proves them right. They'll tell you, patronizingly, that it's a done deal, and your belief in humans being more than obsolescent bio-robots just proves that you're a particularly obsolescent bio-robot. Being proud to belong to the species that aspires to reach for the stars is a dangerous delusion of grandeur, they tell you.

This book is an attempt to vaccinate you against the brain-eating anti-humanism bug. Giving cynics a taste of their own medicine. Debunking the debunkers.

This book is a little science-y, so I'm going to bribe you to read it, like a gym that gives you bonuses for showing up. There are Facebook superiority bonuses scattered throughout the pages. Once you get to another one of these, feel free to use it in your next FB brawl. But you only get them if you really get that far. No cheating, okay?

Be forewarned: there are a lot of discussions in this book about subjects that I haven't studied formally. I don't have credentials in every field I discuss. And you may be tempted to ask yourself, *Then why should I listen to an engineer's thoughts on cognitive biases?*

Gotcha! That's your first bias. It's called the authority bias. I'm not an authority on the authority bias. I'm just a fellow sufferer who happens to have given a lot of (biased) thought, who has done a lot of (biased) research, and who is ready to share my own (biased) opinions.

If you think that some—if not all—of the views expressed in this book are controversial, then that's something we can agree on. You see, I'm no oracle or professor. Professors profess, and they have a hard time admitting that they might be wrong. We mere mortals—including yours truly—don't have that luxury. Maybe I'm full of it, but then maybe it's you. Come to think of it, maybe it's both of us.

So let's argue because that's how we imperfect humans get things right often enough to take us from the caves to the Moon.

Figure 7– Human evolution.

Brandolini's law (a.k.a. the bullshit asymmetry principle) is idea that refuting bullshit takes an order of magnitude more energy than producing it. For example, demonstrating Brandolini's law to be bullshit (which it is, and it's not an order of magnitude; it's at least three) would take a lot more effort than it's worth. More ominous examples include Thomas Malthus's "An Essay on the Principle of Population," Paul Ehrlich's *The Population Bomb*, and other pearls of anti-human wisdom.

Semmelweis reflex is a knee-jerk reaction to any suggestion contradicting an existing dogma. Yes, you guessed correctly, it's outright rejection. Ignaz Semmelweis was a Hungarian physician who thought it might be a good idea for a doctor who has just performed an autopsy to wash his hands before attending to a patient who's still miraculously alive in spite of the doctor's best efforts. It was in mid-1840s. The practice reduced patient mortality 10-fold, whereupon it was summarily rejected by Semmelweis's learned colleagues – chiefly on the grounds that gentleman's hands couldn't possibly transmit disease. Semmelweis was conveniently tucked away at a mental institution and murdered there.

2 Lay of the Land

> **Failure is success in progress.**
> *Albert Einstein*

2.1 *The most successful species on the planet*

We're the champions. No, really. Sure, we started out as a few thousand unappetizing apes on the fallback lunch menu of big carnivores. But from these unremarkable beginnings, in only a million years or so, we have progressed and become nearly eight billion masters of our domain. Meanwhile, the descendants of the merciless carnivores rummage through our dumpsters. We have conquered the highest mountains and the deepest trenches and both of Earth's inhospitable poles. We have covered the planet with the World Wide Web, filled with an immense amount of knowledge. We have learned about stars and galaxies and the Big Bang and cells and molecules and atoms and particles. We have walked and driven on the Moon. We have deciphered our own genetic code. We can leave the Old World in the morning and get to the New World before lunch. We can have a relaxed dinner conversation with people thousands of miles away. We have mastered nuclear fission and fusion, quantum mechanics, and general relativity. We have built robots to automate almost every mundane task. We have genetically engineered plants to feed more large mammals than this planet has ever carried, and most of these mammals are us, humans and our symbiotic species (a.k.a. our life support system). Human biomass on this planet today is nearly twice the biomass of all of the terrestrial vertebrates that lived more than 12,000 years ago.

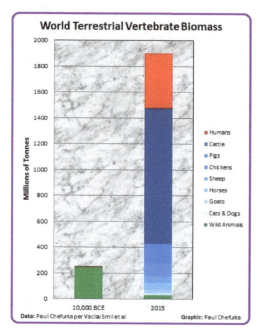

Figure 8 – *We are the champions. Image courtesy of Paul Chefurka.*

We've got it made. By any objective measure of success, we're a success story. We're the only species on this planet that has nuanced language, mythology, religion, science, philosophy, engineering, and art. We're the only species on this planet that knows what species are. We're the only species on this planet that has what it takes to ask the questions we ask in this book, and many others that we don't. We're the only species we know that can read this book or print it or write it.

So, where do we go from there? What does the biggest, meanest kid on the block do once all obvious competition is squashed, and the biggest challenge is to find a challenge?

We could rest on our laurels. We could say that we've seen it all and that we've learned all that's worth learning and that we've conquered all that's worth conquering. What we have is all there is. We've earned our place on top, we're kings of the castle, and we're just going to bask in glory up here, enjoying the view, roaring every once in a while like the MGM lion to remind every creature down there who's the boss.

Arrogant and smug and cynical and dismissive—that's exactly how Goliath felt when he met David. That's exactly how ancient Romans felt right before Rome fell to the barbarians. That's how official science felt when Copernicus died so timely as to not face ridicule and ostracism for his silly heliocentric ideas. That's how established rocket scientists felt when they first heard of Elon Musk.

That's also how the Ming emperors of China felt when they ordered the destruction of their own navy, the biggest in world history, in 1525 and hid the country behind the iron curtain of smug superiority. Less than a century earlier, hundreds of navy ships in the expedition fleet of Admiral Zheng He had completed its seventh and final voyage of world exploration. The formidable fleet had been assembled to search far and wide for anything worthy of notice, from the opulence and grandeur of the mighty and wealthy Chinese Empire. Any prosperous lands, wise rulers, skillful artisans, knowledgeable scientists. But everything they found looked primitive compared to what they already had back home in China. So they sneered at the rest of the world and decided there was nothing out there that they wanted.

By the time the mighty fleet was destroyed, a bargain-priced expedition under Christopher Columbus had found the New World. Columbus' three ships were small, their equipment and provisions were limited, and the navigation was so primitive that it didn't even account for magnetic declination, which the Chinese had known about for 400 years before Columbus' crossing. The navigator died fifteen years later, still thinking that he had found India rather than a new continent. Descendants of the folks he met on the shores of the New World are still sometimes called Indians. An educated Chinese navigator at the time wouldn't have made such an embarrassing mistake.

The Spanish crown had every reason not to support Columbus' voyage in 1492. Columbus had asked for funding to find a sea route to the riches of Asia, which Bartolomeu Dias had already found when he rounded the Cape of Good Hope. The conquest of Asia was also unthinkable for the modest European fiefdoms. Even their provincial sovereigns knew of the Chinese might. Asia already had a master—capable and potent and local—and the best the Europeans could hope to accomplish in Asia was establishing a foothold as humble traders. The rulers of Portugal, Venice, and Genoa—the maritime powerhouses of the time (by European standards)—all turned Columbus down, and the Catholic monarchs of Spain almost did, too. But he did sail, and he discovered a path to the New World—and the struggling Europeans rather than the mighty Chinese reaped the rewards. Three and a half centuries later, China, which had drowned its curiosity and drive in hubris, was a shadow of its former glorious self. It suffered a series of humiliating defeats at the hands of comparatively small but ambitious countries half a world away, and it lost control of its own affairs. It took the Chinese another century and a half to recover.

In the meantime, the European powers were competing to claim center stage, via industrial might and military conquest. Soon after World War I broke out, H. G. Wells coined the phrase "the war to end war." When the war was concluded with the Treaty of Versailles, the victorious Allies had every reason to think that, at the very least, the Germans would never again make war. The other Central Powers (namely, Austro-Hungary, the Ottoman Empire, and Bulgaria) were in tatters, and the big trump card of European conflict, Russia, had been weakened by revolution and civil war. Germany seemed the only remaining cause for concern, but the Treaty of Versailles supposedly took care of her, too. German armed forces were limited to 100,000 men; tanks, armored cars, military airplanes, modern capital ships, submarines, and border fortifications were prohibited; the Polish Corridor split East Prussia from the rest of Germany, which also lost Alsace-Lorraine, Danzig, overseas possessions, the entire output of the Saar coal mines, and control over the Rhineland territory. Germany, it was announced, also had to pay reparations in an amount (132B gold marks) that was chosen to please the public in the victorious Allied countries, but they secretly negotiated downward to 41 billion gold marks, to make it (it was hoped) realistic to demand actual payment.

That arrangement made the Allies feel confident, and justifiably so. They had just beaten the best-trained military on the planet, nearly 5,000,000 strong, well led and backed by the German industrial juggernaut in full militarized swing. Compared to that, containing a demilitarized Germany with just 100,000 riflemen seemed childishly easy. The British had their empire, where the Sun never set, and their mighty naval forces to protect their possessions. The French occupied Rhineland and bridgeheads from Germany to France, and they watched over the Germans like hawks. There was no way any clandestine war preparation would happen on their watch. The French were so confident that they were in no hurry to modernize their military. The French Char B-1 tank, conceived in 1919 (when it would have been a formidable weapon), only entered service in 1936, when it could frighten only the French taxpayers.

Four years after that tank entered service with the French army, the German military overran France in six weeks flat, matching it man for man (although with half the artillery and two, still primitive, German tanks to every three, mostly better, French tanks). The Maginot Line, allegedly impregnable to frontal attack, held its reputation but not much else, as Germans didn't bother with a frontal attack on it but went around through Belgium instead. In their way to Belgium stood Fort Eben-Emael, the most advanced fortification complex in Europe, reputed to be completely impervious to ground assault. The Germans, taking the Belgians' word for it, didn't even try to assault it from the ground. They landed paratroops in gliders on its roof, instantly disabled its weapons, and took it over. The Belgian and French defenders' confidence evaporated, and all organized resistance soon collapsed. The British expeditionary forces, sent to help the Belgians and the French gain battle experience, had to be evacuated by sea from Dunkirk, leaving their heavy equipment and their hubris and their allies behind. Sportsmen, weekend boaters, professional fishermen, Thames water taxi operators, and anyone else who could safely navigate a boat across the English Channel—and many who couldn't—lent a hand in the desperate rescue. If the Germans had been equipped for a cross-Channel invasion, the British would have little to repel the landing force with.

Nazi Germany had occupied Poland, Czechoslovakia, Belgium, the Netherlands, Norway, and France; Japan, Italy, Bulgaria, and Romania had allied with Germany; the USSR and Sweden were supplying war materiel to Germany; the former US Ambassador in London had "informed" the Americans that Britain's resistance was futile, and the German submarine blockade had a tight grip on vital shipments to the UK. Britain was rapidly running out of options. It needed help badly and urgently.

Help came from an unexpected quarter: the subjects from the colonies and protectorates of the British Empire and the Commonwealth. Many of them had fought for independence from Britain, which Britain naturally suppressed, often with a heavy hand. They could reasonably be expected to use that moment of British weakness to gain their independence. The Empire certainly couldn't force Canadians, Australians, New Zealanders, South Africans, East Africans, Indians, and others to provide supplies and facilities and troops and labor and raw materials, the payment for which was very much in doubt (as was the survival of the intended recipient). And they were dealing with the folks whose "civilizing" was not too long ago regarded by the British as the "white man's burden." The imperialists, to be fair, didn't only regard folks with a different skin color as inferior. They also derided the Irish, the Poles, the Boers, and the Americans.

The folks on the receiving end of the British sneer—and all too often at the business end of "civilizing" British guns—came to rescue the struggling Britons. They sent planes and ships and pilots and sailors for those planes and ships. They shipped guns and ammunition and soldiers to shoot those guns. They sent medical supplies for dressing the wounds of soldiers up so they could send them back out to shoot the guns some more. They sent all of that across oceans full of German submarines and surface raiders, all so they could risk their lives fighting side by side with their oppressors. The imperialists had an object lesson on the better side of human nature. Humility, however, is a hard virtue to learn. Even after the hard-won victory over fascism, the British deeds in Iran, Egypt, and India—among other places—had all the hallmarks of old imperial arrogance.

World War II was an expensive, brutal, and unforgiving lesson for many. For Stalin, the dictator of the USSR, it was crushing.

From the Russian Empire, the USSR had inherited vast territory and immense natural resources. The European part of the USSR was the biggest country in Europe. The Asian part of the USSR, Siberia, was the biggest country in Asia. The imperial capital, St. Petersburg, is the gem of European architecture. No foreign capital was allowed to outshine its magnificent palaces, theaters, music halls, museums, and cathedrals. The Hermitage in St. Petersburg, painstakingly stocked by imperial art buyers all over the world, is still by far the biggest collection of art on the planet, even after the Soviet government pillaged its treasures for decades in exchange for (a lot of) Western technology and machinery. For two centuries, the Russian Empire came out victorious in every war it fought. Russian Emperors had every reason for their pride and arrogance. They had no reason whatsoever to think that they were doing anything wrong. Anyone suggesting otherwise was an insane rebel and was treated as such.

So the Russian Empire kept most of its people enslaved until 1861, delaying industrialization and urbanization by about a century, as compared to Britain. The Russian Empire didn't support technological innovation, and Russian inventions like the light bulb, radio, welding, and many other technologies were never commercialized. The Russians ended up importing the high-tech items they could have been exporting. By 1903, the Russian Empire still had no constitution, and it was ruled by a monarch of unlimited power. Or so it seemed.

That year, one of the emperor's advisors coined the phrase, "To contain a revolution, we need a little victorious war". Indeed, discontent was brewing in Russia, especially among the educated class. Consolidation in the face of a common enemy is a tried-and-true tactic to quash dissent, so using it again seemed like a good idea at the time. We'll never know how real the threat to the powers-that-be would have been, if they hadn't adopted the idea of "a little victorious war," but we know what happened when they had. To limit the risk, they chose Japan as the enemy. Weak Russian garrisons in contested Manchuria were neither withdrawn nor reinforced when Japan openly prepared to take it over. Russia and the rest of Europe traditionally discounted Japan as a second-rate power, and they sneered at Japan's recent modernization.

In 1904 and 1905, the Russian Empire suffered a crushing and humiliating defeat at the hands of the Japanese. Discontent with the Tzar and His Majesty's Government came out in the open and left little else to talk about in public. Agents of the much-feared secret police were seen leading public protests against the Tzar. The desperate monarch declared citizens' rights and instituted a parliament, but it was too little, too late. Twelve years later, the last Russian emperor lost his throne, and soon thereafter he lost his life as well.

At first, the Bolsheviks who took over the huge country were anything but smug and complacent. They were hanging on by their fingernails, and they knew it. The whole world fought them. The Germans took Ukraine under the humiliating Treaty of Brest-Litovsk, and they menacingly hovered over the western border. The recent allies, Antanta, occupied Odessa and Baku in the South, Vladivostok in the East, and Archangel in the North. An uprising rocked the Kronshtadt naval base, and White Russian units advanced as far as Gatchina—thirty and fifty kilometers, respectively—from the seat of the Bolshevik government. Close calls were the norm.

Twenty years later, when the opening salvos of World War II were fired in Ethiopia, China, Poland, and Finland, the Bolsheviks were comfortably and confidently in power in the biggest country on the face of the planet. No one in their sane mind would have dared to mount an attack against the mighty Soviet Union. Its Red Army had more tanks than the rest of the world combined. The Red Army had the indestructible KV, the only true heavy tank in the world; and the best medium tank—by far—in the world; and the fastest light tank—by far—in the world. It also had amphibious tanks and flying tanks. Yes, you read that right—the Red Army had gliders that attached to a light tank that was towed through the skies by a tug plane and then released to land on the battlefield, where it shed its wings and immediately went into action. The Red Army had the first paratroop units in the world, and these were not just for show. They perfected division-scale airborne drops. Each city park in the vast country had a jump tower, and each town had an aero club. Trained parachutists and pilots numbered in the millions, and drivers numbered in the tens of millions.

In the Far East, whose remoteness from European centers of industry and population was used by the Russian Empire as an excuse for the scandalous loss to Japan, the Soviets mounted massive operations with overwhelming force against Japan's Kwantung Army. The results were so impressive that even after Soviet divisions left for Europe, the Japanese never dared to attack the almost undefended border.

But most of the Red Army was stationed in Europe, and that army wasn't idle. Its march into the Baltic countries and Bessarabia was unopposed, and the German onslaught wore out the Polish army before the Red Army crossed the border. But the Spanish Civil War and the Winter War with Finland gave the Red Army a cadre of battle-tested officers and generals. In June 1940, the invincible KV tanks in Bessarabia stopped 200 kilometers short of Ploesti, the main source of fuel for the German war machine. The USSR was itself an important vendor of oil to Germany, not to mention an important vendor of a variety of other war materiel. But oil was the switch wired to stop Hitler cold, and now Stalin's finger was on it. No wonder Stalin was confident enough to demolish the old border fortifications of—you guessed it—the Stalin line, and they weren't in a hurry to build the new fortifications farther west. It's no wonder that land mine and demolition charge stocks and secret weapon depots that had been left for guerilla resistance behind enemy lines were all decommissioned and destroyed. The Red Army was the strongest, most confident ground force on the planet. No sane person would attack the USSR, for USSR could now squash any aggressor. It no longer had any use for the defensive measures it was resorting to when it felt weak and vulnerable.

Soviet intelligence reinforced this confidence. The German military made no preparations to take on the USSR, and Soviet spies knew all about it. Germany built no long-range bombers to reach deep into the vast Soviet territory, ordered no winter clothing to survive the unforgiving Russian winter, built no wide-track tanks to cope with infamous Russian roads, and stockpiled no cold-resistant lubricants to keep everything moving when hell freezes over. Which happens regularly in Russia. Even if some deranged mind could imagine taking over the entire USSR in a single summer campaign, winter was going to come anyways. Disregarding this little nuance required a level of complacency that the Soviet spies couldn't imagine. So they didn't, and they happily reported that the Germans weren't ready to attack.

The spies were right. The Germans weren't ready to attack. But they attacked anyway. Hitler probably decided to attack for a variety of reasons, including a complete lack of appreciation of Soviet strength. But one look at the map of Romania in the fall of 1940, with the Ploesti oil refineries within 200 kilometers of Soviet divisions, makes Hitler's train of thought irrelevant. He simply had no choice. The golden beaches and granaries and wineries of capitulated France and its (and Belgium's) undefended African colonies were no less attractive than the freezing swamps around Smolensk or Pskov. Even better, they didn't even have to be conquered, just occupied. But it still wouldn't do the occupiers any good without oil, and Stalin could take that oil away at any moment.

Hitler couldn't have that. There could be only one king of the hill. So in a desperate gamble, the Germans attacked.

One hundred thirty days later, German divisions stood thirty-five kilometers from Stalin's Kremlin office. In 130 days, more than five million Soviet soldiers, sailors, and airmen were dead, wounded, or taken prisoner. Most of the mighty tank force and the vast air force and much of the artillery was gone. So were enormous stockpiles of fuel, lubricants, food, medicine, and ammunition. And so were the resources needed to replace those lost items. The enemy had captured territory where forty percent of the Soviet people used to live, sixty-three percent of coal had been mined, and fifty-eight percent of steel and sixty percent of aluminum had been produced. The lost industrial capacity included more than two million bombs, eight million artillery shells, and five million shell casings—every month. Rolled ferrous metal production fell three-fold, and rolled non-ferrous metal and ball bearing production practically ceased altogether. You can't make guns and tanks and planes without rolled metal and ball bearings.

In the end, it didn't help Hitler. But there's no reason to doubt that the reports of the German attack on early June 22, 1941, ruined Stalin's plans for more than just the rest of the weekend.

If hubris begins to sound dangerous, that's because it is. Nature abhors a vacuum, and it seems to react particularly violently to a vacuum of humility. Kings of the castle tend to think they've seen everything worth seeing, learned everything worth learning, conquered everything worth conquering. Kings of the castle perch on the high tower, looking down on the hapless peasantry below. The high tower is a perfect position to get zapped by any passing thundercloud. Checking overhead is a very useful habit. And it can do us a lot more good than just warn about incoming thunderbolt, Wile E. Coyote or bird poop.

If we look up on a cloudless night, we get a glimpse of the magnificent Universe. Yes, it's The Exercise. Humbled and awed and open-minded and curious, we can open our eyes and see that there's no way we've seen it all. There's no way that we've learned all that's worth learning. There's no way that we've conquered all that's worth conquering. There's plenty more left. There's far more out there that we don't know than that we do know. There's far more out there that we haven't seen, heard, smelled, or touched than that we have. There's far more out there that we don't have words to describe than that we do.

Our minuscule castle is on the modestly-sized planet we happen to live on, a planet that we know embarrassingly little about. The planet is itself a tiny speck of cosmic dust, one of countless billions of such specks, orbiting their stars in countless billions of galaxies. And we know literally nothing about almost all of those worlds. There certainly are problems out there, but running out of selfie scenery ain't one of them.

> Let's add to your Facebook superiority arsenal. Let's talk about the Dunning-Kruger effect. Just roll this expression around in your mouth like good cognac. It sounds sophisticated and double-barreled at the same time. With a weapon like this, you can troll some serious game. So what does it mean?
>
> The Dunning-Kruger effect says that there are two kinds of people in this world: those who shouldn't be making decisions but do and those who should but don't. And the effect is that the decisions are really messed up most of the time. I'm not positive, but I suspect that Dunning was one kind of person and Kruger was the other. The first kind of people (let's call them "Dunnings" for convenience) know so little that they have no clue how little they know. So they think the world of themselves and their competence. They believe that whatever they may not know is useless anyways. They think common sense is a lot more common than it actually is. Gears in their heads are few and far between, which is wonderful for freedom of random rotation, as they don't mesh. Left to their own devices, Dunnings fall into every rabbit hole, get suckered into every shell game, subscribe to every conspiracy theory. They inevitably grow tired of themselves, convince themselves (and each other) that the game is stacked against them, and live haplessly ever after, resentful and plotting revenge.
>
> The second kind of people, the "Krugers," are the opposite. They can quote Homer in Ancient Greek. They can solve Schrödinger's equation with paper and pencil. They can recall the atomic weight of scandium, the thrust of the V-2 rocket engine, and the name of every sailor on Christopher Columbus' ships without consulting Wikipedia. Hell, they wrote Wikipedia. And, of course, they doubt and check and recheck every comma because they know that's what it takes to get reliable information. Such an unnatural amount of data stuffed into one regular-size human head inevitably inhibits some of the head's functions, and the first casualty is often decision making. It's like an antique shop with six-inch-wide passages between flimsy, overpriced paperweights, where the sign reads, "You break it, you buy it." That policy may well be the only reason the place is still in business.

2.2 What did Adam do for a living?

So how did we get to where we are? Why exactly is *Homo* (reluctantly) *sapiens* such a smashing success so far? What makes us so fundamentally different from ants, rats, chimpanzees, and Neanderthals?

An impartial observer would immediately notice that we're light-years ahead of all Earthly competition in one respect: we engage in irrational behavior. Well, not everyone, and not all the time. But sometimes some of us do. No ant voluntarily approaches fire. No rat makes musical instruments. No chimp paints. No Neanderthal scouted far and wide just out of curiosity. And when famine or flood or fire finally forced a Neanderthal tribe to move, every promising-looking valley already had a "Tribal Property, Trespassers Will Be Eaten" sign posted by our Cro-Magnon ancestors.

Some of the ancestors did some really reckless stuff, most likely accompanied by a lot of grumbling and occasional ostracism from the rest of the tribe. Common sense said it was foolish to waste a perfectly good meal on someone who was going to do something stupid, like getting himself killed by trying to control fire or build a raft or explore unfamiliar lands. But our ancestors weren't as good at suppressing their oddballs as the ancestors of modern ants and rats and chimps. Enough human oddballs actually made it for the oddball species to succeed spectacularly.

Let's saddle up the time machine and go to France in 30,000 BCE. When we step out of the time machine, grasses cover the rolling tundra. Streams gather into a river in a home valley of a Cro-Magnon tribe. The few trees in the tundra are too small to hide the carnivores: lions, bears, hyenas, saber-toothed tigers, and, of course, the great-great-grandpa and great-great-grandma. The latter claim to serve the best mammoth steaks in the neighborhood, cooked to order and darn near perfect. They've learned the art of survival from their ancestors, and it serves them well. Nutritious mammoth, bison, goats, and aurox are everywhere, and their migration patterns are well known, as are the methods of cooking their flesh, saving leftovers in permafrost fridges, making flint tools, creating clothing from animal hides and fur, and chasing predators from the home cave using the first two wild creatures that humans domesticated: fire and dogs. Life is good. Life is so good, in fact, that the few black sheep that every family has are no problem. When some geek paints images of mammoth and ibex and rhinos on the cave walls, the rest of the tribe just mocks the crank rather than throwing her out to the wolves.

Part of the reason that they're so forgiving of the painter is that she isn't the only crackpot in the tribe. She isn't even the worst one. That title belongs to a particularly fierce male named Ahd-Amm. The guy is completely out of control. He comes and goes as he pleases. He has his own personal dog—can you believe that?—and he speaks more to his dog than to any human. He spends weeks at a time away from the cave, all alone but for his dog. When he comes back, he tells fairytales about faraway lands and exotic animals and plants and odd-looking people doing odd things. It's nonsense, of course, and everyone knows that. Who can seriously believe that a stream could be so hot that it fogs over even in winter? Who can seriously believe that you can make fire wherever and whenever you need it after Shaman clearly explained that Holy Fire is a gift from the Sky Spirits, passed to us through the Legendary Ancestors? Who can seriously believe that after a ten-day hike facing the mossy sides of tree trunks (that's how you tell north from south—with the moss or against the moss), you'll see trees taller than wooly mammoths when everyone knows that trees aren't even as tall as people? And this guy, completely disconnected from reality, has the temerity to argue with Chieftain, elected by the whole tribe, and to question Shaman's hunting forecast. And get this: he apparently has designs on the tribe's most eligible bachelorette, Eh-Wa. She's the painter.

Offences like these would get anyone else indicted, convicted, sentenced, and eaten the same day. But in Ahd-Amm's case, the grumbling was muted: Ahd-Amm's warnings had a nasty habit of proving true, and everyone knew that. He had tried to warn them about a pack of wolves moving into the tribe's area, and everyone ignored him. They went on a hunt and killed a bison, then they spent a whole day fighting off the wolves, and they came home empty-handed and some wounded. He had tried to warn them that a flood was bound to come to the valley any day now, telling them that the old hunting shelter by the river needed to be moved. Then one day a wall of water with mud and boulders came roaring down the river, sweeping away the shelter and the three hunters in it, never to be seen again. Then Shaman refused to give Ahd-Amm a jar with a piece of Holy Fire for one of his reckless expeditions. Shaman said that if people of faraway lands made fire any time they wanted, like Ahd-Amm had said, then Ahd-Amm could do the same. Shaman was just going to teach Ahd-Amm a lesson, certain that he'd stay home. But Ahd-Amm sneered and went anyway.

Everyone was afraid he'd try to steal Holy Fire from the Neanderthal tribe that lived in the next valley over, and that would start a war. But nothing happened. He was away for a really long time, and everyone thought he was dead. But then he came back, and he had no fire jar with him. So Shaman said Ahd-Amm was in cahoots with evil spirits, for no human could possibly survive that long without fire, and everyone got excited, because they thought it was, finally, time to eat Ahd-Amm and to have no more of his foolishness. But Ahd-Amm told his dog to let no one near him, then he sat down on the flat rock stage and made a fire right in front of everyone's eyes. Whatever he used to make the fire couldn't have been as hot as a fire jar because he had pulled it from under his furs, and neither the furs nor Ahd-Amm were burnt. Shaman, the keeper of Holy Fire, yelled that it was all a trick and further evidence of evil spirits.

But fire is fire, and every hunter knows that babysitting the fire jar slows the hunting party. You can't swim with it. You can't keep moving in the pouring rain, and even if you ran and hid in one of the known shelters, the fire still could die without anything dry to feed on. And if you're far enough from home cave, you'll die with it too, especially in winter. Besides, asking an able-bodied hunter to look after the fire jar was a really big deal when you hunt big game and have to fight off lions, bears, wolves, and Neanderthals. The ability to make fire on demand was hard to dismiss.

If our time machine had at least a six-ton capacity, we could have it paid for in no time (no pun intended) by trading one lighter for one ready-to-eat mammoth. Every hunter knew it wasn't a good idea to eat a guy who can make fire on demand. Saving his hide could one day save yours. And no one knew that better than Chieftain. He was the judge, jury, and executioner. He was also chief lawmaker and head of the executive branch. The buck stopped at his desk, long before desks were invented and back when "buck" still meant a male elk. Democracy in the tribe was very unsophisticated. As long as cratos did an OK job of telling the demos what to do, the demos tolerated the cratos. If cratos messed up, the surviving demos was cold and starved and sick and tired and miserable and in no mood to mince words, so they summarily ate the cratos and declared the position open. After seeing the fate of the predecessor, it took some guts to apply. And a lot of wisdom to stay alive if you got the job.

The current chieftain was wise indeed. A few years ago, Shaman declared Eh-Wa's painting blasphemous, and he demanded justice. By which, we remember, back than they meant eating the offender. Shaman claimed that Ancestor Spirits came to him in his sleep and told him they were offended by the paintings and that the Spirits wouldn't protect the tribe anymore if they didn't stop Eh-Wa, a woman, whose job was raising children, mending clothes, and cooking. And since no one else was inside Shaman's head at the time, no one could confirm or deny what Ancestor Spirits had or hadn't told him.

Chieftain saw through this right away. He, too, was educated in Ancestors' Ways, and he was a good student. He knew that Ancestors' Way for man was to hunt and defend the cave, and for woman it was to raise children, mend clothes, and cook. But they taught something else, something Shaman kept silent about, and Chieftain suspected that he knew why.

The ancestors taught that a woman's job was also to gather herbs and berries and nuts and mushrooms and seeds, which were used for food and spices and medicine. But practicing medicine was Shaman's job. The trouble was that the ancestors weren't particularly clear about what to do if a woman collecting medical herbs happened to be observant and noticed which herbs sick animals used to recover from each particular malady—and eventually learned more about the herbs than Shaman knew. That's what had happened with Eh-Wa. At first, she only discussed her observations with Shaman, who didn't mind at all: Eh-Wa was a good-looking girl, and to the rest of the tribe it looked like he was teaching her—not the other way around. That felt good, and it increased his social status.

But Shaman was an ailing man. The exhausting spiritual practices with hallucinogens had taken their toll, and sometimes he was in no shape to heal the sick. There were times when he himself needed to be taken care of. That job fell to Eh-Wa, and soon everyone noticed how good she was at healing. That was the other reason everyone tolerated her drawing hobby: everyone in the tribe was—gratefully or grudgingly—her patient.

So when Shaman emerged from one of his mushroom-induced trances and banished Eh-Wa from Ancient Rituals, Chieftain immediately recognized the alleged sign from the ancestors as good ol' fashioned professional jealousy. Chieftain believed that the ancestors wouldn't mind their favorite tribe having both a shaman that made people's souls feel good and a healer that cared for their bodies. Shaman's mushrooms and rituals were good at defusing tensions in the tribe and keeping folks in a compliant stupor around the Holy Fire. But when they ventured outside the cave, they needed to be alert and fit.

So Chieftain ate some mushrooms and went into a trance in preparation for his announcement of his decision. That was the part of the job he used to hate the most. The mushrooms always made him sick, and if he showed weakness, everyone would eat him and call for an election. So he learned to pretend to eat the mushrooms, which he flicked into a dark corner of the cave, where they kept old bones for making tools and ritual jewelry. That worked well until someone went into the corner with a torch to look for bones and found the mushrooms. The tribe almost ate him then. That was the biggest scare of his political career, and he knew he couldn't continue like this. So he shared his secret with Eh-Wa and asked her to find an antidote to the mushroom poison. It was a pretty safe bet: no one would believe her word over his, and she knew it. Eh-Wa went above and beyond the call of duty: she found mushrooms that looked like the real ones but had no effect whatsoever. All Chieftain had to do was to fake a mushroom-induced trance, which was childishly easy.

The decision he announced was pure genius. More than 30,000 years before the advent of the Dilbert Principle, he decided to promote Shaman to Vice Chancellor of Religious Affairs. Eh-Wa also got an official title. From that point on, she would be Custodian of Healing Supplies.

And it worked. Shaman happily left lowly Healing Supplies to Eh-Wa and focused on higher matters. Peace reigned in the cave – until Ahd-Amm made fire in front of everyone. The tribe could really use portable, on-demand fire, so Shaman had to be pacified again.

One mouthful of Eh-Wa's special mushrooms and a bout of expertly faked hallucinogenic trance later, Chieftain made Shaman Minister of Heavenly Fires, and Ahd-Amm became Custodian of Pocket Appliances. What started as a nightmare, threatening to destroy social order, became the first day of happily ever after. Ahd-Amm and Eh-Wa got married, and Shaman conducted a beautiful ceremony. Eh-Wa opened a medical herb school and required every female student to bring a male hunter to class so they also knew what herbs to use when out hunting. Ahd-Amm opened a lighter-making school and required every male student to bring a female gatherer so they also could make fire any time they wanted when out gathering. Chieftain got so confused coordinating the schedule of classes, rituals, and hunting expeditions that he coined the phrase, "I'm too old for this shit," 30,000 years before Danny Glover—but then he remembered what happened to the last guy who was too old for something, and he shuddered and buried the phrase so deep that archeologists only dug it up 30,000 years later.

Years passed. Children grew up. Ahd-Amm showed hunters several caves he had discovered, which the tribe used for temporary shelter on hunts, which took longer and longer. To get good game, the hunters had to travel several days against the moss. And the berries and mushrooms and herbs and seeds were better there. There was also a lot more firewood there. It was too far from the home cave to bring a whole mammoth there, so after a hunt they cut up the carcass, hid in the permafrost all that they couldn't carry, and returned several days later with the whole tribe to take the rest.

They did that several times until one day a blizzard forced the entire tribe to spend the night in a cave at the intersection of Cro-Magnon Valley and Neanderthal

Valley. The best hunting grounds were in the broad valley of the merged river. The new cave was bigger than the old one, the entrance was narrow and easy to defend, a stream passed through the cave, and a crack in the roof let the smoke from the fire escape to the outside. That was the new home for the tribe.

That's when Ahd-Amm told everyone about an ice wall a kilometer high, 300 kilometers to the north. It was advancing a kilometer per year and freezing everything in its path. That's where he went every year when he disappeared in the spring. Twelve days with the moss, then twelve days against the moss to get back home. He called the glacier The End. It spread left and right as far as the eye could see. And Ahd-Amm said it was getting closer, moving slowly against the moss. Each year he noticed landmarks getting closer to the wall, and eventually they disappeared under the ice. In the years since he first saw the wall, it took him almost a day less to get to it from the old cave—and he wasn't even moving as fast as when he was younger. The End was coming.

The hardy Neanderthals in the other valley didn't notice anything for many more years. Of course, their Old One complained that game was getting scarcer than it had been when he was a child, but then he was always complaining about something. Just a grumpy old Neanderthal. Every hunter knew that you can't get lucky all the time. Natural variation, capeesh?

When, generations later, a band of starving, freezing, wobbly, and apprehensive Neanderthal hunters reached the intersection of the valleys, the place was occupied, settled, and fortified by the many descendants of Ahd-Amm, Eh-Wa, and their tribemates. No Neanderthal scout ever returned to their home cave (legend had it that a couple of young Neanderthals were taken prisoner and were eventually adopted by the tribe). Soon enough, the Neanderthal cave was a tomb. 300 years later, it was under a kilometer of ice. In the meantime, Ahd-Amm and Eh-Wa's great-great-grandchildren were busy peopling the planet. Explorer genes apparently gave them an evolutionary edge [5].

Among the great-great-grandchildren were proto-Indians, who left hospitable Asia for the icy wastes of the Bering Isthmus. Without a map or GPS, one could wander for generations before getting to a prairie with nutritious bison and mammoths and other groceries. And that's exactly what they did: they froze, they starved, but they also learned survival skills they could use in the new environment. They raised children, and each generation went farther than the previous one. Some made it.

Among the great-great-grandchildren were Polynesian seafarers, who took off into the unknown from Taiwan about 5,000 years ago. Over the next 4,000 years, their descendants settled all habitable islands of the Pacific, from the bountiful Philippines to remote Hawaii and austere Easter Island. Among the great-great-grandchildren were Moses and Ibn Sina and Curie and Bacon and Dali and Ulugh Beq and Da Vinci and Amundsen and Ibn al-Haytham and Newton and Gagarin and Bosch and Einstein. All *H. sapiens'* proud achievements started with somebody's courage to venture into the unknown.

Humans are an odd species. No charismatic ant can convince the colony to go on an island-hopping expedition to settle magic faraway lands, larvae and worldly possessions in tow. No charismatic chimp can convince their troop to pick up the noisy infants and take off for that snow-covered ridge on the horizon in the hope of finding a more abundant supply of bananas. Only we *Homo sapiens* sometimes buy those fairytales. Only we *Homo sapiens* can up and leave our comfort zone on the promise of a better tomorrow. The descendants of Ahd-Amm and Eh-Wa—wandering and stumbling, trying and failing and trying again—inherited the Earth.

So it's time to debunk one of the most popular myths about humans: the oldest human profession isn't what you've been told it was. The oldest human profession is exploration.

2.3 Us and them

Birth is a person's first adventure in the magnificent new world. She has never breathed air before. She has never heard herself cry before. She has never seen other people before.

But soon enough, those moving ghosts come into focus, and she can tell them apart, then they turn into people, each with his or her role and quirks. Here's Nurse, a confident angel. If anything goes wrong, the nurse knows how to fix it. Here's Mom, exhausted and scared and excited and loving and feeding and learning to take care of the baby. Here's Dad, flat out panicked, eyes bloodshot and hands strong but unsteady when others prompt him to pick her up. Here's Grandma and Grandpa and other Grandma and other Grandpa. They're smaller, more wrinkled, but also more confident versions of Mom and Dad. They nap a lot, and they often disappear to some mysterious place Grandmas call "cafeteria" and Grandpas call "chow hall," and yet they're usually the first to notice that she needs to be fed, changed, or entertained. And here's Doc, who shows up on occasion. Doc speaks to everyone in a very authoritative voice. No one interrupts him, and once he's done talking, everyone he speaks to does something different.

It's hard to blame the kid for thinking that she's the center of the Universe. Everyone, including Doc, seems to be there at her service. Some never shake off that first impression, despite all the hints to the contrary.

The first hint, which is quite a shock, comes when she's taken to the nursery, where all hell breaks loose. She discovers herself among other newborns, and all of them are centers of their own private universes. The cozy world where catering to her every whim is everyone's job is, for all she knows, gone forever. She now competes with fifty other babies for Nurse's attention. Leaning on the horn. Pressing the panic button. Yelling at the top of their lungs. Demanding attention. Demanding to be unborn.

The hell they raise, collectively, could send a military marching band packing its tubas and drums. It's deafening, both in decibels and, especially, in emotional intensity. An adult who can keep his sanity in this environment for any length of time is a special kind of human. If you can take this, you can take anything. A couple of months in a nursery should be a mandatory part of training for special forces and submarine crews.

That's where some newborns get a lifelong dislike for other humans. Mom, Dad, Grannies, Nurse, and Doc aren't yet included in the "other humans" category. They're part of a life support system, so she doesn't dislike them. Yet.

That's also where newborns get their first lessons of observation and adaptation. That they can't see Nurse's earplugs is beside the point. What matters is that they notice the overwhelming decibel level and get the idea that if all it makes you want to do is to go deaf, maybe Nurses can't hear very well in that cacophony either. That's the first hint of two important points at once. First one is that your life-support system is made of creatures who, while looking and behaving oddly, still have something in common with you. The second is that if audible cues don't work, you'd better try something else. Fast learners adapt and get to the head of the class. They learn to make cute faces at passing nurses. They smile and they wink. They make it impossible for even the most harried, bored, and sleep-deprived nurse to pass that cute furball without smiling. Click, decision made, outcome checked, lesson learned. Wanna get noticed? Notice others.

Slow learners, meanwhile, keep teaching the world to ignore them. The congenital culprit radar instantly suggests who's to blame for the "neglect." Click, the first conspiracy theory is born. Parents, teachers, classmates, teammates, professors, supervisors, subordinates, spouses, and neighbors beware. Another resentful human is coming your way, and you'd better hide from his wrath. Populists, get ready. In eighteen to twenty-one years, blaming the faceless "them" for real or imagined ills of the world will earn you the loyalty of this bitter kid. If this brain tumor doesn't get excised—and it seems to get harder and harder to cut out with age—he's doomed to live in the world where only one person is always right, and most of the nearly eight billion others are always wrong. That world sucks.

From the maternity ward, babies start to go their separate ways. Some will do things, and some will have things done to them. Some will decide for themselves and others, and some will wait for someone to take the decision out of their hands, then they will resent that someone for doing so.

The crybaby, of course, can't know where it's all going. But we, the adults, are supposed to know. Plenty of data out there.

> Belief is 50% lie and 67% beef.

- More than 90% of people believe that they know the truth about God, and they believe at least 80% of others don't.
- About 94% of Americans claim to pay their taxes fully and honestly, and they believe that 34% of others don't.
- About 70% of people believe that other drivers are extremely dangerous when texting and driving, but only 25% believe the same about themselves.
- Only 2% of high school students self-reported below-average leadership ability.
- Roughly 88% of American students (and 77% of Swedish ones) believe that they're better-than-average drivers.
- About 75% of people believe that millionaires inherited their millions, but fewer than 3% of the millionaires actually inherited a million or more.

You think you're not as biased as participants of those studies? You're not alone! Of the 600 study participants, more than 85% rated themselves less biased than average, while only one person—one person, not one percent!—believed that he or she was more biased than the average.

The bitter, the angry, the resentful, and the perpetually outraged are a species apart. If a relationship falls apart, it's always their partner's fault. If they get into a car accident, it was the other driver who was driving like a maniac. Other poor people are poor because they're lazy and obtuse, but the perpetually outraged person isn't rich because life isn't fair. They know of no one else putting in an honest day's work. They know no one else who can follow the simplest instructions.

The resentful crowd is a great audience for opinion pieces like these: "Are rich people more likely to lie, cheat, steal? Science explains the world of Manafort and

Gates." Of course, none of the research cited in the article indicated that Bill Gates is a liar, cheat, or thief; the fact that the author, the news outlet and its owners are still in business is largely due to Gates' charitable decision to leave them be, rather than to sue their pants off for libel. But they do have a business, so they must have readers.

And their readers are really easy targets. You can sell them any drivel, as long as it's nasty, angry, and derogatory—and directed at someone else. Rich are OK, but poor will do fine, too. Who cares that 85% of the jobs Americans lost lately were lost to robots, not to humans of any nationality, immigration status, or income level? If you tell folks to be angry at robots, it sounds silly. China, Mexico, and illegal immigrants are much better culprits-on-call.

A big meta-study, which studied 1,779 different policy issues, found that it's not average citizens on one side of the issues and the rich elite on the other. It's average citizens and the rich elite on one side, and interest groups on the other. Millions of young people inherit more money from their parents than Bezos, Gates, or Zuckerberg did, and more than 99.999% of them never get to be one of ten richest people on the planet. Your chances of making a billion are very, very small—and so are the chances of the kid up the street who grew up in a mansion.

You, dear reader, most likely had an easier starting point in life than did Diogenes, Mendel, Michael Faraday, Alfred Nobel, Konstantin Tsiolkovsky, Linus Pauling, Oprah Winfrey, Arnold Schwarzenegger, Eminem, Celine Dion, Leonardo DiCaprio, Sarah Jessica Parker, Jim Carrey, Jennifer Lopez, Tom Cruise, Francisco Pizarro, David Livingstone, Tenzing Norgay, or Edmund Hillary. You probably weren't, at the age of seven, kicked out of the family house—which had a thatched roof and no plumbing—by foreign invaders and forced to live in a dugout, as did Yuri Gagarin, the first human to orbit the Earth. You probably never had lunch atop a skyscraper, sitting on a beam 840 feet up in the air with no belay whatsoever, like the folks in the famous 1932 Charles Ebbets photo. You probably had better access to education than Christopher Columbus, Benjamin Franklin, Michael Faraday, the Wright brothers, or Marie Curie. You could be easily cured of the diseases that killed Pascal, Riemann, Fresnel, Livingstone, or Tutankhamun (if you ever catch these diseases in the first place, which is extremely unlikely nowadays). You can, in a few clicks, access information that Mendeleev and Koch and Nobel and Schrodinger and Bohr and Einstein and Alexander the Great and Henry the Navigator would give their right hand to glance at (although the last two would perhaps give somebody else's right hand). You probably have at least one arm, unlike painter Peter Longstaff. You probably have vision, unlike sculptor Giovanni Gonnelli or painter

Lisa Fittipaldi or Mt. Everest climber Erik Weihenmayer. You're perhaps not a quadriplegic, like painter Michael Monaco or physicist Stephen Hawking. You most likely have at least one foot, unlike Everest climber Mark Inglis or Olympic runner Oscar Pistorius.

The people listed here, and millions more like them, are the elite of our species. Unlike those born with a silver spoon in their mouths, they inspire others. And, by the way, don't for a moment imagine that being born without money is less of a handicap for an aspiring industrialist than being born without an arm is for an aspiring athlete. They both have a dream. They both have a passion for making their dreams a reality. They both put in a lot of hard work. And yet they can fail. The ones who succeed are the ones who got lucky, right?

Yep, and right now I'll tell you how anybody with a dream and a good work ethic can get lucky. That's the second secret I'm going to let you in on in this book. If you choose to become the elite of humankind, no minor detail like a lack of money or eyesight or arms can stop you—if you have a dream, are ready to work hard to make it a reality, and do just one more thing.

Just get others to bet on your success. That's it. I said it. All someone with a dream and a good work ethic has to do to belong to the elite is to have others bet on them. But don't take my word for it. Go out and check. See if you can find anybody who succeeded without getting somebody to bet on them. See if you can find anybody who failed despite having a dream, working hard to achieve it, AND getting people to bet on them.

If somebody buys into your story, you've got it made. Whether it's crossing an ocean in a reed raft, circumnavigating the globe in pedal-driven vehicles, skydiving from the stratosphere, making an intuitive computer interface, building a city or a Large Hadron Collider—once you have convinced people that it's worth doing, your dream goes into the repository of human treasures, to be redeemed when and if its time comes. Your portrait—for now small and unimposing—goes to the portrait gallery of human heroes. It may grow in size and move to a more prominent spot over time, depending on how many lives your idea eventually impacts and how significant the impact turns out to be.

If you want to see the elite of the human species, don't turn on the TV. Just look in the mirror. You're the elite. Elite is "us". The folks manipulating you into believing you're not good enough are "them." It's up to you to prove them wrong.

2.4 The shrine of Buridan's ass

Fourteenth-century French philosopher Jean Buridan's claim to fame can't be found in his writings. His great contribution to the philosophy of science was that he was apparently so obtuse that someone—after endless attempts to get through to him—dreamed up the term "Buridan's ass" and a paradox to go with it.

> Tautology isn't an actual scientific discipline.

To begin with, Buridan preached moral determinism, which in layman's terms means that you should always choose the course of action that's most "good" unless you're an ignoramus, a deviant, or an agent of evil. And Buridan was a professor of philosophy and logic at Sorbonne, so quite naturally he ignored the next obvious question: How the heck are you supposed to decide what's "good"? And isn't that the same as deciding what to do in the first place?

Some of his more astute students noticed that the prof's explanation explained nothing whatsoever. All it did was pass the buck. When you make your choice, you can't know if its consequences are going to be mostly positive or mostly negative. You can't even know if your decision to make a decision—any decision—is going to turn out to be a good or a bad one. So you pretty arbitrarily choose something, and often you even more arbitrarily decide that it's time to actually make your choice. Then you rationalize the heck out of it if anyone asks. The kids were smart and eager and naïve and didn't have the good sense to keep their observations to themselves, so they went to reason with Buridan. As you have guessed, they all got F's for the class, demonstrating that knowing what's "good" wasn't a problem for the prof. And if it was a problem for them, then they were ignoramuses, deviants, or agents of evil. Come to think of it, maybe all three at once. With that, he threw them out of his office.

"Buridan's an ass" was perhaps the mildest expression heard as they discussed their options afterwards. Under consideration were 1) burn down the Sorbonne, or 2) douse their exasperation with cheap Beaujolais at St. Nicholas' Tavern around the corner. Sorbonne is hard to burn as it was built of stone, so the tavern idea won. Again. It usually did. And there on a table—the cheap establishment didn't offer napkins—they drew the story of a donkey that couldn't make a decision if its life depended on it. And one day its life actually did depend on it, so it died of hunger, standing halfway between two perfectly edible (for a donkey) bales of hay.

Numerous schemes to save Buridan's ass[3] have been hatched over the years, mostly along the lines of Buridan's own denial that there was a problem at all. The solidarity of many scientists with an obscure medieval philosopher is understandable. Their asses are on the line too. And they appeared to put a lot of effort into it on their own free will, the existence of which they vehemently denied. More on that later.

> The one exception to the rule that what goes up must come down is the landing gear.

In 1984, Buridan's Principle was apparently mathematically proven under certain assumptions. I say "apparently" because what Buridan's Principle said was that "a discrete decision based upon an input having a continuous range of values cannot be made within a bounded length of time." Let's step back and consider that for a moment. Let's say you have a pilot looking at an altimeter—or a radar or visual markers or ILS—to tell him whether the plane has touched down on the tarmac so he can reverse thrust, engage the brakes, and initiate whatever very time-critical (read feverish) actions are necessary to safely bring the darn thing to a stop without hitting anything. The altimeter gives an input with a continuous range of values. The decision to reverse thrust and lean on the brakes is a discrete decision, and Buridan's Principle says that no matter how long the runway is, it still isn't possible to decide that the plane has touched down, and act accordingly. Buridan'. Buridan's Principle predicts that the ass will be spread all over the tarmac and beyond every time it tries to land. But ask any of the four billion passengers who entrust their asses to airplanes every year if that prediction reflects reality. The passengers are okay, which means that the principle is bunk. The idea that no battle plan survives contact with the enemy is evidently not restricted to military affairs.

But wait! Something like Buridan's ass comes into play in electronics. There's a whole class of circuits called comparators, whose job is to produce a digital output (0 or 1), depending on whether or not an analog input exceeds a threshold. Every once in a while, a comparator gets stuck in a meta-stable state, unable to decide on an appropriate output. If you used that output to control Buridan's ass's brain to make the decision, the ass would be just as stuck. The wired ass would be stuck until some random noise in the circuit made it flip into one of the truly stable states

---

[3] In Nature, Buridan's asses don't die of hunger: they get eaten long before that.

(namely, 1 or 0), which stand for the left and right haystacks. At room temperature, it happens in nanoseconds. Donkeys don't die of hunger in nanoseconds. The ass is fine.

So it looked like the idea of the ass being doomed was itself doomed. But in 1994, a scientist galloped to the rescue. This time it was a neurologist, Antonio Damasio. His book *Descartes' Error: Emotion, Reason, and the Human Brain* analyzed a number of people who suffered a severe brain injury. Their ability to make decisions was grossly impeded, and so was their ability to feel emotions. Damasio suggested that our decision-making is emotional rather than rational. A particularly unemotional ass could die of hunger between two haystacks after all, it seemed.

You may be asking yourself, dear reader, What's the big deal? Why all the fuss about a theoretical donkey's imaginary quest for hypothetical hay? Who cares?

It turns out that a lot of folks do, and for a good reason. The ass is smack in the middle of a controversy that dates back at least 2,450 years, to a Greek philosopher named Leucippus, whose student Democritus came up with the idea that the world is made of atoms. Leucippus wrote that "nothing occurs at random, but everything for a reason and by necessity," which is the fundamental principle of determinism.

About a century later, another great Greek philosopher, Epicurus, disagreed. He wrote that "some things happen of necessity, others by chance, others through our own agency." And he knew the implications, noting that "necessity destroys responsibility and chance is inconstant; whereas our own actions are autonomous, and it is to them that praise and blame naturally attach."

So in the debate about who we are, the battle lines were drawn. The Leucippus deterministic camp thought that all we are is a collection of atoms, like everything else in the Universe, and all our actions are completely determined by past causes. If you did something, it was because that was predetermined by some past events, not because you decided to do it. There's no agency, no "you" in "your" decisions. To determinists, there's no "self" other than the current condition of a particular collection of atoms, and that condition rigidly and uniquely determines that heap of atoms' reaction to any set of circumstances in the future.

Epicurus thought that there was a "self" that can choose from among possible courses of action. And that self can be praised for making good choices and blamed for making bad ones. According to Epicurus, when there's a choice to be made, some of the available choices are better than others, and it's not always possible to tell which is better based on past collisions between atoms in the Universe. Sometimes your "self" has to make a stand, not based on any rational, measurable factors demanded by a smug determinist. Epicurus believed that you have what later came to be called "free will" to make choices. Determinists believe that you don't.

Determinism seemed like a great foundation on which to build science. It was a belief in an ordered Universe, and science loves order. Order is neat and predictable and beautiful, and it impresses the uninitiated. For thousands of years after Leucippus, science was busy looking for order in the Universe, and it found plenty. Science developed a great tool to expand knowledge: the scientific method. Armed with that highly useful tool, science proceeded to explore the world, which is a very big place, where you can find plenty of order, if order is what you're looking for. Humans love patterns and regularities—real and imagined—and we're really good at noticing or imagining them in the world around us.

> "Pareidolia" is the inclination to see familiar patterns where none exist, like faces in the Moon, giraffes in the clouds, intelligence in a calculator, or a nude (or a staircase) in Marcel Duchamp's 1912 painting "Nude Descending a Staircase, No. 2."

Yet Epicurus couldn't bring himself to believe that Leucippus was predetermined to declare everything predetermined. "Everything" includes the Leucippus' declaration itself. Making such a sweeping statement based on a rather limited knowledge of the Universe seemed to require free will, whose existence Leucippus was so fiercely opposed to. Didn't Leucippus choose to say what he did?

It's a delusion, determinists reply. It only seems that other outcomes were possible. Leucippus was predetermined to claim that free will doesn't exist, and Epicurus was predetermined to disagree. And free will deniers are predetermined to be right, and free will believers are predetermined to be wrong. The modern deniers claim that contemporary science doesn't support free will. They also claim that free will is no more than a myth developed by Christian theologians to justify praising saints for making good choices and blaming sinners for making bad ones. Deniers claim that mighty positivist science has reduced human behavior to physics and chemistry, which are, in their minds, deterministic. Thus everything we do is deterministic. There's no room for freedom in the scientific reality, they claim with feigned sorrow. Science, they repeat, doesn't support free will.

"Science doesn't support X" sounds like a death sentence to X, until you notice that it's a thoroughly confusing expression that could mean two more or less opposite things. It could mean that science examined X thoroughly and with open mind, using the scientific method that gives science the authority of the unbiased arbiter of our worldviews - and found it to be false. Or it could mean that it didn't do any of that.

Let's see for ourselves. Let's decide for ourselves if scientific evidence has, as some claim, resolved the centuries-old dispute between Leucippus and Epicurus, the deniers and the believers. And let's be scientific about it. We'll use the scientific method, which works like this: 1) observe the world around you; 2) make a hypothesis, consistent with your observations, about how it works, 3) based on your hypothesis, make predictions about something you haven't observed, and 4) create an experiment or make further observations to determine if your predictions are accurate. If they aren't, your hypothesis goes to the wastebasket, and you try to develop a new one. If your predictions are accurate, and if others can reliably confirm that accuracy, then your hypothesis eventually becomes a theory.

To qualify as scientific, your hypothesis has to yield predictions falsifiable by experiment or observation. An alternative hypothesis is that you're full of it. Which hypothesis better describes reality? Scientists call selection of a better hypothesis "discrimination" (scientific discrimination is perfectly legal and moral, by the way). There's only one scientific method to perform this discrimination: you make predictions about something from both hypotheses and compare the outcomes of both with observations. Whose hypothesis does the evidence support?

If the predictions are identical, then they're "non-discriminating," which means that observations can only falsify (or not) both hypotheses. To distinguish between the two hypotheses, you need to find something that the hypotheses predict differently. Then it's possible to falsify one but not the other. That's how you get your winner.

Can we apply that method to determine if free will exists? Do the competing hypotheses make discriminating predictions? Does a world with free will differ from one without it, and can we tell which one of these we actually live in?

Buridan's Principle is an example of a discriminating prediction. It shows that producing a rational, discrete output from a continuous input would take infinite time. The perfectly predictable deterministic world with only one possible outcome for every perfectly predictable deterministic situation is incapable of determining what this outcome should be. Not this side of eternity.

And the world we live in appears to be one where discrete outputs are made from continuous inputs all the time, without much trouble. A pilot lands a plane and engages reverse and the brakes in time to avoid smashing it to smithereens. A helmsman changes course as another ship grows in his view. A diver decides that it's time to come up for air. A chicken looks at traffic and decides to cross the road.

The world we live in, where we make countless decisions every day, appears to be compatible with free will and incompatible with rigid determinism. Issue settled?

Not quite. Actually, it's nowhere near settled. As Upton Sinclair famously quipped, it's difficult to get a man to understand something, when his salary depends upon his not understanding it. A successful career in science and philosophy, like elsewhere, depends on meeting the Guild's appearance standards – and for centuries, it has been safest for science to appear to be studying a perfectly ordered world. Ordered, of course, by God. The Guild's standards were developed while the Church watched over its shoulder. When the best minds of humankind labor for thousands of years under the handicap of having to frame their results in a way acceptable to the Church, they can rationalize the heck out of their compliance with political correctness of the day. Their rationalizations make it into their books, their lectures, and their students' minds. And then most folks can no longer tell where science ends and dogma begins.

Dogma is the dark side of science, which prides itself on being enlightened. Determinist dogma began with the noblest of intentions: to help the folks doing science avoid the dungeons of the Inquisition. In return, Guild members were supposed to toe the party line, lest they endanger themselves and others. Worshipping order became an initiation rite for the Guild.[4]

---

[4] [...] annoyed that the movements of the world machine, created for our sake by the best and most systematic Artisan of all, were not understood with greater certainty by the philosophers" [6].

"The Scripture and Nature both derive from God, the Scripture as His dictation, the Nature as the obedient executrix of His orders. The purpose of the Scripture is to persuade humans of those propositions which are necessary for service of God and salvation. To adapt to the understanding of unlearned people, the Scripture speaks many things which differ from the bare meaning of words, and it would be blasphemy to accept them literally by attributing to God human feelings like anger, regret, or forgetfulness. Nature, on the other hand, never transgresses the laws imposed upon her, or cares a whit whether her recondite reasons and ways of operating are understandable to men. God has endowed us with senses, language, and intellect not to bypass their use and give us by other means the knowledge we can obtain with them. Therefore, whatever sensory experience and necessary demonstrations prove to us concerning natural phenomena, it should not be questioned on account of Scripture's

Worshippers substitute belief for reason when no one's looking. Then they implant something like "contradiction between free will and contemporary science" in their sacred texts, making it sound as if contemporary science actually has evidence that free will doesn't exist. When you hold their feet to the fire, they'll give you plenty of examples of verifiable facts and established theories compatible with reductionist materialist determinism. They hope you won't notice that all of these examples are equally compatible with quite a few alternative models, which don't require your decisions to have been made at the time of the Big Bang 13.8 billion years ago. They hope you won't notice that the examples of contemporary science they give are perfectly compatible with both the non-existence and the existence of free will. For contemporary science to be incompatible with free will, it's necessary for it to be compatible with denialism. It just isn't sufficient.

> Sattinger's law: It works better if you plug it in.

Any scientist over five years of age is supposed to know the difference between "necessary" and "sufficient." To publish a scientific paper, it's necessary to write it, but writing isn't sufficient for publication. For something to be nonexistent anywhere in the Universe, it's necessary that it doesn't exist anywhere you have checked, but that's not sufficient. Astrophysicist Neil DeGrasse Tyson once said, "Claiming there is no other life in the Universe is like scooping up some water, looking at the cup and claiming there are no whales in the ocean." Sounds like an invitation to keep an open mind, doesn't it?

But when it comes to determinism's rearguard action against our free will, minds slam shut with a bang, like tank hatches before engaging an enemy. "You have the illusion of free will, but, in fact, that illusion comes about because you don't know the future. Because you are a prisoner of the present, forever locked in transition, between the past and the future." Says who? Well, that's the familiar voice of Neil DeGrasse Tyson, the suave, knowledgeable, and incredibly smart and logical scientist who just mocked folks for declaring something a fact just because they freely chose to.

---

words which appear to have a different meaning. This is especially so for those sciences about which we can read only very few words in the Scripture which does not contain even the names of all the planets, and so it was not written to teach us astronomy"[7].

Of course, in a world without free will, it's really hard to have illusions of free will or any illusions of anything at all. To have an illusion, you have to have a "self," a you. *Cogito, ergo sum.* I think, therefore I am, like Descartes said. That is, identity has to have a meaning so you can have your illusions and I can have mine, different from yours. And you can't have that in the reductionist, deterministic world.

There's no meaning to anything individual in the reductionist, deterministic world without free will. There's no "I" that can be blamed for wrongdoing or praised for accomplishments. Your body is unlikely to contain more than a few of the atoms you were born with. It also contains about ten times more nonhuman cells than human ones. Then who exactly is the "you" who's reading this? Who exactly is "you" who remembers your first day at school, your mom's elation when she learned you were admitted to college, the smell of grandma's cooking - when most of the atoms currently in your body have been elsewhere?

The self-identification problem doesn't start at our level of complexity. Far from it. Elementary particles, the favorite heroes of reductionist lore, have identity crises of their own, only theirs are much worse than ours. Elementary particles, which make up all the particles in the Universe, live in four fields—gravitational, electromagnetic, weak and strong—of all the particles in the Universe. Every one of the roughly 10^{80} particles that make up our world contribute to the total field that acts on any single one of them. With one exception: itself. Each of the four fundamental interactions has infinite energy at zero distance, so if a particle couldn't somehow tell itself from 10^{80} others, its energy—and therefore its mass—would be infinite. Split personality disorder is nothing compared to glancing at the scale one day and seeing "∞."

In a perfectly deterministic world, you can't have any illusions or different views. The perfectly predictable outcome of a perfectly logical consideration of a perfectly deterministic world would yield only one perfectly sound prediction about the future. There's no good excuse in a perfectly deterministic clockwork Universe to not know the future or to have different opinions, wrong predictions, or illusions. A deterministic "block" Universe knows where each billiard ball is going to go even before the cue touches the cue ball. It knew that even before the players were born. It knew everything since the Big Bang 13.8 billion years ago. In the block Universe, everything has, effectively, already happened, in the only way it possibly could happen.

Of course, scientists–the other favorite heroes of reductionist lore—are in the business of having different opinions and making hypotheses falsifiable by making wrong predictions. Then they use—or at least they're supposed to use—the scientific method, which gives science the authority of arbiter of truth, to test the predictions experimentally. If they have no free will, then nothing that happens in those experiments is up to them, so they aren't actually setting up the experiments, soldering circuits, flipping switches, and processing data. In the world without free will, all of that is an illusion. The block Universe, where everything has already happened at some moment of creation, isn't amenable to study by scientific experimentation. All scientists are inside the Universe, so they can't change a single setting on their apparatuses freely at will. They have no free will. And if the experiments (and experimenters) are pre-programmed, then so are the results and the interpretation of the results. There can't be an objective test of anything at all. By denying free will, reductionist, deterministic materialism pulls the rug out from under its poster child, its symbol of objectivity, and the yardstick of Truth: science. If scientists' free will is an illusion, then so is all of science.

It's hard to hope that no one from the outside ever notices such a glaring inconsistency. And science, as we have seen, cares a lot about projecting a solid, authoritative image to the outside world in general and to funding agencies in particular. Funding agencies have their own reputations to uphold, so they stay away from controversies if they can help it. Inconsistencies itch. They give people a type of mental indigestion called cognitive dissonance. Victims of cognitive dissonance used to burn the alleged offenders at a stake, but in today's tame world, they just reject your papers and grant applications. It doesn't hurt as much, but it makes it hard to have a successful career in science.

So some dodging is urgently called for. Scientists are a very inventive bunch. No one—but no one—can out-dodge a trained scientist. There are three ways of dodging a contradiction: you can pretend it doesn't exist, you can pretend it doesn't matter, or you can pretend it's not a bad thing. Orthodox reductionism is nothing if not thorough: it does all three. We'll look at them in the next chapter.

2.5 *Free will denial as an act of free will*

The three ways of dodging a contradiction are an example of a trilemma (a.k.a. logical hamster wheel) [8]. Trilemmas abound in the high art of getting oneself out of a tight corner in an argument. For example, everyone loves 1) low taxes, 2) balanced budgets, and 3) good roads. Any halfwit bureaucracy can deliver one of the three. A disciplined government can do two out of three. But doing all three at the same time is a unicorn no one has seen yet – which, among other things, guarantees that any aspiring politician anywhere on the planet will find something to be righteously indignant about. Just remember that the next time you vote.

> Epicurus, the free will guy, has a namesake trilemma: 1) God is omnipotent, 2) God is omnibenevolent, and 3) evil exists. The mental contortionism demonstrated by folks trying to reconcile this triad is

A trilemma that deals with dodging a contradiction is called a Münchhausen trilemma. That's the epistemological gem you discovered as a kid to drive your parents up the wall every time without fail. Epistemology, by the way, is the study of how do we know that we actually know what we think we know. Long before you knew what it was called, you already used epistemology as a reliable on-demand exasperator of any adult you wanted to get off your back. A Münchhausen trilemma deals with the impossibility of logically proving any certain truth. It goes like this: you ask Dad to prove that something is true (for example, 2+2=4). When he gives you a proof, you ask him to prove that his proof is true, and so on ad nauseum. Sooner or later, even the dumbest dads learn to use an ice cream as a gag. If no ice cream is handy, there are three ways to deal with you, none of them entirely satisfactory: 1) regressive argument (the ice cream truck is always one block away), 2) circular argument (the ice cream truck is always right around the corner), and 3) axiomatic argument (Mom comes and explains that no universe where $2+2 \neq 4$ has any ice cream in it).

Let's get back to the contradiction between the worldview of free will deniers and their own behavior. Let's start with the idea that contradiction is okay. Famous historian Yuval Noah Harari postulates that "consistency is the playground of dull minds." That sounds like a great snub of anyone seeking consistency, right? Well, a lot of folks use that barb to do just that. Fortunately for scientists, funding agencies don't. If they were to use this principle when deciding which projects to fund, inconsistent proposals would get rejected because they make no sense, and consistent ones—because the proposer is dumb. But that would require funding agencies to be consistent, which would put them in danger of looking dumb, a danger that they consistently avoid. If you're starting to think that this playground thing makes no sense whatsoever, that's because it doesn't. Not if it means that making no sense makes the most sense.

Is Humanity an Apprentice God?

Figure 9– Reality Check.

So, to make any sense it must mean something else. What could that something else be? Let's try this statement on for size: "Resolving inconsistency is the playground of sharp minds." That makes sense, and that's actually how the scientific method works. In the scientific method, a new concept is called for when the old one is found to be inconsistent with observations. Sharp minds get to work and expand our understanding of the world when old understanding proves inconsistent with observations (or with itself) and a new one is needed. The contradiction is a signal that something is wrong and that we need to do something about it.

Let's look at the history of modern physics. By the time Max Planck came to the University of Munich, physicists were an unhappy bunch, bored out of their skulls. Physics looked like a done deal. All that really mattered had been adequately explained by the intellectual giants of the past. The physical worldview looked very complete and slightly dreary, and there was no obvious place for an inquisitive mind to play. Engineering, for example, appeared a lot more exciting: railroads and telegraphs and ships and bridges were changing human lives every day, and building such marvels could—and did—use a lot of talent. Seeing that Max was an obviously smart kid, Philipp von Jolly, a physics professor at the University of Munich, warned young Planck about physics: "In this field, almost everything is already discovered, and all that remains is to fill a few holes." Luckily for the world, Planck was stubborn, so he chose a career in physics anyways.

One of the few holes was the theory of electromagnetic radiation. Planck got involved in the field in 1894 through an early conservationist effort by electric companies, which commissioned him to help maximize the electric bulb's per unit light output per unit electricity the bulb uses. They needed a theory of how the bulb works, and they needed it for very practical purposes indeed. The best theory that conformed to the Newtonian clockwork worldview was the Rayleigh-Jeans law, which proved so hopeless at describing short wavelength emissions that it led to the term "ultraviolet catastrophe." By 1896, Planck's colleague Wilhelm Wein had conjectured a formula that worked at short wavelengths, but it failed at long ones. Using empirical formulae in theoretical physics like a hammer to fit a square peg into a round hole is a sure sign of desperation. And "despair" was exactly the term Planck used to describe what happened next: "The whole procedure was an act of despair... I was ready to sacrifice any of my previous convictions about physics." He fiddled with two formulae, each of which worked for one end of the spectrum and failed on the other end. Eventually he dreamed up an ad hoc combination that fit both and, more importantly, the data.

Planck's formula fit the data fine. But it was unexplainable by known physics. It didn't logically follow from known physics. So Planck reluctantly started formulating a new physics that his formula could be derived from: quantum physics. Yes, quantum physics was born from a conservationist quest of electric utility companies.

At about the same time, another drama was unfolding in physics, and it also had to do with electromagnetic radiation. Once emitted by a source, light moves through space, and scientists since long before Newton were interested in learning the details of light propagation. In 1887, Henrich Hertz demonstrated light to be an electromagnetic wave. The wave was thought to be carried by a hypothetic medium called luminiferous ether, which was supposed to resemble the water that carries ocean waves. Ether gave everyone endless headaches. No one could think up an ether that would behave in a way that made any sense. The tight community of researchers of electromagnetism was falling victim to a cognitive dissonance epidemic.

On the one hand, there was no particular reason that ether should be immobile with respect to the Earth, which was known to spin around the Sun at a dizzying speed. Even if it happened by chance at some point in time, a half year later the Earth would be traveling at the same speed in the opposite direction. Ether can't be stationary with respect to Earth (or, to put it more modestly, the Earth can't be stationary with respect to ether) both times.

Or can it? Maybe Earth drags, or entrains, ether as it moves? If so, do they move completely in synch, or is there any residual ether wind at the Earth's surface? One set of theories and experiments appeared to support incomplete entrainment, the other complete. One predicted that you can feel the wind of ether as Earth moves through it; the other said that you can't.

In 1886 and 1887, two very exasperated physicists, Albert Michelson and Edward Morley, did a series of experiments that verified two apparently contradictory results from the past. One was Michelson's own experiment from 1881, which failed to detect any ether wind. The other was the measurement of the speed of light in moving liquids, first done in 1851 by Armand Fizeau. That one failed to detect the match in velocities that complete (windless) dragging would predict. The results of the old experiments made no sense taken together. It was as if you could feel a gentle breeze but somehow failed to feel a hurricane. Michelson and Morley carefully repeated the measurements. The results stood. Ether with wind didn't fit the real world. Ether without wind didn't fit the real world either.

That's when a bunch of really smart and generally rather dignified gentlemen went into a bout of mental contortionism worthy of a mechanic explaining how the darn car still refusing to start ain't his fault. They used a lot of obscure technical terms with progressively vaguer meanings. They attributed to luminiferous ether combinations of properties that didn't look possible to combine. They seriously discussed the possibility of Nature conspiring (with itself) to hide ether behind a veil of mutually cancelling properties designed specifically to defeat their attempts to detect it. They sounded less and less confident and increasingly came to rely on private correspondence rather than public papers to discuss their ideas. They didn't want an innocent passerby to stumble upon them and suffer serious injury. In a word, they were well and truly stuck.

Einstein couldn't find a better time to offer a fresh look at the situation. The field was ready. Einstein's approach was so refreshing that a less deflated Guild would have rejected it out of hand. Einstein was a patent outsider with no standing among the distinguished and sophisticated fraternity. Yet he had the temerity to propose a revolutionary approach based on a very simple idea: if completely entrained ether, incompletely entrained ether, and completely un-entrained ether all give us mental indigestion, shouldn't we at least consider no ether at all?

In place of ether, Einstein used two postulates to describe the propagation of light. One was the relativity principle guessed by Galileo in 1632 (you can run, but you can't hide from laws operating in the Universe). The other was the principle of invariance of light speed guessed by Einstein himself in 1905: you can run, but you can't hide from light propagating at exactly the same speed in empty space. He hoped it would be possible to derive the rest of it from these two principles. He did precisely that in an elegant, straightforward, and seemingly effortless manner. It was two sparks of intuition, 273 years apart, that gave us special relativity.

Searching for consistency in electrodynamics turned out to be a playground for the sharpest minds our species ever had produced. That itch to make sense of the world gave us both relativity and quantum mechanics.

Back to our trilemma. The next option is that the contradiction doesn't exist. It goes like this: sure, the Universe knows everything since the Big Bang, but you don't. You have no access to all the information in the Universe, so you can make wrong guesses based on the limited information you possess at the moment. And, of course, the limited information sets are different for different people, so it's perfectly understandable that we have different opinions, all of which could turn out to be wrong. The reductionists say that everything is preprogrammed, but some programming is faulty.

To get the mounted trumpeter of reductionism off his high horse, you may start by innocently asking what caused the Big Bang. It turns out that the determinists' clockwork Universe starts with a fuzzy miracle of staggering proportions. They claim that the event that has determined everything afterward is itself not determined by anything they can put their finger on.

Modern neurophysiology found that it takes a reductionist less than 100 milliseconds to respond to a perceived threat to his cherished cozy reductionist worldview. Which means that the first reaction you get is likely preprogrammed, in full compliance with the reductionist's own beliefs. But when the (slightly deflated) free will denier comes up for air (to yell something disparaging at us), we'll be ready.

See, the Big Bang isn't the lone example of a gaping hole in this clockwork Universe. Freedom didn't end 13.8 billion years ago. Actually, all you have to do to get back to the real world from the illusion of perfect determinism is to turn on an old Geiger counter. Its crackling never fails to give a smart, educated determinist a Wile E. Coyote moment.

Spontaneous radioactive decay, where each unstable nucleus freely decides when to go, is a huge rusty nail in the coffin of the neat, ordered Universe where everything was decided 13.8 billion years back. Every nanosecond, an unimaginable number of nuclei throughout the world commits suicide in apparent protest against the clockwork Universe delusion. The time course of decay of any radioactive isotope is exponential, which means that each particular nucleus that hasn't blown itself out of existence yet is as likely to do so in the next nanosecond as any other nanosecond. There appears to be nothing outside that nucleus that tells it to go at any particular moment.

And it doesn't stop there. Fluorescence, phosphorescence, and first-order chemical reactions all happen the same way. Each individual molecule goes whenever the heck it pleases, and there's no evidence whatsoever that when one goes after the other, they have been somehow programmed to do so. Every time you smell ozone after a thunderstorm or see a firefly or a phosphorescent sign or a luminous watch or an instrument panel, the non-programmed, free-willed Universe is staring right at you.

As we remember from the brief excursion into the history of relativity and quantum mechanics, the unexplained itches. The glaring discord between the illusion of an orderly Universe and observations itches really badly. And reductionist scientists invent really impressive contortions to scratch at the itching cognitive dissonance. Which inevitably leads to attempts to resuscitate our old buddy the luminiferous ether.

What if some spooky influence tells the nucleus when to blow itself up or tells a molecule when to emit a photon? Can't there be something somewhere that causes all events? Some hidden variable that controls the behavior of quantum objects in a way that we can't detect?

The hidden variable theory has originated a way out of a quantum mechanical dilemma. Physicists have found that interacting particles become somehow entangled, meaning their properties and behaviors become mutually dependent. You can't describe them individually anymore but only together. What's really odd is that the entanglement is maintained after the particles have flown far apart from each other. Really far apart. Like on a galactic scale. Yet one particle of the entangled pair instantaneously "reacts" to a physicist performing a measurement on the other particle. Say you have a "blue" particle and a "yellow" particle, and after the interaction, you can't tell which is which until you actually measure its "color." Before you make the measurement, for all you know they're both "green." But when you measured one and found it to be "yellow," the other will instantly be "blue." But not a nanosecond earlier. And the damn things may be light-years apart by then.

The hidden variable theory tried to make sense of it all by saying that something in the particle's memory tells it what color to show the unsuspecting experimenter. As if the particle always knew what color it was and the experimenter didn't know until they actually made the measurement. So in the hidden variable theory, there's effectively a memory of that particle's "color" out there somewhere. The particle itself may carry this memory, in which case it's a local hidden variable. Or the memory is separate from the particle, somewhere else in the Universe, in which case it's called non-local hidden variable. The hidden variables were suggested in a 1934 paper by Einstein, Podolsky, and Rosen (hence the name the "EPR paradox").

In 1964, John Stewart Bell worked out some predictions from the local hidden-variable model that various experiments have since repeatedly and conclusively falsified [9]. Deterministic contortionists tried to resuscitate the model's ghost by assuming some hidden signal that the Big Bang Almighty sent to the experimenters just to fake the results of the experiments (that conspiracy theory is characteristically called the "superdeterminism loophole"). The beauty of this idea is that it's not falsifiable; the flaw of this idea, like any other non-falsifiable idea dressed up to look scientific, is that it belongs on the religious side of the science-religion divide. Determinists can choose to believe that we live in a terminally boring Universe that exists for the sole purpose of fooling them. Whatever you do to test Bell's predictions, they say, is caused by a 13.8-billion-year-old invisible hand that drives your decisions so you obtain fake data. That hand knew all along what you were going to do, what equipment you were going to use, where each electron was located in that equipment, and where each atom in your brain will be located at each moment for all of eternity. That invisible hand forces your hand to press a button, or whatever, at the exact moment when the result of the measurement would be misleading. And it does the same to different people in different labs running different experiments using different equipment. If you believe that, you'll believe anything.

What about nonlocal hidden variables? OK, it's not the particle itself that secretly knows what color it is, say the deniers—but maybe it's the Universe that does? Maybe the whole Universe tells the particle if it's blue or yellow, or when it's time to fall apart, and the Universe has known the answer ever since the Big Bang? This is their luminiferous ether 2.0: instead of using its trickery just to fake the measurable results for light propagation, this one is sophisticated enough to counterfeit the entire observable Universe. It is, by design, unknowable, unobservable, untestable, unfalsifiable and, as such, completely unscientific.

> Science is like a teenager: once it hears a question, it starts talking, never shuts up, and answers all the questions in the world. Except the one you asked.

As Carl Sagan once famously said, extraordinary scientific claims require extraordinary evidence. In their rush to buttress determinism, the free will deniers manage to completely miss just how extraordinary their claim is. Let's assume for a moment that they're right and that scientists' impression that they're free to choose the details of their experiments is an illusion. It wouldn't only apply to experiments whose outcomes the deniers happen to dislike; it would also apply to any experiment by any scientist. That would, in one stroke, make all of science an illusion. All experiments are an illusion to exactly the same extent, and for the same reason, as entanglement experiments. So the defenders of determinism ultimately destroy science. Scientists only think they study the Universe that really exists, or we only think that scientists really exist who think they study the Universe that really exists. Thanks, but no thanks.

The third option to explain away the inconsistencies between the reductionist, materialist, determinist worldview and observations is that it doesn't matter. It goes like this: the real world is perfectly deterministic, except there's random noise in it. "Random noise" is scientific for "I have no clue where the heck it's coming from, so I'm going to make it sound insignificant." Determinists predictably claim that the noise is also deterministic but unknowable, which makes it impossible to calculate predictions with the precision needed to compare those with observations. This excuse is popular among the followers of determinism unlucky enough to work in disciplines that deal with complex systems with lots of interacting parts and lots of ways that those parts can interact. The only problem with that excuse is that it kills the scientific method (just as mercilessly as superdeterminism did) because you can't falsify a hypothesis if any discrepancy between the prediction and the observation can be explained away as random. And without falsifiability, science is dead. More on that in the next chapter.

2.6 The Causality Delusion

On October 29, 2018, a Boeing 737 Max plane—a beautiful, sophisticated, and advanced flying machine—plunged into the Java Sea twelve minutes after takeoff, killing everyone on board. On March 10, 2019, another 737 Max crashed six minutes after takeoff from Addis Ababa. All 157 people aboard died. This model of aircraft was grounded worldwide. More than a year after the second of these tragedies, the entire worldwide fleet of 737 Max planes—worth more than $30 billion—sat idly on tarmacs around the globe, burning holes in airlines' budgets, Boeing's reputation, and flyers', crews', and investors' confidence. More than 400 of these marvelous but apparently flawed machines have been built in the first nine months since the grounding, but none were delivered to airlines. When Boeing finally decided to halt production, their decision affected tens of thousands of suppliers in the US and abroad.

When a plane crashes, aviation authorities have their hands full. They want to know what caused the crash and how such tragedies can be averted in the future. No one believes there could be a crash without a cause, and if you're certain that there's a cause, you'll find it. In the investigation of the first tragedy, the final report, which took a year to deliver, listed nine possible causes of the crash. Which seems like a lot, until you see that a preliminary version of the report had listed forty-one causes, and an even earlier one had a hundred.

A few days after the announcement that production of the 737 Max planes would be suspended, a space capsule failed to reach its intended orbit. Boeing had also built the CST-100 Starliner astronaut capsule, under a contract with NASA worth more than $4 billion. The Atlas V rocket—built by Boeing's partner in United Launch Alliance, Lockheed Martin—pushed it to space. The capsule was undergoing an unmanned test before it could be human-rated to shuttle astronauts, primarily to and from the ISS. The failure was quickly attributed to a faulty timer—a minuscule part in the millions of parts that make up the spaceship. The astronauts slated to fly the first manned mission of the capsule announced that they could have corrected the problem if they had been aboard this flight.

So what caused the failure? Was it the timer or the absence of humans aboard the capsule? Was it a test procedure that allowed the faulty timer to be installed? Was it a design flaw that compromised the fault tolerance of the vehicle? Did corporate culture allow this to happen? Did government oversight miss some warning sign? What's the ultimate cause?

We humans love ultimate causes. We look for cause-and-effect relationships everywhere. Is a flat tire caused by catching a nail? Is an inflated tire caused by air pressure in it? Is the fall of a brick caused by Earth's gravity? Is the flight of a satellite caused by orbital velocity?

Do vaccinations cause autism? Does the Moon cause tides? Does fluoride in water cause you to get dumb and docile? Do chemtrails cause infertility? Does burning fossil fuels cause climate change? Do genetically modified crops cause cancer and, again, infertility in some racial groups but not others? Do black cats cause bad luck?

All of these allegations are based on correlations—real or imagined, documented or anecdotal, weak or strong, consistent or erratic. But we've all heard the mantra that "correlation does not imply causation." The number of drownings per day clearly correlates with ice cream consumption. The average global temperature clearly correlates with a number of pirates on the planet (see the plot below). The number of Japanese cars sold in the US clearly correlates with the number of vehicular homicides. It just happens to be inconceivable that there's a cause-and-effect relationship between these.

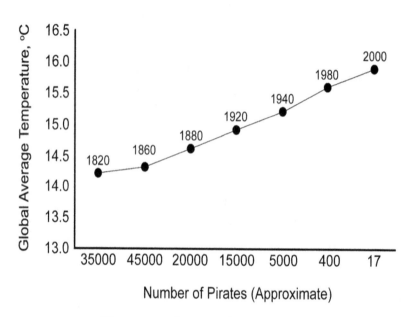

Figure 10 – Pirates and climate change.

But if correlation doesn't imply causation, then what does?

Apparently, our minds do. Our minds have noticed that we live in an exasperatingly complex, interconnected world that needs to be made sense of somehow. So they deploy two large-bore weapons as the first line of defense from menacing confusion: reduction and induction. Reduction reduces the complexity of the real world to simple, linear cause-and-effect relationships. Induction says that because some observed relationship has held true to this point, it's okay to assume that it will hold true forever and ever.

Let's look at reduction first. Reductionism is a philosophical approach that suggests that in order to understand a process too complex to comprehend as a whole, one needs to take it apart – and keep doing so until its components are small enough and simple enough for us to understand. Then—hopefully—we can reconstruct the whole from the parts.

The reductionist's world is made of bouncing pebbles, whose interactions are governed by immutable universal laws. In this world, if you can learn enough about the pebbles now, you should be able to predict their positions at any point in the future. This world is neat and ordered.

In the seventeenth century, Newton pioneered a reductionist approach to physics, and it proved incredibly powerful. It turns out that if you ignore everything about a falling apple except the fact that it's accelerating downward, you can build the foundation of a very successful scientific discipline: Newtonian mechanics. Generations of school kids have cursed Sir Isaac for forcing them to learn those darn equations. Generations of astronomers have praised him for helping them find planets and moons at any given time. Newtonian mechanics are great at describing interactions among very few pebbles. Newton's laws very accurately describe a pebble swinging on a string, shooting out of a cannon, sliding down an inclined plane, or even whooshing around a planet on the invisible string of gravitational attraction.

But as the number of pebbles in the system grows, we quickly run into trouble. All it takes is three gravitating pebbles, and you have the infamous three-body problem. No general formula can describe the three pebbles' trajectories. In special cases, the so-called closed-form solutions exist, but in general, the world is only approximately predictable with just three interacting pebbles in it. Newtonian mechanics speak the language of calculus, and we make predictions about the future by performing calculations. The closed-form solutions don't lose accuracy over time. You just input the time into the formula, crunch the numbers, and get the results. But if we can't find a closed-form solution, we have to use numerical approximations to make our predictions. To predict where the pebbles will be the next time we look, we start at some point in time with some initial conditions and increase the time, step by step. We can use the results from each increment as the initial conditions for the next one. In the real world, time doesn't advance by some arbitrary increment, so every time we do this, we introduce an error in our predictions. Errors accumulate, and trying to make predictions for some distant future puts us between a rock and a hard place. If we choose a small time increment, we have to do a lot of calculating steps, each taking time and introducing errors. But if we increase the time step, the number of calculations decreases, but then so too does the precision of each step. Looking into the future without a concise formula is a dicey proposition.

It gets worse. The whole idea of bouncing pebbles is based on the concept of an "isolated system." This means that all forces that influence the behavior of the system are contained within the system. Once additional interactions are introduced, the neat previous model flies out the window. An apple falling in the Earth's gravitational field can be described using a single force in the fleeting moment of its flight, but once the apple knocks somebody on the head, all bets are off. Most objects in the real world are involved in a lot of interactions at any given moment, and even more over time. The level of abstraction required to get Newtonian mechanics to yield predictions for most down-to-Earth systems is, frankly, ridiculous. Spherical cows in a vacuum are a rare breed.

If the connection of the reductionist worldview with reality is so tenuous, how did it become so influential? After all, historians credit Sir Isaac Newton with facilitating the Industrial Revolution no less—even though none of the early inventions of the Industrial Revolution has been, as far as we know, enabled by the inventor actually using Newtonian mechanics. Does Newton deserve the credit?

The Industrial Revolution was enabled by a new mindset, an enlightened worldview. Humans came to believe that Nature was governed by laws that humans could learn and use to control Nature for their benefit. And it wasn't just the scientists who thought so. When Newton presided over The Royal Society of London for Improving Natural Knowledge, two-thirds of its duty-paying members were non-scientists. Enlightenment wasn't confined to the groves of academe. Its ideas were shared and advanced by the society at large. Non-scientists—engineers, tinkerers, businessmen, lawyers, physicians, nobles, and tradespeople—participated in the cross-pollination of ideas. The scientific community promoting the concept of a world made of isolated systems was, ironically, itself anything but isolated.

The isolated system concept proved fruitful for both the Scientific and Industrial Revolutions. Watt's steam engine, which enabled the Industrial Revolution, was a fairly complicated contraption with dozens of interacting parts (see Figure 11 below). If somebody tried to compute the dynamics of that machine using Newtonian mechanics (known for half a century by then) with the means available in the dark, pre-Google ages, he'd still be at it today. Thankfully, James Watt didn't. Instead, he took the principle of an "isolated system" and ran with it. Watt was no scientist. He started his career as a scientific instrument maker, which exposed him to the idea of excluding undue influences and extraneous interactions.

In Boulton and Watt's steam engine, functions are assigned to specific parts and assemblies. Thus, we can think of them as "isolated systems." But they're all linked, right? Yes, but they're linked in a limited number of prescribed ways, allowing you to optimize one without considering the operation of another in detail. The governor Q, for example, is a rather complex assembly of many parts, which converts the speed of the rotation of a shaft into a displacement of some sort. In steam engines, it typically controls the speed by controlling the flow of steam. You don't need a detailed understanding of the governor mechanism to use it in a steam engine. Most other parts of the steam engine can be altered without altering the governor, and vice versa. Different engineers could develop the governor and the crank, and different companies can fabricate them and supply to the system integrator that puts the steam engine together. The "isolated system" of the governor Q consists of the governor itself, with all its delicate parts, intricate connections, and flawless kinematics; the input (angular velocity of a shaft); and the output (displacement and pressure exerted). The only folks who care about the innards of the governor are the ones who develop and build it. The others can focus on other parts. Even if the same person ends up developing more than one subsystem, it's still incomparably easier to develop each in turn and then, if necessary, tweak them until they work well together than to develop the whole system from scratch.

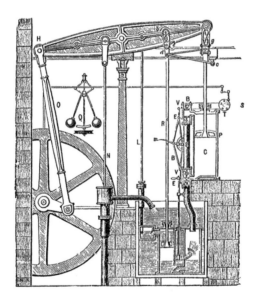

Figure 11 – Boulton and Watt steam engine, 1784.

The power of reductionism isn't its ability to reduce the complexity of Nature—it is what it is, and you can't reduce it—but its ability to reduce the complexity of the mental picture of Nature that we need to create useful approximations. Those approximations aren't perfect, but they're often good enough. Reductionism is a technique for focusing the mind's eye on a piece of the limitless Universe small enough to comprehend. It's a mental shortcut.

When used as an engineering tool, reductionism has proven incredibly useful. The Saturn V, the mighty rocket that took humans to the Moon, was comprised of more than 3,000,000 interacting parts. You think that's a lot? The largest number of transistors on a single chip made so far is roughly 1,200,000,000,000. That's how many grains of sand it would take to fill your bedroom to the ceiling. That's five times the number of stars in the Milky Way galaxy. That's fourteen times the number of neurons in the human brain. And even this breathtaking number pales in comparison with the number of components in the Internet. So how can we mere mortals organize a system with more cooperating parts than we have neurons to even consider each part?

By never considering each part individually, that's how. We build artificial systems as hierarchies of subsystems, each with its own self-contained innards and very limited—and strictly controlled—interactions with anything outside the particular subsystem. Together with the prescribed inputs and outputs, the innards make an "isolated system" that we can imagine, design, prototype, test, outsource to a place that can make a million replicas of it cheaply, and join it together with other subsystems that went through the same process. When subsystems of our artificial systems fail to interact in a strictly prescribed way with their environment—including each other—planes fall out of the sky, bridges and buildings and giant radio telescopes collapse, hammers hit walls and fingers instead of nails, and rockets blow up on the launch pad. We have learned to avoid most of that. We have become experts at building a whole civilization out of predictable, isolated subsystems.

We're surrounded by artificial things that reductionism helped create. Most of the objects that we modern humans deal with were developed that way. For people who live in a highly artificial world, it's only natural—pardon the pun—to think that everything in the Universe works the same way.

And science is glad to supply some glorious examples of Nature's apparent reductionism. Newton's law of universal gravitation made sense of the movements of planets and moons. The periodic table of elements illustrates how just one parameter (namely, the number of electrons in a neutral atom) largely determines the chemical properties of that atom. The Central Dogma of modern biology, proposed in 1958, postulates unidirectional information flow, from the DNA in your genes to the RNA intermediaries to the final product, which is functional protein. Neat, clean, logical, and sterile. Intellectually attractive. Teachable. Perfect for study-aid cartoons.

It's extremely tempting to think that we can make sense of all of Nature using a reductionist approach. But as Neil DeGrasse Tyson once said, "the Universe is under no obligation to make sense to you." There's no logical reason why the entire Universe should be made of bouncing pebbles, and there's no evidence that it is. To the contrary, there's a lot of evidence that, if all you choose to see is bouncing pebbles, you're missing a lot.

In physiology and sociology, geophysics and climate science, economics and behavioral science, materials science and meteorology, the reductionist approach yields embarrassingly inaccurate predictions about the behavior of the systems in question. Studying components of a system in isolation from the rest of that system fails to provide useable information about its interactions within the system as a whole. We can stare at a monkey in a zoo for ages but remain entirely clueless about what it's going to do in the jungle. Complex systems have emergent properties that can't be guessed, predicted, modeled, or computed based on any amount of data collected for their components in isolation from the rest of the world. Context matters.

The pebble bouncers dismiss this little inconvenience as a mere computational problem. Give us the positions and velocities of every atom in the system at a given time, they say, and with sufficient computing power, we'll tell you what the system's going to look like at any given time and with any given precision. Read out every atom in, say, a human brain, and you can 3-D print its perfect copy elsewhere. Beam me up, Scotty.

The Star Trek teleportation transporter is a direct descendant of Laplace's demon. What later came to be called Laplace's demon was a beautifully poetic formulation of the reductionist causality myth: "An intellect which at a certain moment would know all forces that set Nature in motion, and all positions of all items of which Nature is composed, if this intellect were also vast enough to submit these data to analysis, it would embrace in a single formula the movements of the greatest bodies of the Universe and those of the tiniest atom; for such an intellect nothing would be uncertain and the future just like the past would be present before its eyes." The normally hectic Paris is an unexpected place to dream up a perfectly predictable, ordered world, but that's precisely where Pierre-Simon de Laplace came up with the demon idea—in 1814, while bearded Cossacks galloped down Champs-Elysées. Laplace was a past master of abstraction.

The universe of bouncing pebbles, however, is seldom taken to be an escapist poetic metaphor. Its adherents believe that it is the true nature of Nature, the cornerstone of Almighty Science, the yardstick we should use to measure the Ultimate Truth.

This would be all well and good if not for a couple of little problems. It turns out that bouncing pebble world is incompatible with both quantum mechanics and the theory of relativity (among other things). First, Heisenberg's uncertainty principle says that you can't know the positions and velocities of every atom in the system at a given time with arbitrary precision to begin with. Second, there's supposed to be no such thing as a "given time" either. Any galaxy far, far away—as we see it today—is far, far in the past. For all we know, today it may not even exist anymore. At what point in time is the demon supposed to know "all positions of all items of which nature is composed"? In what sense can we even talk about "positions" of moving stuff at a given time, especially after Einstein shot the universal clock off the wall with his double-barreled relativity gun?

And if that weren't enough, any practical attempt to approach the theoretical limit set by Heisenberg for a system of a reasonable size—say a brain—would look like a really big explosion to any observer unfortunate enough to happen by. The explosion would be particularly devastating if the brain were a big one, like the one owned and operated by Jacob Bekenstein (who, among other things, worked with Stephen Hawking to find leaks in black holes). Bekenstein discovered that there is a limit to how much information one can stuff into a finite space. It comes to about 2.6×10^{42} bits of information to read out each and every atom in a human brain. According to Boltzmann's entropy formula for conversion of that information into energy at, say, 36.6° C, we need 8×10^{21} J, the equivalent of about two million million tons of TNT. In the volume of a brain. That's the energy required to map the brain to Bekenstein bound of precision (which is nowhere near infinite).

How much time do you have to read out that information before the pebbles shift out of position and you have to start from scratch? Well, you'll be doing molecular dynamics simulations of a brain, and there's a lot of hydrogen in a brain. In molecular dynamics simulations of something containing hydrogen bonds, the time step is on the order of 1 to 2 femtoseconds (10^{-15} second). That's how fast you need to read out everything if you ever hope to map the atoms making up the brain. That's how long you have to spend the energy equivalent of about two million million tons of TNT. In the volume of a brain. The power required is on the order of the entire output of the Milky Way galaxy. In the volume of a brain.

The energy equivalent of the brain mass—the famous $E=mc^2$—yields a mere 10^{17} J. So in order to keep up with the brain using matter-antimatter annihilation as your power source, you would need to burn matter in the amount 40,000 times the mass of the brain in the 10^{-15} seconds, and the identical amount of antimatter. The brain in question has a femtosecond to somehow interact with matter and antimatter 80,000 times its own mass—to get mapped to a precision infinitely lower than the infinite precision the demon asked for. And that's as much precision as you can ever get. Can you imagine anything more dissimilar to an "isolated system" than a brain being mapped as you build a Laplace's demon model of it? I know I can't.

And we're just getting started. We haven't submitted the data for analysis yet, as Laplace's demon asked. We have on the order of 10^{26} bouncing pebbles to analyze in a human brain. And they interact all the time. A vast majority of them for the vast majority of time probably don't do anything to write home about, but in the bouncing pebble model of the Universe, Laplace's demon doesn't have the luxury of losing track of even one of them. It has no choice but to follow each of them all the time. Incrementing time, step by fleeting step, and creating 2.6×10^{42} bits of information every time. You can't skip any steps because you need the results of each as initial conditions for the next. And you'll need 1 to 2 femtoseconds for the time step. Doing calculations costs energy, and so does writing the results somewhere. A lot of energy. About as much as mapping.

So it's not just in the first femtosecond that the demon would annihilate countless millions of tons of matter/antimatter to fuel the creation of the map of the little isolated brain. It's every femtosecond just to keep up with what's going on. At that rate, the equivalent of Earth's mass would be consumed in about one day, and the Sun's mass would be gone in about 700 years. You'd need to keep pumping all the energy of the Milky Way galaxy just to keep up with the pebbles in a little brain, and that little brain is still an isolated system. You'd never know anything about the brain owner's breathing and eating and playing soccer. You'd never learn from the energy-gobbling simulation anything about the brain owner who built and operated the simulation. The bouncing pebble model is incapable of running itself.

If that's not enough, Hans-Joachim Bremermann has put yet another fence between Laplace's demon and reality. Bremermann calculated the limit to how fast a real digital computer of finite size—however cleverly designed—can perform its calculations. It comes out to 1.36×10^{50} bits per second per kilogram, so an ideal computer weighing as much as an average human brain would calculate at 2×10^{50}

bits per second. And to keep up with itself, it has to calculate 2.6×10^{42} bits every 10^{-15} second or 2.6×10^{57} bits per second. That is, 13,000,000 times faster than it can. To put it another way, an ideal digital computer is 13,000,000 times too slow to do what it would need to do to predict what it's going to do before it actually does it. It would take more than half a year for an ideal brain-sized computer to "predict" just one second of the brain's work with questionable precision.[5]

Enough already. If all the resources of the Milky Way galaxy are required to do a real-time molecular dynamics simulation of one isolated brain using the bouncing pebbles model, then the model is useless for making predictions. And if it's useless for making predictions, then its predictions can never be compared with observations. Which means that it's not a falsifiable (a.k.a. scientific) hypothesis.

But maybe it's doable using a hierarchy of "pebbles," like we do with computer chips and rockets and cars and aircraft? Bigger pebbles could be made up of smaller pebbles, and those of even smaller ones, and so on all the way down to atoms and subatomic particles.

This is where a big difference between science and engineering comes to play. Engineers design things the right way—the way that looks right to them, that is. They deliberately cut the system into more manageable subsystems, define interfaces between those systems, then develop each subsystem. And if a subsystem proves too cumbersome to develop as a whole, they repeat the process until all the pieces are within reach. Simplifying the heck out of a system is what gets engineers promotions, bonuses, and respect.

Scientists don't have this luxury. Scientists love simplicity as much as anyone, but Nature seldom cooperates. Studying a system of two balls acting upon each other through vast empty space, 100 times the size of the larger ball—those were the good old days. We have since learned that isolated systems are a rare exception in Nature. Natural systems usually are messy and have lots of interactions, and you never have the luxury of knowing in advance which of the interactions will turn out to be important and when and where they will happen. The exhaustive list of significant interactions in your system may be spelled out in a physics homework assignment, but in Nature, you need to find out for yourself. More often than not, it is the interactions that you are looking for, if you are doing actual science rather than homework. Isolating the pebbles snaps connections among them. It reduces the reality to what you have included in the model.

---

[5] That's how badly we need scientific theories. Without the abstraction shortcuts they offer, we'd never predict anything in time to do us any good.

When engineers model something, they aren't interested in confirming the laws by which their pebbles bounce. The engineers start with the assumption that the laws work. If you're busy building a bridge, you can't afford the distraction of verifying Hooke's law. What you're asking a model to tell you is whether your design works or not.

When scientists model and test something, they aren't testing that "something." They're testing the model itself. If predictions of the model fail an experimental test, then the model is wrong. If predictions of the model survive an experimental test, they may still fail the next one. Every model is a priori wrong under some circumstances—it's an abbreviation of Nature, imperfect by design. What scientific testing doesn't do is "prove" the model. What scientific testing does do is find situations where the model isn't good enough to yield useful predictions and (hopefully) others where it is.

Multi-scale hierarchical models are an instant win for engineers because they know the boundaries between the pebbles at each scale. Engineers often design boundaries between the pebbles for the express purpose of making their interactions testable every step of the way.

It's a lot harder for scientists. How do you cut up, say, a whole human brain into top-level bouncing pebbles? More than a century ago, Korbinian Brodmann tried to do just that following histological clues. Except, of course, the pebbles—the fifty-two Brodmann areas—weren't bouncing much because the brain under his histological microscope was dead. And it's very hard to run an experimental test of any hypothesis concerning live pebbles if the only pebbles you can study are dead.

Ever since, people have drilled skulls and poked electrodes into live brains, trying to find some kind of a universal law that fundamentally controls interactions among the Brodmann pebbles. For the last thirty years, neuroscientists have had an additional weapon in their arsenal: the fMRI. This imaging technology shows the flow of energy to replenish what's recently spent by active areas of the brain.

The problem with Brodmann super-pebbles, which is the same problem with any natural subsystem bigger than an atom, is that there doesn't appear to be anything fundamental about the "laws" governing interactions among them. We may one day discover otherwise, but there's only one tool at our disposal to discover it, and that's the scientific method. If you look at interactions in Brodmann area 17, which lights up in fMRI when you see a fly approaching your eye, and a blink of that eye, it looks nowhere near as neat and orderly and set in stone as Newton's $F=ma$. Today you see the fly and choose to blink; yesterday, under similar circumstances, you chose to butt it with your head; and tomorrow you may choose to go after the darn thing with a vengeance and a fly swatter.

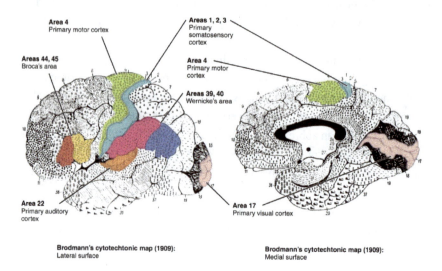

Figure 12 – Brodmann areas. Image courtesy of OpenStax (via Wikimedia).

Of course, the pebble bouncers will tell you that the rest of your brain was in a different state in each case, and the fundamental laws of the Universe inexorably led it to three different reactions to the same stimulus. When they do, ask them to please predict what you're going to do next time.

Science, unlike religion, is supposed to be strictly evidence based. For a postulate to qualify as a scientific hypothesis, it must produce falsifiable, discriminating predictions. To become a theory, it then needs to survive lots of attempts to falsify it. Falsifiable means someone can make an observation or design an experiment and compare its outcome with what the hypothesis has predicted. Discriminating means that a competing theory would predict a different result for the same experiment or observation. Without any evidence, anything is possible, and science tries to avoid assuming a priori knowledge. With evidence, the possible shrinks to what's possible given the evidence. When they sent Gagarin eastward to fly around the Earth and he came back from the West and reported seeing no turtle with elephants on its back, the space of cosmological possibilities shrunk considerably.

A good scientific hypothesis is one with a lot of discriminating power. It makes predictions that are so specific that any observation or experimental result kills a lot of alternative explanations about how else the Universe might otherwise work. In other words, it shrinks the possibility space a lot. Possibilities are opposite of knowledge, so the more we know, the less remains possible given that knowledge.[6] Using Newtonian mechanics, Urbain Le Verrier predicted, from irregularities of Uranus' orbit, where to look for an extra planet no one had seen before. He then looked there and found Neptune. Then, using Newtonian mechanics, Urbain Le Verrier predicted, from irregularities of Mercury's orbit, where to look for another extra planet no one had seen before. He was so confident that he would find a planet that he even gave it a name before looking: Vulcan. Then he looked and found... nothing. They kept looking for more than seventy years, which is how long it took to propose an alternative hypothesis. The hypothesis was Einstein's general relativity theory.

If nothing in the observable world depends on whether a postulate is true or false, then the postulate is irrelevant and can't add anything to knowledge. There are two ways for a postulate to never make it as a scientific hypothesis. The first is that it fails to make any testable predictions at all. The second is that it makes predictions that would be the same for a large number of alternative postulates.

For example, a statement could be that the world is made of a hierarchy of bouncing pebbles, and that the bigger pebbles are made of the smaller ones. In this multi-scale bouncing pebble model, there are fundamental laws at each level governing the interactions among the pebbles—the bouncing. How do you make this statement contribute to the scientific understanding of Nature? You derive predictions about Nature from it, predictions specific enough to check against observations or experiments and discriminating enough so alternative theories give different predictions. The trouble is that you can't make any specific, testable predictions without first getting specific about what your pebbles are and what the "fundamental laws" of their interaction are. Therein lies the rub.

For fifty-two Brodmann super-pebbles, you'll need 1,326 pairwise "laws." Each law is, in fact, at least two laws: a reaction of area A to the stimulation of area B, and vice versa. Do these 2,652 laws act independently of each other? Do interactions between Brodmann areas 26 and 42 somehow affect interactions between 8 and 14? You need to ask 7,033,104 of these questions over a range of stimuli and their relative timing and over a range of study subjects. Each answer requires a multi-year study by several Ph.D. researchers, hundreds—if not thousands—of subjects.

---

[6] That's another big difference between science and engineering. In science, the possible shrinks as you learn more, moving from "anything goes" to what's allowed given what you've learned. In engineering, you start from scratch, and possibilities grow with knowledge.

This project would exceed the Manhattan Project in scale by as much as the Manhattan Project exceeded Edison's experiments with light bulbs. And we're just getting started.

There's no a priori reason to exclude the possibility of triplets of the "laws" mutually influencing each other. Or quadruplets. Or any number, up to and including all of them. And every time you add a potentially dependent law, the number of experiments you need to run rises by a factor of 2,652. By the time you get to checking combinations of thirty interactions, the number of experiments you need to perform exceeds the number of atoms in the observable Universe. This way lies defeat.

Could be, instead, build the multi-scale hierarchy the other way around—from the atoms up? Could we get from ab initio molecular dynamics of the molecules involved, to subcellular structures—organelles, synapses, etc.—to cells, to Brodmann areas, to the whole brain? It works for engineers, after all—from atoms to transistors, from transistors to circuits, from circuits to integrated chips, from integrated chips to electronic modules, from modules to complete computers, servers, Internet. What's different about modeling Nature?

The short answer is... everything. In engineering, you can assume the bouncing pebble worldview as a given, and you can make sure you build your system so that, for your system, it's reasonably accurate. In science, the hypothesis that the world is nothing but bouncing pebbles has to be falsifiable, like any other hypothesis that aims to contribute to our knowledge. And the "nothing but" kind of hypothesis in science is the easiest one to falsify. If you need any additional assumptions on top of your model to make any predictions you can compare to an experiment or observation, then it's not "nothing but" anymore, and the hypothesis is false.

Do you need nothing but oxygen atoms and hydrogen atoms to make a snowflake? If you take this to be a falsifiable (a.k.a. scientific) hypothesis, then it's false. No one has so far predicted the shape of a snowflake starting with "nothing but" models of hydrogen and oxygen. Not without, ahem, peeking at the answers. If there's nothing but hydrogen and oxygen atoms in the freezing water, then all possible snowflake shapes could be predicted starting with nothing but hydrogen and oxygen. But so far, not a single snowflake has been "built" from scratch, much less the infinite variety of them observed in Nature. The claim that a snowflake is "nothing but" bouncing pebbles has zero support in modern science. And as of this writing, that's where we are with snowflakes. Emergent properties of these relatively large ensembles of atoms don't appear to be reducible—in a meaningful traceable way—to the properties of the atoms themselves.

And if you can't predict a simple snowflake shape starting with just two kinds of pebbles, try predicting a mitochondrion, synapse, neuron, or the nervous system of C. elegans with 302 neurons. C. elegans, by the way, is a tiny round worm that has no brain, and its life experience is somewhat limited compared to ours. Never mind the human brain with its 86,000,000,000 neurons and 1,000,000,000,000,000 synapses. Never mind general relativity and the *Mona Lisa*.

Pebble bouncers—each equipped with 86,000,000,000 neurons and 1,000,000,000,000,000 synapses—are a very inventive bunch. You think that you've cornered them with your demand that they produce something tangible, but they easily wiggle out. Sure, they say, we can't build a working model of the brain from nothing but bouncing pebbles today, but if we keep trying long enough—and get funded generously enough—maybe we can do it tomorrow. Well, in a decade.

In 2009, Henry Markram promised to create—in ten years—a hologram to talk to a human on equal terms. In 2013, his Human Brain Project got $1.3 billion from the EU for those ten years [10]. To date, HBP has produced more Europe-wide scandals than scientific models of bouncing-pebble brains of any kind: 1 and 0, respectively. The scandal, which focused on project management issues, has—IMHO—missed the point. Billed as Big Science, the project sure was big, but it never had much use for the scientific method. There was no falsifiable hypothesis to begin with, and without one, all you get for $1.3 billion is a bunch of really cool animations that add nothing to our knowledge of the nature of Nature.

Yet this fiasco failed to convince the pebble bouncers to reconsider the nothing-but-bouncing-pebbles model of the human brain. In the best traditions of plausible deniability, the reductionists claim that the nothing-but-bouncing-pebbles model is The Received Truth. It's just computational difficulties that prevent us from getting any testable predictions.

No statement is falsifiable if we don't ask for testable conclusions (in other words, if we take it on faith). Ernest Rutherford once quipped that all science is either physics or stamp collecting. It's not about a particular discipline. It's about the approach. A historian can have falsifiable hypotheses and—literally—dig up evidence; conversely, an alleged physicist can claim "mere computational difficulties" as an excuse for a hypothesis failing to yield testable predictions.

There's nothing trivial about the "incomputability" of predictions. Testable predictions are the language of science, and a postulate doesn't get to enter the exclusive club of scientific ideas unless it's substantive enough to make predictions without peeking at the answers. One of the common ways of failing to make computable predictions about the real world is the butterfly effect. For many complex systems, a small variation in initial conditions can, over time, completely change the behavior of the system in question.

Edward Lorenz, a mathematician involved in meteorological modelling, noticed that a small change in initial conditions in weather simulations got amplified over time, and eventually the forecast had nothing in common with the original one. "Does the flap of a butterfly's wings in Brazil set off a tornado in Texas?" was the title of a talk Lorenz gave about the effect. His research gave rise to chaos theory, a branch of mathematics that studies dynamic systems highly sensitive to initial conditions. Chaos theory shows no signs of running out of systems to study. Neurons, their dynamics, and their networks are among the favorite subjects of chaos theorists. The dynamics of clouds and interpersonal networks, economics and populations, epidemics and asteroid trajectories are all chaotic. Small variations in initial conditions grow over time and trigger widely different behavior in all of these systems.

In 1936, Alan Turing—later credited with founding computer science no less—published a paper addressing computability. He mathematically proved that there are numbers that can't be arrived at by any computational procedure. What does it mean for systems with a butterfly effect, which are ubiquitous in the real world? Let's imagine that Turing's incomputable numbers happen to be the initial conditions for some dynamic scenario of a chaotic system. Any iterative procedure takes output from its previous step as initial conditions for the next one. That means that this scenario can't be predicted by any iterative procedure, and over time, the unpredictable scenario may grow very different from any predictable one. In other words, what Turing and Lorenz have shown together is that some scenarios of the evolution of an arbitrary, complex system differ substantially from any scenario that we can predict by any iterative procedure. And the real world is chock-full of complex systems.

Chaotic systems are chaotic not just when you try to predict the future. They work the same way looking into the past. A small inaccuracy in measuring today's world not only makes a lot of radically different futures possible, but also it makes possible a lot of radically different pasts. We don't know where each butterfly in the world is right now, and even if we tried to determine that, we would only get a (very) limited resolution in space and time: it takes an inordinate amount of energy to collect precise information about any macroscopic object, as we have seen with the brain. A lot of radically different pasts are, for all we know, perfectly compatible with the world we see today. The limited resolution of mapping the world today gets amplified by the bouncing-pebbles dynamics, be it forward in time or backward. As far as we can tell, the past rapidly loses the ability to influence the present—and, of course, the future—in any testable (a.k.a. scientific) way. That appears very different from the Universe where everything is inexorably guided by immutable laws and precise initial conditions. But at least this works in the approximation of the Newtonian mechanistic world, right?

No, that's wrong, too. The gravestone of the myth that Newtonian mechanics are deterministic is called the Norton Dome (not to be mistaken for Notre Dame), an example of Newtonian indeterministic system. In the mid-1970s, the non-deterministic behavior of Newtonian systems was found with the tip of a pen, much like the planet Neptune was found. The trouble was that the systems included either an infinite number of objects or infinite distances between them, not an easy thing to observe or experiment with.

Then in 2003, Professor John D. Norton found an indeterministic Newtonian system with just three components in it: the Earth's gravity, a specially shaped dome, and a ball precariously balanced on the top of the dome [11]. Newtonian mechanics can't determine if the ball ever rolls off, and if it does, it can't determine which way it will go. It has nothing to do with anything disturbing the ball, like an irritated determinist blowing a lot of hot air on it or the seismic effects of a bunch of resentful reductionists stomping their feet at Professor Norton. If it did, the Newtonian equations of motion would have to include these disturbances to predict the ball spontaneously leaving the apex at some indeterminate point in the future in some indeterminate direction. They don't. Clockwork Newtonian mechanics predicts that the ball can leave whenever and wherever it darn well pleases without any help from a passing garbage truck or a determinist falling out of his chair in a lab next door.

So much for reduction. The other cornerstone of the causality temple is induction, the belief that it's enough to see some number of white swans to conclude that all swans are white. Being a swan "causes" a bird to be white.

Inductive reasoning is an extremely potent tool in practice. Seeing folks cross a wobbly suspension bridge gives you confidence—justified most of the time—that you'll make it across just fine, too. Multiple fines for speeding at the same spot will eventually teach you to avoid the damn place. If your Scotch and soda doesn't agree with your stomach (and the rest of your body), and neither do bourbon and soda, tequila and soda, or vodka and soda, then it won't be long before you recognize the common denominator and exclude the soda.

Since at least Sextus Empiricus, a second-century physician and philosopher, thinkers have recognized that inductive reasoning is no more than a mental shortcut, lacking any logical foundation. Is induction useful? Hell yes. When our esteemed ancestors heard a rustle of leaves somewhere, they usually had no opportunity to scientifically investigate if it was a lion or a rabbit. They had to choose which way to run, and they had to choose fast. We're the descendants of those who happened to make the right choices most of the time.

Figure 13 – Black swan.

Is it scientific? Hell no. The favorite argument for induction is that "it works," which indeed it often does. Until it doesn't. The guy hit by enemy fire is always someone else, until it's you. It's always winter on Christmas, until you're in Australia.

Induction isn't even logical. Induction is, after all, the idea that if something works today, it's going to work just as well tomorrow. If you take the fact that induction works today as evidence that induction is going to work just as well tomorrow, you have just assumed the result. Get off the hamster wheel already.

Like reduction, induction is an exceptionally useful mental shortcut. It offers enormous savings of processing power in familiar situations. It's a reliable cornerstone for our common sense. If Grandpa and Pops made spearheads by flaking this kind of rock, then the first thing I'm going to try if I need to make a spearhead is making it from the same kind of rock and in the same way that worked before.

The trouble begins when we use such shortcuts in science and forget that we did. Say we're trying to find out how old a spearhead is. How do we go about it? We use radioactive decay. Rocks contain potassium, and some of it is radioactive isotope ^{40}K. The ^{40}K nuclei spontaneously decay into ^{40}Ar, and the ^{40}K half-life is over a billion years; so, story goes, you measure the ^{40}Ar/^{40}K ratio and, voilà, you have the age of your sample. The longer version of the story is that about 90% of the decay isn't into ^{40}Ar but ^{40}Ca, but there's so much of that lying around that ^{40}Ca/^{40}K won't tell you much because most of the ^{40}Ca has nothing to do with the ^{40}K. It could have come from lots of other sources, so we use the ^{40}Ar/^{40}K ratio.

We have just skipped over a whole lot of assumptions without even mentioning—much less explicitly admitting to—any of them. We implicitly postulated that, unlike ^{40}Ca, ^{40}Ar can only be introduced in the sample from ^{40}K decay. We implicitly postulated that ^{40}Ar formed in the sample stays in the sample, either completely or in some known proportion (that's a particularly tenuous assumption because argon is a noble gas that loves its freedom so much that it puts libertarians and escape artists to shame). We implicitly postulated that the only process that can ever change the concentration of ^{40}K in the sample is its radioactive decay, and the proportion of the decay that results in the formation of ^{40}Ar is a constant over time. And so is the rate of decay.

Each of these assumptions has the distinct advantage of being just about the simplest scenario we can imagine, but is that good enough? After all, the theory that the world was created in six days about 6,000 years ago is even simpler, and Whoever can create a whole world in six days would have no trouble forging fossils with any ^{40}Ar/^{40}K ratio He chooses. Scientists are reputed to be a lot pickier than to accept something for no better reason than that it's apparently simple.

For example, are the constants—including isotope decay rates—really constant? It turns out that we don't know. Everyone and his brother know that Einstein postulated the invariance of the speed of light in his 1905 theory of special relativity; fewer people know that Einstein was also working on variable light-speed models for much of the rest of his life. The possibility of variable light speed has come back to light in the 1990s, when physicists learned to measure the temperature of cosmic microwave background. They looked around the cosmic horizon and found what is now called the "horizon problem." The darn cosmic microwave background temperature looked uniform across the sky, as if all thermostats were at the same setting. That includes parts of the sky too far apart to coordinate the settings of their thermostats—if, that is, the speed of the coordinating signal didn't exceed the constant speed of light. The easiest proposed way out of this dilemma, which doesn't in any way "prove" that it's true, is to assume that the light speed in the early Universe was 1,000,000,000,000,000,000,000 times higher than it is now. The alternatives suggested so far are even worse than that.

Other constants don't get nailed down just because they're called "constant" either. Each constant's constancy is a hypothesis, and each of these hypotheses have an unbounded number of competing hypotheses, which hold that the "constant" does, in fact, vary over time in one way or another. For all we know, it can be anything—until we know better (that is, until we have observations or experimental results that narrow the field). The hypothesis that the fine structure "constant" is an actual constant, for example, hasn't survived experimental testing [12]. And the fine structure "constant" is a combination of three other fundamental "constants" (the speed of light, Planck's constant, and the electron charge), so at least one of these has to be variable as well.

We can, in principle, study the constancy of constants over many billions of years by looking at objects billions of light-years away. For example, the gravitational constant nine billion years ago can be checked by looking at a supernova whose light took nine billion years to reach us. What we're looking at today is what the supernova was doing a long time ago. Conclusion? The upper limit of the gravitational constant's average change over the nine billion years is 10^{-10} per year. Huh? Well, in plain English that means that it could have been $9 \times 10^9 \times 10^{-10} = 90\%$ different from the present value back then. That is, tenfold lower or two-fold higher. And, of course, it could have been changing all the time in between, either within these boundaries or outside them. And this Earth-shattering conclusion still depends, by the way, on the supernova being what astrophysicists call "a standard candle," meaning that it works today exactly the same way it did nine billion years ago. Wait, aren't the constancy of the laws that run the Universe and the constants that go with them what we were trying to test in the first place? Didn't the number of assumptions piling on top of each other make the whole exercise useless?

Well, not exactly. We did indeed learn something: the models of the Universe that are incompatible with what we have just found out are all wrong. That includes both the models that didn't work and the ones we never put together in the first place, so any future theoretician trying to explain how the world works will have to do it in a way compatible with the facts at hand. And that's nowhere near useless. We managed to get rid of an infinite number of possibilities. We just didn't reduce the number of remaining possibilities to anywhere near one.

Why would anyone believe that Einstein's cosmological constant is a constant? Because Einstein said so, that's why. And Einstein introduced the constant in 1917 to accommodate a static Universe. Lacking any way of actually finding out if the dang thing expanded or contracted or swirled or whatever, he assumed it was static: that was the simplest scenario we could imagine at the time. Then in 1927, Georges Lemaître dared to doubt, and in 1931 Edwin Hubble bothered to check if we actually live in a static Universe. It turned out that we don't. Our Universe is expanding. So the constant was out, to the delight of Einstein, who is reputed to have called it his biggest blunder.

Except it wasn't. Throwing the cosmological constant away turned out to be an explanation for something that cosmologists, again, assumed to be the case just because it was the simplest scenario they could imagine at the time: expansion at a constant rate. Even before Hubble's observations, Russian cosmologist Alexander Friedman had identified multiple solutions of Einstein's original equations of general relativity, which all led to alternative scenarios: accelerated expansion, decelerated expansion, pulsation, etc. Almost eighty years later, the expansion was found to be accelerating, which means that the "cosmological constant" term is real and measurable. We know its value (at least we think we do). And it's puzzling—again.

It's puzzling because the prevailing interpretation of the general relativity equation with the cosmological constant term in it is that the term stands for the energy density of a vacuum. It's that "dark energy," which people have so far failed to detect in the laboratory, that prevents the gravitational attraction of the matter in the Universe from slowing down the Universe's expansion. To explain observed behavior of the Universe, a lot of "dark energy" is needed, enough to make up about three-quarters of the Universe.

And it's missing. A force holding up the sky isn't exactly easy to miss. Yet people keep looking for it and finding nothing [13].

If that's not enough of a puzzle, the quantum theory of vacuum gives an estimate for vacuum energy density. So does cosmology. And the estimates differ 1,000,000,000,000,000,000,000,000,000,000,000,000,000,000,000,000, 000,000,000,000,000,000,000,000,000,000-fold. Stop counting already. That's 120 zeros. The situation has been called "the worst theoretical prediction in the history of physics." And the only solution [14] even proposed to deal with this gargantuan faux pax starts with doubting the convenient assumption that the Universe is uniform, an assumption so patently false that one wonders why it took a lot of very smart physicists almost a century to shake off its spell.

If this isn't a crisis in science, then I don't know what is. Postulating the simplest scenario we could imagine is like betting on a horse that wins every race—unless there happen to be other entrants. All complex phenomena have simple, easy-to-understand wrong explanations. And our Universe is very complex. Trying to reduce it to a set of simple linear cause-and-effect relationships is, at best, folk science: a set of memes somewhat useful only within our puny experience.

Figure 14 – Holding up the sky.

"Causation as a folk science" is the title of a 2003 article by John D. Norton in *Philosophers' Imprint*. Professor Norton argues that causality is like a vacuum. Vacuum sucks. And Nature abhors it. For a vivid image that's enough, but if you have to calculate the actual forces, you'll have to abandon the illusion of a vacuum acting on things and look for something else, like pressure of the air outside the vacuum.

Causality dogma isn't benign or harmless. Once we refuse to see everything that has no apparent cause, we ignore or disbelieve a lot of the world around us. And then we stare in puzzlement at the reproducibility crisis in science, when way over half of the results published in respected peer-reviewed journals can't be duplicated. In the bouncing-pebbles world of isolated systems, this can't be happening: an isolated system of bouncing pebbles, where you know and control all interactions with the outside world, will respond to the same test in the same way today as it did yesterday. The evidence is in: there's a lot out there that the deterministic cause-and-effect paradigm fails to account for. For the bouncing pebbles to do their flawless act on curling ice, a bunch of oddly serious guys with regulation brooms feverishly remove all the imperfections they can, knowing full well the damn curling stone is going to stop in a matter of seconds anyway.

Isolating systems from the world, so their behavior briefly looks causal, takes a lot of ingenuity and hard work. That's the business of scientific instrument makers, and they're among the most inventive folks on the planet. No wonder James Watt, the father of the Industrial Revolution, was a scientific instrument maker by trade. No wonder it took the genius of John Michell, the discoverer of black holes and double stars, to build the devilishly clever torsion balance for the so-called Cavendish experiment, which weighed the Earth.

But reducing interconnections in the real world to linear cause-and-effect dependencies usually throws the baby out with the bathwater. We start snapping connecting threads in the natural web, and the web inexorably changes. The tension on the remaining threads adjusts, and the nodes move. The cause-and-effect worldview is a filter, a bias. Simplifying the real world to fit into our mental picture limits our perception of the world. We then only see the stuff that can be jammed into a causal picture frame. It took more than 300 years after publication of Newton's *Principia* to even consider that there might be something indeterministic in a simple Newtonian system. Determinists still summarily dismiss any connection between the potential fate of a newborn and the position of planets on that particular day (a.k.a. astrology) as contrary to the principles of the Almighty Science and, therefore, impossible. Wild horses couldn't drag them to look at any astrological data, far less to do their own research on this outlandish thing. That is, until one tells them, in their own causal language, that the gravitational pull of the planets may shake the plasma that the Sun is made of, like a storm shakes oil in a tanker; and sunspots may reflect that motion; and that radiation may, in turn, interact with the electromagnetic field on Earth, which a fetus is shielded from with conductive amniotic fluid, until it's born. On a certain date. So that date can be a lot more relevant than the pebble bouncers assume, without even looking.

Assuming stuff—believing something without evidence—is religion. Science, on the other hand, is supposed to require evidence. It's supposed to be so objective that it even calculates the probability of being wrong, then dutifully reports that about each hypothesis, as a confidence level. It reports the hypothesis, the data collected, and the probability of it being wrong. The probability looks low, so the hypothesis is true, right? Well, not so fast.

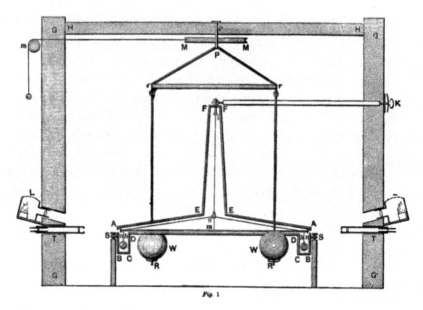

Figure 15 – *Cavendish experiment: the balance that weighed the Earth.*

Here we come upon the dark secret of the current scientific paradigm: the null hypothesis. The null hypothesis is The Sacred Truth of reductionist science and the foundation of its current paradigm. Like any foundation, it's supposed to be inconspicuous. Indeed, it's frequently—and conveniently—overlooked.

The null hypothesis, the default position of reductionism, goes like this: any two phenomena are unrelated unless proven otherwise. The onus is always on whoever wants to prove the interdependence of the world. So the world made of isolated systems is assumed by default, with no evidence required. If you see things as interconnected, then in the eyes of the current scientific paradigm, you're guilty until proven innocent.

This military maxim is attributed to Helmuth von Moltke the Elder: no battle plan ever survives contact with the enemy. Just as an illustration of how quickly onus-pushing fails even the simplest reality tests, let's apply the null hypothesis to reductionist science itself, as related to objective reality. Remember, the null hypothesis says that "A" is, by default, unrelated to "B," whatever "A" and "B" are, unless proven otherwise. So if we take "A" to be reductionist worldview and "B" to be learning about the nature of Nature, then, by default, using reductionists' favorite commandment, the reductionist view has nothing to do with understanding reality, unless we have measured and published in a peer-reviewed journal a P-value for the scientific hypothesis that it does. Which no one has done so far.

Nothing conveys the sense of belonging like shared biases. Ever wondered why "peer review" sounds so much like "peer pressure"? It's hard to publish anything without chanting the accepted mantras. Causality is what one uses to swear allegiance to the Guild. All you have to do is write something like "Illusions of causality at the heart of pseudoscience" [15], and everyone knows that you're on the side of the angels, and no causality you allege can possibly be illusory. No cardholding member of the Guild will ever point out the glaring omission of any recipe for distinguishing between illusions of causality and the allegedly real thing.

With the Guild in habitual denial—despite ample evidence to the contrary—that it has a systemic problem, much less that any particular conclusion could possibly have anything to do with that problem, it's hard to blame waning public trust in science [16] exclusively on the public. Take, for example, this gem: the up-and-coming discipline of attribution science. In full compliance with the cause-and-effect tradition, attribution science strives to provide expert evidence connecting any particular disaster with the actions of a particular alleged wrongdoer, preferably one with deep pockets [17] so it can be sued for the particular tornado or flood that dropped a tree on your porch. Or better yet, your Porsche. In the backward days of Plato and Ibn Sina and Ulugh Beq and Newton, the barriers between science and racket may have been somewhat higher. But modern attributologists can offer jury-dazzling services using the best statistical and visualization software packages your money can buy, unavailable to the idealists of the bygone era. They can expertly giggle at any suggestion that these very packages predicted, with 96% confidence, that Hillary Clinton would win the US presidency hours before Donald Trump actually won it. A humble reminder that the pebble-bouncing reductionist models—allegedly accurate to hundredth decimal place or whatever—completely missed the 2008 economic meltdown, or confidently predicted worldwide famine to kill four billion people during 1980s, and an ice age by 2000, will likely earn you just a patronizing smirk if you are poor—or a lawsuit if you aren't.

Or maybe not. In a court of law, you're allowed to argue, and if your arguments make sense and your opponent's arguments don't, then you win. At least in theory. And the idea that causality is somehow inextricably linked with science can't survive legal scrutiny. Look at it sideways and you'll see Wile E. Coyote in mid-air, supported by nothing but the cartoonist's free will.

In a perfectly causal world, the scientific method is dead: no scientist has free will to perform even a single experiment. All the experiments we thought we performed were, in the causalist's view, preprogrammed into us by previous events, so we didn't really have the freedom to perform them. Thus, we can't take their results as evidence of anything. What we get to see as results has been preprogrammed by prior events as well, so if we're misled by seeing some preprogrammed fake, we can never tell because the fake is elaborate enough to include preprogramming us and all of our equipment and each and every particle and wave that we thought we measured. So we can never use the scientific method to actually learn anything about a perfectly causal world because we can't perform any experiments in it.

The idea that the nonexistence of free will anywhere in the world applies to the scientific experiments done anywhere in the world is called superdeterminism. The reason it's "super" is because it applies determinism to determinists, whereupon trained observers report amazing mental contortionism by said determinists.

> Mirroring is the simplest known BS detector: apply some postulate to itself and see if it holds.

In the end, causal materialistic determinism isn't just unsupported by modern science. It's not even compatible with the scientific method. If you assume that no thinkers were free to think what they thought they thought and that no experimenters were free to ask Nature the questions they thought they asked, then all their conclusions aren't supported by any evidence at all. Oops.

Eternalism, or the block Universe model, is the extreme version of causalist conspiracy theories. That's the view that everything isn't just rigidly determined for all eternity but that eternity has already happened and we just haven't noticed. For an eternalist, the past, present, and future coexist simultaneously, and it's only our limited perception that prevents us from seeing the Universe in its static, glorious perfection—terminally boring, unfalsifiable, and, as such, completely unscientific.

Thankfully, the world we live in isn't boring. Actually, it's anything but boring. While the merchants of deterministic boredom peddle their wares, the real world continues on its own awesome way [18], and if someone chooses to ignore this, it's their loss, not the Universe's. Remember, the Universe is under no obligation to make sense to you.

Causality, like most folk medicine, is helpful—when taken in moderation. And the label on the causality pill bottle should warn about harmful side effects, such as refusing to believe your own senses when they tell you something interesting.

2.7 What else could it possibly have been?

If the linear progression of cause to effect doesn't rule our world with an iron fist as pebble-bouncers allege, then what are the alternatives? The journey from the simplistic causality myth to the entangled reality is long and fascinating. One of my favorite trails on that journey is the feedback loop, an arrangement whereby processes are their own causes and effects. It works like this:

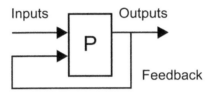

Figure 16 – Feedback loop.

The system "P" in this diagram uses its own "effects" (outputs) as "causes" (inputs). Say you have an A/C system in your house. You input a desired temperature, the thermostat compares the actual detected temperature with the target you set and turns on heating or cooling to correct the difference. When the actual temperature gets close enough to the set goal, heating or cooling is turned off.

This familiar feedback system illustrates a number of concepts common to feedback loops of various kinds. One of these is positive and negative feedback, which has nothing to do with "good" or "bad," except by accident. Systems with negative feedback are self-correcting. For example, if the temperature deviates from the setting, the A/C system counters the discrepancy. If it's too hot, it removes heat; if it's too cold, it adds heat.

Systems with positive feedback, on the other hand, are self-reinforcing. Let's say, adherence to a certain point of view becomes advantageous for advancing a scientist's career. Then, naturally, more scientists in advanced career positions would adhere to this point of view, thus making it even more advantageous for anyone in the field to hold this view.

Another important concept is that of an objective. Once you have an objective or a goal, evaluation becomes meaningful. System P in the previous picture can compare a desired value of a variable with its actual value, can detect a difference, and can try to do something about it. It can tell "good" from "bad". Too cold or too hot is "bad" for an A/C system, and the target temperature is "good." Spinning one's wheels without publications in prestigious journals or with a steady stream of research grants is "bad," and having lots of both and being pursued by reputable institutions trying to get you on staff is "good."

And there are also related concepts of optimization and free parameters. Once you know which way is up, you can get to a good spot. If, that is, there are things you can change. The things you change are called free parameters, and optimization is a general name for a variety of procedures changing the free parameters to achieve some desired outcome, often to minimize a deviation of some quantity (linked somehow to the free parameters) from its target ("good") value. The branch of math studying optimization is called variation calculus, which was founded by none other than… Isaac Newton, the guy who discovered the ironclad laws that, the determinists claim, don't allow any freedom to change the parameters. Oops.

The humans who first discovered the feedback principle weren't scientists; they were engineers. Specifically, ancient Egyptian engineers designing a water clock. The clock worked by filling a large tank with water that lifted a floating indicator; the indicator showed time. For that arrangement to work, the flow rate of the water into the tank had to be stable. The engineers found that it could be stabilized by arranging another tank above the one with the float. The other tank had a small outlet and a constant water level. But how do you keep the level constant when water keeps flowing out?

This was in ancient Egypt, so the first thing that came to mind was to assign a slave to keep the water level constant. When the system's accuracy was found to leave a lot to be desired, a whip-wielding slave driver was added, one per shift. Then the driver crew and the slave crew required a manager, an assistant manager, and a cook, and the whole system started getting completely out of hand. The customer wasn't happy. And back in those barbaric days, the dissatisfied customer (namely, the Pharaoh) expressed his frustration with the clock's accuracy by chopping body parts off everyone involved in the project. After a few iterations, the remaining mutilated engineers were running out of spare parts and getting pretty desperate. Necessity is mother of invention; and float valve, the first known manmade feedback system, was born.

The float valve let water into the small tank when the level in it dropped beyond some set value. When the level was high enough again, the valve closed and stopped the water inflow. You can see a remote descendant of that system if you lift the lid off the water tank of any modern toilet bowl.

Since then, relieved engineers use feedback systems everywhere. Power supplies and electric ovens, cars and rockets, irrigation systems and cell phones all use feedback to operate as intended. And most of these have lots of interacting feedback loops, nested like matryoshka dolls, branching like a tree, diverging to control separate variables like oven temperature and cooking time, and converging again to produce a common result like a Thanksgiving turkey cooked to perfection. And, of course, the 1's and 0's that fill our digitized world are held by memory circuits designed around feedback loops, where strong positive feedback loops prevent noise from accidentally flipping the circuit from one "state" to the other.

Once the concept of feedback loops was recognized, they kept popping up everywhere, and not all of them were ours. In fact, most feedback systems we know are not designed by us humans. Living systems—from biomolecules to the biosphere—are full of feedback loops. The activity of enzymes depends on the product of the reaction they catalyze—and vice versa. The foraging, drinking, or scratching activity of an animal depends on it feeling hungry, thirsty, or itchy—and vice versa.

There are two important differences between the humanmade feedback systems and the ones we haven't designed. First, the humanmade ones can tell "good" from "bad"—or, in control systems engineers' parlance, they have a goal function—because we told them so. We, the designers of these systems, set some goal and design the feedback system to counteract any deviation from the goal. A drop in voltage causes a system we humans built for keeping voltage constant to react in such a way that the deviation is reduced. There's a causality there because we put it there.

The systems that developed without our input work differently. Say a small island has foxes, rabbits, and no humans. A particularly crafty leash of foxes can do serious damage to the local rabit population. When rabits get hard to find, the foxes starve and die. Dead foxes don't eat rabbits, so the few remaining rabbits breed like rabbits, making more food available for the few remaining foxes, who, in turn, feast and breed. There's no "good" or "bad" in this system. No one sets goals for it deliberately. We can, and often do, ascribe objectives to the rabbits and to the foxes and even to the grass that the rabbits eat before being eaten by foxes. We can anthropomorphize the heck out of anything we want, even the soil that the grass grows on or the microbes that convert foxes' poop back into the soil.

Microbes and grass and rabbits and foxes just don't care, and neither do worms and clouds and hawks and the Sun and everything else under the Sun. They just do whatever the heck they do, interacting in whatever ways they interact, and it's up to us to explain all of that to ourselves. Again, as Neil DeGrasse Tyson once said, "The Universe is under no obligation to make sense to you." So how do we make sense of it? How do we distill the Universe down to something we, mere mortals, can comprehend and deal with in a somewhat deliberate fashion? How do we figure out what things and interactions need to be taken into account when we try to predict stuff that matters to us?

Gradually, that's how. We accumulate observations, notice trends, and use our intuition to create mental shortcuts or presumptive causes (a.k.a. biases). Our mental shortcuts yield predictions. Then we check predictions against further observations. If the predictions work, we grow more confident in our mental shortcut. Eventually we start calling the shortcuts more and more flattering names: hypothesis, theory, principle, law, standard model. If this sounds suspiciously like the scientific method, that's because it is.

Accumulating observations so you can notice trends takes more than just staring at the darn thing. First, something has to be happening, changing somehow. You need some variables, descriptors of your objects that can take on different values. The Sun rises, moves across the sky, and sets. The whole night sky, with all its constellations, spins around. Trees grow leaves, blossom, bear fruit, change color, and lose leaves. Things happen.

And when they do, observant humans notice that some variables vary in unison. The Sun goes up in the sky, and everything looks lighter and feels warmer. When migrating birds leave, the Sun follows a different path in the sky than when they return. The sunrise is at one place when the first buds open in spring, and it's at a different place when fall foliage first appears.

When things change in unison, that's correlation. Sometimes a correlation is very obvious, like sunrise's correlation with daylight. Sometimes it takes some doing to detect, as with a particular direction of sunrize and the beginning of spring. And sometimes it's really obscure, like the recently discovered correlation between the severity of Covid-19 in a patient and the presence of a particular chunk of Neanderthal DNA in the patient's genome.

The more obscure a correlation is, the better the tools you need to detect it. Some of the tools are instruments for collecting precise data, like the grandiose megaliths precisely aligned to the stars. The other tools are the mathematical theories and methods helping to fish out the corellations from the collected data: probability and statistics.

Imagine that you know two important things about something: it's not impossible (it's been known to happen), and it's not certain either (it's not seen everywhere all the time). And imagine that you know nothing else about it. What do you think its chances are of it happening? If no additional information is available, most folks would guess 50/50—it's either going to happen, or it ain't.

Congratulations to those of us who think that they don't know how to make probabilistic estimates: you just did. Statistically speaking, you just found the ratio of the size of an event space to the size of a sample space. It sounds complicated, but it's not... yet. Event space is all the events of interest that count. In our case, that's "X" happening. Sample space is all of the events of interest that can happen. In our case, that's "X" happening and "X" not happening. Heads or tails—N = 2. One event that counts over two that could happen is ½, which is 50%. A coin toss. It's really that easy.[7]

Figure 17 – Compound event (left image courtesy John Fowler via flickr.com).

Actually, you just discovered Laplace's principle of indifference. And, no, it's not the principle of indifference to what Laplace had to say. It's a rather bold statement that says that if all we know is that N mutually exclusive things may happen, the default probability of each of these actually happening is 1/N.

It quickly gets more interesting. Say you toss a coin twice. What are the chances you'll get heads both times? That's what's called a compound event, meaning that it's made of two or more separate events. The first toss yields either tails (T) or

---

[7] Why is it important to learn about probabilities? Because probabilities and statistics are the language that science, our best tool of exploring the world, uses to tell us how confident it is about the rest of what it tells us. It's a great reminder that it ain't perfect, but it's the best we've got. Just remember that it ain't perfect.

heads (H), and so does the second one. So your compound sample space looks like this: HH, HT, TH, TT. The event space is only HH, so the probability is ¼. The probability of each toss yielding heads independently is ½, so the probability of a compound event is exactly the product of the individual probabilities of the simple events. In our case, ½ x ½ = ¼.

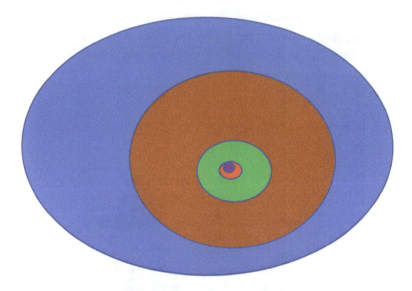

Figure 18 – Compound probabilities.

When you have a compound event that depends on many other component events, its probability is a combination of all component events' probabilities. Say you have a pebble pyramid like one shown in Figure 17. The top pebble can only stay in place if all pebbles underneath it stay in place. That is, the bottom piece has to stay in place AND the next one AND the next one and so on and so on, all the way to the top. So the probability of the top pebble still being there an hour from now depends on the probabilities of all pebbles underneath it still being there, too. Figure 18 illustrates how the dependence works.

If Figure 18 kind of looks like the top view of the pyramid in Figure 17 that's because it's meant to. The blue area of the big oval is the "event" of the bottom pebble being there after an hour. The orange oval within the blue one is when the next one up is still there, too. The orange part is smaller than blue since it stands for a subset of the blue "events." Within the orange area, not only does the bottom pebble stay, but so too does the next one up. The blue event is necessary for the orange; it's just not sufficient.

For any pebble to stay up, each of the previous ones staying up is necessary but not sufficient, so the area representing each event is smaller than the previous one. Their ratio is the conditional probability, the chances of the next pebble holding given that all the ones underneath it were okay. And, of course, the overall probability is the product of all conditional component probabilities:

$$\frac{P_N}{P_{N-1}} * \frac{P_{N-1}}{P_{N-2}} * \frac{P_{N-2}}{P_{N-3}} * \ldots * \frac{P_1}{P_0} = \frac{P_N}{P_0}$$

So if the conditional probability of each pebble staying put is ½, then the 15th pebble's overall chances of still being there are $½^{15}$ = 1/32,768. We ought to be (a lot) more impressed with the pyramid on the right of Figure 17 than the ready-to-topple-any-moment pillar on the left: the pyramid has a lot more opportunities to go.

This, by the way, is very important to keep in mind when you decide how much trust to invest in what you're told. The more assumptions that have to be true for a statement to also be true, the flimsier the whole pyramid looks. And the less faith we can afford to put in it without checking the end result by direct experiment or observation.

> Every time the word "truth" is mentioned in an article, the amount of accurate information in it decreases by 50%. If the word is in the title, it's 99%.

Two things are important here. First, the two simple events are combined in a special way to yield the compound event of interest: they're both required to yield that particular outcome. This determines how the probabilities of simple events are combined to produce the one for the compound event, as in Figure 19 below.

The sample space for the first toss is on top of the figure. The second toss is on the left. The sample space for the two tosses is two-dimensional: it's the 2 x 2 square filled with all the possible combinations of the results for the first and second toss. The event space is the smaller square in the upper left corner of the bigger one. The area of the square is the product of its dimensions. So the probability is the product of the length and width of the smaller square divided by the product of length and width of the bigger one. But that's the same as the ratio of the length times the ratio of the widths, and that's the product of the probability of heads in the first toss and in the second. QED (which is short for quod erat demonstrandum, which is Latin for "whew").

The second important thing is the independence of the two consecutive tosses. What you get in the second toss doesn't in any conceivable way depend on what you got the first time. And don't even mention the possibility of the SECOND toss somehow influencing the FIRST one, at least not when there are militant causalists around.

Why not make the game more interesting and pull cards from a full deck of fifty-four? There are thirteen each of hearts (♥), diamonds (♦), clubs (♣), and spades (♠), plus there are two

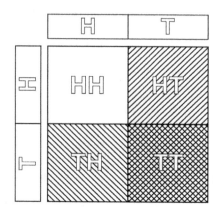

Figure 19– Heads or tails.

jokers without a suit. For those who have never seen a deck of cards: no, jokers are NOT in their underwear, and what's meant by a "suit" is hearts, diamonds, clubs, or spades. Fifty-four here is the N in Laplace's principle of indifference, or the size of the sample space, so the probability of getting any particular card is 1/54.

What are the chances that a card you pull at random is hearts (H)? The sample space is the full deck, and the event space is thirteen hearts, so the probability is 13/54. T, in this case, stands for "the other ones." Notice the important distinction between the coin toss: the probabilities of H and T aren't 50/50, even though they're still mutually exclusive. We're aware of some additional information (which cards make up the deck), which makes for different expectations.

What if you pull two cards, each coming from its own deck of 54? What are the chances of both being hearts? The decks are separate, so each "event" has no influence on the other. If you draw a square like the one for coin tosses, you'll find that each side of it is 54 possibilities long, divided between 13 hearts and everything else. The small square (a.k.a. the event space) is 13 by 13; the big one (a.k.a. the sample space) is 54 by 54. If the result you got wasn't $13^2/54^2$, then yours truly shouldn't be explaining probabilities to unsuspecting strangers. Let's hope you got it right.

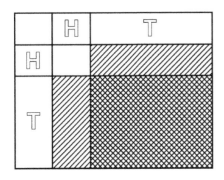

Figure 20 – Heads and the other ones.

If you think that serving two cards from two decks complicates matters, try serving both from the same deck. That's when the assumption of independence (of the simple events) falls apart, and calculations get more convoluted.

When the first card was served, there were thirteen possibilities to get a diamond out of the 54 cards. But serving the first card changed the deck because there were 53 cards left, and (if you got diamonds the first time), then 12 diamonds are left. So the sample space isn't a square anymore; instead, it's a rectangle. And the event space is a rectangle also. The total probability will be $\frac{13}{54} \times \frac{12}{53}$. No big deal, right? It's almost the same as it was for the previous example. The difference is a mere 6%, which is okay to ignore in most situations.

But what if the simple events are strongly dependent? Say your decks only have two cards in them: one hearts card and one clubs card. If the simple events are independent (different stacks), then the chances of pulling the same suit twice in a row is 50%. Whatever color you have the first time, the one you pull from the next deck is either the same color or the other one. If they're dependent (same deck), the probability is exactly 0%. You can't pull the same suit twice from a deck that doesn't have two cards of the same suit. So there is a degree of dependence, or independence, of events.

Let's change the game a little. This time, you don't get to pull the cards yourself. You don't even see the deck. There's a wall in front of you, and you can't see or hear what's happening behind it. There's a small window in the wall, and the cards pop up one by one in that window for a few seconds, then they disappear again. What can you tell about a deck—or the decks—they appear from? Can you decipher the algorithm of their selection?

Hold on, that's not fair! You just had access to all the rules, the sample space was mapped out, and all you had to do was to compare some areas on the map. Now, all of a sudden, there's no map, and you have to figure it out on your own, based on glimpses of cards popping up in some window? Ridiculous!

Welcome to the world of science. When we do science, we don't get a map at the entrance. It's our job to draw the map. We don't know how many cards are behind the walls or how many copies there are of each kind or if they're subdivided into decks. We don't know if the cards we have already seen are returned to the pool or thrown away. We can fill an encyclopedia with what we don't know. Science is tough. As Stephen Hawking concluded from his research of black holes, "Not only does God play dice, but... he sometimes throws them where they cannot be seen."

Say, we see a sequence like this: A♥, 3♦, A♥, 3♦, A♥, 3♦, A♥, 3♦, A♥. Does this mean there are only two cards behind the wall? Only two suits? A special deck where the first 9 cards are the ones you just saw, and the rest are all 5 ♣? Is there a UFO—unfair flabbergasting obfuscator—behind that wall, with no other mission than to confuse a naïve observer? Like, there's every imaginable card in there, but all you ever get to see in the window are these two? What if the entire setup is an illusion, and it's just some magician making you think there are any cards at all?

There's no end to it. I mean, literally, no end. For any finite sequence of observations, we can generate an infinite number of hypotheses that are perfectly compatible with every observation in the set. Within our puny experience, there isn't much you can tell about the mysterious hidden mechanism that has shown you those nine cards. Without more information, you can't tell much about what's behind that wall.

There are different ways to go about obtaining that information. You can wait for more cards to show through that window and hope something more interesting eventually happens. You can take a more proactive approach and start doing experiments, like shining UV light or gamma-rays at the window or elsewhere at the wall or drilling the wall or banging it with a sledgehammer. You can also up and leave in search of other walls with windows to see how those behave. You can consult historical records and scientific publications to see if anyone has ever seen anything like this. You can ask around.

Of course, even after doing all of that, it's still perfectly possible that what we have seen in the first window through the first wall was completely unique to that one window in that one wall, observed at that particular time. It's still perfectly possible that the results of any experiments on that particular phenomenon—with gamma-rays or a sledgehammer—reflect more on the experiments themselves than on the phenomenon we're trying to get a grip on.

It just gets less and less likely as we accumulate experience. Exploring this world, we notice things that tend to repeat themselves, and these trends, within our experience, become laws. Then we explore further and see those laws violated, so we replace them with other laws that account for what we have learned.

Say we have seen a hundred sequences of nine cards at a hundred different walls with windows in them. Then imagine that all the sequences were the same. Can you tell how likely it is that tenth card in any one of them will not be 3♦? Can you tell the probability that a 101st wall will show an entirely different sequence of nine cards?

The only probabilities you measure in the experiment are called, naturally, "empirical probabilities." They're nothing but ratios of the number of times something happened to the number of times you tried. So in the example with one window and nine tries, we have two empirical probabilities: 5/9 for A♥ and 4/9 for 3♦. We also have an 8/8 empirical probability of two consecutive cards being different, 7/7 empirical probability of two cards that are one apart being the same, and so forth. That's the extent of our knowledge of the world, as far as those cards are concerned. Everything else is conjecture.

We can put together any number of models to explain what's hidden behind the wall, and then we can calculate the theoretical probabilities of getting the result we just saw if one of the other models were true. We can then compare the models and rank them. Which ones are less unlikely to produce the combination we have observed?

First, we would exclude models that are entirely incompatible with what we have just seen—like a model where the cards are drawn from a regular deck of 54 cards, shown in the window, and then discarded—is incompatible with observations. There aren't five A♥ cards or four 3♦ cards in such a deck. We're on pretty solid ground so far.

But can we move any further with what we have? Can we make a probabilistic argument that at least some of the remaining models are better than the rest?

It turns out that sometimes we can. Let's consider a less artificial situation than the mysterious cards behind the wall. Say an archeologist is digging for pottery shards at a site that hasn't been precisely dated yet (the example is adopted from [19]). How would she go about dating it?

Assume that the prevailing wisdom in the field is that tenth century pottery in that area was only 1% glazed and 50% decorated, whereas by the fifteenth century, it was 80% glazed and 5% decorated. Each glazed shard found would be, therefore, less likely to be tenth century than fifteenth; and for each decorated one, the likelihood would be the other way around. The archeologist would, therefore, enter the number of glazed fragments and the number of decorated fragments into a software package, and the computer would spit out an estimate of the site's age, complete with error bars and confidence intervals.

The software she would use performs Bayesian hypothesis testing. Without going into too much detail, Bayesian hypothesis testing ranks hypotheses according to the likelihood of the observed evidence if the particular hypothesis were true.

Assume that the shards that the archeologist dug up are 80% glazed and 5% decorated. Care to hazard a guess what the program's answer would be? Yup, that's right: it's going to be very confident that it's fifteenth century. And the confidence grows (the technical term is "updates") every time you find a piece of pottery, so the next time someone finds 80% glazed and 5% decorated pottery fragments, the pile in the fifteenth century bin is going to be even higher, and so is the confidence in dating them as fifteenth century.

Please note that reinforcement of the fifteenth century belief didn't require actual independent dating by any other method. In other words, once folks in the field have come to believe that these kinds of attributes are "caused" by a certain age, the Bayesian hypothesis testing software would reinforce that belief without a shred of further evidence. The site would be reported as "confirmed" fifteenth century. Kids at school, science reporters, visitors at local history museums, and activists of the preservationist society would all be quite certain that it's a fifteenth-century site.

If it's beginning to seem as if "Bayes" is somehow related to "bias," that's because it kind of is. Specifically, to the confirmation bias. If all they ever got was twenty ceramic pieces that were actually carbon dated and 20,000 more were added by the Bayesian procedure, the mound of evidence you would need to climb has grown 1,000 times taller. To suggest that a mostly glazed piece of pottery was made in the tenth century instead of the fifteenth, you now need 20,000 pieces of evidence, not twenty. If you just carbon-date twenty and get a different result, that's not good enough to convince anyone anymore. The onus is on you, and it doesn't take much to add weight to it.

That brings us to the infamous Russel teapot. British philosopher Bertrand Russell envisioned a Chinese teapot in an elliptical orbit around the Sun, too small to be detectable by any available telescope. The image was intended to ridicule the idea of God, whose undetectability by scientific instruments was supposed to convince a rational reader that it's unlikely that God exists (the mockery apparently backfired, dooming the publication of the commissioned paper by Russell the Nobel Laureate). It's interesting to see what a Bayesian hypothesis testing software would do with the Russel teapot hypothesis. The hypothesis would likely become an unassailable instant winner: every time someone looks up through a telescope and detects no Chinese teapot, this observation is in full agreement with the hypothesis' prediction that it won't be detected. So every time you see no teapot, the hypothesis that says that it's there gets more likely. As ridiculous as that sounds, you never have to actually see the teapot to get increasingly confident, in a statistical sense, that it exists.

However preposterous the orbiting teapot may be, Russell still believed that enumerative induction, or Bayesian inference—as in the glazed pottery dating example—may hold water. What's enumerative induction? In this approach, instead of declaring a theory outright "true," evidence would adduce pointers, making some models less likely than others. Then the more likely theory, inductivists say, should rationally be preferred. It's the philosophical rationalization for Bayesian hypothesis testing.

If you find a philosopher who says that X may be true, then you can rest assured that you can find another one that says that X may be false. That, by the way, applies to the previous sentence. Remember epistemology from Chapter 2.5? Arguing about how we know that we know what we think we know is one of the particularly bloody battlefields in philosophy. Russell the skeptic was uncharacteristically lenient toward Bayesian epistemology—that is, the idea that we can actually infer something useful about things we didn't empirically test or observe. Another giant of modern epistemology, Karl Popper, was sharply critical of the idea. Popper's position was that the riskiest theory—that is, the easiest one to falsify by observation or experiment—is rationally preferable, as long as it hasn't been so falsified.

One thing is clear from this battle: philosophers' rationalizations are themselves not all that rational. While they do indeed push the boundary between knowledge and belief, belief survives just fine, thank you very much. There's enough room for interpretation left for the two titans of modern philosophy to take apparently incompatible positions that both kind of make sense.

In quite a variety of very practical circumstances, one's choice of a "winner" may well depend on individual experience and personal preferences (and peer pressure) much more often than we'd like to admit. All things being equal, two reasonable people can reach, rationalize, and justify very different conclusions that are perfectly compatible with the same sum total of accumulated relevant evidence. Sometimes it's just a false dichotomy, and the models may not be as incompatible as they look at first glance. Sometimes it's not that the models are incompatible but that the domains where they work—meaning that they give useable predictions—just don't overlap.

Say you're in the habit of listening to news on a particular radio channel at a particular time every morning. Your car radio is preset on that frequency, and as soon as you turn the key, a familiar voice tells you what's going on in the world. Until one day it doesn't. You turn the key, and the radio is silent. What's wrong?

Let's try to be scientific about it. The scientific method tells us to formulate hypotheses and to use evidence to test them. Is the radio broken? Is the car battery dead? Is the station off the air? Did a military junta stage a coup in the capital, shutting down all civilian broadcasting in the country? Did space aliens invade Earth and destroy human civilization, somehow missing just your neighborhood? Or maybe the whole routine of listening to the news every morning has been an illusion?

Karl Popper would prefer the easiest hypothesis to falsify. How would he know which one it is? He'd be already in the car, so perhaps he'd first look at the dashboard and check if any lights were on. If they were, the dead battery hypothesis is out. Next, he'd turn the dial on the radio and check to see if he could hear any other stations. If he could, all scenarios that involve a dead radio—as well as all global disaster scenarios—are out in one fell swoop, and that includes the ones that aren't on the list. The list is actually pretty short: it makes no difference if the station is shut due to planned maintenance, power outage, thunderbolt strike, alien invasion, or a newly adopted austerity program. If all you can check is whether or not this particular station is off the air while others are still on, no additional detail beyond that is warranted.

Bertrand Russell, on the other hand, would prefer the most likely hypothesis. How would he know which one is most likely? His initial guess would have to be from prior experience, just as the hypotheses he would choose from were formulated from prior experience. If Russell had experienced a dead battery before, this hypothesis is likely to pop first in his mind. It would also become an instant favorite. First come, first served. Being thorough though, Russell would come up with a few alternative hypotheses, but in his mind, he would already have a winner. Then, using the Bayesian procedure, Russel would collect evidence and sort it all into bins. The evidence that doesn't contradict his favorite hypothesis would go in the "hakuna matata" bin. Say, Russell sees a neighbor's car: the car radio is off, and so is everything else. That's perfectly consistent with the dead battery hypothesis. The Bayesian approach is to count that as supporting evidence. It's weak, but it's still supporting.

If Russell went to a junkyard, he'd quickly collect a huge amount of supporting evidence. Any car there would count as one with a possibly dead battery, which is consistent with the hypothesis. He could add thousands of instances without checking a single battery.

Eventually, confidence would grow so high that even running cars would be consistent with the dead-battery model because they could have been jump-started or something. The hakuna matata bin would fill up even faster.

Please note that both Russell and Popper, following the scientific method, would proceed to collect additional evidence to test their hypotheses. They just wouldn't collect the same evidence or interpret it to mean the same thing. There are perfectly legitimate ways to justify different conclusions while starting at the same point. There are perfectly legitimate ways of collecting and treating additional evidence differently, depending on nothing more than unprovable beliefs.

If your car mechanic happens to follow modern philosophy, you'd better hope he sides with Russell. Checking the likeliest possibility first is a terrific strategy for all routine problems, and he'd save his customers lots of time and money, save himself aggravation, and establish a great reputation for his garage. Like every approach based on statistics, it wouldn't work every time, but most of the time it would.

If you were aboard the *Titanic* and your captain happened to be a modern philosophy buff, pray that he's on Popper's side. An experienced captain with hundreds of safe ocean crossings to his credit would be very confident that rogue icebergs are extremely rare 400 miles south of Newfoundland in mid-April. He'd also be very confident that an alert and properly trained crew is capable of detecting and avoiding any obstacles on a routine voyage. And he'd be very confident in his ship, a marvel of modern engineering, equipped with such advanced safety features as remotely controlled watertight doors.

For the actual captain of the *Titanic*, Edward Smith, all this confidence was backed by an enormous amount of evidence and experience. This was to be his last voyage before retirement, and he had a lot of successful voyages under his belt, which he could infer from. His inferences were so unshakeable that the inductivist captain ignored no fewer than seven iceberg warnings from his own crew and from other ships in the area. Seven warnings, Karl!

A follower of Popper would come up with two competing hypotheses. The first one is that the alarmists are full of it and that everything is okeydokey (with the obvious exception of mass hallucinations among seamen in this particular corner of the North Atlantic). The second one is that the 'bergs are there for real. Whichever hypothesis is easiest to falsify is the one Popper would like best. Without proper facilities to test the sanity of numerous seamen, most of whom are on other ships miles away, falsifying the insanity hypothesis would be rather difficult. On the other hand, all it takes to check for actual icebergs is to post lookouts on the bridge, which is very, very doable. Sure, the owners of the *Titanic*—in their Bayesian wisdom—didn't equip it with searchlights. And, sure, the top brass of the *Titanic*—in their own Bayesian wisdom—left the keys that opened the bridge binoculars locker back in Southampton, England, an ocean away. And, sure, captain Smith never bothered ordering a crewmember to break the damn lock. Those blunders reduced the iceberg-detection range to the distance the naked eye could see. And a 46,000-ton ship couldn't be stopped or turned instantly, so in order for the lookouts to do anyone any good, they would have had to employ a device that the bridge, luckily, did have: the machine telegraph. They'd have to reduce speed so an iceberg big enough to sink them could be detected far enough to evade collision. The captain chose not to, and we all know what happened next.

So when operating in familiar, calm waters with well-mapped probabilities of every outcome of every action on the bridge, everyone tends to use Russell's inductivist approach. Experience matters when you have it and it's relevant. But without a time machine, you can't know for sure if the experience you have is enough. Maybe the 'bergs are different this season. Maybe your lookouts had one drink too many. Maybe someone used brittle rivets when they built the ship and a good knock would split it wide open. Maybe anything. You just don't know.

And here we come back to the onus pushers. It's currently fashionable to insist that the burden of proof is always on folks who doubt the theory that the majority of experts currently accept. The theory that the majority of experts accepted at the time of the *Titanic* held that it would be the safest voyage of all time. The seven iceberg warnings failed to meet the burden of proving otherwise. It took more than 1,500 people drowning to convince some that expert consensus could be wrong after all.

Some folks learned useful lessons from the *Titanic*. In aviation, for example, the theory that the majority of experts currently accept is that flying is the safest way of getting from point A to point B. The theory is backed with an overwhelming amount of data. Yet in aviation, the burden of proof is always on those who agree with the accepted theory, not on those who doubt it. The burden is heavy and expensive – there is an enormous amount of testing going on all the time, and a good portion of your ticket price pays for that testing. Which is how flying has actually become—and demonstrably continues to be—the safest way of getting from point A to point B.

Not everyone got it, though. In stock trading, for example, the theory that the majority of experts currently accept is one that holds that markets are efficient. That's the idea that market players are all busy rationally processing the same information, which is equally accessible to all and perfectly adequate for making rational "decisions." The suckers who accept the currently accepted theory are nowhere near as successful at investing as George Soros, who doesn't subscribe to it. Apparently, being the most successful American investor alive still fails to meet the burden of proof.

In epidemiology, the currently accepted theory holds that quarantines save lives by preventing the transmission of pathogens. The onus is therefore pushed on the folks trying to warn that the cure may eventually cost more lives than the disease itself. The data [20] that one in nine Americans seriously considered suicide (and so did one out of four Americans aged eighteen to twenty-four) during the pandemic lockdowns of the summer of 2020 failed to meet the burden of proof. We're still waiting to see the outcome, but whatever it is, epidemiologists and virologists have disclaimed any responsibility for it. Talk to another department.

And that's how a lot of rational folks come to discount expert advice. Any theory—prevailing or otherwise—is an abbreviation of reality. A good theory works, more or less, within the past experience of the experts in the field, and they also know the boundaries of that experience (unless they're really dense—the experts, not the boundaries). If the theory is really good, it can be extrapolated beyond the existing precedent, but it's a risky exercise, depending on whether new, unaccounted-for factors kick in and invalidate the model. Short of having a time machine, you just can't know for sure, although there are some useful indicators of what to look for and where. Extrapolation is a gamble. Once an expert takes responsibility for the overall result, that's one good reason to take her seriously. Not only does she know the prevailing theory (that goes without saying: she's, after all, an expert), but also she understands the limits of its applicability, and she feels confident enough about the situation at hand to give a straight answer. She looked holistically beyond the domain where the model has been tested, considered the shadows of latent demons that could be lurking out there in the dark, and felt confident enough to bet on us against them. That's golden, and when you hear expert advice like that, it's worth listening to.

But getting unequivocal advice this way is rare. The usual expert-speak is full of caveats, conditions, and disclaimers. An auto mechanic tells you that unless there's something wrong with wiring somewhere, then the repair should take an hour and cost $400. How the heck are you supposed to know if your wiring is okay? He's the one with experience, and experience tells him not to pretend to know more than he does, which is still a lot more than you do.

As Dr. Hickam once quipped, "Patients can have as many diseases as they damn well please." Yes, a cardiologist can treat you according to prevailing theories in her field, and a urologist and a dozen other specialists can do the same, but eventually your body may well succumb to the accumulated side effects of their pills, even if each of the pills was, by itself, beneficial. The ultimate responsibility to keep breathing is on you, the patient. The doctors are the ones with degrees in medicine and board licenses and years of experience, but the ultimate decision is yours.

> To spot the expert, look for the one who predicts that the job will take the longest and cost the most.

Say you're investigating a black box. On its surface are two input dials and an output display. You input 2 and 2 and get 4. What have you learned? What's the latent, built-in function of the box? Is it $Y = X_1 + X_2$? $Y = X_1 \times X_2$? $Y = 2 \times X_1$? $Y = X_2 \times X_2$? $Y = 4\sin(X_1)/\sin(X_2)$? The answer is that in the three-dimensional space X_1, X_2, and Y, one point doesn't define a useable answer. No divine intervention, in the popular form of Ockham's voice from the sky, is going to tell you anything useful about the system's inner workings. All you can tell about the black box innards is that they can't give any output other than 4 for 2 and 2 as inputs.

And maybe you can't tell even that. The assumption that the black box always produces 4 if you enter 2 and 2 is just that—an assumption. The next time the result could be different. So it's not a 3-D puzzle; it's a 4-D one. The extra dimension is time, represented by the number of tries. You just don't know what the output is going to be next time. Of course, your confidence grows with every test that yields the same result, but it's completely up to you to decide when to quit trying. And if all you have is a bunch of 4s, then all you know for certain about the mechanics of the box is that they allow the output 4 for inputs 2 and 2, not necessarily that they require it.

So what else could it possibly be? Anything except what it couldn't. How do you tell if you've seen enough to decide what to do? As with most good questions, the honest answer is that it depends. First of all, it depends on how willing you are to trust your experience. In other words, it depends on your free will.

2.8 Our interconnected world

Galileo Galilei, whose allegedly blasphemous heliocentrism cost him his freedom for the last twenty-seven years of his life, never said, "Earth and other planets orbit the Sun." Not once. For the sufficient reason that he didn't speak English.

Galileo was credited with being the father of the scientific method. His *The Assayer* (*Il Saggiatore*) essay dismissed authority (Aristotle's no less) as the ultimate judge of truth in science. Instead, he promoted the mathematical formulation of scientific ideas to yield testable predictions and experimentation to do the actual testing.[8] Meanwhile, the selfsame Galileo was looking so hard for evidence to support heliocentrism that he even advanced a flimsy theory about tides that he thought would help. According to that theory, as Earth goes around the Sun as well as around its own axis, water sloshes around in cups and buckets, lakes and oceans—and is sloshes a lot more in oceans than in cups. The trouble was that Galileo's sloshing tides would occur once a day at the same time, in sync with an Earth day, —in stark contrast with the real tides, which sync with the Moon day, nearly an hour longer, and happen twice in that time. Accommodating these facts, which our observant ancestors have known since time immemorial, took a considerable deal of ingenuity. So besides the scientific method, Galileo apparently fathered dark matter, hidden in convenient locations at the bottom of the Earth's oceans and shifting tides to fit observations. When it came to evaluating the evidence of the supporting models he happened to favor, Galileo was a lot more forgiving than with models he happened to dislike. Moving goalposts for one's favorite team (namely, oneself) isn't a new idea. Our brightest minds—the scientists—are humans, and they have human strengths and human weaknesses.

That's not to say that goalpost moving doesn't evolve with time. Remember the elections of tribal chieftains from Chapter 2.2? The ones when folks ate the ex-chieftain after an unsuccessful job performance review? We have advanced a lot since then. Our elections often involve live incumbents running for the chieftain's job. We grew so soft that any incumbent in an election nowadays has an unalienable right to claim credit for anything good that happened while she was in charge. If

---

[8] Ibn Al-Hatham advocated the same thing six centuries before Galileo, but our textbooks couldn't credit the Arab with fathering the scientific method without official paternity test results.

she's really thorough, she will claim credit for all the bad things that didn't happen during her tenure as well. On the other hand, any challenger in the same election has an unalienable right to blame the incumbent for anything that went wrong during the same period and, of course, for anything that could have gone right but didn't. Anything will be counted as evidence of anything, as political expedience demands. No nuance, no details. Just a linear cause and effect. Keep it simple, stupid.

Got a fire in your backyard after decades of throwing combustible trash there? Blame climate change deniers (never mind that warm climate has been, throughout Earth's history, wet and rainy) [21]. Any problems in the U.S. from the years 2009 to 2016? Blame George Bush (you have two to choose from). Take a look at this article, written after almost eight years of Obama's "Change We Can Believe In" presidency, which boasted two years with both a Democratic House and a Democratic Senate [22]: "It's George W. Bush's world, and we're just living in it. Not Donald Trump's. Not Hillary Clinton's. Not even Barack Obama's." Screwed up testing for a virus discovered three years after Obama left office? Blame Obama anyways [23].

Assigning blame and credit wherever you damn well please isn't an exclusively political phenomenon. Say you picked up a nail and got a flat tire. Was it because some careless idiot spilled demolition junk all over the street a month ago? Or was it because someone bought the land where the demolished shed used to be and cleared the place to build something else? Or because Google Maps told you to take this street? Or because the town has no public transportation, so you had to drive your own car? Or because tires are made of rubber, while nails are made of steel? Was it because you got a letter in the mail telling you to go wherever the heck you were going when you got the flat? Or because the Second Continental Congress in 1775 established the U.S. Postal Service, which delivered that letter?

You know the right answer as well as I do: all of the above and more. Lots more. Whatever we choose to be righteously indignant about, we will have no trouble finding evidence of that in your flat tire. Climate change and illegal immigration, government overreach and world hunger, underpaid maintenance crews and the scandalous schedule of the county landfill—you can make a convincing story about any of that, starting with the damn nail in your tire. Lots of folks make a pretty decent—if that's the word—living doing exactly that.

Instead of driving, you could choose a much safer form of transportation and fly to wherever it is that you want to go. Say you made it without incident, just like statistics suggest you most likely would. Was it because the Earth's atmosphere is filled with air dense enough to fly in? Or because the Wright brothers figured out how to make flight controllable? Or because the military potential of aviation left no choice but to heavily invest in aviation technology in the first half of the twentieth century? Or because the FAA is doing a good job of keeping flying safe?

Airport security will have you believe that if not for them, you wouldn't have made it. The Aircraft Mechanics Fraternal Association would make a very convincing argument that they really make it all possible by keeping all the critical parts of the plane properly attached. The Airline Pilots Association would point out that it's their members' job to make the actual decisions about flying that gets you from point A to point B safely.

And all of them are right, at least to some extent. On top of that, that nail you'd otherwise have caught in your tire was on a different street, not on your way to the airport, which has yet another endless list of contributing factors.

Do you hear that drumbeat, like when a circus gymnast is about to perform a particularly daring aerial stunt? That was me, about to make one of the boldest statements in this book. Here we go: no event ever results from a single cause or produces a single effect.

Figure 21 – Entangled world.
Image courtesy of Gordon Beagley via unsplash.com.

The world we live in is a tangled web. Everything that ever happens is related to everything else that ever happens. An isolated system that doesn't interact with the rest of the world is a unicorn no one has ever seen. Approximating an isolated system on purpose, such as measuring the gravitational constant (see the Cavendish experiment in Chapter 2.6), takes an impressive amount of ingenuity, patience, and manual dexterity: in the real world, things really love interacting with each other in all kinds of ways. None of the 10^{80} or so particles that make up the observable Universe are, as far as we can tell, equipped with any fence, beyond which they no longer act on each other. There's no reason to believe that any particular one of them doesn't interact with all the rest of the Universe, including you and me, right now.

That's not to say that a particular helium atom in Alpha Centauri significantly affected the likelihood that you would pick up the nail (or catch the flight). Most likely it had less impact than the flap of a butterfly's wings in Brazil had on a tornado in Texas. But when 10^{80}—unbelievably weak—latent interactions add up in some way, the cumulative effect may become very noticeable indeed.

The cumulative effects of a massive number of (individually utterly insignificant) events are often hard to even identify, let alone explain. Some of these are so conventional that we don't even recognize them as such, like the myriads of photons that are going into your eyes right now to give you the picture of this page as you're reading it, —helping convey the meaning of what this page actually says. Spring melt and forest fire, fall foliage and bird migration, market crashes and seasonal flu are common examples of emergent effects of lots of—individually inconsequential—events.

Some emergent phenomena, like simple phase transitions, are for the most part made of events of one kind. Take away the kinetic energy of lots of identical liquid molecules (a.k.a. cool it down), and at some point, the liquid is going to freeze. Add kinetic energy to lots of identical metal ions and electrons in a magnetic needle (a.k.a. heat it up), and at some point, the needle is going to forget which way is North. But even for these, bridging the gap between the microscopic quantum wonderland and the visible, macroscopic events in the world we can actually experience is no small feat.

No single snowflake has ever been predicted *ab initio* by quantum mechanics (by the way, "ab initio" is Latin for "without fudging"). For a theory that is supposed to describe the whole wide world with miraculous accuracy, it's rather embarrassing to require empirical props (a.k.a. peeking at the answer) to explain something as relatively minuscule and simple as a snowflake. Once we get to real macroscopic objects, like water in a teapot—no, not Russel's teapot in circumsolar orbit, but the one on your stove—it gets even more awkward. No quantum theorist, even with all our modern computing power, managed to accurately calculate the water boiling temperature at 1 atmosphere of air pressure using nothing but quantum mechanics.

Sure, folks have tried to predict the whole phase diagram of water (that's where you plot the state of the water—ice, liquid water, and vapor—against temperature and pressure) using quantum mechanics [24]. The result, calculated more or less from first principles of quantum mechanics (okay, that's what *ab initio* really means), would instantly sink the *Titanic* with everyone on board.

As you'd expect, when the component events come in many different flavors rather than just one, it's even harder to figure out what's going on. Waves in the ocean and the clouds over it and the ripples in the sand and the foam at the shoreline are mesmerizing in their irregular regularity. Care to name a single "cause" for that particular bubble?

And then bubbles coming up through the water interact with dissolved gases, some of which get concentrated and react with each other to make simple organics. And then the bubbles get to the surface and burst, and the simple organics interact with atmosphere and UV light and lightning and get more and more complex. And then at some point, they make a protocell, a lump of organic matter sophisticated enough to behave (or misbehave). That protocell merges with other organic matter and occasionally splits into two or more lumps. Different lumps interact with each other and their environment in all sorts of ways, which changes both them and the environment in all sorts of ways. The ones that are particularly good at splitting off progeny are at an evolutionary advantage, so their descendants develop into cells and worms and me and you. That's how life allegedly developed on Earth. The understandable lack of eyewitness reports makes it rather hard to know for sure, but that doesn't stop folks from trying to reproduce the process in the lab.

The trouble with this is not just trying to reproduce something that was supposed to have taken hundreds of millions of years (an experimental series duration that funding agencies justifiably frown upon). It's also pretty hard to tell if you have succeeded or not without knowing what life is. Just a brief sketch of the main biochemical components, their interactions, and their transformations look pretty intimidating (see the picture below), and that's not even close to the complexity inside you and me. This is a simple *E. coli* bacterium that lives in my gut. Add organelles, tissues, organs, organisms, herds, colonies, species, biota, and biosphere—up to and including Gaia—and you'll appreciate the exasperation of a parent whose kid innocently asks, "What is life?"

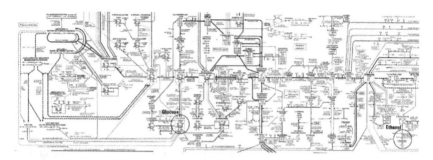

Figure 22 – Biochemical pathways of one microscopic cell. Image courtesy of US DOE, Office of Biological and Environmental Research.

And as the system in question grows, so too do the number of interactions that define its behavior. Below is a sketch for just one aspect of the planetary dynamics: the climate system [25]. Each arrow in that chart has far more interactions than *E. coli*, which is just a couple of microns long. The Earth's hydrosphere, atmosphere, and biosphere weigh as much as 2,000,000,000,000,000,000,000,000,000,000,000,000 (2×10^{36}) bacterial cells. That's how many different realizations of the previous chart would physically fit into the next one, and all of them would be interacting at least with their nearest neighbors, some of which are at least as convoluted as the chart above.

The promise of reductionism is that when something is taken apart to be examined and then painstakingly put back together, the system as a whole works just as it did before, which is evidence that all important parts were properly reattached. Analysis and synthesis. But as you have discovered long ago at a toy store, taking something apart is the easy part. Putting it back into working order often proves to be the bigger challenge.

In using the synthetic phase of the reductionist paradigm to forecast a system's behavior (a.k.a. putting it back together), we describe the system mathematically as a system of partial differential equations (PDEs). PDE terms correspond to arrows on the system diagram: identified interactions between (or among) identified components of the system. Usually very, very few of them. The vanishingly small atoms and the vast spaces between them are ignored and replaced by a continuous medium completely described in terms of several continuous, differentiable variables. Differentiable with respect to spatio-temporal coordinates, that is. In weather forecasting, for example, PDE variables are observables: temperature, pressure, wind speed, vapor concentration, radiation density, etc. They're things that we can measure. PDEs reflect the fundamental laws of Nature as best as we know them: conservation of mass (continuity equation), momentum (Navier-Stokes equation for fluid dynamics), and energy (heat balance).

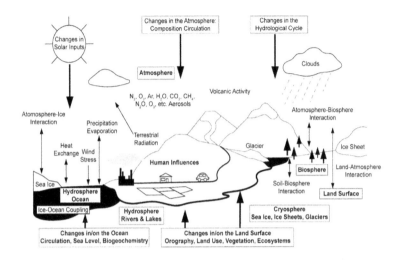

Figure 23 – Main components of climate system and some of their interactions.

The volume we're modeling is divided into cells in a process called "meshing." On its outer boundary we add some boundary conditions. Initial conditions—initial values of the variables throughout the system—are defined at the beginning of a simulation run. The boundaries are the only places where discontinuity is allowed. You can have a roomful of (initially) cold air and suddenly, at t = 0, introduce a hot surface on the floor. Hit Enter, and your computer increments time and solves the PDEs by computing the results of prescribed interactions among variables within every cell and between each cell and all of its immediate neighbors. Variables evolve according to known laws from old values into the new ones, and the new ones are the forecast. In the cold room with a hot plate on the floor, you'll soon see a convection column developing over the plate, and eventually it will reach the ceiling and develop into a circulation pattern. Using observable variables we can measure at the outset is what makes this whole approach possible. The variables are, thank heavens, not the velocities and positions of every atom that the Laplace demon asked for (and that the Heisenberg uncertainty principle declared unobtainable). They're integral characteristics of an unimaginable number of atoms. Masses and velocities and charges and spins and everything else about the atoms in a cell are folded into the (very) few state variables characterizing its contents.

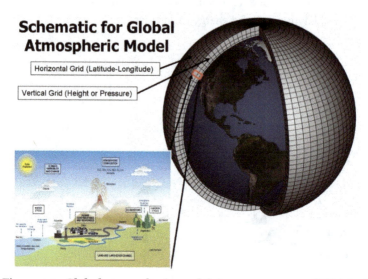

Figure 24– Global atmospheric model. Image courtesy of NOAA via Wikipedia.

We have just made a lot of assumptions. We have assumed that the variables that are explicitly written out in our PDEs are the only ones that matter. We have assumed that the interactions between them explicitly written out in our PDEs are the only ones that matter. We have assumed that the nearest neighbors are the only ones that any cell interacts with.

And oftentimes that's the way things actually appear to work, judging by the fact that short-term weather forecasts are, believe it or not, pretty accurate under most circumstances. Yes, you heard me right: the lame meteorological excuse that their forecasts are, most of the time, pretty accurate in the short term is itself perfectly accurate. They are.

That helps no one, however, because of the caveats "most of the time" and "short term." Most of the time you don't expect the forecast to warn you of the sudden arrival of a hurricane at your doorstep. And, quite accurately, most of the time it doesn't. Most of the time it doesn't need to because hurricanes are, thankfully, rare.

Even better, some hurricanes rather credibly imitate a pissed-off rhinoceros, and their trajectories are about as hard to predict once they take off. That's when you get lucky—with plenty of advance warning to evacuate everyone and everything that needs to be evacuated, and safely shut down what needs to be shut down, and preposition your emergency assets while roads and ports and airports and gas stations and cell towers are all still working.

The rest of the hurricanes stumble along, sometimes wandering hesitantly for days around some point in the vastness of the ocean, which looks no different from most of the rest of the ocean in any respect. Then it suddenly chooses a direction for the next sweep, or it disappears altogether. And all hurricanes start as a few innocuous clouds, cute as a kid and white as driven snow, and it's impossible to believe that an embryo of a monster lies within. In the next ten days, that monster will kill thousands and cost billions in damage. Most of these clouds never become such monsters. And our current weather models can't tell which ones will, until they already have, and we have run out of time to do something about it.

To begin with, the models are nowhere near as deterministic as advertised. The laws that are supposed to rule the weather with an iron fist are, in fact, so ambiguous—mathematically, that is (a.k.a. chaotic)—that they amplify any small variation in initial conditions until the forecasts are completely unrecognizable. How fast does it all fall apart? That depends on the cell size (the technical term is "granularity") and the precision of initial conditions. And you simply can't know the initial conditions with infinite precision at every point in space. With current weather radar and satellites and everything else, useable predictions should be computable out to about ten days, which should be plenty long enough for hurricane warnings. It's not.

> Corry's Law: "Paper is always strongest at the perforations."

It's not, because our assumptions, the ones that held most of the time just fine—about the interactions we account for being the only ones that matter—fail us when we need them most. The path that the system in question chooses from among an infinite number of very diverse paths is perfectly compatible with all data at hand, and it appears to depend on data that aren't at hand. NOAA doesn't send entomologists to study butterfly wing flaps in Brazil when it tries to forecast the next hurricane in Texas. Maybe it should. Or maybe they could at least consider the schedule of school soccer games at Nouakchott, Mauritania. The dust those kids kick up gets blown right over the very area of the East Atlantic which spawns the hurricanes that eventually arrive to batter the American East Coast. The dust is great for ice nucleation in any nascent clouds, which kind of tells those clouds what to do next while they hang in a precarious Navier-Stokes equilibrium.

When titanic forces like heat and pressure are balanced so perfectly that the evolution of the system can be nudged by much weaker forces, wherever the heck they feel like nudging it, it is. I mean, at times like these, the system's evolution does actually get nudged by the much weaker forces we have justifiably ignored before. Things that you can normally discount matter at those special moments of truth.

And after building a whole model by abstracting from all those frustrating minutiae, it's hard to backpedal and put them back in. We just don't know which ones to add back. And there are so damn many possibilities that checking them one by one would keep a lot of folks gainfully employed forever—it kinda already does—but it's unlikely to help much.

Instead, the ignored phenomena and the disregarded connections and all the latent variables associated with them are covered under a magician's tablecloth with an inscription that reads "Random Fluctuations." The trick we're being prepared for is called "ensemble forecasting," which involves taking a lot of forecasts you can't trust individually and lumping them together one way or another. That's supposed to produce, from multiple deterministic forecasts, a single probabilistic one.

From a practical standpoint, this is a great idea. That approach tells a lot of people what to do and how to justify their actions if asked. And rest assured, they will be asked. Say you have an ensemble forecast that predicts a 40% probability of $2 billion in damages from the hurricane coming to your town. The way they get there is by having an ensemble of fifty forecasts, twenty of which predict that your town will get whipped and the rest of which don't. If boarding things up and piling sandbags and whatever else would reduce the damage—after accounting for the cost of the sandbags and whatever—from $800 million (40% x $2 billion) to some lower number, then you do it. If it wouldn't, then you don't bother, and you keep your fingers crossed and tough it out. Ensemble forecasting is supposed to give you some rational guidance about whether all that plywood and nails and sand and labor and aggravation are worth the trouble.

Figure 25 – Butterfly effect.

As usual, the devil is in the details. If the models we started with were deterministic, then where do the probabilities come from? The only place to introduce fluctuations into a deterministic PDE-based model is the initial (and boundary) conditions, and that's exactly what happens. The initial conditions are assumed to be randomly distributed in one way or another, and multiple runs are conducted using the randomly distributed starting points. The ensemble of random initial conditions evolves according to deterministic laws programmed into the model, which yields a distribution of random forecasts. Since the original distribution of initial conditions corresponds to the precision and granularity of their actual measurements, it seems like a great way to eliminate the uncertainties arising from the uncertain initial conditions. Unfortunately, it's not. You just swap one uncertainty for another. You can't afford an infinite number of runs. In fact, since the models require enormous computational resources to run, you can't run the models enough times to thoroughly map the variable space. Instead, you have a multi-dimensional crapshoot (a.k.a. the Monte Carlo method).

The Monte Carlo method is the best thing since sliced bread if you're exploring something huge and smooth like the shape of the *Titanic*'s hull. Each data point costs a fortune: it's difficult to dive to its present depth of 3,840 meters to take measurements. According to the frugal Monte Carlo method, you'd randomly sample it at as many points as you can afford, and then you'd safely interpolate between the points. Safely—because you know the thing you're measuring is smooth, so it's okay to interpolate. You know you'll introduce an error, and you know the interpolation error on a smooth surface is small. If you're really thorough, you can even estimate the error; and if it's too high for your liking, you can apply for a grant to keep adding measurements until you get the error down to where you want it.

The trouble starts when the assumption of smoothness is violated at the scale of interest, which happens in weather forecasting every time anything really interesting appears out of thin air. The updraft that seeds a monster hurricane that's 500 km in diameter may be comfortably less than 1/1,000,000 the area of the eventual storm. Just for comparison, the hole that sunk the *Titanic* takes about 1/20,000 of its hull area. If you probe the shape of its hull at 100 points, your chances of missing that hole are about 99.5%. Even with 1,000 points, which would cost ten times as much and take ten times as long to measure, the probability of missing the hole is still 95%. At which point your funding agency grows really apprehensive about hearing from you ever again. That's what the law of diminishing returns looks like. The thing you're trying to understand looks pretty much as baffling after spending $100 million on studying it as it did after the first $10 million.

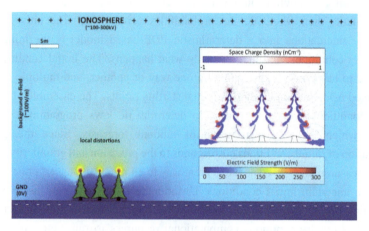

Figure 26 – Electric fields around trees. Image courtesy of Dominic Clarke, Erica Morley, and Daniel Robert [26].

Why is the assumption of smoothness violated? Interesting atmospheric physics—clouds and thermal columns and volcanic craters and airplane contrails and towns and factories and fields and chimneys and ice floes and dust devils and tornadoes—are all much smaller than the cells used in global modeling. And the gradients associated with these variables are orders of magnitude steeper than anything the model is equipped to handle. The interesting physics ain't smooth. When we look at cells big enough for things to look smooth from one cell to the next, we have already missed the birth of all the monsters and their far more numerous but harmless twins that disappear without a trace.

What's worse, much of interesting physics isn't a part of the model at all. Traveling spiders know more about atmospheric electricity (yes, that's how they do the spider balloon fest in the fall, in case you ever wondered) than our forecasting models. The PDEs that the models are made of don't model corn harvesting in Nebraska or nucleation of ice in the clouds over Newfoundland or the source of Northern Europe heating fuel this winter. These variables just don't explicitly figure into the calculations at all.

So not only is ensemble forecasting supposed to take care of the uncertainty in the initial conditions, but also it's charged with accounting for the phenomena missing from the model altogether. Putting these back could allegedly be done by jiggling the model's parameters (these approaches richly deserve their collective name of "perturbed parameter schemes"), combining results of multiple different models running the same physics with ad-hoc corrections (super-ensemble forecasting) or even different physics (called hyper-ensemble, although the "r" in "hyper" so far appears unwarranted: without looking at the answers, this method has thus far had a hard time predicting the trajectory of a drifting buoy for a day and a half, which is supposed to be somewhat easier than actually forecasting global weather). The ensemble forecasts are "calibrated," which means that they're assigned weights for averaging or subjected to some other ad-hoc corrective procedure, according to how accurately they retro-cast some weather that has already happened. Then the results of different fudging recipes are compared, and the best one is deemed to be state of the art—the super-fudge, if you will—and used in actual forecasting. By then, all pretense of comprehensive determinism and unwavering causality is long gone. Never mind that soccer game at Nouakchott. This thing would ignore a Krakatoa eruption or a hit by a 5-km asteroid, neither of which is an easy thing to ignore.

Neither of them is an easy thing to predict, either. And it's kind of the same as the trouble with the weather: the sum total of reductionist all-there-is-to-it pieces just keeps resisting attempts to put it together in such a way as to yield useable predictions. Our models of Earth structure are compatible with neither the existence of a magnetic field around Jupiter nor periodic flips of the Earth's magnetic poles, both rather firmly established. And most of the space rocks that can end human civilization aren't even identified, much less tracked.

It's not just an occasional rock from way out there that's connected to happenings down here. It's also the magnetosphere of our planet that shields us from the Sun's radiation, which might have otherwise sterilized the Earth. It's the Moon, whose motion around the Earth stirs the core of our planet, which might otherwise have no magnetosphere. It's the Sun's radiation that faces off with radiation from deep space at the so-called heliopause and creates a protective bubble around the Solar system. The bubble is called the heliosphere, and it shields the Solar system from the galactic cosmic rays, which might also have otherwise sterilized our planet. The heliosphere, by the way, is fluid and, much like the atmosphere, has weather and climate. Distant stars measurably affect events on Earth [27]. For example, when neutrinos from distant stars up there are gravitationally lensed by our Sun, they temporarily speed up radioactive decay down here.

We humans intuitively felt this interconnectedness of the Universe long ago. Our observant ancestors appreciated their connection to the Cosmos. Ancient myths and rituals link events on Earth with events in the heavens. So did ancient calendars and almanacs and navigation clues. The first known astronomical observatory, Nabta Playa, was built by cattle-worshipping nomads 7,000 years ago in Nubia, before there were any permanent settlements in the region. It's a stone circle with markings for the summer solstice and the arrival of the monsoons. Nabta Playa is about 1,100 km south of the Great Pyramid of Giza, which—with its cardinal alignment and other tantalizing astronomical clues—is itself a monument to ancients' awareness of the Universe.

The ancient idea of using distant stars to make sense of things down here on Earth has transformed through the millennia, but it's still very much alive. With humanity learning more about our Universe, it may be getting more relevant than ever.

Austrian physicist and holistic philosopher Ernst Mach was credited with what Einstein called Mach's conjecture, the idea that local physical laws are somehow related to the large-scale structure of the Universe. It's often stated as the "mass out there influences inertia here." Inertia, by the way, is resistance to acceleration. Einstein was an early convert to this concept, going as far as saying—in 1930, fifteen years after Mach's death—that "it is justified to consider Mach as the precursor of the general theory of relativity," although Mach apparently rejected the theory.

What Einstein found inspiring was Mach's analysis of Newton's bucket argument. Let's retrace the footsteps of the three giants.

First, Newton sought a way to buttress his absolute space idea. In Newton's world, objects move in a space and time that are independent of whether the objects (matter) are there or not. To illustrate the concept, Newton suggested the following thought experiment: let's pour some water into a bucket, hang the bucket on a rope, and twist the rope. Now release it. At first, the bucket starts spinning and sliding around the water, which remains stationary. Soon, though, the bucket drags water with it, and the water itself starts rotating. That produces a very visible effect: the entrained water climbs up the walls of the bucket, and its surface goes from flat to parabolic. Why? Because rotation is absolute, said Newton. Linear motion might be relative, but when things rotate, you get forces that can tell you if you're spinning or not. It's those forces, in the rotating body of water, that make it go up the wall of the bucket. Since these are real, as anyone can plainly see, absolute rotation is a real thing, and so is absolute space. The same is true for linear acceleration, which requires measurable forces so you can detect acceleration just like you do with rotation (every point in a rotating body that isn't on its axis of rotation accelerates toward the axis, and preventing a spinning body from flying apart requires a force that you can measure).

Not so fast, said Ernst Mach. All we know is how water behaves in a regular bucket, which is not all that big. What if the bucket were the size of a planet? The

Solar system? The Milky Way galaxy? Entire observable Universe? When a spinning ice skater controls the rate of spinning by extending her arms or pulling them in close to her body, what if she actually interacts somehow with all the distant stars that make up her frame of reference? What if rotation is as relative as uniform linear motion, only what it's relative to is so vast and remote that we don't even recognize it as having anything to do with the little skater?

There's a good deal of controversy surrounding Mach's principle, starting with the fact that George Berkeley, Newton's contemporary, published the same analysis in 1721, long before Mach. It's not even certain if Mach thought that "inertia originates in a kind of interaction between bodies": the phrase is from a 1913 letter that Einstein wrote to Mach, not the other way around.

In that letter, Einstein described an effect he predicted while working on the theory of general relativity, later known as the Einstein-Lense-Thirring effect. If a Foucault pendulum, a deceptively simple contraption used to study inertia, were surrounded by an immensely massive rotating shell, the pendulum's plane of rotation would—imperceptibly slowly—follow the shell's spin. Ninety-one years later, the effect was claimed to be successfully confirmed, although the number of additional assumptions needed to pull the minuscule effect of Earth's rotation on satellite orbits out of the noisy data is affected by—perhaps literally—everything under the Sun, which leaves room for debate.

But what if frame-dragging effects, predicted by the theory of general relativity, are real? And what if when the "body" that drags the frame of reference is our entire Universe, it entrains the frame completely—like the ghost of luminiferous ether physicists used to scare students in the nineteenth century or the ghost of the co-moving observer used for the same purposes in the twentieth? And where do remote parts of the Universe drag the skater's frame of reference? Toward the mass distribution as it was long ago, when light from there started its journey to illuminate the skating rink today? Or toward the location of those masses at this instant? And is there such thing as a "this instant," which makes the same sense over there as it does down here?

Recalling the Greek cosmology of celestial spheres that went out of fashion after Kepler, what if outside the observable Universe actually is a massive hollow sphere that spins around like a giant flywheel, giving everything inside inertia, just as Mach suggested? The recent puzzling discovery of the Universe's anisotropy—aptly called the "Axis of Evil" by the exasperated folks trying to explain it away—may turn out to be a manifestation of the flywheel that we can't see, just like we can't see dark matter or the Flying Spaghetti Monster (it may be that the matter in the visible Universe is spinning around the Axis of Evil, which we can't see from inside the Universe for the obvious lack of reference points). Any light that the spherical flywheel might have ever emitted our way wouldn't have had time to reach us, but gravity may well be a good deal faster [28]. Then again, a considerable amount of light is apparently coming at us out of nowhere [29]. Maybe that mysterious glow is somehow connected with the Wheeler-Feynman absorber idea, which holds that any photon ever emitted has to somehow find its absorber in the vastness of the Universe. If it sounds as wild as a hollow, solid sphere surrounding the visible Universe, that's because it is.

The trouble is that Wheeler and Feynman were dealing with a problem at least as serious as the Axis of Evil: they were trying to explain the Arrow of Time. It turns out that we don't know why light moves from the past to the future: according to Maxwell's equations, it might just as well go the other way. Since causality in physics involves the speed of light, the stakes are really high for causalists to explain which way is tomorrow, from the point of view of a photon somehow managing to get there from yesterday and not the other way around, despite Maxwell not telling it how to. The Wheeler-Feynman absorber theory doesn't appear to explain much, especially compared to the monumental assumptions made to hold it up, but it shows the promise of an approach whereby the search for a lost key isn't limited to the well-illuminated spot under a streetlight.

The world is full of wonders that keep turning out to be interconnected in all sorts of unexpected ways. Even the very tools we use to learn about the world around us aren't exempt. For example, quantum computing, one of humanity's most ambitious current endeavors, is based on the quantum entanglement of tiny qubits. Their "memory" eventually fades in what's called decoherence, limiting the performance of the computer. It turns out cosmic rays are the next barrier to improving the performance of quantum computing [30]. The number-crunching power available to the future interstellar explorers may well critically depend on how much radiation shielding their ship can carry.

It doesn't take a quantum computer, though, to become fascinated with numbers, particularly if, like Paul Dirac, you do science for a living. Dirac was captivated by the approximate coincidence of two ratios. The ratio of electric forces to gravitational forces in hydrogen, the most common atom in the Universe, is about 10^{40}. So is the ratio of the size of the observable Universe to the size of the hydrogen atom's nucleus—proton. Not only that, but the square of each of these numbers—or their product—happens to be roughly the same as the number of particles in the Universe. An obsession with numbers sometimes leads to interesting developments in science, like Pythagoras' research of fundamental frequencies and harmonics of strings in sixth century BCE, which seeded the whole science of acoustics. Pythagoras' concept of *musica universalis* inspired Johannes Kepler so much that he entitled his book on dynamics of the Solar system *Harmonics of the World*.

One of Dirac' conjectures from these observations was that the gravitational constant G, along with other "fundamental constants" and the amount of matter in the Universe, may not be a constant at all. Instead, it may vary with the age of the Universe. The trouble was that within the context of the theory of general relativity, as originally formulated, a variable gravitational constant would violate the conservation of energy. Not one to do things by halves, Dirac promptly offered both ways out of this apparent contradiction: Einstein's theory might need to be modified, or the conservation of energy might have actually been violated at the scale of the whole Universe. Maybe, he suggested, matter (and hence energy) actually is added, either uniformly throughout the Universe or preferentially around existing concentrations of mass. After all, the conservation of energy and mass—verified to impressive precision for small, artfully isolated systems—hasn't been tested for the whole Universe. Once we accepted the creation of our Universe—with all the energy and 10^{80} particles of matter and time and space—in a Big Bang, accentuating brushstrokes that add a photon here and a muon there really pale in comparison. There's a lot of room between big and small.

Alan Guth, who was later awarded the Kavli Prize (with Andrei Linde and Alexei Starobinsky) for the cosmic inflation theory, published in 1981 one of the first theoretical papers [31] linking the big (the Hubble parameter for the expansion of the Universe) with the small (the quantum phase transition in the primordial vacuum). Assuming the creation of our Universe opens a lot of possibilities. One of those is that our laws are different on the small and the large scale, and maybe even such apparently fundamental laws as the conservation of energy and matter are observed in the breach. Maybe there are things that look like laws within our puny experience exactly because it's so ridiculously small compared to the really big questions some of us dare to ask.

Our theories of big and small—gravity and particle physics, respectively—so far fail to click together. Our leading concepts in these fields, GR and QM respectively, paint pictures of this world so different that they have resisted a century's worth of effort by the sharpest minds on the planet to reconcile them. Their predictions for energy density of vacuum differ by 120 orders of magnitude. There have been attempts to attach significance to this number (10^{120}) as well. It happens to coincide with the number of nucleons (protons and neutrons) we can pack into the volume of the observable Universe, and it's alleged to account for the sum total of all information in it.

The information content of the Universe is central to Dutch physicist Eric Verlinde's theory linking quantum mechanics and cosmology. In his (evolving) model, space is a network of entangled qubits containing—collectively—all information about the Universe. Some have hypothesized that the Universe is holographic, in the sense that a surface—in this case, cosmological horizon—holds what amounts to a complete copy of all information in the network. The entangled qubits "talk" to their neighbors, thus propagating information through the network. As information percolates through the network, the entanglement gets weaker, and information gets noisier. Noise is entropy, so Verlinde invokes thermodynamic reasoning to derive Newton's law of gravitation [32]. Actually, he does one better: he also derives MOND.

What's MOND? It stands for "MOdified Newtonian Dynamics," a hypothesis that Israeli astrophysicist Mordehai Milgrom offered in 1983. He was exasperated by the fact that the standard cosmological model needs twenty kilograms of invisible pseudomatter to explain the behavior of each kilo of matter we can see. It all started with the rotational curve catastrophe, when astrophysicists learned to measure the speed of stars' spin around the centers of their galaxies. They found that if Newton's gravitational law kept working on that scale AND if all matter in the galaxies was the star matter they saw and dust and planetary matter they kind of saw, then the speeds they measured were all wrong. Beyond some distance, stars were flying too fast. Newton's gravitational law said that those galaxies ought to have flown apart. Observations suggested that they didn't. Something had to give.

The default approach was to invent dark matter, an invisible, undetectable, transparent, and non-refractive substance that stubbornly refuses to interact with anything—including our detectors—in any way other than gravitational attraction. It just happens to be conveniently distributed, for no apparent reason, so as to hold the galaxies together, despite their outer stars spinning too fast.

The nice thing about invisible dark matter is that it's impossible to disprove. Just add some here, subtract there, and you'll get any distribution of that fake mass you want, so there's really no way for dark matter to be inconsistent with any experiment or theory. It's got infinite freedom to fit anything. It's not falsifiable.

Then it turned out that a Universe with all that dark matter in it wouldn't be expanding at an accelerating rate, as it appeared to be doing. Another prop was promptly found: dark energy. The magic wand of dark energy conveniently tweaks gravitational attraction to hammer the galaxies' rotational curves into compliance with Newton's gravitational law. Whereupon every observation consistent with omnipotent dark matter—which, again, is any observation, already made or otherwise—was sold as evidence of its existence. Maybe Milgrom wasn't the first to notice that by using this method one could prove a whole zoo of unicorns, but he did offer an alternative.

Milgrom proposed that the inverse-square-of-the-radius law prescribed by Newton isn't universal for every distance or, more accurately, for every acceleration. In MOND, after gravitational acceleration falls beyond a certain threshold, it keeps falling, but as the inverse of the radius, not the inverse square. The threshold acceleration was taken from experimental galaxy rotational curves, and that was the only empirical parameter in the theory, not the infinite number of invisible masses distributed by a magic wand.

One rabbit pulled out of a hat is a lot more believable than an infinite number of invisible elephants pulled from the same hat, but it would be even better to know how the rabbit got into the hat in the first place. And that's what Verlinde's emergent gravity model aspires to explain [33]. According to his theory, gravity on a cosmic scale emerges from interactions of microscopic qubits that individually don't possess any gravitational properties at all. Gravity—and, therefore, inertia—isn't then an inherent property of just the body in question. Instead, it emerges from its interactions with the rest of the Universe. Mach's conjecture may turn out to be correct after all.

In science, experiment or observation is the ultimate judge. Mach's conjecture predicts that the rotational curves will be significantly affected by neighboring galaxies, with MOND yielding testable predictions for what this effect should look like. And a recent survey of 153 galaxies [34] found—surprisingly and significantly—that MOND predictions are accurate. In the meantime, another survey found that satellite galaxies in a galactic cluster around Centaurus A don't just fly unexpectedly fast. They're also kinematically synched in a disc-like alignment around the central galaxy [35]. Standard cosmology, using Newtonian gravity and general relativity, tells us that the galaxies are too far from the center and from each other to be so choreographed. The Universe appears to be full of spooky actions at a distance [36]. As we explore our magnificent Universe, we realize that the stars out there—and the humans down here—keep turning out to be related in more and more ways. We get closer to the stars as we grow up.

2.9 Holistic science for a holistic world?

Every student at every school has heard the story of great Galileo using the leaning tower of Pisa for experiments that conclusively proved that bodies in free fall accelerate independently of their mass. You want a passing grade in science? Then this is the right answer: Galileo Galilei has proven, by meticulous experiments, that light and heavy objects in free fall take the same time to fall to Earth. If you want an A+, you'll add that he performed those experiments in 1589.

It doesn't take long to realize that the prescribed answer is specifically wrong: Galileo couldn't prove anything experimentally about bodies in free fall in 1589. The first vacuum pump was invented in 1650, sixty-one years after Galileo was dropping things on gawking tourists in Pisa. So whatever Galileo may have dropped wasn't in free fall. It was falling through the air. As a result, they were subject to—besides gravity—both Archimedes' buoyant force and air drag. A brick, a feather, and a hot-air balloon[9] wouldn't hit the bottom of the tower at the same time if they were released simultaneously at the top. To do that, they'd have to be falling in a giant evacuated enclosure, unavailable at the time—unless helpfully supplied by little green men.

Galileo pulled the "experiment" out of thin air, pardon the pun. He did it all in his mind. Just like, 2,000 years before him, Leucippus and his pupil Democritus in Greece posited, with no evidence whatsoever, that the world is made of indivisible atoms of all sorts and the void between them.

It turned out that Galileo guessed kind of right, and so did ancient Greek natural philosophers Leucippus and Democritus (there are atoms of various sorts, and space between those), but Thales missed (he said that everything is made of water), and so did Anaximenes (he thought everything was made of air) and Empedocles (his list of elements included fire, air, water, and earth) and Aristotle (he added ether to Empedocles' list). How do you tell who's right? I mean, now we can Google what's kosher in ten seconds flat, but someone somehow figured it out first, right?

The architectural peculiarities of ancient Greek gyms provide a hint. There were at one time three popular gymnasia in Athens—the Academy, the Lyceum, and the Cynosarges—where followers of three respective philosophical schools could

---

[9] Galileo worked in Pisa 160 years before the Mongolfier brothers' flights but 1,400 years after the Chinese invented Kongming lanterns, which float in the air when lit—unmanned, of course, but perfectly adequate for Galileo's purposes.

congregate, exercise, attend classes, and host debates.[10] Cynics, predictably, went to Cynosarges; Platonists attended to the Academy; and Aristotelians belonged to the Lyceum. The part of each gymnasium devoted to wrestling, boxing, and ball games was called the "palaestra." That's where, under covered porticos, philosophers gave lectures and threw punches, polemic or otherwise. There was no better place in all of Greece where philosophical disputes with visiting scholars could turn from metaphysical to just physical. Duke it out. Plato, who had a secondary appointment at Aristotle's Lyceum and who regularly lectured there, must have been the inspiration for Master Yoda or an early incarnation of David Carradine's character from the *Kung Fu* series, Kwai Chang Caine (Plato was actually a competitive wrestler).

On a (slightly) more serious note, we're going back to epistemology—the study of how we know if we really know what we think we know—and the general philosophy of science. The three gyms had a good reason to wrestle: the worldviews of the crews, and the crew bosses, were very different.

Cynics believed truth to be unknowable to mere mortals, who—by their primitive, ignorant nature—aren't privy to the deep meaning of the Universe. The best we can hope for, according to this cynical view, is to describe, encode, and catalog our direct experiences. And that's the sum total of what we can ever learn about the nature of Nature.

Let's illustrate cynical "science"—a simple data compression/cryptography exercise—with a contemporary example. Say you're shooting a 4K video of a moving train with a 12-bit RGB camera at 24 frames per second. You get flooded with 37 Mb of mostly useless data 24 times every second, so instead of paying through your nose for sending all this junk around, you compress it. You squeeze out as much of the stowaway burden as you can via data compression, and it turns out that humans are ingenious enough to get rid of between 80% and 99.5% of the junk. So you can go from 888 MB/s down to 4.44 MB/s with little loss of information. Yet the cynics believe you can't take a moving picture of a train and derive general conclusions about nature of Nature from it – the conclusions about the train movement that will allow you to predict where the train will be in the next

---

[10] By the way, the word "gym" is short for "gymnasium," which is a derivative from the Greek word "gymnos," which means "naked." This was before Nike and Puma and Reebok, so athletes had to practice and compete without any uniform, and only adult, male Athenians were admitted in the gym. Gender disparity in science may well be traced to Athenian gym rules.

frame—until you actually see that next frame. Remember *Roadrunner* cartoons, where Wile E. Coyote got flattened by heavy objects miraculously condensing out of thin air? Cynosarges' movie theater must have run *Roadrunner* all the time.

Cynicism traces back to Antisthenes, a pupil of Socrates. He had plenty to be cynical about. A son of an Athenian father and a foreign mother, he wasn't considered equal to the real, red-blooded citizens. A veteran who fought for Athens in many battles, he still had to go to Cynosarges, the hall of bastards, the gymnasium reserved for those born to slaves, foreigners, and prostitutes. He was a heathen beyond the pale. And the trial and execution of his revered teacher, Socrates, didn't mellow Antisthenes any. He spent a considerable part of the rest of his life plotting revenge on those responsible.

Plato, the founder of the philosophical school at the Academy, was twenty years Antithenes' junior, but, like Antisthenes, he was also Socrates' pupil. Plato's philosophical approach was somewhat different from Antithenes'. Plato wondered if abstract ideas—perfect, eternal, immutable Forms that select few humans can grasp by pure reason—were the only things true and real, whereas all of the material world is no more than an image of reality distorted by our limited and imperfect senses.

The "select few" part is important. Plato famously came up with the cave allegory, the first recorded conspiracy theory in the history of humankind. In the allegory, he pictured humans as chained slaves, living in a cave and watching an endless shadow play. They are restrained so they can't see what makes the shadows, so they mistake the shadows for the real world. Only a select few can see the ugly truth, and then only with their minds. They realize that perfect, eternal Forms guide everything, and the shadows that we mere mortals see are pale imitations of what's really going on. Anticipating Harry Houdini by twenty-three centuries, a superhero (a philosopher, of course—preferably Plato or one of his students) breaks free of the chains, then climbs out of the cave and gets to see the real world outside. The philosopher will at first be blinded by the Sun, but then the Truth will show itself to him. What comes next, in the allegory, is a warning: the philosopher, full of pity for the cave dwellers, returns to share the newly obtained knowledge and to induce the cavemen to go see the light—whereupon, naturally, he'd be blinded by darkness, and as the cave prisoners watch him blunder around, they inevitably conclude that the world outside the cave is a dangerous place where folks go blind. According to Plato, the philosopher is then killed by the cavemen for urging them to go outside and expose themselves to the dangers of the unexplored reality.

Socrates' pupils seem to share his rather low opinion of common humans. But then their beloved teacher was tried, convicted, and executed with poison for what amounts to making ordinary citizens feel like idiots.

The surviving works of Plato (and there is a lot of surviving text attributed to Plato with some level of confidence) are vague and ambivalent enough for some folks to hold that Plato rejected the theory of Forms mid-career in "Parmenides," although others interpret "Parmenides" and later texts as an argument in favor of the theory of Forms. That makes studying the views of Plato, twenty-four centuries after his death, rather—ahem—platonic. What we really study are the records made by folks arguing about what they thought Plato thought, which, as everyone knows, ain't the same thing as what he actually thought.

Plato's writings are a lot clearer about the concepts he attributed to his teacher, Socrates, than about his own. Maybe he just didn't notice. It's fairly common to notice holes in someone else's reasoning while being oblivious to your own. But in Plato's case, it was more likely by design. He wrote that "the subjects that I seriously study… there does not exist, nor will there ever exist, any treatise of mine dealing therewith." He also said that "every serious man in dealing with really serious subjects carefully avoids writing." The trouble is that if we take seriously one of the thoughts he did commit to writing, then we shouldn't take it seriously. See the problem?

Plato's student, Aristotle, did. Aristotle is credited with single-handedly creating formal logic,[11] defining and thoroughly investigating deduction and "discovering" induction ("argument from the particular to the universal," in his words). Aristotle also addressed the issue of how we know that we know what we think we know. In his *Posterior Analytics*, he spelled out the problem: to claim that we "know" something, we need to "demonstrate" that we actually do. That "demonstration" is based on something we claim to "know," and so on ad infinitum. If you have a first statement in the chain, it has nothing backing it up – so it cannot be known. Since, for Aristotle, "to be acceptable as scientific knowledge a truth must be a deduction from other truths" – nothing downstream from first statement hanging up in the air can be acceptable as scientific knowledge. Oops.

Aristotle's first solution was to loop the whole train of thought in a tail-chasing circle. The conclusions from conclusions somehow looped back to make their own premises. The obvious advantage of a hamster wheel like this is that the hamster is kept occupied indefinitely. The disadvantages, though, are numerous and obvious.

---

[11] Logic is a systematic method of coming to the wrong conclusion with confidence.

For all its heroic efforts, the hamster ain't going anywhere. Worse, any attempt to modify the wheel ruins the whole thing and sends the hamster flying. The hamster wheel has to be perfect, unalterable, and eternal. Logical rigor turns out to be rigor mortis.

It takes a mind much less brilliant than the one owned and operated by Aristotle to notice that the hamster wheel solution is less than satisfactory. It contacts reality exactly nowhere, which gives its designer wonderful freedom to put in any nonsense, as long as it's logically self-consistent.

There has to be a better way, and Aristotle knew he had to look for it. After all, what's to prevent a gymnasium across the street from building their own hamster wheel and declaring it superior to Aristotle's? The answer Aristotle came up with was induction: arguing from the particular to the universal. While watching the world, you notice what looks like commonalities and trends. If you look "right," you can inductively argue from specific instances to general rules. If you went to the right school – that would be Lyceum, if you haven't guessed yet—you get "the universal" right. But perceived commonalities and trends don't add up to "knowledge" of some fundamental first principles, do they? I mean, somebody could have noticed another set of trends and argued for another set of first premises, couldn't they?

Aristotle urgently needed something to hobble the competition, necessity is the mother of invention, so he offered this pearl of wisdom: "We do not know a truth without knowing its cause." It goes without saying that Aristotle knows best what the cause is—he literally wrote the book on it.[12] The book, however, is so incomprehensible that it requires a live interpreter to be present at all times, and the interpreter gets to tell the rest of us the Truth. Plato is my friend, but patented Truth is a better business.

Inventing criteria for the Truth that were so vague that your services are required to tell what they mean helped a lot—but in the irreverent culture of Ancient Greece, this wasn't enough to establish a firm monopoly. That's where, in *Posterior Analytics*, Aristotle introduces a cryptic word: nous. Yes, our "knowledge" is, in all likelihood, the badly mangled Aristotle's "nous". Aristotle taught that nous was an altered cognitive state that wise men enter for insight or intuition about the deep fundamentals related to how the world works. You just get it, and by "it," I mean Truth. Presumably, that Truth comes from Above.

---

[12] It's actually two books: *Physics* and *Metaphysics*—but their chapters on causes are very similar.

As an advertising vehicle for a struggling philosophy school in dire need of revenue,[13] selling membership in the exclusive Club Nous was pure genius. Students who wanted to learn the secret nous from the teacher of Alexander the Great just had to pay a membership fee. Alexander the Great, meantime, was seriously pissed at Aristotle for teaching anyone other than Alexander himself and his (presumably loyal) inner circle. Alexander had this to say on the matter: "Thou hast not done well to publish thy acroamatic doctrines; for in what shall I surpass other men if those doctrines wherein I have been trained are to be all men's common property?"

There were several ways of dealing with the issue raised by Alexander. The Western thinkers view learning about the nature of Nature as a private enterprise, which has pros and cons. Socrates, who was son of a mason and a midwife, couldn't afford to own a gym, so he practiced philosophy as a street performer. It speaks volumes about the state of mind of common Athenians back then that Socrates' lectures on obscure philosophical subjects could compete with the performances of acrobats, musicians, and fire eaters. It's hard to imagine this happening in a society that dished out $1.27 billion to shoot *Pirates of the Caribbean*, which returned a 250% profit, yet wouldn't give 2% of the *Pirates'* budget to the Arecibo radio telescope[14] for another facelift. Even in ancient Athens, though, the citizens' charity wasn't enough for Socrates to earn a decent living, so he performed philosophy as a hobby, earning his keep elsewhere. Plato, on the other hand, was born into wealth and influence, and he owned his Academy. In the privately owned institution, he taught that rulers had to give up not only private property but also private families. His *Republic* leaves the reproductive rights of a ruler (a.k.a. the "philosopher king") in the hands of the community, which would tell him when to reproduce and who to reproduce with, in the best interests of the state. Many of those justifiably scandalized by reproductive communism are entirely unaware that the idea originated with Plato as an early and clumsy concept that was to evolve, twenty-two centuries later, into checks and balances.

---

[13] Aristotle, the resident alien, couldn't own property in Athens, so he had to cover rent, in addition to all his other expenses.

[14] The giant radio telescope, now officially deceased, earned its keep—literally—with a long string of discoveries, including ice on Mercury (yes, the one with a surface hot enough to melt lead), fast radio bursts from mysterious invisible sources, and pulsars that play hide-and-seek. Arecibo's last renovation was finished in 1997, and it cost $26 million. Twenty-three years later, it was gone.

Is Humanity an Apprentice God?

Clearly, the idea of state-sponsored philosophy was all Greek to the Greeks. Passing fancies of the high and mighty notwithstanding, Western philosophers were on their own. That could hardly fail to reflect on the beliefs they held. After a revenge poisoning of Socrates, a kidnapping of Plato by King Dionysius of Syracuse, Plato's subsequent refusal to entrust his deepest thoughts to paper, and Aristotle's tutoring of kings to make ends meet, the pattern was set. The Western state and Western philosophers cooperated only under duress, and they felt it best to keep at arm's length otherwise. The world conqueror Alexander the Great and Diogenes the Cynic famously expressed that attitude when, at the height of his might and glory, the former visited the latter at his barrel dwelling. Alexander asked Diogenes what he could do for the philosopher, who had only one request: would the Emperor please move the heck to the side so as not to block the sunlight, thank you very much. Alexander reportedly loved the retort and said, "But verily, if I were not Alexander, I would like to be Diogenes."

Meantime though, Alexander never forgot to send samples of plants, animals, and artifacts—including Babylonian science libraries on clay tablets—to his old teacher Aristotle in Athens, where the fellow Macedonian had triumphantly returned after skipping town as an undesirable alien (he would have to flee again after his patron's death, allegedly by poison, in which he was said to have played a role). Aristotle had counseled the young Alexander about Persia and the rest of Asia, telling him to be "a leader to the Greeks and a despot to the barbarians, to look after the former as after friends and relatives, and to deal with the latter as with beasts or plants." One wonders what Alexander's three wives would have thought of this advice if they had heard it, given that all three were Asian and two were Persian. One also wonders how many of the ideas credited to Aristotle were appropriated from the barbarian libraries.

For all that, state helped science in the Occident only by accident. Elsewhere, such cooperation was more of an established norm (with its own pros and cons). Jixia Academy, the first known institution of higher learning under state patronage, was established by Duke Huan of Qi (in what is now China) in seventh century BCE. We know very little of the teachings of Jixia Academy: the exclusivity that Alexander the Great sought in vain from Aristotle is not, it turns out, all that difficult to procure. All you have to do to have exclusive rights to your philosophers' time and talent is to pay enough for said time and talent so the eggheads don't have to seek a second job elsewhere.

Eastern scholarly thought is traditionally (and often dismissively) presented in the West as vague, tangled, holistic, esoteric, secretive, and mystical—as opposed to the West's own crisp, defined, atomistic, exoteric, open, and rational ideas. There is a variety of explanations for this disOrientation, which aren't necessarily mutually exclusive. The most obvious possibility is a (distinctly bigoted) professional jealousy. There's plenty to be professionally jealous about.

Rig Veda of ancient India—I mean really ancient, as in Stone Age, fifteenth to twelfth century BCE—contains a cosmological theory of a cyclical or oscillating Universe of the type only rediscovered in twentieth century CE. In this concept, a "cosmic egg" ("*Brahmanda*" in original Sanskrit) containing the whole Universe mushrooms out of a single concentrated point called a "*Bindu*," which has no dimensions, and eventually it collapses back onto itself and starts all over again. And it does this in a series of indefinite Big Bangs and Big Crunches, the terms coined in the West thirty-five centuries later.

The Babylonians used precise measurements and calculations to predict the positions of planets in the sky centuries before Greeks did. Early Babylonian astronomers (called "*Chaldeans*" by the Greeks) left no record of their cosmological theories, but the accuracy of their actual predictions proved hard to beat. They produced the first useable *Farmers' Almanac* around 1700 BCE, eighteen centuries before Ptolemy the geocentrist, of epicyclic fame, was even born. And a clay tablet from 1800 BCE shows an unknown Babylonian scribe using Pythagoras' theorem thirteen centuries before Pythagoras.

Indian astronomer and mathematician Aryabhata described elliptical orbits around the Sun at the end of the fifth century CE, twelve centuries before Kepler. So did Ja'far ibn Muhammad Abu Ma'shar al-Balkhi, four centuries after Aryabhata but eight centuries before Kepler. No, these aren't the names you get to learn (and promptly forget) at school.

Chinese scientists documented a solar eclipse in the twenty-first century BCE, noted the magnetic attraction of a needle in the first century CE, made the first recorded observation of a supernova in the second century, put together the first atlas of comets in the fifth, researched climate change (with a proper scientific method) in the eleventh, and discovered light refraction in the eleventh century too—500 years before Willebrord Snel van Royen in Europe—and used it to calculate corrections to astronomical data.

Meanwhile, Arab polymath Musa Al-Khwarizmi invented algebra in the ninth century (the word "algorithm" bears his—badly mangled—name). Omar Khayyam, known in the West only for his poetry, calculated the length of the year to within five decimal places in the eleventh century. In that same century, Islamic scholars made several other consequential contributions. Arab intellectuals corrected

Aristotle's error (Aristotle thought that velocity, rather than acceleration, is proportional to applied force) and brought to light Ptolemy's and Euclid's mistakes (they thought that vision involved your eyes emitting something toward whatever you see). They proposed the action-reaction principle, the idea that no material object can act without being acted upon, which is the concept behind both Newton's third law and John Archibald Wheeler's relativistic notion that "spacetime tells matter how to move; matter tells spacetime how to curve." They also beat Willebrord Snell van Royen to Snell's Law in optics by five centuries, just like the Chinese did. Ibn Sina started the first systematic clinical trials. But, most importantly, they (specifically, Ibn al-Haytham) came up with the idea of scientific method: testing of hypothesis' prediction by reproducible experiments. Ibn al-Haytham also believed that mathematics is the language that science needs to express itself—so its predictions are tight enough to actually be testable.

Al-Khwarizmi didn't invent the first recorded algorithm in the ninth century. Hero of Alexandria put on paper the first recorded algorithm for iteratively calculating a square root of a number in the first century CE, so Western historians wasted no time in calling it Heron's method. There's evidence, however, that Babylonian mathematicians figured it out some seventeen to nineteen centuries before Hero (yes, the evidence is very tangible: it's a damn clay tablet with a very precise value for the $\sqrt{2}$ written on it, which they somehow managed to calculate).

So maybe—just maybe—the story we are taught – the one about the West single-handedly building modern civilization, is, ahem, somewhat embellished. While it's hard to trace each particular baton pass, it appears rather naïve—well, not so much naïve as arrogant, ignorant, condescending, bigoted, and plain stupid—to imagine that the Greeks single-handedly built the glorious temple of knowledge from scratch in a couple of centuries, then abandoned it for millennia until the Renaissance, whereupon the inherently superior West, with no contributions from anyone else worth mentioning, miraculously revived it and proceeded to discover and build everything we know and enjoy today. But that's largely the picture you get from the popular books on the history of human knowledge in every bookstore in the West.

Another possible explanation for the West's condescension and pointed scepsis toward the holistic Oriental philosophy is that Eastern philosophers' employers were really good at keeping their employees' discoveries to themselves. The Orientals' intellectual contributions are just not nearly as well known to the outside world as the works of their Occidental colleagues, and the Occidentals were glad to take the absence of evidence of rich Oriental intellectual traditions in every Occidental bookstore to be evidence of the absence of said tradition. It wasn't.

But it does suggest a degree of isolation that Eastern thinkers had to accept in exchange for their job security. The trade wasn't without benefits: state sponsorship of the Eastern intellectuals gave them the peace of mind to focus on the Big Picture, millennia before an astrologer and an alchemist became a must-have status symbol for European courts. For that, they gave up the freedom to go to any competing gym they wanted and offer their ideas up for an open debate. That's a significant handicap: we humans rely on each other to find holes in our thinking, and in the process of duking it out, we improve the ideas that need improvement and weed out the unsalvageable ones. The cycle of inspiration and validation repeats itself, and the outcome depends on both whoever gets inspired and whoever does the validating. Competing colleagues – peers with similar interests and knowledge base, but (!) different points of view on what it all means – tend to make the most useful sparring partners (yes, maddeningly reluctant to concede anything – and very useful for that very reason).

The advantages of an open contest of ideas don't come cheap. There have always been—and I am sure always will be—brilliant sparks of intuition that didn't survive peer assault and had to be reinvented centuries later. Ptolemy killed Aristarchus of Samos' heliocentric model of the Solar system, which was forgotten for millennia, until Copernicus resurrected it. Plato and Aristotle rejected Democritus' atomism, which was largely forgotten until 1905, when Einstein published his paper on the Brownian motion of pollen. The existence of atoms remained purely speculative for another fifty years, when we took the first blurry pictures of them.[15] But to paraphrase Churchill, open debate is the worst form of nature-philosophical inquiry, except for all those other forms that have been tried from time to time. Given that fact, whose heads could the Eastern thinkers, pretty well locked up by their masters, bounce their ideas off of?

The masters' heads, that's whose. We here in the West assume, by default, that wisdom, knowledge, and information all flow one way: from the eggheads to the brass. Hollywood says so, and so do the talking heads on TV. It's hard for us to visualize an emperor trading polemic blows with a philosopher to benefit the latter's theories. But if we imagine that possibility happening in the ancient Orient, then the Oriental holistic approach becomes much easier to comprehend.

---

[15] No one may ever know how Lucretius, in his 60 BCE opus *On the Nature of Things*—seventeen centuries before the first microscope and nineteen centuries before Robert Brown—managed to accurately describe the Brownian motion of dust particles.

Is Humanity an Apprentice God?

Rulers earn their keep by ruling. Decisions—mostly resource-allocation decisions—are their end product. Which makes a holistic view of the world the only viable option for a successful ruler, —especially in ancient times, when resource-allocation mistakes were typically punishable by a de-throning by middle management or a very hostile takeover. You can't afford to forget about finances, or you die. You can't afford to forget about agriculture, or you die. You can't afford to forget to build granaries and tax everyone on good crop years, or you die in hunger riots on a lean year. You can't afford to forget about defense, or you die. You can't even afford to forget about damn arts—or foreign visitors ain't properly impressed, report your fiefdom to be a dump, neighbors leave you out of their alliances, aggressors-to-be are encouraged by seeing you as an easy prey, and you die. Basically, you learn to keep everything, and every conceivable connection between things, in mind, and take it into account every time you decide on anything, which is all the time. Or you die.

"Look out!" is what we yell at someone in danger. If sharks are circling outside your little comfort zone, then zoom out, and you'll see them and maybe manage to do something to save your skin. Rulers who last are good at zooming out. It's a dangerous world out there, and all kinds of monsters may be waiting for their chance to pounce. The farther out you see something, the more time you'll have to decide what to do about it. It helps if you live a bit longer. This, by the way, is one of those things you'll never learn by the statistical analysis of the tunnel-vision type so popular nowadays. Myopic blunders of the kind described in the film *Without Warning*[16] usually go unreported: there ain't no one left to report them.[17]

---

[16] The 1994 sci-fi film depicts a myopic humanity that slices its own throat with Occam's razor. Odd meteorites fall in an odd pattern around the globe, and odd things start happening in the places where the meteorites fell, and then all around the planet. The powers-that-be disregard the possibility that alien intelligence has anything to do with it, and when another object shows up, they nuke it. Whereupon... no, I'm not going to spoil it for those poor souls who haven't seen it.

P.S. It's not—certainly not, emphatically NOT—the low-budget 1980 namesake that stars flying jellyfish sent by aliens to hunt humans for sport. If you see that film somewhere, RUN! The mental damage it will cause may be permanent.

[17] Want a real-life example? Here's one related by Robert McNamara, the US Defense Secretary during the Cuban Missile Crisis. During WWII, he was doing statistics for the

The lookouts aren't posted on the guard tower just for show. The spies in the foreign lands are paid handsomely to report on the first whiff of cool air blowing this way. Expeditions are outfitted and sent overseas, observatories are built and staffed to keep an eye on the skies, and libraries are stocked with information and ideas from around the world, all in an effort to reduce the probability that one day some unannounced disaster will wipe you out just because you never gave yourself a chance to prepare. Looking out—into space and time—is what leaders do for a living.

Imagine spending time with a guy like that. He's your employer, and whatever you tell him, he can't help but to relate it to whichever issue might be on his mind at the moment. Which can be anything. In response to anything you say, he might

---

US Army Air Force. As you'd imagine, repair reports data on B-17 bombers during WWII were very thoroughly analyzed to improve the machine itself, crew and mechanic training, and logistics. In particular, they wanted to add armor to the areas that got damaged the most. But you can't add armor all over a bomber or it will be too heavy to fly. You need to be smart about it. They thought they were, but they were dead wrong.

A Jewish mathematician and refugee from Austria named Abraham Wald worked on the project, gathering data for the Air Force. He had a chat with an armorer at some airfield. We may never know the name of the kid, but his blue-collar common sense saved a lot of American fliers. The observation he shared with Wald seems obvious in hindsight, but every higher-up managed to miss it and its implications.

The armorer said that they only needed to write repair reports on the repairs they actually did, and they only did repairs on the planes that made it back from a mission. The ones that were shot down or that were too severely damaged to make it back to base didn't get any reports.

Wald slapped his forehead, drew up a B-17, and marked all the areas where they had data, then he reported that those areas weren't vital for the machine because the planes shot in those places had made it back fine. It was the others that perished, and it was those other places needed that extra armor

He had a hell of a time getting the idea across to his superiors, which is what makes him—and the anonymous armorer who had the actual idea—the hero in this story. But eventually the notion percolated, and armor was added where he suggested. As a result, aircrew survival rates shot up.

ask you a question about anything else, anything that looks completely unrelated at first glance. And you can't afford to look unprepared and unworthy of continued tenure: the heads of your predecessors, who were insufficiently prompt in answering apparently random questions, were bitten off, shrunk, and mounted on the wall. Saves a lot of retirement paperwork. So you have to anticipate, which is impossible unless you adopt an outlook at least as broad as his. As a selective pressure mechanism for keeping a broad, inclusive, holistic view of the world, employment as a wiseass-on-call at an ancient Oriental court is very hard to beat.

The first scientific activity that we know about in any detail was the Mesopotamian *sumero-akkadian* astronomy of the nineteenth century BCE. Written documents of its earlier origins are—so far—lost in the mist of time. But it only takes one look at the map to see that Mesopotamia is located between Egypt and Persia. Egypt is where folks were developing math at least in the thirty-second century BCE, and the three largest pyramids precisely aligned with the cardinal directions (0.067 degrees, counterclockwise, off true cardinal alignment), which weighs heavily—pardon the pun—against the idea that Bronze Age Egyptians were astronomically ignorant. The three pyramids in question were all built in the twenty-sixth century BCE. In Persia, recent excavations unearthed the remains of a culture that traded with the Elam in the West and the Indus Valley civilization in the East in the third millennium BCE. All three of these advanced civilizations left behind documents, written in a script very different from Mesopotamian cuneiform and Egyptian hieroglyphs, and they haven't been deciphered yet.

The Chaldeans, who came to Babylon later, built upon the existing tradition of astronomical and mathematical research. Then the Greeks joined in and had their Olympic run with Prometheus' fire (*"pramathyu-s"* means "a thief" in Vedic Sanskrit. In *Rig Veda*, a hero named Mātariśvan steals the fire of wisdom from the Gods to give to humans. A hero named Enki does the same in Sumerian lore).

The Roman conquest of Greece in 146 BC didn't stop the intellectual tradition. While Rome did conquer Greece militarily, culturally it was the other way around. In fact, even after suppressing Greek insurrection in 86 BCE and taking to Rome Aristotle's papyrus scroll library as a trophy, general Sulla (Lucius Cornelius Sulla Felix) had the priceless texts restored as best he could after centuries' worth of worm and mold damage. Every Roman family that could afford the fees hired an educated Greek to tutor their children. At the height of its might, the Roman Empire was an incredibly successful enterprise for its time: diverse and largely tolerant, pragmatic and making good use of available resources to benefit its citizens.

And then it all went south in the West. Corruption, income disparity, and nepotism punched holes in the Roman economic and political fabric. What amounted to a state religion replaced religious tolerance, the emperors started calling themselves *dominus et deus* ("lord and god"), and they progressively lost touch with reality. Primitive technologies left humans vulnerable to unpredictable climate swings. The main sources of energy in the Roman Empire were muscle power (human or animal), firewood and animal dung, and all of them were critically dependent on climate conditions. For a while, the Roman warm period, which lasted until the fourth century CE, kept everything peachy. Until the fourth century, Romans felt no need to build water mills, although they were fully aware of the technology. Practical windmills didn't get built until at least 250 CE, although Hero of Alexandria had made wind-driven toys two centuries earlier. Roman society stagnated and decayed; decadence and hubris ruled. Roman soldiers found cuirasses and helmets too burdensome, and none other than their "lord and god" the emperor officially granted the soldiers permission to abandon them. So when the climate changed and desperate, starving Huns attacked the bruised but decadent Romans, the Huns had the upper hand. The already weakened Empire disintegrated, and Europe sank into darkness.

The next Golden Age of human scholarship started in the ninth century in Baghdad. Not surprisingly, it took advantage of the treasure trove of earlier knowledge, particularly the Greek manuscripts on science and philosophy. These were largely contributed by the Christian community, who found themselves custodians of ancient wisdom after the disintegration of the Roman Empire. Persians pitched in with the rich cultural estate left by the Sassanid Empire, which outlasted the Roman Empire by more than two centuries. Just like the Romans (and Alexander the Great before them), the Muslims started off as ambitious, cosmopolitan, and tolerant. And just like the Romans, they were eager to provide secure and lucrative employment to educated foreigners. In just a few decades, the newly founded Baghdad became the largest city on the planet. There, Caliph Harun al-Rashid established a house of wisdom: a library and an institution of learning. Scholars from all over the world gathered there and translated every piece of human knowledge and thought they could lay their hands on—just like others, sponsored by Ptolemy II, did at the Great Library of Alexandria eleven centuries earlier. Arabic became the language of science and philosophy, just as Greek had once been. Like the Romans before them, Muslims got lucky with a good run of warm, wet climate called the Medieval Warm Period. And like the Romans, their early ambition and drive eventually faded into hubris, corruption, and inefficiency, accompanied by religious squabbles among progressively less tolerant factions.

The caliph and his viziers lived in luxury. Gold, priceless carpets, and imported slaves and concubines were everywhere you looked. That violated traditional interpretations of Islam by religious scholars, and it was the caliphs who actively sponsored the rationalist, Greek-influenced "Mu'tazilism" school of thought. But as the caliphs lost their grip on power, it became a crime to copy books on philosophy. And Baghdad wasn't providing services to the provinces that were commensurate with the taxes that the provinces were paying. Naturally, the provinces started seeking independence (a.k.a. refusing to pay taxes). Predictably, this separatism happened exactly when Baghdad needed the money the most—to subdue the provinces with military force. To make the long story short(er), when the Arabs were hit with the triple whammy of the Crusader invasion from the West, the Mongol invasion from the East, and climate change (this time it was the Little Ice Age), the Golden Age of Islam faded into the mists of history.

In 1021, during the Islamic Golden Age, Ibn al-Haytham—a mathematician, astronomer, and physicist—wrote his *Book of Optics*, which completed the development of the scientific method. Again: scientific method as we know it exists since 1021. Presocratic natural philosophy – Babylonian, for instance – was empirical and descriptive. The Greeks introduced logic and mechanistic approach. Aristotle taught induction – arguing from particular to the universal – and deduction, its reverse. Just add the powers of observation for noticing trends and intuition for proposing mechanistic hypotheses to explain phenomena, and voilà, you can explain the world.

The trouble is that induction is (very) imperfect, and so is intuition, which means that someone else could explain the same world differently. So is there a way to tell which explanation is the right one? Not really, but Ibn al-Haytham came up with the next best thing: he suggested how you can tell which explanation is wrong. The way you do that is by working out predictions about something you can empirically test and then testing it. If the data you collect isn't what your hypothesis predicts, then your hypothesis is wrong, so try again.

Incidentally, Ibn al-Haytham was a big fan of math: using math to express a hypothesis yields predictions tight enough to actually be testable. It also helps to process the raw observational data that you start from. Merging a mechanistic approach from the West with an empirical approach from the East, Ibn al-Haytham completed the circle: you start with empirical data, then you go back for more empirical data to test your mechanistic ideas of how the world works.

The scientific method as we know it is based on empirical observations. We repeat the observations again and again to see if they're reproducible. Then we publish our experimental protocols so others can repeat our experiments in their labs to check if they get the same results. And we change the conditions under which we make the observations—in other words, we manipulate the system from outside it— and start over so we can separate the wheat from the chaff. If your model of the world says that X has nothing to do with Y, but every time you change X, something happens to Y, then your model is wrong. And vice versa. If your model says that X "causes" Y but empirically nothing happens to Y when you change X, then you need another model.

This is all good and well, but if you're interested in the Big Questions like cosmology, this approach gets you in trouble [37]. The Universe you're trying to explain only happened once, so any observation you make of the Universe as a whole is unique and irreproducible. You have no chance to look at it from the outside, so the observer is always a part of the system. And forget about tweaking any parameters to see what wiggles as a result. We can't even get any empirical data from anywhere that doesn't lie on the paper-thin 2.5-D surface of the r=ct cone in 4-D spacetime. The empirical data set we use to make big claims comes from a vanishingly small sample of the Universe we are trying to comprehend. If we want to claim the authority of the scientific method—the authority earned through centuries of discovery—we have to actually apply its methods with the same rigor as earlier scholars did. And in cosmology, you can't do that.

And it's not just cosmology, either. Our best theory of the small, quantum mechanics makes the observer—and the very act of observation—an inseparable part of the system. And problems with our current theories of the big and messy are even bigger and messier. As far as we know, our species only happened once, just like the Universe did. So, strictly speaking, did our Earth. Outside observers of humanity as a whole aren't available. We aren't at liberty to tweak the parameters of humanity or the planet we live on in order to obtain empirical data for hypothesis testing. Every branch of human knowledge that deals with these systems is laboring under these incapacitating handicaps. Sociology and history, geophysics and climate science, economics and environmental science, epidemiology and meteorology all study systems that the scientific method, as it has existed for the last 1,000 years, plainly fails to cover. Are they all condemned to linger in the gray area between rigorous science and handwaving?

This question is getting pretty urgent. Humans are an increasingly global species, and the systems we create—deliberately or otherwise—are also increasingly global.

To engineer global systems deliberately, one needs reliable models to predict the global systems' behaviors before we build them. So far, engineers have borrowed their models from science. Use Hooke's law to design a bridge. Use Newtonian mechanics and design a crane. If we want to be as deliberate about managing the climate, environment, or economy as we are about bridges and cranes, we need models that are as at least as accurate and reliable as Hooke's law and Newtonian mechanics. Otherwise, it ain't physics; it's stamp collecting. If someone tells you that you should bet the future of humanity on a collection of stamps, you can bet your bottom dollar that he's selling you something. Probably the stamp collection.

The rest of us (a.k.a. the sane majority) would dearly love to know what the heck we're doing. It would be really helpful to be able to predict the consequences of our actions in the real, entangled world we happen to live in. And not just the obvious ones but all the consequences that matter. There might be a reason that "comprehensive" and "comprehension" sound so much alike. If a model fails to cover, comprehensively, all the factors linked to the system's behavior in a substantive way, is it any good at helping you comprehend the system accurately enough for engineering or even just forecasting?

We can deliberately control something only to the extent that we can predict how it will respond to our inputs. Just ask Wile E. Coyote what happens when we can't. In the engineered world of isolated systems, our inputs (usually) produce predictable outputs through an artfully restricted set of prescribed interactions. Outside this artificial domain of bouncing pebbles, we don't have the luxury of exclusively controlling just the parts of the whole we're trying to control. The rest of the system, intertwined in all kinds of ways, can't help but change in response, —which, in turn, modifies the response we're after. It's more like bouncing kids on a trampoline: each of them affects all the others.

Reductionist models describe bouncing pebbles on a frictionless plane and the other varieties of a spherical horse in a vacuum. Bouncing kids on a trampoline require holistic modeling. But besides the reductionist-holistic dimension, models can also be either mechanistic or descriptive (heuristic).

Mechanistic models try to predict the behavior of the system in question based on some concept of its innards. Their variables describe a surmised list of, and supposed interactions among, the parts that allegedly make up the observable system. You don't get to introduce latent variables and constants willy-nilly. All of them have a meaning, like the mass of a brick or the charge of a particle. You can learn things about the system by examining its parts. If your approach is both mechanistic and reductionist, you can take a brick or particle out of the system, measure its mass or charge in the lab, and put it back, and what you measured is supposed to stay the same. Reductionism assumes that properties of parts taken out of the whole are enough to fully characterize the whole; the holistic approach regards that statement as a falsifiable hypothesis.

Mechanistic models (the ones we know how to build) work when all parts that matter and all their interactions are accounted for in the model. If something is missing, the model gives inaccurate predictions that don't survive testing, which is a great thing: that's how you know that something is missing. If your model used to work great, you extrapolated it to a new set of conditions, and it failed the new tests, —then something was missing, something that didn't matter before but started to matter when you changed the conditions. The missing thing has properties that interact with the rest of the system in a way related to the parameters that you changed the last time. That gives you a hint of what it is you're looking for. Mechanistic models are a tool for exploring Nature.

The problem with mechanistic models is that once the system you're trying to understand is complex enough, it becomes a challenge even to list all the interacting parts in it. And trying to track the interactions among them is far harder still. Emergent properties miraculously pop up whenever and wherever the heck they choose, and there's no reason to expect a quantum-mechanical atomistic model to ever tell us anything useful about the weather in Timbuktu next weekend. At some point, reductionism becomes a handicap for developing mechanistic models.

Descriptive models, on the other hand, don't bother with the meaning of their latent variables, —which makes their accuracy, in principle, unlimited. You can introduce as many fitting parameters as you damn well please. If you want to describe the trajectory of a falling brick using a descriptive model, then all you have to do is use enough terms in the formula for data interpolation to yield any precision you wish. None of these will be derived from the Earth's diameter or the mass of the brick or the relative positions of the Earth, the Sun, the Moon, the brick, or anything else. All you have to have is a bunch of measured positions at some points in time, and you'll have the coefficients in your formula. Then you'll be able to tell where the brick was at any point in time between your first measurement and the last one, and you can extrapolate after the last measurement, assuming that the formula continues to work in the future.

In principle, you can also get an arbitrary degree of data compression by throwing away as much of the data as you choose and conveniently calling it "noise." But you can't do both at the same time. Improved accuracy of the output requires more inputs (or more significant digits in each input, which is, entropically speaking, the same thing), while data compression requires exactly the opposite.

But the proliferation of meaningless parameters every time you look away isn't the only problem with the cynical descriptive approach, and it's perhaps not even the worst one. The worst one, in my view, is this: however much you learn about a particular brick falling under particular circumstances, you still won't know anything about any other brick—or a feather or anything else in the Universe—or even the same brick falling in a different place or at a different time. Descriptive models aren't portable. Every time anything changes, the unbounded accuracy of the descriptive model goes down the drain, and you get no rules that would let you transfer knowledge from one event to another. If you want to know the weather forecast for Timbuktu five days from now, the best you can do with descriptive models is to find out what was happening there five days from some date in the past when every input was exactly like it is today. If you can't find a precedent like that, you're out of luck.

Mechanistic models are a very different story. A falling brick acted upon by nothing but gravity will experience the same gravitational acceleration as a feather or hot air balloon in the same place, so once you have probed that acceleration using a brick, you don't need to test it again with anything else: the acceleration should be the same. If, that is, you're prepared to bet that nothing but gravity acted on the brick.

Furthermore, you can relate the acceleration you measured in the vicinity of Earth to the mass of the Earth—as Henry Cavendish did in 1797—and then your theory gets to work in the vicinity of any celestial body with a known mass. It also gives you a "scale" for measuring that mass from your observatory right here on Earth. Mechanistic models give you portable knowledge you can take with you and apply elsewhere.

That portability makes engineering possible. Hooke's law lets engineers use material constants measured in a lab to design structures that have never existed before. With portable knowledge, you can extrapolate to unprecedented situations.

How about the Timbuktu forecast? In a mechanistic model of atmosphere, the inputs are measurable: temperature, pressure, humidity. Wind, cloud cover, the position of the Sun in the sky. Terrain, vegetation, agriculture. And the inputs have to be measured over a sizeable area around Timbuktu: in five days, wind can deliver weather from quite a way away. In fact, weather forecasting has little chance of predicting anything more than a few days out unless it considers the entire planet. In this interconnected world, the further out you want to look in time, the farther out you have to look in space, and the greater the chance that butterflies in a remote forest will change the weather where you live. So the number of inputs rapidly gets out of hand, as does the computational burden of producing the actual forecast. With computational difficulties come errors, which build up and eventually gum up the works so nothing useful comes out at the other end. You get hit with the law of diminishing returns, whereby adding input data and data crunching power no longer makes much difference in the quality of your forecast. You drown in chaos.

The drowning weather forecasters (and other modeling folks) try to keep their heads above the water by parametrizing their models. On a global grid with a cell 150 kilometers on a side, you can't do physics of cloud formation: all relevant physics happens on a much smaller scale. As I wrote this sentence, a ski resort in the next state over was doing a brisk business after a seven-inch snowfall, and all nearby hotels were packed at completely ridiculous prices. Another resort about 4 km away barely got a single snowflake. The 150-km grid is way too crude for modeling the cloud that brought that snow. So the clouds in the cell are reduced to a set of generalized parameters, whose connection to anything real and measurable is often rather tenuous.

> Jones's law: the man who can smile when things go wrong has thought of someone he can blame it on.

Here's a quote from an actual recipe for calculating how much it's going to rain: "Precipitation formation is adopted such that condensate in convective updraft is converted into precipitation when its amount exceeds a threshold value. The threshold value of 8.0×10^{-4} kgkg^{-1} in 10-km MSM is increased to 1.0×10^{-3} kgkg^{-1} in 5-km MSM to eliminate precipitation calculated by the KF scheme and to improve the representation of weak precipitation in summer season." Just like that. No fundamental laws changed; no Platonic forms discovered. Just put your finger on the slider and miraculously improve your model.

Put enough sliders in, and your postdictions—that is, the "retrocasts" of past weather—will be as accurate as you want them to be. Parametrization is the gray area between mechanistic and descriptive modeling. It uses terms from the real world (for example, clouds, precipitation, evaporation, convection), but what it means by these words is a bunch of rather ethereal abstractions that couldn't get you soaked if it tried. There's nothing fundamental about the laws the parametrization uses to describe these abstractions, their interactions, and the evolution in time. The 8.0×10^{-4} kgkg^{-1} threshold isn't something you can derive from quantum mechanics of hydrogen and oxygen and nitrogen and all the rest, nor is it something you can measure in a lab. Outside of the model, it simply doesn't exist.

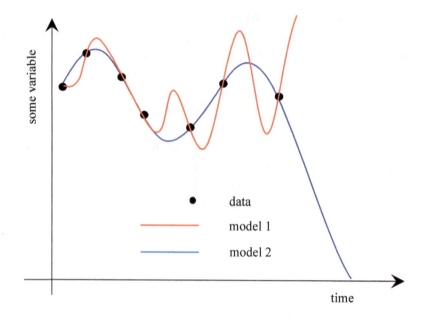

Figure 27 – Alternative hypotheses: same data, very different predictions.

Hence, we get the degeneracy problem. I'm not cursing (yet), though I probably should. Degeneracy in science (usually) has little to do with slobbering imbeciles. Instead, it has to do with explanatory redundancy. When you have lots of alternative hypotheses, each perfectly compatible with available data, that's Nature's hint that you're talking through your hat and that you don't have enough data to discriminate among the hypothetical explanations of whatever's going on. If, as is usually the case, there's nothing unique about a descriptive model, and lots of alternative models (explicitly spelled out or otherwise) can fit the past data equally well, then you don't have data to justify preferring any of them to any other. That's fine if all of them yield the same predictions for the future, but most of the time they don't. And there's no rational way of telling which of the different predicted futures is the one that's going to actually happen, unless it exactly repeats some past precedent. No situation without precedent can be reliably forecast by a descriptive or parametrized model. Neither can you engineer a new system using a descriptive or parametrized model, however good the model might be at describing the past.

That puts us between a rock and a hard place. Mechanistic models quit yielding any useable predictions once the system in question is complex enough. Descriptive models give you any prediction you can think of—and more—but no criteria for choosing the right one until it's too late. And parametrized models seem to inherit the problems of both parents.

How, then, do we get models we can trust? Let's try to look at both dimensions (namely, holistic-reductionist and mechanistic-descriptive) at once. Academics currently prefer the reductionist-mechanistic worldview, except it often stops giving useable predictions long before we get to the level of complexity and interconnectedness of the real stuff of interest. Reductionist-descriptive models have become a default fallback position when we need some numbers to show the boss, but the system in question is so damn convoluted that we can't get any numbers without fudging. Holistic descriptive models have advanced very little since Nostradamus—understandably so, since Michel de Nostredame has already predicted absolutely everything that will ever happen. He achieved this impressive result by the simple expedient of being sufficiently vague for his predictions to be interpreted as accurate after something happens. Anything, really. Just add dark matter. That left the rest of us with little to do but to admire his handiwork– other then, of course, figure out some ways to get usable predictions before the events they predict (a.k.a. while they still can do somebody some good).

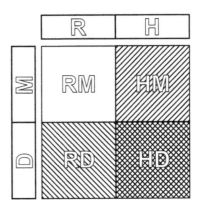

Figure 28 – Model types.

We may find these ways in the one quadrant of the 2-D diagram that has been least explored so far: the holistic-mechanistic worldview. In mechanistic models, you can learn things about the system by examining interactions among its identifiable parts. In the holistic worldview, you don't throw the baby out with the bathwater by assuming that what you noticed so far is all there is. It might be good not to have to choose between mechanistic and holistic approaches. Can we take advantage of both at the same time?

Zhang Heng, the inventor of the first known seismoscope, at first glance appears to be a naïve causal reductionist. From the horse's mouth: "The chief cause of earthquake is air, an element naturally swift and shifting from place to place. As long as it is not stirred, but lurks in a vacant space, it reposes innocently, giving no trouble to objects around it." But wait for the next sentence: "But any cause coming upon it from without rouses it, or compresses it, and drives it into a narrow space… and when opportunity of escape is cut off, then 'With deep murmur of the Mountain it roars around the barriers,' which after long battering it dislodges and tosses on high, growing fiercer the stronger the obstacle with which it has contended."

That's a pretty accurate description of how pressure waves propagate. That's what modern seismologists are taught, and that's what their computers model. The only part of the story Zhang Heng got grossly wrong was the reductionist part: the "chief cause." Earthquake waves mostly go through rock, not through air. The rest of it—the holistic part, the "any cause coming upon it from without"—worked well enough to construct a practical device that even indicated the approximate direction of an earthquake, which operated fine despite the fact that it was made with second-century technology. Could it be that our seismologists, nineteen centuries later, still can't predict earthquakes largely because they still don't take into account "any cause coming upon it from without"?

We have learned quite a bit since the times of Zhang Heng. Some of the big questions that pique our curiosity remain: if remote events appear correlated (for example, an earthquake in Tibet and Earth shaking in Chang'an), then what is the mediator that links them? Does it even need a mediator? Now we ask these questions about entangled photons, and (in Einstein's words) some spooky action at a distance that links them. We have learned to ask even deeper questions: Does the mediation propagate at a finite speed? What, if anything, does it propagate through? Does the mediator only affect the events we happen to observe? Are some latent players with hidden variables also interacting with the system in a way that we haven't noticed yet?

So far, answers to these questions are few and far between. But the ones we have are fascinating, and they're encouraging further exploration. They challenge the most foundational assumptions of our most fundamental theories. They destroy the illusion that we have already discovered all the basic laws of the Universe and that future explorers only have insignificant gaps left to fill in. The last time we broke that illusion, at the turn of the twentieth century, we discovered the theory of relativity and quantum mechanics and triggered an explosion of new technologies. There's no reason to think this time will be less productive. In fact, the coming scientific revolution may prove far more fruitful than the last one.

Our ancestors waited for millennia for astronomy to develop to the point where it could provide the Babylonian *Farmers' Almanac*. Then the cross-pollination of ideas between science and engineering accelerated. By the time of Newton, the delay between advances in fundamental knowledge and progress in everyday lives shrunk, sometimes to well under a century. When Wilhelm Röntgen took the first X-ray photo of his wife's hand in 1895, the pace changed so much that the first radiographic clinics opened the very next year.

And then we stepped on the brakes. The healthcare revolution promised after the Human Genome Project is nowhere to be seen, almost twenty years after we deciphered the human genetic code. In the seventy years since we pioneered numerical weather forecasting, all the satellite data and supercomputers and other resources poured into it managed to extend relatively reliable forecasting range by a mere few days. Cheap and abundant fusion power remains out of reach, almost a hundred years after the fundamental physics were worked out. So what happened?

We got hit with the law of diminishing returns, that's what. We have run outta low-hanging fruit. At the dawn of Industrial Revolution, Newtonian reductionism in science was a progressive, productive idea that drove advances in engineering for centuries afterwards. Not anymore. Many of the systems we are dealing with now are so complex that reductionist models are no longer good enough to predict their behavior with useful accuracy. Too many latent variables, too much chaos in dynamics, too many emergent properties for reductionist approach to yield meaningful predictions. Taking the system of interest apart works just fine, thank you very much—it's putting it back together that's been getting harder and harder. The threads we snap and don't restore during reassembly are lying around the shop, and the whole contraption looks plausible enough if the lights are dim enough—but then the dreaded test comes, and the darn thing sputters and coughs and refuses to catch. The ensuing excuses sound particularly lame in light of the latest round of chest-pounding and boasts that, "There ain't nothin' 'ere but the stuff we know everythin' 'bout."

We can't leave science behind and move forward with ad-hoc fixes. The finished product of science (a.k.a. the explanation of how the world works) is our only rational guide when we need to predict the world's behavior under unprecedented circumstances. Which is most of the time. You woke up today in a world different from the one you went to bed in last night, and a lot of butterflies in Brazil have flapped their wings while you were asleep. Today has too many moving parts to be an exact replica of yesterday or any other yesterday, so history may be a guide, but it certainly isn't a recipe book. There's nothing more practical than a good theory, which can predict things that have never happened before. Including the outcome of any frantic action you may cook up once you've seen the forecast.

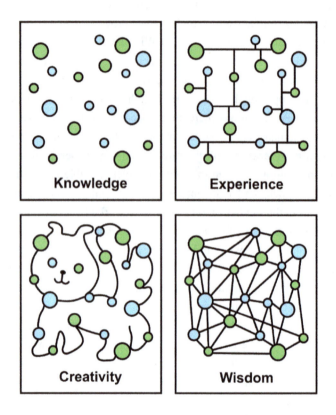

Figure 29 – Data to wisdom.

The next book will deal with some opportunities for the new holistic-mechanistic approach to creating theories in science. Meanwhile, there are arguably two systems that already use it to determine what happens next. One of them is Nature. The other is discussed next.

2.10 Humanist hypothesis

Russian President Vladimir Putin recently announced that Avangard hypersonic weapons are operational and in service within the Russian military. Apparently a whole regiment is armed with them. However secretive any military force may be—particularly the Russian Strategic Missile Forces—about targeting the most advanced weapons in their arsenal, one thing is certain: some are sure to target the capital of their main adversary. That would be Washington, DC. There is no known defense from a hypersonic glide missile like the Avangard: the darn thing actively maneuvers to avoid interception.

The announcement made it to American mass media on December 27, 2019. On New Year's Eve, Washington, DC, papers reported the rescue of two kittens from a fire, announced various venues to celebrate the 2020 New Year, and invited residents to join the mayor for the 5K run on January 1. What they didn't report was panic, the evacuation of the government to secret underground bases, a mass exodus from the city, real estate sell-off for pennies on the dollar, families refusing to return home after the school break. None of that actually happened.

The residents of Washington, DC—adults and kids, right and left, rich and poor, the elite and the bums, seasoned military experts and wide-eyed pacifists—collectively and accurately predicted that they would be fine right where they were. Most of the folks making this accurate prediction had no access to, nor any interest in, detailed information about the new weapon, including its capabilities, location, targeting, command structure, or whatever. How did they do that?

Figure 30 – Gestalt intelligence?

How do laypeople get it right even when experts often don't? What possessed Neville Chamberlain in comfortable Great Britain in 1934—before Anschluss, Czechoslovakia, Norway, Poland—to reflect on a "universal feeling of apprehension about the future"? How do folks in Florida make the decisions to get out of town or stay put when a hurricane is menacingly heading in their general direction? How do we decipher the picture above to mean that something's afoot, and we better start packing? How did rank amateurs start social distancing and using homemade masks during the Covid-19 pandemic long before experts and authorities caught up?

We can, and usually do—even before the Earth quits shaking—get out of the house to see what the neighbors are doing. The couple wearing camo looks like Burt and Heather Gummer, with all weapons, ammo, and survival gear already packed into the M35 surplus military truck that will go 8 miles per gallon. They were born ready. Their preparations for hell or high water are so comprehensive, they look somewhat disappointed every time nothing happens. The old guy in his robe and pajamas picks up a newspaper, looks around and nods to nobody in particular. The couple from across the street is arguing on the porch, beside an overflowing mammoth suitcase, the terminally bored goth daughter and the lying-down pooch trying to look cool and eager at the same time and failing miserably on both counts. Birds cautiously try chirping again. The single mom from the house next door, a recent arrival from out of state, loosens the grip on her kid—who exhales for the first time since the first shake. And you, in the split second it took you to take in all of this, don't need all these seismologists with their sensors and supercomputers to tell you what to do. You put the car keys back in your pocket, drag the damn suitcase back into the house, and reemerge on the porch with an open beer in ten seconds flat.

In that fleeting moment you didn't, of course, have any opportunity to compute your survival chances in staying where you are and compare those with the chances you'd have on the road. You were just guessing, like everyone around you. So were the geologists with their supercomputers and sensors. The geologists had a lot more objective information and a lot more number-crunching power available to them. All you could rely on was your own perception, your neighbors' perceptions, and any public announcements you might have heard during the commotion. But most of the time, your evaluation will be at least as good as the experts'. How can you be that good?

A honeybee collecting nectar and pollen zigzags through fields and orchards, apparently at random, flying wherever the next foraging clue takes it. Once fully loaded, it takes off and follows the shortest straight line directly home. The dang insect has no GPS chip, and it doesn't stop at a gas station every couple of blocks to ask locals for directions. It just goes straight in, deploying landing gear and aerobrakes right before the hive entrance. Most people can't do that with a map and a compass, which keeps attendants at the Met and Louvre gainfully employed, telling the bewildered visitors which way the exit is. How come humans are so much better than bees at complex tasks when we are so hopeless at the easy ones?

A hint can be found in the way we approach the most demanding cognitive tasks. Say you have a pile of painstakingly collected evidence about a murder. The prosecutor is eloquent and argues that the defendant did it. The defense lawyer argues just as convincingly that he didn't. How do we make sense of it? Should we ask a judge, an experienced professional with a law degree and a lot of experience in these kinds of cases, to actually judge? Why do we cling to the system of jury trials for the most serious crimes, believing, apparently, that twelve laypeople with no experience can untangle the most perplexing situations better than a pro who has seen it all?

Why do we pay outsiders to sit on a board of directors of a business where they have never as much as screwed in a light bulb, inviting them to make decisions vital for the firm? Why do we elect fishermen and engineers, nurses and farmers, stockbrokers and physicists, car dealers and ministers to our parliaments to make laws for us?

Because we make sense together a lot better than even the smartest ones of us do individually, that's why. That's the gist of the hypothesis from *The Enigma of Reason*, a wonderful book by Hugo Mercier and Dan Sperber. The two cognitive scientists argue—quite convincingly if you ask me—that human reasoning is drastically improved when we do it together. A group's decisions are usually much better than those of the smartest member of the group.

To begin with, who the heck is a cognitive scientist? Say you grow up in a perfectly normal family. Your parents and grannies and aunts all have a dream for you. What you want for yourself is to make a decent living out of your hobby; and your hobby happens to be to confuse the heck out of everybody. Your parents also want you to make a decent living and be happy, but they also want to look dignified in your college graduation photo. They want bragging rights. If you are a true rebel, you'll become a stage magician. The considerate ones become cognitive scientists.

Sleight-of-hand tricks abound in both professions. Cognitive science's David Copperfield is Peter Wason. His four-card selection task is a very neat peephole into the gearbox of human reasoning. Details are unimportant for our story. What's important is that test subjects are asked to untangle a logical puzzle. The puzzle obviously has a logically precise answer in there somewhere, and you'd inevitably arrive at that answer if you only meticulously followed the steps. A long sequence of boring and very obvious steps. If you have ever had a fishing line tangle, you know what I'm talking about. Half a beer later, you made the wise decision to, quite literally, cut your losses. You cut out the tangle, spliced the line, and went back to actual fishing.

The test participants weren't allowed any beer during the test, so they arrived at the same decision even faster. They guessed. And they guessed wrong eight or nine times out of ten. Peter Wason was that good.

Then they changed the rules and let participants argue in groups. They made the person suggesting a solution actually justify it to her peers, and they let peers ask questions and offer alternatives. Then a miracle happened: instead of eight or nine wrong answers out of ten, folks got it right eight times out of ten. No member of the group got it right more than two or three times out of ten when working alone, but the group as a whole was more than three times smarter than its smartest member.

It's all very clear in hindsight. Remember the 175 biases that make every individual individual? You can hardly see your biases from the inside—I can't see mine very well either—but we have 20/20 vision of each other's biases (if they're different from our own). So when I look out and see something through my individual filter set and you do through yours, we see different worlds and come to different conclusions, and that's the best we can do on our own. But when we compare our views, voilà, we get a more accurate picture together than either of us can get individually.

We compare the pictures, for the most part, using words. Language. I, for one, learn a lot by paying attention to human language. There's a lot of collective wisdom in it. We know more than we know that we know. A lot more. And there's plenty to discover just by listening to each other.

Take, for example, this expression in English: "makes sense". That's what people – Rational Humans - make: sense. Bees make honey, beavers make dams, humans make sense. It's the product of our species. You "pay" attention, "make" sense, and "earn" respect. It sounds suspiciously like capitalism: investment, product, revenue. And then you reinvest your "revenue" and start all over again to make more "product," more sense.

It takes more than just an investment to make a product. You need technology, and components. You can't make sense just by paying attention. What are the components that we make sense out of? And what's our technology to make sense with?

I suggest that the "components" that *H. sapiens* (a.k.a. Perceptive Humans) acquires by paying attention are the observations of the world around us. We then make sense of what we perceive. How do we do that? I suggest that our preferred technology for making sense is zooming. You can zoom in or zoom out. By zooming in, we decompose a complex picture into smaller and simpler pieces until they start making sense. That's the reductionist approach we discussed in the previous chapters. Zooming out is a matter of putting things in context, and it's the alternative, holistic approach. *H. sapiens* (a.k.a. Wise Humans) does both.

Making sense is a process of abstraction of essentials from the world overloaded with minutia. Abstraction is, strictly speaking, always wrong: it never tells the whole story. But telling the whole story in real time is impossible anyway, only Nature can do that. Abstraction is the best we can do. Abstraction is how we, with our frugal sensory abilities and pathetic processing bandwidth, manage to get a sense of what's going on without any help from Laplace's demon.

You can make sense of a big chunk of marble by imagining David and chipping away the rest of the marble. Michelangelo did that, and since then, billions of people know what the master imagined David looked like. But that's not what the original marble boulder looked like.

The boulder might have looked like a sheep or a bear or an alien spaceship. Especially if you were, respectively, a shepherd or a bear hunter or Erich von Däniken. But all three would agree that what's left of it looks like an apprehensive, naked, muscular kid with a sling in his left hand. At closer look, a trained cardiologist can even diagnose the kid by the distended jugular vein in his neck. The distention is suggestive of heart disease, in which case swelling would be expected around the kid's body. There is none. A temporary jugular distention is also common in people exerting themselves – or getting ready to. Which David clearly is, once we remember the context, it makes sense. David is depicted getting ready to fight Goliath, and the only air support available to him is the sling in his left hand.

At even closer look, the marble statue no longer looks like a statue at all. Look at it through an atomic force microscope, and it won't look any different from any other piece of polished marble. In this context, the shepherd and the hunter and von Däniken would have to agree again. But this time they would agree on something other than the first time. Context matters. It matters even when the only thing you can play with is the scale. And it matters a lot more when things you consider aren't unflinching stone statues but objects that change over time.

What's the context for the transient, real-world events that we're interested in? The point of the "making-sense" exercise seems to be to find a way to make some actionable predictions —before we actually see things happen—so we can do something about it. Making the whole wide world the context would make the "predictions" precise but useless. We have seen in the previous chapters that if we take everything in the world into account, computing even the computable predictions takes forever, so they aren't available in time to help anyone. Predicting precisely what should happen after it has already happened doesn't do anybody any good. Abstraction is a compromise between the precision of predictions and their availability, and that's what makes our product useable. Abstraction is a gamble; when you abstract whatever you're interested in from the intertwined world web, you can snip the wrong threads and lose it. But if you don't abstract at all, you won't have any prediction until it's too late, so you'll lose for sure. Choosing a context to make sense of the world is a bet you have to take if you want to have any control of your future.

And if you must bet on something, why not bet on yourself? You're the context. You are what gives your experiences meaning. You are what looks out the window, sees snow, and chooses what to do: snuggle inside or have fun skiing. The difference between information (raw observation) and knowledge is meaning. Information means something in a context, and out of context it's meaningless. You look at data and say what it means to you. You provide the context. We Rational Humans make sense of information and, thus, convert it into knowledge by rationalizing the information within our personal worldviews. It snaps in place and becomes a part of us, and the next time we try to make sense of something, we take it into account as an inseparable part of the context.

The same information could mean different things to each of the 7.9 billion humans on the planet. Individual knowledge is very subjective and, thus, has low fidelity. We can't survive and strive if we base important decisions on skewed subjective worldviews. We need something better. The sense an individual makes of things is for a niche market: there is only one person in the world it's a priori good enough for. This is a pathetic market size, and we deserve better than this. We paid attention and made sense, so we want our investment back—with interest. So we try to earn respect by marketing our worldview. We tell stories that make sense to us, and we hope they will make sense to others.

Others will be in no hurry to abandon their worldviews in favor of yours. If what you're saying doesn't call for a change in their worldview, you will be welcomed to the ranks, issued a dog tag or whatever that particular tribe uses, and thoroughly ignored thereafter. But if your story deviates from the conventional wisdom your audience holds near and dear, then get ready, pal, they're coming for you. Making anyone doubt even a small piece of the whole picture earns you a lot of grief. The picture is a web, and it only makes sense as a perfect whole. If someone tore a hole in your favorite T-shirt, wouldn't you be pissed? Folks protect their worldview as if it were their immortal soul or their nest egg or both, which for all we know, it may well be. And everyone knows that the best defense is a good offense, so they're going to attack your story and try their best to find what's wrong with it.

Which is the best thing they can do for you and your story. That's how you can make your product better: by engaging with the folks whose opinions differ from yours. For most really consequential stories, that's everyone and his brother. That's how you know that you managed to squeak out something nontrivial: there are a lot of folks announcing that you're full of it.

Most of the announcements are no more than pledges of allegiance to a tribe, guild, hive, or herd. Yet you can't afford to ignore them: there are gems in that pile of manure that aren't available elsewhere. And they have your name on them.

The gems are the arguments of folks telling you what they believe to be wrong with your story and why. They're reasoning with you. They're the first to get through the first two stages of grief – denial and anger – and to move on to the third, bargaining. They're your audience. They are—for the most part—unwittingly talking about you to the members of their hive, who otherwise would never notice your stream of consciousness. For all intents and purposes, they're your agents. You've made it. Congratulations!

Before you climb on the damn pedestal and try to look regal, please note that the guild/hive/tribe has been around since long before you graced the scene with your arrival. It couldn't have been wrong every time it whacked an opponent on the head, otherwise it wouldn't still be there. When they say you're full of it, may well be one of the cases of them being right. It has happened in the past, and it can happen again. Some of their arguments are actually sound, so you'd better tweak your story to address them. Other arguments miss the point. You use the same words to mean different things, and you argue past each other. You need to tighten up your definitions so folks know what the heck you're talking about. And yes, there are also completely idiotic arguments that only a True Believer could possibly buy. When your opponents publicly make fools of themselves, that could make a most valuable marketing tool too, especially once you have honed the invaluable skill of milking every last ounce of humiliation out of every comma they may have gotten wrong.

And then somebody somewhere makes a guarded remark that in some other Universe, on some planet that has nothing in common with ours, some species entirely unrecognizable as our relatives may have a small village where something like what you're saying may have once made sense. Wowsers! You've just done something that nuclear-powered aircraft carriers, guided missiles and millions of trained men under arms routinely fail to do: you changed someone's mind. The piece of the Universal jigsaw puzzle that used to make sense to no one else has been checked by someone who actually agrees that this one may fit.

When it fits, it clicks. That's the aha moment. We crave those. We celebrate them. We wham ourselves on the forehead and thump ourselves on the chest and yell from rooftops and slap unsuspecting strangers on the shoulder. We work outward from what has clicked already to assemble unattached pieces, like in an endless jigsaw puzzle.

What has clicked together is our island of knowledge. *The Island of Knowledge* is the title of an outstanding book by a Brazilian physicist named Marcelo Gleiser. You can thank me later. That's what the jigsaw puzzle is: our habitat, the island of knowledge that we humans build to live on. It's an island of what we have made sense of in the endless ocean of unknown. Our farms and factories, hospitals and universities, courts and governments are all built on that island. Staples and Moon rockets, microchips and bridges, guns and bandages are all made here on that island. Our lookouts are on shore with grappling hooks, and they catch and rope in the new pieces. The Hubble telescope, the Fermilab Holometer, the Large Hadron Collider, and the XENON1T dark matter detector are sophisticated, enormously expensive harpoon guns that we use to hook big pieces of flotsam, which we haul in and add to our island. We examine each piece and decide if it's a good enough fit with what the island is already made of. If it is, it becomes a part of our island, right there at the seaboard. "As far as we know" just became a little farther.

The island of knowledge is a floating island that stays afloat by growing. The old knowledge gets waterlogged and weighed down by barnacles, and it doesn't have much buoyancy. Some of the old knowledge decays and falls to the bottom of the ocean of the unknown. Then you need special divers (a.k.a. historians) to retrieve it and try to fit it back into our island.

Every time we notice what looks to us like a promising fit, we do a war dance on the beach. We light a big fire and make smoke signals. We blow conch shell horns. We act crazy and hope everyone notices. We want them here and now with their grappling hooks. We can't do it alone.

Sometimes someone else reels in a piece that fits just as snugly as an existing piece, and we argue about it. Every once in a while, we throw away something that only yesterday seemed like the best thing since sliced bread. Something like epicycles or phlogiston or luminiferous ether or Laplace's demon. Our reward for bold moves like these is often not a better fit with what we already have. Galileo's heliocentric model didn't yield more accurate predictions than the pre-Galilean geocentric ones, but it helped us lose that thing that stuck out like a sore thumb and got in the way every time we tried to fit anything else.

Sometimes the piece that just snapped in place turns out to be a great match for something that had bothered us for a while, bobbing out there in the waves and refusing to fit anywhere else in our island. Like one hard-to-fit spot in a jigsaw puzzle that, once filled, triggers an avalanche of other pieces falling into place. At the turn of the twentieth century, a few aha moments in physics triggered a massive shift in our understanding of the physical world. A couple of key insights into the nature of the genetic code in the mid-twentieth century precipitated a parade of discoveries in scientific fields as far apart as pharmacology and archeology.

It takes a lot of us to make all of this happen. To begin with, someone has to have the luxury of spearfishing for knowledge rather than actual fish. So somebody else has to get the fish and bread and houses and roads and aqueducts and all the rest of the tangibles of human civilization. Cavemen and nomads couldn't afford to build Large Hadron Colliders, even if someone told them how. They were too busy dealing with more immediate problems, like the minuscule size of their island of knowledge. Among the tiny island's inhabitants were first-rate dreamers—remember the Stone Age folks in India who imagined the Big Bang?—but they hadn't yet learned to ask the questions that the Large Hadron Collider is supposed to answer.

When your knowledge base is small, you don't know what you're missing. Your world is full of what Donald Rumsfeld called unknown unknowns: dangers and opportunities you don't know even exist. You then hunt wooly mammoths off the face of the planet to feed fewer than a million humans. You can't imagine that it's perfectly possible to feed ten billion humans while at the same time having national parks and Nature preserves and letting even the damn deer chewing on your wife's cherished tulips live, against wiser counsels. You don't know that the dirt under your feet can be turned into cars, airplanes, computers, and rockets—and energy to power all of these. You can't imagine any threat from a dinosaur that had been wiped out by an asteroid millions of years before you—or from another asteroid that may do the same thing to you. Ignorance is bliss, until it ain't.

When you don't know what you're missing, you can't rationally justify spending precious resources to look for it. So, rationally, you don't. Neanderthals, for example, were rational, pragmatic, unimaginative, dogmatic folks [38], whose lifestyle didn't change much over hundreds of thousands of years. The alleged extinction of Neanderthals—if true, despite frequent encounters with the type in modern life—may be evidence of the evolutionary advantage of imagination, sort of selective pressure for an explorer gene.

It was our slightly irrational ancestors who changed the game. With the Ice Age breathing down everyone's neck, no one had a particularly easy time 40,000 years ago, but Grandma and Grandpa were nimble enough to adapt and survive, chiefly by chasing the remaining mammoths all over the Northern hemisphere and incidentally exploring a good part of the planet. Their Neanderthal cousins weren't nearly so enterprising. So once global warming gave our Cro-Magnon ancestors a break from the damn cold, things started happening apace: the domestication of plants and animals, irrigation, settlements, the invention of writing, civilization. Altogether, it's called the Neolithic Revolution.

At first, it didn't seem to work all that well. Irrigation and agriculture required a lot of work, and the variety of domesticated species was narrow, so the quality of diets declined compared to the free-roaming nomad days. And yet they—we—persisted, and won. It turns out that trading occasional feasts for some measure of control over our food supply wasn't such a bad deal after all. From an evolutionary standpoint, eating regularly and working a lot are apparently better than an accidental all-you-can-eat buffet. Better good than lucky. Our numbers went up, and that's how Nature tells a species that they're doing something right.

Our numbers went up, and so did the scope of the problems we faced. We were rank amateurs at everything we were doing. We didn't know how to dig irrigation ditches or how to plow the fields or how to figure out the right time to plant or how to save the harvest and the seeds. It took a lot of trial and error to get it right, so it's a good thing we had enough folks around to keep trying different ways.

The bigger the pool of talent, the greater the chance of somebody getting it right, even if everyone works alone. But we humans do better – we cooperate and compete and argue and combine our experiences and points of view to produce better solutions than any of us could ever dream up in isolation. Just try to build Stonehenge with nothing but stone-age tools, and you'll immediately see the value of collective intelligence (collective muscle power doesn't hurt either).

But before you get around to building Stonehenge (with its precise astronomical alignment) or its contemporary Warren Field (the first known calendar, about 10,000 years old), you'll need data. Astronomical data, that is. Astronomical data is something you accumulate over time, a rather long time. That's pretty difficult to do without not just modern instruments, but even a written language to jot down your observations. Especially when you try to do multi-year observations at a time when life expectancy is below the typical astronomer's graduation age. Individual stick-to-itiveness isn't enough. You need transgenerational persistence.

And size does matter in this case. The size of your tribe, that is. The bigger the tribe, the greater the chance of it sustaining progress from generation to generation. Neanderthals, after all, must have had a genius at the outset—some genius inventor who launched the Mousterian stone tool industry that survived for 400,000 years. But to pass on the creative Promethean fire to the next generation—especially before the invention of writing—and to keep innovating and exploring, each generation has to have students good enough and interested enough and lucky enough to take it from the teachers. Drop the ball once, and you have to start all over again. In a small tribe of nomads with a short life expectancy, the chances of continuous preservation and the development of some obscure knowledge—something like preliterate astronomy—are rather slim. You need a critical mass of people to produce nerds often enough so that one of them can pass the baton to another while (s)he is still around.

Collective intelligence, collective muscle, and a continuous trickle of nerds to take care of abstruse issues are synergistic. They are intertwined positive feedbacks that conspire to give us an evolutionary advantage, not just to survive but to thrive.

Let's start with tangibles. Economic data suggests that we are each other's resource—for palpable material prosperity, that is. Our wealth (a.k.a. per capita GDP) grows as humanity expands. Actually, the per-person dividend of collective knowledge and creativity outruns the population growth (see Figure 31). As Robert Zubrin puts it, each human is born not only with a mouth but also with a pair of hands and a mind. Yes, including that jerk you wanted to ask about, however hard it might be to believe.

But tangibles are just the beginning of the story. The material wealth is, IMHO, not the biggest advantage we have over hunter-gatherer societies. Rather, it's the wealth of knowledge and creativity, accumulated due to (among other things) our ancestors' choice to accept challenges. It's the *Mona Lisa* and Bell's theorem and Rodin's *Thinker* and Planck's constant and Joe Dassin and the periodic table and Tolstoy. It's the schools and universities and museums and theaters and the chance to travel around the world and explore unfamiliar environments and share your experience with others. In a word, it's culture.

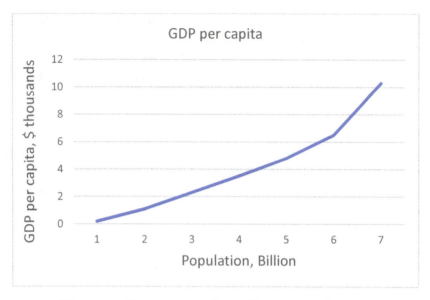

Figure 31– Human prosperity and human population.

Give every kid in a country a hockey stick at birth, and one of them one day will turn out to be Wayne Gretzky. Make it a soccer ball instead, and it'll be Pelé.

It's not always this direct, though. Culture is ambient and diffuse. It's the lullaby and your crib and the school desk and the books and the other kids and teachers and soccer practice and your first kiss and dreams of the future and college and parties and movies and the first job and marriage and your own firstborn and the lullaby again. It's everyone around you, not just the big enchiladas. It's the folks you actually get to deal with. It's also the tangibles and intangibles touched by folks you may never meet. But mostly it's your immediate circle.

Six degrees of separation (a.k.a. the "six handshakes" theory) is the idea that Bill Gates is your buddy's buddy's buddy's buddy's buddy's buddy, and so is Barack Obama, George Clooney, Tu Youyou, Xi Jinping, and anyone else you care to name. And yet most of the time we communicate with just our immediate environment— Mom and Dad, relatives, classmates, coworkers. They are the folks we value most: that's who we have a chance to bump heads with. It's these interactions that have the most influence on who you are. They influence what your filter set looks like. They influence the options you happen to be aware of at the moment you choose to make your choices. They influence how you choose to choose. And you do it for them in return.

Let's make the reasonable assumption that each of your contacts personally knows about as many people, on average, as you do. In other words, each circle is a fixed number of times bigger than the one before it. Then you'll have N folks who know you, N^2 people[18] who know you through a common buddy, N^3 people who know you through two intermediaries, and so on. The six shakes hypothesis can be then expressed as N^6 = 7.9 billion. In other words, everyone on the planet knows you through no more than six intermediaries.

That yields roughly N = 44. So your immediate circle should have 44 people in it. The second circle—the folks in the first circle of your first circle—has about 2,000 people in it. There are 87,000 in the third circle, 3.9 million in the fourth, 171 million in the fifth, and all 7.9 billion of us in the sixth.

That 44 estimate is somewhat lower than Dunbar's number. In the 1990s, British anthropologist Robin Dunbar suggested a cognitive limit to the number of steady social relationships we're able to keep, somewhere between 100 and 250. The most commonly used number is 150. Companies and governments use this number to plan how big offices and office parking garages have to be. The next time you're late for an appointment, blame Dunbar. At a 150x growth factor at each step, it would be not six handshakes to reach Bill Gates, but less than five. But at higher degrees of separation, new factors are likely to kick in, such as the available pool of potential contacts you can choose from before hitting serious obstacles like the language barrier.

How important are the folks in those circles to you? How much are you willing to give to solve their problems? There's actually data on that. In the US, only 4% of charitable donations go to global causes [39], but 96% of humanity doesn't live in the US. That means that 96% of the average person's donations goes to 4% of her fellow humans who happen to be her compatriots (the US population makes up 4% of the world's population), while only 4% goes to the remaining 96% of humanity. So just by living in a different country, somebody becomes 576 times less important to us than an average fellow citizen of our country – and we all know that that average includes quite a few rather objectionable characters.

Thankfully, that's not the end of the story. In 1847, the Choctaw people sent donations to starving Ireland during a potato famine [40]. The Choctaws weren't particularly well off. In fact, twenty years before the famine in Ireland, the Choctaws were forced to abandon their ancestral lands and travel 500 miles along the Trail of Tears in a forced resettlement in Oklahoma. But after learning that

---

[18] Strictly speaking, it's fewer, but we're doing back-of-the-envelope estimates here.

Is Humanity an Apprentice God?

Ireland was an occupied country and that the starving Irish had been forced to abandon their native culture by the same "civilizers" that were displacing Native Americans, they felt compelled to do something about it. So they collected money and sent it overseas. Now, 174 years later, during the Covid-19 pandemic, some Irish donors have returned the favor.

The Choctaws and many other Native American tribes didn't have much of a technological civilization by the mid-nineteenth century. Even now there still are, in some corners of the globe, whole tribes of people who don't drive, fly, build telescopes, or attend universities. They didn't go to Cambridge, Yale, or Sorbonne and then freely choose to go back to Nature. Most of them were denied the opportunity to choose. There's no reason to disrespect any of them individually - they are victims of what turned out to be bad choices made by some long-gone ancestors.

When I look at these folks, I see a huge lost opportunity. They're resilient, observant, and cooperative. They carry the explorer genes that helped their ancestors cross glaciers and oceans and mountains and swamps, and they learned to survive in wildly different environments on the way to settling this planet. They'd be a huge asset to any enterprise set to explore the Universe. Yet their circumstances deny them any chance to be part of the first crew to set foot on Mars or to develop a theory uniting relativity with quantum mechanics or to invent a way to control Earth's climate. And their missing achievements and contributions are your loss and mine, too.

Looking back at the mid-nineteenth century Choctaws makes me appreciate how fortunate we are to have choices. Our schools expose us as kids to arts and sports and sciences and technologies. We can apply our talents and ambitions to endeavors completely incomprehensible to a hunter-gatherer or a subsistence farmer, who never had a chance to learn that these opportunities exist. We stand on the shoulders of giants, whose combined toil and talent gives us incredibly diverse options to apply ourselves.

The most ambitious of us choose more than one field and find synergies in unexpected places, like Einstein did when he played the violin or examined patents. Max Planck, the father of quantum mechanics, was a concert-level pianist and a talented composer (look for a record of Planck and Einstein playing Mozart together). When Leonardo DaVinci wasn't painting the *Mona Lisa*, he made several biomedical discoveries, and he had a successful engineering career as well (besides quite a few things that actually worked, he also invented a muscle-powered ornitopter—and, just in case, a parachute to go with it). Omar Khayyam, the famous poet, was a mathematician and an astronomer on the side. A diversity of interests evidently helps. Ancient Greece, the cradle of the modern Western school of thought, put a premium on raising well-rounded youth: kids were schooled in the arts, philosophy, music, and rhetoric. They also perfected their bodies through sports, all in pursuit of beauty and virtue. The fertile, multifaceted Greek culture paid rich dividends in philosophy, science, math, engineering, art, and literature.

Fertile cultures, cooperating flexibly in large numbers, are diverse and collaborative. They take advantage of the whole spectrum of human talent available to them, and they nurture that entire spectrum. Diversity is a collaborative renewable resource. Even the alleged solitary geniuses don't create in a vacuum, and their interactions with the rest of contemporary culture aren't limited to professional correspondences with fellow celebrity eggheads. When you're trying to pack enough exploration into a single life to revolutionize our understanding of the nature of Nature, having a working plumbing system in your home helps a lot. So does living among folks who appreciate and encourage nerds. Sure, Newton eventually corresponded with Locke, Hooke, Halley, Leibnitz, and Huygens. But he started by going to King's School, Grantham, which boasted a 325-year history at the time. While there, he was bullied by a schoolmate, but he won the popularity contest by excelling at studies and science-y pursuits (constructing sundials, for example). That speaks volumes about what his schoolmates thought was cool.

When Newton's mom tried to pull him out of school and make him a farmer, a school master cared enough to talk her out of it. Newton then enrolled at Cambridge University, which had more than 440 years of scholarship. None of Newton's former classmates or teachers at Grantham or Cambridge invented Newtonian mechanics, but there's no reason to doubt that they helped prepare Newton to do so. So did uncountable anonymous people who built his home and stitched his pants and cooked his food and played Shakespeare's plays in London theaters. Newton's portrait as a reclusive nerd is as accurate as a spherical horse in a vacuum. The real Sir Isaac served in the British Parliament, presided over the Royal Society (whose members were, for the most part, non-academics), and served as Warden and Master of the Royal Mint (where he didn't feel it was beneath him to do undercover work, including pretending to be a drunk in London pubs to collect evidence against counterfeiters).

It's not hard to imagine that Einstein's work on patents—like the ones dealing with clock synchronization—may have nudged his thoughts, leading to the theory of relativity, just as Planck's work on efficient lighting prompted the creation of quantum mechanics. It's not hard to imagine that living in Bern, a small but sophisticated town of just 90,000 people that built an opera house in 1903, stimulated Einstein's burst of creativity in 1905.

But it would have taken just three handshakes for Einstein to reach everyone in Bern—barbers, doctors, bricklayers, street peddlers, bureaucrats, teachers, janitors. He probably bumped into every single resident of town during his Miracle Year, when he published four seminal "Annus Mirabilis" papers on the photoelectric effect, Brownian motion, special relativity, and the equivalence between mass and energy. It was just four degrees of separation for him to reach everyone in Switzerland—farmers, lawyers, carpenters, painters, plumbers, musicians, handymen, engineers, hotel maids, soldiers, clergy. Did they have anything to do with Einstein's breakthroughs?

Figure 32 – Bern, where Einstein lived and worked at the Swiss Patent Office during the "miracle year" of 1905. Image courtesy of CucombreLibre via Flickr.com.

Pebble bouncers would have you believe that the only way a plumber in Bern could have contributed to Einstein's insights was to make sure plumbing worked properly in his home and at the office so that the genius could focus on higher matters rather than fixing some damn leaks. I suggest otherwise.

I suggest that the Olympia Academy, the circle of Einstein's close friends founded in 1902 to discuss philosophy and physics, was an indication of the mindset of the time and the place. It's not every day and not in every small town that you can bump into half-a-dozen folks who would regularly meet for years to discuss the details of writings by Mach and Poincare, Spinosa and Hume.

I suggest that there was something in the air in Bern that got into Einstein and helped him in some mysterious way.[19] I suggest that that something may be vaguely described as *esprit de corps*, that "yes we can" feeling. The pride of belonging to a species that can create something as wonderful as the town in the picture above. It makes one want to do her best, to be her best. It's a bit like the Greek Olympics, where everyone cheers for the runners and wrestlers and javelin hurlers and discus throwers and artists and musicians. It's like basketball, where the home team wins twice as often as the away team. I suggest that it's not just the players on the court who feel buoyed by everyone in the stadium, but also the aspiring future stars no one knows yet—like Einstein was before his inspiration and his discoveries and his fame. I suggest that it's not just the folks who happen to be at the stadium who deserve the credit. It's also the folks who built it decades ago and the folks who made the hotdogs served in the stands and the folks who built the plane flying ten kilometers above the stadium during the game. Civilization is a package deal.

I suggest that, like necessity is the mother of invention—culture is the mother of ambition. Culture is where we get that exciting feeling that we're going places, that faint hint that we're part of a bigger whole that supports our quest, that feeling in the back of the mind that what we're doing is worth doing. Humanity is behind you. The cultural environment is the incubator of explorers. It's the evolving, interwoven web of our collective consciousness (a.k.a. culture) that we, its dynamic nodes, make sense in. It's that web that develops emergent properties that none of us mere mortals have—emerging from the stories we tell each other.

It's culture that knows, in its collective consciousness, which way's up. It's culture that tells good from bad and whether bullies and cynics or nerds and dreamers are better to be friends with, and to eventually empower to decide how we will spend society's resources. And so far, by and large, human culture has been

---

[19] For those who think this idea is BS: if you mean beyond science, then we're in complete agreement. Science requires falsifiability. There's no way to experimentally falsify conjectures that deal with unique events. You can't, for example, wind the clock backward, tweak something in the environment Einstein was exposed to, and check if Annus Mirabilis would still turn out fine. Not having a time machine really sucks.

diverse and competitive and sprouted exploratory branches. Many of those branches failed, and some of those disappeared forever and others got amalgamated into the few spectacularly successful ones, and this whole messy process seemed maddeningly inefficient compared to some imaginary linear, rigidly algorithmic Master Plan. Yet by trial and error, we did somehow get from the caves to the Moon, and our youth dreamed of Mars and Jupiter and stars and galaxies.

And then we hit a huge pothole, and the generation that grew up knowing that one of them would be the first human to set foot on another planet now looks in the mirror and no longer sees the optimistic dreamers who were going places. What they see in the mirror is gray-haired, disillusioned cynics.

Houston, we have a problem.

3 Quo Vadis?

> "If you think you can, you can.
> And if you think you can't, you're right."
> *Henry Ford*

It took us billions of years to get from stardust to the first flint tool, millions more years to get to the first library, thousands to the first spaceflight, and only decades to land on another celestial body. We were on an accelerating path. Time flies when you're having fun, and we were having more and more fun.

In the half century from 1870 to 1920, we learned how to use electricity to illuminate our homes and streets, transmit energy and information over huge distances, and power factories and cars. We learned how to capture nitrogen from the air and put it into fertilizer and how to disinfect drinking water. We built internal-combustion engines and put them in all kinds of vehicles that moved across land, seas, and skies. We discovered radioactivity and viruses, atomic nuclei and continental drift, elementary particles and quanta of radiation. We learned of the redshift in the spectra of galaxies (back then called nebulae) flying away. We discovered stellar nucleosynthesis, establishing the link between stars and our fragile bodies. We visited both the North and the South Poles, and we lived to talk about it. We formulated thermodynamics, the theory of relativity, and quantum mechanics. We made a first—admittedly clumsy—attempt to regulate our affairs on a planet-wide basis by founding the League of Nations. We instantly doubled the intellectual resources officially available to our species by opening the institutions of higher education to women. We created national parks, where whole nations put resources together to preserve and showcase the best of their natural treasure. We dreamed of controlling weather and flying to space and reaching the Moon.

By 1920, the grandkids of folks born before the first lightbulb had taken over the business of human progress, and the trend continued apace. In 1927, in the capital of the USSR, a poor and technologically backward country, an exhibition was opened that reflected the spirit of the time. The exhibition [41] was entitled "The First Worldwide Exhibition of Interplanetary Apparatuses and Devices." Projects and research materials by Tsiolkovsky, Kibalchich, Goddard, Valier, Oberth, and others were on display. The USSR was about to embark on a number of grandiose projects that, to a sober impartial observer, would look completely crazy given the shortage of technology, technologists, and pretty much everything else—besides naïve enthusiasm.

The USSR was looting the art collections and gold reserves it inherited from the Russian Empire to hire Western technologists and to buy Western equipment – it didn't have much of its own. The country had large trade deficits to cover. Its main exports were raw materials and (despite domestic shortages) agricultural staples. The quality of domestic industrial goods was so low that, once the decision was made to spend export revenues chiefly on equipment rather than consumer goods, bread shortages ensued: farmers preferred to keep the harvested grain rather than sell it for the money they couldn't spend. A realistic forecast would have been a complete collapse in a few years. From the giant DneproGES hydroelectric power station to the mammoth Stalingrad Tractor Factory to tripling industrial production in five years, the ambitious Soviet plans sounded like a desperate gamble. Which they were. Rationally, there was no reason to believe that the enthusiasm would pay off. But in the end, the technologists trained during that push eventually sent the first humanmade satellite to orbit. And soon thereafter, they sent the first human into space as well.

In the half century between 1920 and 1970, humanity learned how to get electricity by nuclear fission and how to build computers and helicopters and supersonic airplanes, television sets and electric refrigerators, radars and copy machines, lasers and communication satellites, solar panels and defibrillators. We made antibiotics and insulin and vaccines, and we learned how to send humans beyond Earth's atmosphere and get them back alive. We visited the Moon and Mt. Everest and the Mariana Trench, and we lived to talk about it. We discovered other galaxies and Hubble's law, induced nuclear fission and the formation of basic blocks of live matter in a simulated primeval soup. We formulated the uncertainty principle and quantum electrodynamics, the central dogma of molecular biology and the standard model of particle physics, the information theory and Gödel's incompleteness theorems, the Big Bang theory and the Universal Declaration of Human Rights. We founded the United Nations, hoping to better manage our global affairs. We made a first—admittedly clumsy—attempt to regulate our affairs in space via the Outer Space Treaty of 1967. We dreamed of flying cars and colossal habitats in orbit, interstellar travel and elevators people would ride to space like a bus. Our species' view of the world and our place in it was, by and large, positive. We were going places.

But then the mood changed. In 1968, Paul Ehrlich published *The Population Bomb*, telling people that there were too many of us around for his liking. Just six years later, the 1974 Club of Rome manifesto "Mankind at the Turning Point" declared that, "The Earth has cancer, and the cancer is Man." Here's a long quote from *In Defense of Homo Sapiens*, a 1975 book by Joan Marble Cook:

Bookstore shelves are cluttered with volumes by zoologists, anthropologists, and scientific popularizers who claim with feigned alarm that man is a dangerous animal with instinctive drives for dominance, territory, and aggression. Popular films and plays are saturated with violence and sadism, and the old taboos against triumph of evil have disappeared. The new figure of fun is the good man, the quiet intellectual, whose unmanliness is shown by his rejection of violence.

…

This narrow concept of man-the-victim, a creature with little control over or responsibility for his fate alternately depressed and baffled men, who secretly clung to the unfashionable idea that they still had a measure of free will. Thus it is not surprising that a revulsion against science is now developing, just as there was a turn against religion a century ago; and men and women are seeking fresh approaches to life through Zen Buddhism, encounter groups, revivalism, poppy smoke, and meditation.

Nor is it astonishing that people listen with extra care when voices are raised which claim that the classical psychologists are wrong about human nature, that the important thing about man is that he is an animal, and a bad animal at that. A whole school of pseudo-anthropological writers have gained astonishing prominence in the

Is Humanity an Apprentice God?

last few years with books which charge that man is nothing but a "naked ape," a territorial hunter, or a "child of Cain." These books are lively, spiced with bedroom details and hints of the evil that lurks beneath our breasts, and we tend to swallow them uncritically, quaking inwardly as we contemplate the depth of our own debasement.

What's astonishing to yours truly is how little time it took to get from celebrating the Moon landing to writing books in defense of our species, a defense from the backstabbing by our own alleged scientists and science popularizers. Such a sudden change in direction is a telltale sign of some forceful feedback working overtime. What could it be?

Like God allegedly created Adam from mud, Rabbi Judah Loew Ben Bezalel of sixteenth-century Prague is rumored to have created Golem out of clay and breathed life into the cadaver. Golems were supposed to be obedient servants of their masters, efficiently going about their set task. Karel Čapek, who coined the term "robot" in a 1921 play, insisted that robots had nothing to do with the Golem, but doubts persist to this day. Just like robots, Golem starts as a perfect slave to its master's wishes, but then, like robots do in the movies, develops hubris and independence and has to be destroyed. According to Jewish mythology, destroying some Golems has cost their repentant creators their lives. The sacrifice looked justified: Golems' original jobs were to guard the communities. Hubris corrupted these trained soldiers, turning them into very efficient racketeers.

The Golem meme has, over time, grown to mean a lot of different things to a lot of different people. Most memes do. The one of immediate interest to us is the Golem effect. That's the term used to describe the self-fulfilling prophecy of low expectations. It goes like this:

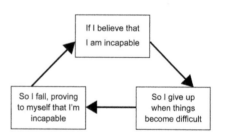

Figure 33 – Golem effect.

The Golem effect has a companion self-fulfilling prophecy: the Pygmalion effect. The idea is that setting high expectations stimulates higher achievement, like this:

Educational psychologists have made quite a few studies of the Pygmalion effect and some on the Golem effect too—declaring the original study that first demonstrated the latter seriously flawed.

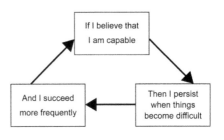

Figure 34 – Pygmalion effect.

Which it probably was. But the most telling sign here doesn't come from the research the psychologists did. Instead, it comes from the research they mostly avoided and the reasons they gave about why they avoided it.

The scarcity of the studies of the Golem effect is actually justified by... the Golem effect. Specifically, psychologists believe in the potential to do people real harm by convincing them that they're bad, and they believe it so strongly that most wouldn't touch this research topic with a ten-foot pole.

If you couple the Golem/Pygmalion effects with the lemming effect—the alleged tendency of folks to do something for no reason other than seeing lots of people doing the same thing—then you have a ready-made explanation for some really odd group behavior. Like, for example, the sixteen-fold market valuation increase of GameStop in 2020 and 2021 and AMC's almost ten-fold increase, while both companies were in deep trouble [42]. Or the 1929 Wall Street crash or the Salem witch trials of the 1690s or the Tanganyika laughter epidemic of 1962, and so forth.

Such one-size-fits-all explanations of one-off events are entirely BS: beyond science. You can't very well formulate a separate hypothesis for each of the possible factors involved and then test each hypothesis by changing conditions and checking if the outcome changes the way the particular hypothesis said it would. So—lacking a time machine—you won't know when the next mass craze is going to happen or what it's going to be about. Maybe another witch hunt. Maybe another Moon race. Maybe starting human civilizations on other planets. Maybe exterminating the one on Earth. We just don't have the tools to rationally, scientifically predict the future. The unavailability of a time machine is a firmly established fact, yet we keep waiting for science to declare, authoritatively and precisely, what tomorrow will look like.

How dare you, we ask indignantly, not deliver my guaranteed future on a silver platter?! How dare you expect us to take risks?!

The Magratheans in *The Hitchhiker's Guide to the Galaxy* built the Deep Thought, a supercomputer oracle that has one job: calculating the answer to the Ultimate Question of Life, the Universe, and Everything. About 7.5 million years later, it produced the answer: 42.

Are we setting ourselves up for a royal letdown? Are we going to wait for 7.5 million years for an answer to a question we never learned to ask? Are we looking for guidance on how to build a better tomorrow—or an excuse not to?

3.1 Which way's tomorrow?

Tomorrow. It's about time.

Picture this: the gold medal basketball game at the 1972 Olympics. Team USA wins, and folks step onto the court to congratulate the Olympic champions... except that there are three more seconds on the clock, and that's just enough time to change the outcome. A mere three seconds before the end of the game, no supercomputer could have predicted the winner. A mere three seconds before the end of the game, no scientific, reductionist model could have been programmed into that oracle to compute that forecast.

Half a century later, we still haven't got that scientific oracle. And the emergent properties of complex systems that we discussed in the previous chapters are only part of the challenge. Another problem is that our scientific understanding of time itself is, so far, rather tenuous.

How could that be? Our reality (a.k.a. life) is the process of getting from yesterday to tomorrow. Time is our natural habitat. We experience time all the time (pardon the pun). But where is it going? How can we tell, rationally and scientifically, which way is the future?

For us mere mortals under normal circumstances, it's child's play. Literally: fill a movie theater with kids, start playing a movie backward, and you'll have an instant riot on your hands. Shards flying off the floor and reassembling into a window, a ball passing through that space right before glass seals it—those are strong hints that something is amiss. A lot of processes in our life are time-irreversible. We're very familiar with them going forward, but we never see them go backward. We call this the Arrow of Time. We feel it's pointing somewhere, as if it had a mailing label with clearly marked origin and destination addresses.

But that's just a gut feeling, not science. Can science guide us on the matter? Is there a rigorous, scientific way to tell which way the Arrow of Time points?

The laws of physics as we know them now – all but one - are completely time-reversible. In the deterministic Universe of bouncing pebbles, you wouldn't be able to look at a movie and tell if it was played normally or backward. The Newtonian laws of their motion just don't care: take any solution in terms of "t," substitute "-t," and it's still a solution. Lord Kelvin has put this predicament in a rather vivid picture: pretend you could in an instance reverse all velocities in the Universe. Then "the course of nature would be simply reversed for ever after. The bursting bubble of foam at the foot of a waterfall would reunite and descend into the water; the thermal motions would reconcentrate their energy and throw the mass up the fall in drops re-forming into a close column of ascending water." We'd instantly know something was amiss, but time-reversible Newtonian dynamics appears to be perfectly OK with all these oddities. Lord Kelvin thought friction could be the culprit, but do bouncing pebbles really violate time-reversible Newtonian mechanics when they do "friction"?

Ludwig Boltzmann suggested, instead, that it's not the individual pebbles we should consider, but the whole ensemble – the entire pool of all their trajectories compatible with Newton's laws. In statistical mechanics parlance, a macrostate is an ensemble of microstates. Isolated systems tend to evolve from a non-equilibrium state to equilibrium as the latter is, in some sense, less unlikely. For a gas molecule closer to the left wall of the tank than the right, it's more likely that its very first collision will be with the left wall, sending it to the right. When your initial and boundary conditions are asymmetric, you can, it turns out, have a pool of perfectly valid solutions of time-symmetric equations of motion whose likelihood is not time-symmetric.

The one time-irreversible law is the second law of thermodynamics. Yup, the cynics' favorite law, the one that says that chaos always wins in the end. Among the endless expressions for it is Murphy's seventh law: left to themselves, things tend to go from bad to worse. Or Schopenhauer's Law of entropy: if you put a spoonful of wine in a barrel full of sewage, you get sewage; if you put a spoonful of sewage in a barrel full of wine, you get sewage.

The second law of thermodynamics is one leg of the oldest of the three elephants holding up modern science's model of the world: statistical mechanics. Its illustrious younger siblings (namely, relativity and quantum mechanics) outshine their older sister as twentieth-century celebrities. Albert Einstein was involved with all three elephants (and reputed to have seen the turtle)—and he was the only scientist ever to be honored with a ticker-tape parade. But it was statistical mechanics that first asked, in a rigorous scientific sense, how you can tell which way's tomorrow. It was also the first to offer an answer. The answer it proposed was the second law of thermodynamics: tomorrow, for statistical mechanics, is where chaos is. And yesterday is where order was.

Figure 35 – The (Really) Big Picture.

Formulating the second law of thermodynamics, by French military engineer Nicolas Léonard Sadi Carnot in 1824, was our first scientific foray into the fascinating world of emergent properties of complex systems. Our understanding of this world is still, two centuries later, in its infancy. There's a lot more to discover where this one came from.

When the system you're dealing with is an ideal gas locked in an ideal tank, the second law provides very clear, falsifiable predictions—and they have passed a lot of tests with flying colors. Say, by some fluke—or artful experimental setup—all bouncing pebbles – sorry, gas molecules – are gathered in the far bottom left corner of the tank. That would be order: unusual, unexpected order of things in this system. The thermodynamic measure of disorder, entropy, would be low. As the pebbles move and bounce off the walls of the tank and off of each other, they randomize their positions so they're more likely to move closer up and to the right than they are farther down and to the left. They move from an unlikely configuration to a more likely one. Order goes down; entropy goes up. You can build an actual clock measuring time with bouncing pebbles by watching pebble patterns dissipate over time.

Ludwig Boltzmann was considering ideal gas in an ideal tank when he came up with the formula for entropy: $S = k_b \ln W$, where k_b is Boltzmann's constant, and W is the probability of the system's macrostate: the number of microstates that would make the system look like it does, divided by the number of all possible microstates.

> "Shit happens" is the original formulation of the second law of thermodynamics. Vague and dire predictions with no deadlines never fail. Just ask the Delphic Oracle, Nostradamus, Baba Vanga, or Karl Marx.

If you leave a system like this alone, it's going to spontaneously go from a less likely state to a more likely one. W is going to go up, and entropy is going to go up with it. Entropy grows in an isolated system, and entropy is a measure of chaos. So if the Universe is anything like ideal gas in an ideal tank, time would flow from a Universe with less chaos—from our standpoint—to one with more chaos. Since chaos is but a measure of our confusion, then does the arrow of time point in the direction of maximum confusion?

Closed systems of bouncing pebbles spontaneously evolve to equilibrium. Trajectories taking them away from equilibrium are less likely than the ones approaching it. That's kind of the definition of "equilibrium," the state a system tends to go to if you leave it alone. Bouncing pebbles at equilibrium are mixed, featureless, uniform. Half the beach of red pebbles and half the beach of identical but blue pebbles are still not in equilibrium—the beach has to be evenly purple. There will, of course, be fluctuations, and a few pebbles of the same color can, by chance, clump together, but as long as there's any motion at all, the fluctuation will be short lived. Mechanical energy of the fluctuations dissipates and becomes heat, and then heat dissipates and becomes evenly distributed. Everything asymptotically crawls to an equilibrium.

If your system includes the whole Universe and the dissipation principle still applies, then all motion in it will eventually cease. The idea was first suggested by the inexhaustible William Thompson in 1851.[20] And in 1927, Georges Lemaitre

---

[20] William Thompson was knighted as Lord Kelvin, not for his contributions to the science of thermodynamics but for his role as engineering advisor to the project to lay the first transatlantic telegraph cable.

wrote the modern story of Creation, the Big Bang. The Arrow of Time got the two ends any self-respecting arrow needs. Kind of. Well, not really.

To begin with, the second law of thermodynamics would require—assuming it holds for the Universe as a whole—the original state of what was to become our Universe (what Lemaitre called the "primeval atom") to have been the Universe's most ordered state ever. In every sense that makes any sense, the act of Creation would really be that: not only was all of the energy—and space and time and matter—there from the outset, mysteriously appearing out of nothing, but so too was all the order ever.

The second law makes this very, very unlikely. Ludwig Boltzmann racked his brain over this paradox until his suicide in 1906. Incidentally, the paradox itself is called the Boltzmann brain. It goes like this: let's assume that universes (in their lowest entropy state) really do randomly pop out of nothing. Nothing has no time, no space, no energy, no matter, no Boltzmann constant, no Planck constant—no anything. Then, by some miracle of Creation, nothing fluctuates, and out comes a universe, complete with seeds of all of the above and much, much more. Now let's compare two hypothetical universes emerging this way. One has Boltzmann in it, with his oversized mental capacity to make sense of things around him, and it also has all the things around him. His pen and paper, his desk, Vienna, Europe, Earth, the Solar system, the Milky Way galaxy, and all the rest of it. The other universe has just Boltzmann's brain in it and nothing else. His pen and paper, his desk, Vienna, Europe, Earth, the Solar system, the Milky Way galaxy, and all the rest of it. The other Universe has just Boltzmann's brain in it, and nothing else. His pen and paper, desk, Vienna, Europe, Earth, solar system, Milky Way galaxy and all the rest of it are all, in the hypothetical Universe #2, mere figments of Boltzmann's unimaginable imagination. The first one takes a lot more order to make.[21] Both

---

[21] Allegedly. There are a number of hidden assumptions there, some of which are rather bold. For example, it is assumed that a mental picture of a world—real or otherwise—can be contained in an isolated brain. It is further assumed that a brain with a mental picture of a nonexistent world has the same entropy as one with a mental picture of an otherwise identical world that really exists. And any attempt to compare the likelihoods of Universe #1 and Universe #2 would have to be based on some assumption about the inner workings of the primordial nothing. Needless to say, experimental testing of any of these—if we were to take them to be falsifiable (a.k.a. scientific) hypotheses—would be rather difficult.

universes share the highly ordered brain, but the first one is chock-full of all kinds of things having some sort of order in them. And the question we're going to ask is this: Which of the two are we more likely to be living in?

If you turn Boltzmann's formula for entropy around, you can use it to calculate probabilities. This has serious, and troubling, cosmological implications. If a universe is born as a random fluctuation of nothingness, smaller fluctuations are far more likely than bigger ones. Assuming, that is, that Boltzmann's constant has the same value in all the universes. One can then use Boltzmann's entropy formula to compute the odds of having any reality in the rest of the universe, besides the brain that imagines it. The chances of the rest of the Universe being real—rather than a figment of the brain's imagination—turn out to be outrageously low. The odds—under a bunch of assumptions, expressly spelled out and otherwise—are astronomically in favor of our Universe being nothing more than a delusion of the most economical brain capable of imagining it. The folks who went through the actual calculations come up with probability ratios that look like $1:10^{50,000,000,000,000,000,000,000,000,000,000,000,000,000,000}$. In other words, the second law of thermodynamics—assuming it's universal, eternal, and immutable—estimates that the chances of everything you're looking at actually being there as 0.0000000000000000000000000000000000000000000001%. Oops.

Figure 36 – Continuum. Image courtesy of eli007 via pixabay.com.

Assumption is the mother of all screw-ups. The assumption of the reality of the world around us and the assumption of the universality and the immutability of the second law of thermodynamics are very unlikely to be compatible.[22] Something has

---

[22] Unless our calculations themselves are way off. See the previous footnote.

to give. And science isn't offering much help in deciding which of these hypotheses to dump.

The scientific method calls for falsifiable predictions. The hypothesis that the outside world only exists in your imagination isn't falsifiable: all of your observations and experiments are, according to the hypothesis, also imaginary. You can't have an objective outside observer to tell you whether reality is real—for how would you know that you aren't imagining whatever communications you get from that observer? That is, without assuming the result?

Trying to test if the second law of thermodynamics is universal and immutable puts us in a similar hamster wheel. How do we know, by observations we make today, if some law has been universally observed, without fail, ever since the presumed birth of the Universe and in every corner of it? Any signal we see today from those primeval events has been traveling through our Universe for all this time—unless, that is, we're delusional and none of this really exists. And we can't interpret those signals that have been in transit for a very long time (or not) without some model of what might have been happening to them along the way. Which is the very model we're testing. We the observers, being locked within our Universe—including its history—are limited to the observations made from the inside of it. There is no rational basis to decide one way or another if the law is universal, eternal, and immutable. There's no rational basis to believe that such a decision can ever be made rationally.

So the back end of the arrow of time looks rather ambiguous so far. How about its business end? Where is it all supposed to be going? The Universe born in Big Bang in an allegedly ordered state is supposed to then devolve through a progression of more and more chaotic states, ultimately losing all order and eventually going very, very dark and cold. For an expanding Universe with a constant amount of energy in it, the equilibrium is supposed to be terminally boring. Stars will quit forming for lack of raw material, and existing ones will run out of fuel, after gobbling up their planetary systems first. Regular "baryonic" matter, the stuff you and I and stars and all the tangible stuff around us are all made of, will be swept up by black holes, which in turn will evaporate until only photons remain. Very low energy—cold—photons, with galactic-scale wavelengths. The baryonic matter, particles that have a rest mass and can't move at the speed of light, will be gone. The leftover photons are eternal and immutable, but they have nothing to interact with. In this dying Universe, nothing happens, so you can no longer build a clock. Time no longer has a meaning. All hell freezes over. Curtains. And it's all supposed to happen a mere 10^{40} years from today.

The scenario above is called the heat death of the Universe. The understandable lack of witnesses makes it a challenge to test this idea. And the observations that can be made don't appear to fit. An expanding Universe with a constant amount of energy in it is supposed to be cooling. It's also supposed to be getting more chaotic (a.k.a. less ordered) in the process. Instead, the Universe is heating up [43] and getting more structured (a.k.a. ordered) as it does so. By now, it's got giant voids a billion light-years across [44], and arcs of galaxies are lined up across 3.3 billion light-years [45]. Oh, and galactic filaments, structures containing billions of galaxies, also undergo concerted motion [46].

On the other hand, the primeval atom, which Lemaitre postulated was the seed of our Universe, wasn't much of an atom after all. It had no structure, space, time, particles, waves, or much of anything else. It then allegedly developed into space and time and elementary particles and radiation, which developed then into the nuclei and atoms and density fluctuations and stars and galaxies and clusters and filaments we see through our telescopes—as well as bugs and slugs and humans and telescopes and the World Wide Web. Our observations of the cosmos—and its evolution from simple and featureless to complex and ordered—challenge the concept of inescapable, one-way devolution from ultimate order to ultimate chaos [36] [47]. Self-organizing structures of the Universe and human brain—recently found to be oddly similar to each other at, of course, vastly different scales [48]—appear to have little in common with pebbles randomly bouncing around in a box.

This cognitive dissonance between the imaginary pebbles inexorably bouncing into featureless, boring equilibrium and the magnificent world in front of our eyes is a wonderful gift to science. Seriously. Paradoxes like this one bug curious people, and some of them start examining old dogmas that no one thought to doubt before. And that's how the realm of scientific exploration expands. Like Richard Feynman said, "Religion is a culture of faith; science is a culture of doubt." As long as we doubt that the current scientific picture of the world is all there is to it, the picture can evolve.

One dogma currently coming under the scientific microscope is the reality of reality. It's hard to bring oneself to doubt that the world we see objectively exists. Boltzmann Brain—not just the organ itself but the idea that the rest of the world is illusory—may have contributed to Boltzmann's decision to leave it. It's reassuring to think, despite ample evidence to the contrary, that what you see is what you get. It's comforting to think, despite ample evidence to the contrary, that what you see and what I see are objectively one and the same thing.

Part of the maddening evidence to the contrary can be written off as mere difference of opinion. You and I see the world from different perspectives through different sets of filters. Facebook be my witness, we pick our facts differently, and we interpret them differently as well.

But evidence mounts that it's deeper than that. It turns out that it doesn't take two human minds to come to incompatible conclusions about what's going on.[23] Even two photons, in actual experiments, have been found to be perfectly capable of having different "worldviews" [49]. Again, but slower this time (don't worry if you're struggling with this one: it took me a while to digest it too): objective reality may not be the same for you and me, even if we're as simple as a pair of photons. Objective, observer-independent reality appears to be incompatible with actual, experimentally testable reality of our world.

Figure 37 – Old lady/young lady: bi-stable perception.

Paradoxes like this one get smart and curious folks whamming their foreheads. What they just realized isn't that the old paradigm was "wrong" all the time. It's just nowhere near as universal, eternal, and immutable as it seemed back when we didn't know any better. A model that used to work fine and then failed isn't necessarily an outdated piece of junk. In fact, it may have just gotten better. It continues to work where it used to work before, but now we can start mapping that domain. When crossing some invisible boundary violates one or more assumptions of a model, that gives people an opportunity to reexamine these assumptions. Then they can take a leap and offer new concepts.

A new concept is a chance, not a guarantee of anything. It may turn out to be a new way to see the world and our place in it, or it might be a dud. Many ideas look smoking hot at first glance, but upon closer look, they don't pan out, even when the authors are as smart as John Archibald Wheeler and Richard Feynman.

---

[23] Even the same mind can argue with itself, arriving at different conclusions at different times about the very same data. For example, which way is the lady in the portrait above looking? And how old is she?

What these two great thinkers noticed was that for a photon to get absorbed by something, it has to be first emitted by something. Light, apparently, knows which way tomorrow is, right? But Maxwell equations that govern light propagation are time-symmetric. They yield two perfectly valid solutions: a retarded wave and an advanced wave, forward and backward through time. A retarded wave is the "normal" one: it's first emitted, then it propagates through space, and only then does it hit a detector. The advanced wave arrives at the detector before it leaves the emitter, raising a lot of eyebrows along its path. Maxwell equations are perfectly compatible with both. Our everyday experience, on the other hand, isn't. Our experience makes us really uncomfortable when an alleged effect allegedly precedes its alleged cause.

Wheeler and Feynman [50] galloped to the rescue of the sacred causality principle with a postulate that holds that the radiation emitted by each particle is completely absorbed by all other particles present in the Universe. The assumption is bold to the point of recklessness and supported by nothing whatsoever. Worse, it didn't even help - retrocausality (effect preceding the cause) survived just fine.[24] Lots of folks immediately saw through the BS (brave semantics) of calling the same particle an absorber and an emitter arbitrarily when it suits you, and they pointed out that swapping the labels—as arbitrarily as they have been assigned—would make time flow backward. Symmetry with respect to time is hard to sweep under the rug. Could it be that our perception of the arrow of time is illusory after all?

There's an elephant in the room that strongly suggests otherwise. For starters, the symmetries in Nature are a temperamental bunch. Negative and positive electric charges in the Universe appear to be perfectly balanced. That's the only way that the electromagnetic interaction, which is about 10^{40} times stronger than gravity, can

---

[24] For those mathematically inclined:

$$E_{tot}(x,t) = \sum_n E_n^{adv}(x,t) + \sum_n E_n^{ret}(x,t) \quad (1)$$

Assuming, as Wheeler and Feynman did,

$$E_{free}(x,t) = \sum_n E_n^{adv}(x,t) - \sum_n E_n^{ret}(x,t) = 0, \quad (2)$$

we can add 0 to anything and end up with

$$E_{tot}(x,t) = \frac{\sum_n E_n^{adv}(x,t) + \sum_n E_n^{ret}(x,t)}{2} + \frac{\sum_n E_n^{adv}(x,t) - \sum_n E_n^{ret}(x,t)}{2} =$$
$$\frac{\sum_n E_n^{adv}(x,t) + \sum_n E_n^{ret}(x,t)}{2} - \frac{\sum_n E_n^{adv}(x,t) - \sum_n E_n^{ret}(x,t)}{2} = \sum_n E_n^{adv}(x,t) = \sum_n E_n^{ret}(x,t) \quad (3)$$

(2) is the clearest example of assuming the result that I've ever seen, but even this doesn't help us tell which way is tomorrow.

fail to completely dominate gravity in the self-organization of the Universe at large scale. Mass, on the other hand, appears to have only one sign, and masses of the only available sign appear to always attract, unlike electric charges of the same polarity. Symmetry for the electric charges; no symmetry for gravitational "charge"—mass. But that's only the beginning: particles have counterparts (a.k.a. antiparticles) of the same mass but of opposite charges (electric and otherwise). For all intents and purposes, antiparticles are nothing but regular particles moving backward in time. What makes regular particles regular, though, is the fact that they massively outnumber their antiparticles everywhere we have managed to check. Why? In experiments, particles and antiparticles appear to form (and annihilate) as particle-antiparticle pairs. The gross matter-antimatter imbalance may not have been there forever. It might have started as an almost perfect balance between a lot more particles and anti-particles than we have today, the vast majority of which have since annihilated each other. But in our Universe now, most of the matter appears to experience time in the same direction you and I do. How come Big Bang apparently created exactly the same amount of positive and negative electric charges but somehow different amounts of matter and antimatter?

Could this be due to some force of Nature that's not time-symmetric? For a long time, every fundamental interaction known to physics—gravitational, electromagnetic, weak, and strong—was believed to work exactly the same way in both time directions. But in 1957, hints emerged that one fundamental force (namely, the weak interaction) may not be perfectly time-symmetric after all. There's a minuscule leak in that presumed air-tight symmetry. In 1966, Andrei Sakharov suggested that if such a mechanism was operational when the big mess coming out of the Big Bang cooled down enough to start making particles—baryons (like protons and neutrons) and leptons (like electrons)—it could have yielded a slightly imbalanced number of particles moving forward and backward in time. Predictions of this model have yet to be experimentally tested. Part of the reason they're so difficult to test is that the time-asymmetry of the weak force isn't predicted to produce any effects in today's Universe as obvious as the arrow of time. Weak force rules some rather obscure, hard-to-observe phenomena, so much so that folks have constructed a hypothetical weak-less Universe that is undistinguishable from ours by any experiment we can do today [51]. In other words, even the very existence of the weak interaction is, so far, BS (beyond science).

A big part of what makes it challenging to test any hypotheses about the nature of time is the butterfly effect. It has been recently shown, for example [52], that three black holes in free fall, modelled with perfectly time-reversible Newtonian laws running forward and then backward in time, sometimes fail to return to their original configuration. What's significant is how little perturbation it took to make the system time-irreversible. The three black holes, each of a million solar masses, were initially separated from each other by roughly one parsec. The runs were done multiple times after introducing a small perturbation. It only took a Planck-length perturbation (10^{-51} parsec) to ruin time-reversibility in 5% of the tests.

That result shows how hard it is to make any falsifiable (a.k.a. scientific) general statements. Can anyone measure initial positions of black holes with a precision down to the Planck length, which is 0.0000000000000000000000000000000016 meters, and synchronize the measurements over a parsec, which is 31,000,000,000,000,000 meters, with such precision that the Planck-length positional accuracy still holds? Our synchronization light signal would take 3.26 years to travel the parsec separating the black holes. Are they going to stand still with respect to each other to within a Planck length for that long?

If we can't test this hypothesis—and we sure can't—then time-reversibility of gravitational interaction at parsec scales is, again, BS (beyond science). This doesn't mean it's false; it just means that our reasons for believing it to be true aren't scientific, even if they use a lot of scientific-sounding terms. Not yet, anyways.

But maybe somebody somewhere already learned how to do the testing of this hypothesis, making it a scientific one. Can we learn from them? And if so, will their science hold here on Earth?

The answer to the second question is, so far, maybe not. If even two entangled photons can have different—and simultaneously perfectly valid—worldviews [49], it would appear that it's even easier for two civilizations separated by cosmic distances to come to different yet perfectly justifiable conclusions about anything under the Sun—starting with which sun is the Sun. On the other hand, as different as our viewpoints might be, they could still have something in common. Red-green color blindness may make it debatable which light is on, but getting a disputant hit by a bus is a great way to settle disputes in an objective, impartial manner. As long as every survivor sees the same thing, that is. Which gets us right back to question #1: Can we, in some sense that makes any sense, learn if the guy got hit by a bus or made it across just fine?

If quantum mechanics leads us to bickering photons and thermodynamics and the Boltzmann brain paradox, then maybe relativity can help tell which way the arrow of time points? At the first glance, it looks promising: in relativity, getting information is supposed to be possible only from inside our causal past-light cone. In other words, the light signal we can see now had to be emitted no farther from us in space than r=ct, where t is how long ago it was emitted and c is the speed of light in a vacuum. According to the theory of relativity, the speed of light in a vacuum is the fastest we can learn something from someone living elsewhere.

Recent experiments [53] suggest otherwise. Entangled photons appear to change their state instantaneously once the other photon in the entangled pair has been found to be in a certain state. Well, maybe not quite instantaneously, but at least 10,000 times faster than it would take light to carry a signal from one of them to the other.

And that's not an unexpected result—if, that is, you're such a firm adherent of quantum mechanics (requiring instantaneous "communication" between entangled particles) that you're willing to ignore the theory of relativity (which strictly forbids such communication).

Supraluminal (a.k.a. faster than light) interactions may even be rather common. Take gravity, for example. Is the Moon attracted to where the center of the Earth is now or where it was 1.3 seconds ago, which is how long it takes for light to get from Earth to the Moon?

Arthur Eddington, the guy whose observation of a solar eclipse in 1916 made Einstein an instant celebrity and the theory of relativity an unassailable Truth, wrote in 1920:

> If the Sun attracts Jupiter toward its present position S, and Jupiter attracts the Sun toward its present position J, the two forces are in the same line and balance. But if the Sun attracts Jupiter toward its previous position S', and Jupiter attracts the Sun toward its previous position J', when the force of attraction started out to cross the gulf, then the two forces give a couple. This couple will tend to increase the angular momentum of the system, and, acting cumulatively, will soon cause an appreciable change of period, disagreeing with observations if the speed is at all comparable with that of light.

Again, but slower this time (it took yours truly a while to let this sink in): the idea that gravity propagates no faster than light would violate the conservation of momentum in the Sun-Jupiter system to an extent perfectly detectable a century ago. No such violation has been detected so far [54]. And it would have been really hard to miss.

Newton, Laplace, and Eddington all knew that if gravitation propagated at a finite speed, that would violate the conservation of angular momentum. Failure to conserve angular momentum so far hasn't been used in horror movies, which is a shame because it's really scary. If gravitational force propagated from the center of the Sun to the Earth in 8.3 minutes—like it would at the current distance at the speed of light—it would be continuously accelerating Earth in the orbit. So according to celestial mechanics, the orbit would get bigger, and in 1,200 years, the average distance between Earth and the Sun would double. That would put us beyond the present orbit of Mars and right on the inner boundary of the asteroid belt. Of course, neither of those would still be where they are today due to the same effect. And missing out on the asteroid mining gold rush would be the least of our problems. The much bigger problem would be that at twice the distance from the Sun, Earth would be getting only a quarter of the energy it's currently getting from our home star. There's no way to compensate for that with any amount of greenhouse gases we could find. And if this was the way that gravity worked, we'd be frozen to death in a few centuries, and so would every living creature we know. Come to think of it, if this was the way gravity worked, we'd never have time to evolve in the first place, and neither would all the rest of the Earth's biosphere because the climate would have been changing too fast in the past as well. Observations and historical records strongly suggest that the Earth's orbit is a lot more stable and, thus, a lot more hospitable than that.

If gravity—or any other interaction—is instantaneous, then is there a global time? Can an instantaneous interaction be used to synchronize clocks independently of their location in space? Is there, for example, radiation that propagates faster than light—up to and including infinitely fast—to synchronize a global clock?

One candidate is longitudinal electromagnetic waves. These are known to be not limited in their propagation by the speed of light in a vacuum; instead, they're limited by fading with distance much faster than the regular transverse waves. They're mostly restricted to a few wavelengths from the source. But this can be, in human terms, a very long distance: for a low enough energy and a long enough wavelength, the near-field can occupy the entire Universe. These ultralow-energy photons would be born delocalized in space—and by Heisenberg's uncertainty principle, they would be born delocalized in time as well.

The Pauli exclusion principle is another example of particles being instantaneously "aware" of each other, apparently without any signals passing between them—what Einstein has called "spooky action at a distance." When Wolfgang Pauli (reluctantly) suggested in 1924 that no two fermions can be in the same state, that sweeping statement was met by skepticism of no lesser authorities than Bohr and Heisenberg. There was a good reason for that skepticism: fermions turned out to be the particles that matter is made of, and there's a lot of these throughout the Universe. Since the exclusion principle isn't limited by how far the fermions are from each other in spacetime, it appears to apply universally to the roughly 10^{80} particles our observable Universe is made of. How do the fermions at some particular location know which states are occupied by the fermions making up the rest of the Universe and which are currently available? And how do they even know what "currently" stands for if some of the particles in question are billions of light-years away from each other? The exclusion principle has been, by the way, experimentally tested to exquisite precision [55]. In 1967, Freeman Dyson and Andrew Lenard showed the exclusion principle to act as a "fifth natural force" that defines the structure of matter. Without it, the balance of repulsive and attractive forces in each atom would be very different from what it actually is. As a result, the atoms we're made of would occupy so little volume that people (and their vehicles) would be able to pass right through each other. So the next time you're sitting in traffic, don't curse the guy in the next car. Curse Wolfgang Pauli.

So what's time, and which way is tomorrow? I don't know about you, but to me it doesn't look like physics is ready to explain time to the rest of us. Not yet. Not in terms that would make much sense. This one is left for future generations to work out.

3.2 Where is my time machine?

Why is there so much discussion of physics in a book dealing with the future of humanity anyways? Science is supposed to be the most reliable way to learn about the world and our place in it, and physics is widely regarded as the quintessential science. Scientists in other fields and countless millions of non-scientists eagerly follow developments in physics. Developments in physics have, throughout history, been the early warning signs of the coming tectonic shifts in the way that we view our world and ourselves. We appear to be in the middle of one of these tectonic shifts right now. In this particular one—like in the ones before it—science and the way we perceive and use its findings continue to play a big role.

In this particular one though, the role may be very different from what it has been before. And science itself may have to change to help us out this time. The systems that we have to understand, forecast, and, hopefully, engineer are complex and entangled. Many of them are also self-organizing, evolving, and/or nested like matryoshka dolls. Physics in its current state wisely keeps clear of messy systems like this. I say wisely because the reductionist-deterministic approach, overwhelmingly prevalent in present-day physics, has a hard time giving us useable predictions for systems complex and entangled enough to resemble the world we're growing into, and the nascent holistic approaches in physics are nowhere near mature enough for forecasting the future to a useable level of detail.

Fortunately, physics isn't the only game in the science town. Other scientific disciplines don't have the luxury of milking spherical horses in a vacuum for centuries to derive intellectually stimulating and practically useable results. The folks working in these disciplines face the unenviable choice between studying the most confusing, intertwined, and messy systems as they are (that is, without much help from the invaluable reductionist tool of picking them apart) or changing professions. Many of these folks study living systems, which stubbornly resist attempts to reassemble the reductionist pieces in a way that yields useable predictions about the whole. So they're really hard to apply scientific method to. Especially the conscious, sentient ones.

> Maslow's hammer is a tendency to interpret any task at hand in terms of tools available to you. As the saying goes, if the only tool you have is a hammer, you treat everything as if it were a nail. When all we have to simulate human consciousness is modular digital electronics, we tend to imagine human consciousness to be modular, digital, and electronic.

Let's try a language experiment again: see if our words can tell us something we never knew we knew or if they can help us find a big, unexpected gap in our understanding. Let's take very common words: "life," "consciousness," and "mind." Let's look up a dozen common definitions of those and take a look.

I don't know about you, but I was surprised when I did this experiment. Everything I got was about a thing, a state, a condition. None of the definitions I found in a brief search had the word "process" in it. It's as if we look at a snapshot of the family album rather than the live baby.

That's odd. After all, every time we check to see if someone is alive, conscious, and in command of her mental facilities, we're checking for processes: pulse, breathing, blinking her eyes, responding to questions.

And I submit that the sad fact that we haven't gotten far in understanding life, consciousness, and mind is very much related to us looking at stuffed animals instead of the real living thing. They're all processes, folks. *We* are all processes.

Life is a process, not an article. You, dear reader, now contain almost no atoms you were born with. We living creatures swim upstream in a river of time, and we can't take a break. We aren't built to stay put. If you want to preserve an airplane, the last thing you want to do is to stop it mid-flight. If you want to preserve an animal, the last thing you want to do is to stuff it. Why do we call freezing Earth in the current fleeting state "preservation"? It's never been frozen in time and prevented from evolving. Neither has humanity, so why do we call someone breaking with the proudest human tradition of change a "conservative"? The most conservative thing humans can do is to keep changing: trying new stuff and keeping what works.

To me it seems altogether backward to call the pastoral societies that chose to leave the path of human progress "traditional", and romanticizing the lives of the folks who, through no fault of their own, are denied the wealth of human culture, knowledge, and experience. I think Spinosa and Confucius and Avicenna and Beethoven and Galileo and DaVinci and Columbus and Mendeleev and Heyerdahl and Gandhi and Armstrong and Curie and Einstein are the real keepers of the human tradition worth keeping. The tradition of accepting challenges and moving forward.

We swim upstream in a river of time. Time sweeps past us and takes people we love and possessions we cherish and carries them into the past. Eventually it takes everything that stands still on its banks—settlements and fortresses and churches and libraries and the Antikythera computer and the Arecibo radio telescope. When in use, these are repaired and remodeled and buttressed against the sweep of the mighty river. Once abandoned, they inexorably erode and fall and are swept away piece by piece. They become less and less recognizable as what they once were. Chaos takes over.

The chaos out there relentlessly probes for a breach of our defenses. We keep plugging the leaks while holding the world up with the other hand. We keep mopping up the chaos that got in and throwing it back out. If it's not one damn thing, it's another. We just can't let go. A sailor in a leaky boat, a guerilla fighter behind enemy lines, a passenger going up a down escalator—we can't take a break. We keep climbing or we go down. Grow tired, and we'll inexorably slide into the heap of what once was.

We humans stay in the present as long as we keep swimming against the current of time. The human race is a race against the clock. When we move faster, we reach into the future. When we grow tired and can't keep up with the flow of time, we're swept back and become fading memories. So are human tribes, empires, and civilizations.

You have heard this parable: two mice fall into a jar of cream. The walls are high and slippery, and there's no way to climb out. One mouse rationally assesses the situation, quits struggling, and drowns. The other keeps fighting, churns cream into butter, and hops right out.

The drowned mouse obeys the second law of thermodynamics. Its corpse moves toward chaos. The atoms it's made of will soon no longer be recognizable as mouse atoms. There will be nothing left of the mouse-like dynamic structure they used to be a transient part of. The atoms will move toward perfect equilibrium, as prescribed by the second law.

The survivor mouse, meanwhile, will try to reproduce. If successful, it will organize some matter into its favorite ordered structures: mouse pups. Does life create order?

The first concise formulation of life as a process counteracting chaos comes from Erwin Schrodinger's 1944 book *What Is Life?* [56]. He noticed that thermal equilibrium—the even distribution of everything everywhere, with no organized structure or activity—looks like death. Assuming that every system big enough to contain a living organism obeys the second law of thermodynamics—that is, its entropy (chaos) always goes up—how does the organism (spectacularly ordered in space and time) stay alive (ordered) for a while? What is the nature of the "marvelous faculty of a living organism, by which it delays the decay into thermodynamical equilibrium (death)"?

Schrodinger proposed that when any organism interacts with its environment, what it's feeding on isn't just calories but order. In his view, "The device by which an organism maintains itself stationary at a fairly high level of orderliness... really consists in continually sucking orderliness from its environment." In other words, what matters for living systems is entropy flux from the environment, which already has some order in it. Where does that order ultimately originate?

It's easy to see how sucking orderliness from its environment could work for a whale that filters a lot of disordered water to feed on ordered plankton. The whale is a heterotroph, meaning that it eats other life forms, making its own ordered biomass out of somebody else's ordered biomass. But heterotrophs actually reduce the amount of ordered biomass: they eat more of it than they make. Plankton, on the other hand—well, the photosynthesizing phytoplankton—is a photoautotroph: it feeds itself on sunlight. It makes its finely structured biomass—lots of it, actually— out of a very disordered, aqueous solution of carbon dioxide and a not-very-ordered photon flux from the Sun.

Or maybe the photon flux is more ordered than it looks? Otherwise, it's not clear what's the "environment" which the primary production (a.k.a. photosynthesis) of plankton, and every other photosynthetic organism under the Sun, can get so much "orderliness" from. The regularly chanted mantra that no living organism can violate the sacred second law of thermodynamics would sound much more convincing if somebody actually explained how tiny photoautotrophs (a.k.a. photosynthesizing cells) on this planet manage to convert 10^{11} tons of carbon annually from a disordered to ordered form. In other words, it would be great if, instead of handwaving and grandstanding, someone actually measured the entropy flux. It's a monumental challenge that no one has met yet. When Jennings et al. reluctantly suggested that photosynthesis may violate the postulated second law of thermodynamics [57], defenders of the second law promptly declared the suggestion "distressing" [58]. Yes, you heard me right: postulated. While it has been experimentally verified in quite a variety of controlled experiments, in many situations of real interest it hasn't. For example, does the entropy of biomass—say an organism—change when it dies? So far, no one has experimentally addressed this question. Even Heisenberg's cautious suggestion that "a living organism tends to approach the dangerous state of maximum entropy, which is death" has yet to be empirically tested.

What about bigger things like the biosphere or the Solar system or the galaxy? Does entropy increase or decrease in the Universe as a whole? No one knows, as the Universe's entropy is kinda hard to define and even harder to measure. So the idea that a law describing a gas in a box with exquisite precision can be extrapolated to a microbe, a human, a galaxy, or the whole Universe is supported by no empirical evidence of any kind. The immutable laws of thermodynamics are actually believed to have been violated in the most violent manner. And the name of that violation is the Big Bang. Why do we nevertheless assume—without any experimental evidence—that the second law of thermodynamics is eternal and universal even if this assumption leads down the blind alley of Boltzmann's brain paradox? Again, where does order in billions of tons of biomass come from?

Does the Sun radiate order? Its light has been declared (again, without much evidence) "high-grade non-entropic form of energy" [59]. Our Sun indeed seems to have its own mysterious source of order stashed somewhere. See, the sacred second law of thermodynamics has many incarnations, and their equivalence to each other is rigorously proven. As Lord Kelvin put it, "It is impossible for a self-acting machine, unaided by any external agency, to convey heat from one body to another at a higher temperature." The trouble is that the Sun's corona is millions of degrees Kelvin hotter than its "surface," under which lies the thermonuclear furnace, the alleged source of all that heat. The relatively "cool" surface is between what's believed to be the power source and the hot corona. According to Lord Kelvin, this requires help from an external agency. Despite much effort, no such agency has been experimentally identified so far, even though Wallace Thornhill and David Talbott have suggested a candidate [60]. They argue that the source of the Sun's heat isn't inside the Sun but outside, and it's the Universe's energy that's electrically transmitted to the Sun and other stars, not the other way around.

Could it be that the Universe as a whole is where order is coming from? The Sun—and about 10^{22} other stars—formed somehow. And they hang around long enough for planets to form and for life to evolve, at least on one of them that we know of. Star formation is governed by physical laws and the values of parameters that go into those laws. And these values—strengths of fundamental fields, masses of elementary particles, the speed of light, the Planck constant, etc.—appear to be made to order so that nucleons, atoms, stars, and humans are possible. This puzzle is called the fine-tuned Universe. The precision – estimates put it at 10^{-55}, the ratio of one hydrogen atom's mass to 10 times the mass of the Sun—screams for an explanation. It's just ridiculously improbable to happen at random. This much order impresses some cosmologists – professional skeptics, but professionally swayed by very big, very small, or very precise numbers – enough to get religion. This particular religion is cryptically called "The Anthropic Principle": it's the belief that if someone tampered with the Big Dials, you and I wouldn't be around to ask why it's a bad idea to tamper with the Big Dials.

As explanatory tools go, the anthropic principle could do with a lot of improvement. Lee Smolin, a cosmologist and natural philosopher, has offered just that [61]. Smolin found inspiration in a biological concept: evolution. He suggests that nothing is pregnant with universes. Universes pop up here and there from nothing, with kind permission from the Heisenberg uncertainty principle, but most of them are extremely short-lived: they don't have the right combinations of parameter values to stick around. But some do, and very few are lucky enough to have the right combinations of parameters to survive long enough and develop what amounts to reproductive organs. Very few of these are lucky enough to have the right combinations of parameters for their reproductive organs to actually work.

Universes' reproductive organs are black holes. The nascent theory of quantum gravity suggests that black holes may produce a universe's offspring – and just like biological reproduction, the offspring looks much like the parent. In a population of universes, most members would be the offspring of the ones "fit" to reproduce like rabbits. This is cosmological natural selection for just the right combination of parameters to make fertile black holes. A natural extension of this idea is that if a black hole's production by chance gives a universe an evolutionary advantage, then a civilization that could make universes on purpose would be even more advantageous. I will discuss this possibility and its implications later in the book.

Figure 38 – Spawning candidates for natural selection. Image courtesy of adage via pixabay.com.

"Fitness," then, emerges as a state variable useful for describing the evolution of systems far beyond its origins in population genetics. It offers a fresh perspective on forecasting the behavior of the hierarchy of the self-organizing systems that our world increasingly appears to be made of (a.k.a. getting better at predicting the future). Fitness is a holistic ensemble variable that makes sense in a population, and in context, rather than isolated individual. Temperature and pressure are other examples of ensemble variables. They have no meaning for a single molecule in isolation, but they are relevant and measurable in a "population" of molecules.

Your fitness to survive and procreate doesn't depend just on you alone. Unless you're a universe, that is. And even for a universe, there could be ways to have an environment and interact with it, as we'll discuss later. The future of anything smaller than a universe clearly depends on everything else in that future that it will interact with. From this perspective, your definitions of "good" and "bad" aren't just yours. You can look all you want at mutations that, about 320 million years ago, split amniotes (the first terrestrial vertebrates) into sauropsids (the ancestors of dinosaurs and sparrows and alligators) and synapsids (the ancestors of humans and cows and lions and mice), and you'd never guess which sequences of "A," "T," "C," and "G" are good for "fitness" and which are bad. The events that make some of the gene variants more advantageous than others hadn't happened yet when these variants formed. When a huge asteroid hit the Earth and changed the rules of the fitness game about 65 million years ago, dinosaurs were the uncontested kings of the hill—and ugly, primitive mammals were anything but. If dinosaurs had science (of the reductionist-deterministic variety), that science could have readily provided 255 million years' worth of data to demonstrate the evolutionary superiority of sauropsids over synapsids. Right up to the moment of the asteroid impact, the Bayesian probability of synapsids ever busting out of their marginal environmental niches to take over as the evolutionary winners would have been ridiculously low.

Events that haven't happened yet can, and do, make a mutation that materialized long ago a "good" or "bad" one. An asteroid falls, and all of a sudden a certain genetic makeup (that's been a premium model—chrome trim, leather seats, the works—for over a quarter of a billion years) turns out to be a death sentence. And this kind of thing doesn't have to be rare and dramatic. For example, in a mixed population of bacteria, mutant variants are often at a competitive disadvantage (in population genetics parlance, their selection coefficients are negative). The microbes that don't "waste" resources on diversity—deviation from time-honored optimum nucleotide sequence—replicate marginally faster, so in just a few generations, they vastly outnumber the mutants. But when you take an antibiotic pill, most of these ultra-efficient bugs die off. If some of the otherwise suppressed population of mutants happen to carry the lucky genes for drug-resistance, then they take over and occupy the environmental niche recently vacated by their deceased competition. The burdensome mutation retroactively becomes advantageous instead. If you take another antibiotic, then a different nucleotide sequence will "cause" survival of its carriers and become preferentially heritable.

Mutations, a form of biological noise, are born neutral. All they do is supply some raw material for natural selection down the road [62]. There's no such thing as a bad nucleotide or good one. It's only the downstream interactions that contribute to the higher or lower "fitness" of the individuals carrying a "G" versus "A." Among the interactions are the ones with the rest of the organism's DNA, including future mutations and all of the organisms that this one interacts with, which don't stop to evolve just because an adenine base in some cell's nucleus in another body has become a guanine. That asteroid lurking in space somewhere didn't stop in its tracks just because of a mutation billions of miles away. It continued to fly for a quarter of a billion years after that mutation occurred before it finally slammed into the Gulf of Mexico and made one version of that gene "fit" and the other "unfit."

A snow leopard's chances of survival clearly depend on availability of ibex and pikas and marmots, whose elaborate adaptation to the hard life in the alpine environment is, in turn, influenced by everything in that environment and by the ruthless competition in the valley below. The bison crowding in the rich pastures below push the light-footed ibex up the steep slope, toward the slim pickings of the windswept mountain ranges, where the heavy bison can't roam. The survival strategies[25] of different species are multidimensional and interdependent. Species and habitats, up to and including the entire biosphere, coevolve.

In coevolving systems, living and otherwise, the retro-causality of emergent kind—where evolutionary value of what happens today depends on events in the future—appears to be rather common. Does a decision to take a particular class, go on a particular date, invest in a particular stock, or vote for a particular candidate increase or decrease your chances of leaving viable offspring? The answer depends on a lot of interactions that hadn't yet happened when you made your choice. The outcome of everything you choose to do—or not do or even choose not to choose—is an emergent feature of the Universe, and you can never know in advance if you have considered everything that's going to matter. So to predict exactly and comprehensively the outcome of what you're thinking of doing, you'll need an actual time machine that takes all interactions in the Universe into account. Failing that, the next best thing is a scientific model that takes into account enough of those interactions to stay accurate for a very, very long time: long enough for the systems in question to evolve and finally be influenced by rare events that are usually safe to ignore on shorter time scales. But with even the best model, you can't be certain. A model is necessarily an abbreviation of reality, so when it comes to the phenomena you choose for your model to account for, you need to draw a line somewhere. And the damn space rock that—very, very rarely—wipes out three-quarters of the species on the planet may be just beyond that line.

Self-organizing systems adapt to changing conditions by, well, self-organizing. Sometimes, to a naïve stranger, it might look as if they knew in advance that the change was coming: a system might have developed an adaptation apparently custom-made for meeting a particular challenge long before the challenge happened. Being prepared especially helps if the changes we're dealing with come faster than the system can adapt.

> The law of the perversity of nature: You can't successfully determine beforehand which side of the bread to butter.

---

[25] "Survival trajectories" would be more accurate. As far as we know, we humans are the only species on the planet whose survival involves somewhat deliberate attempts at strategizing.

There are two ways to be ready in advance. Our preferred way is to try to actually anticipate a challenge. That is, we can try to forecast how the situation is going to develop and prepare for it. In theory, that's a really attractive, efficient approach. If it works, it allows one to be prepared for the future that will happen, without wasting resources on preparations for all the alternative futures that won't. It's really comforting to know, for example, that asteroid Apophis isn't predicted to hit us at least for the next century [63]. It helps to remember, though, that the sky is full of Apophis-class objects, only a tiny fraction of which are tracked. What's worse, the ones that are tracked interact with the ones that aren't tracked, making it hard to predict collisions with Earth five to ten years in advance, the timeframe we allegedly need [64] in order to do something besides cursing and praying. As impressive as it might sound, predicting our relative risk of being hit by a big rock for a century out doesn't really help much, not when there are an estimated four million asteroids in the Solar system at least as big as Apophis, and roughly 25,000 of those asteroids cross paths with Earth. Would you buy insurance that only covers being hit by one particular car?

As I've mentioned before, no battle plan ever survived contact with the enemy. The idea of knowing exactly what to prepare for is no exception—chiefly because our forecasting, as it is now, usually can't hit the broad side of a barn. On March 23, 2021, a container ship suddenly lodged itself in the Suez Canal [65]. The ships awaiting passage on both sides of the canal carried 10% of everything that was moving around the globe—oil, food, components for all sorts of machinery. No car factory manager in her sane mind plans for rogue sandstorms in Egypt, but that's apparently why some parts needed for assembly were sitting in a container on a huge ship in the middle of a desert. So maybe—just maybe—we're a bit too focused on short-term efficiency, and we're unwilling to admit how vulnerable we are to occasional mishaps. The losses to the shipping industry from the blocked Suez Canal ran to about $10 billion per day. The total for the six days it took to unstick the Ever Given (that's the unlikely name of the stuck ship) would have paid for broadening the entire length of the Suez Canal to a width that would make such blockages impossible (35 kilometers had been so widened by 2015, so we know how much it costs to do the rest).

With 20/20 hindsight, any problem like this looks inevitable, and any failure to prepare for it looks like an act of criminal idiocy. The "I told you so" chorus reaches deafening intensity the moment the fertilizer hits the fan, and some of the shipping experts were even telling the truth: they have indeed told us so. But while logistics experts were warning of the urgent need to do something about the choke points of world commerce, cybersecurity experts were speaking (just as convincingly) about virtual bugs, epidemiologists were warning about real ones, city planners were sounding the alarm bell about suffocating traffic, utilities analysts were bemoaning the scandalous deficiencies of the electric grid, *et cetera ad nauseum*. How are we supposed to know which of the experts to listen to? No one knows how to prioritize society's resources in a comprehensively deliberate, justifiable fashion without that darn time machine. While the Union of Conceited Scientists is busy doing "attribution science," which attributes global changes to the emissions traced to individual fossil fuel companies [66], the actual science of complex systems remains in the state somewhere between conceptive and contraceptive. The nearly universal aversion to geoengineering—the idea of deliberately tweaking global variables, like the albedo, to control Earth's climate—is justified (rather convincingly) by our inability to predict, comprehensively and accurately, the outcome of such tweaking. In the meantime, it's been pointed out [67] that SpaceX is about to put more aluminum particles in the Earth's atmosphere than all the meteorites and volcanoes together, and no one has any way of predicting if that will plunge the planet into another Snowball Earth era. It would be great to have better predictive models, but I wouldn't hold my breath for attributologists, with their preconceived notions, to come up with models that can forecast the future without assuming the result. If we're looking for unbiased guidance, we'd better look elsewhere.

If you don't know the future, your only option to prepare for it is to hedge your bets. Which is expensive. When you can't anticipate change by reliable forecasting, you pay a penalty. You get caught in the dilemma of risky efficiency vs. reliability through redundancy so expensive that it can be self-defeating. You pay for getting ready for many different scenarios, knowing full well that any return on that investment will come from only one future: the one that comes to pass. And even then, it better be in the range of what you prepared for. You may spend a lot of resources and still miss altogether. Not having a time machine really sucks. The only option more expensive than paying for good science is paying for the consequences of not having it.

The dilemma is this: if you spend too many resources to prepare for a rainy day, it will start pouring - and, with disturbing consistency, it will happen smack dab at the spot your preparations, thorough as they were, managed to miss anyways. Your more focused competition bet the farm on a single monoculture crop, but without distractions, they perfected growing it. In the short term, they will have you for breakfast, and you will never get a chance to prove how good you were at dealing with some remotely possible scenarios they never bothered considering. When one of those materializes and duly whacks them on the head with a two-by-four, you may no longer be around to enjoy your "I told you so" moment.

Failing to prepare is preparing to fail. Trying to prepare for every eventuality is preparing to fail. Damned if you (over)do, and damned if you don't. So it might be a good idea to look for an optimum in there somewhere between these extremes. But how do we find it without a time machine?

Evolving, self-organizing systems billions of years older than us have been "looking" for this balance for, well, billions of years. And the fact that they're still around strongly suggests that they may have been doing something right. How do other, nonhuman, non-sentient systems search for that elusive balance – quite successfully, too, if you judge by the result? How do they dose diversity?

I don't know the answer, but I think I know where to look. Mutations in biology, like noise in physics and chemistry, are a major source of diversity [68]. They interact with the environment, which "mutates" in turn. Diversity is a long-term survival tool. As Linda M. Van Blerkom explains, "The study of human evolution has concentrated on humans and their hominid ancestors, without as much attention to other organisms also evolving in the same environments. But a population must constantly interact with and adapt to these other organisms if it is to survive and reproduce. Domesticated species, predators, and agents of infectious disease have all played a role in human evolution" [69]. In coevolving systems, long-term selective pressure appears to be against uniformity and for diversity, but the opposite is true in the short term. That applies to nonbiological systems, too. Just look at, for example, the timelines of Toyota, Volkswagen, and Studebaker vehicles.

Mutations are evidently risky. Some are called "lethal mutations," which means that the individuals carrying them aren't viable, like the Edsel car brand. Many other mutations put you at a competitive disadvantage, at least in the short term. Consider the branching of amniotes, into not only the mighty, and mightily successful for a long time, sauropsids, but also the heathen-beyond-the-pale synapsids. Consider also our more immediate ancestors, the hominids, whose oversized brains didn't provide an immediate evolutionary advantage over the existing primates. So risk-aversion—clinging to tried-and-true ways of doing things—appears to be a safe short-term strategy. The sophisticated and elaborate memory mechanisms—genetic and otherwise—ensure that you behave more or less like your parents are there for a reason. There can be no evolution without memory of what works. Wiping the slate clean every generation isn't a heritable trait.

In the long run, neither is perfect uniformity. All it takes is for the rest of the Universe to evolve far enough away from the old state where the old way of doing things was optimal—which it eventually will—and the choice becomes to adapt or die off. Absolute efficiency comes at the (prohibitive) cost of giving up adaptability altogether. In a changing world, risk-aversion is an existential risk.

If faithfully reproducing every minute detail in every generation is a bad idea, and so is starting from scratch every time – there might be an optimum in there somewhere between those extremes. It would be nice to know where it is. Of course, it would be even nicer to know what to change—and when and how—so as to anticipate the evolution of the Universe and your particular corner of it, but that requires a time machine, which we ain't got. Failing that, it would be very helpful to at least get some rational basis for deciding what mutation rate—in the broadest imaginable sense of the word—is optimal for staying competitive in our changing world.

Science is where we humans go for answers for these kinds of questions. We often come back empty-handed or, worse yet, with an earful of useless, arrogant mumbo-jumbo. As is usual in any relationship, both sides share some blame if something goes wrong. In the relationship between humans and our science, we (still) often expect the impossible; and science doesn't yet deliver the possible.

The damn space rock that killed the dinos is, among other things, a useful reminder. It reminds us that what science knows about the world at any given moment is but a subset of what the world knows about itself. Science is reliable as long as it stays true to its empirical roots, but this is both a feature and a bug. The reliability comes from empirical experience, but experience is limited and biased toward common, easy-to-observe phenomena, where plenty of empirical evidence is available for scientific scrutiny. We can't observe everything everywhere, and rare events are particularly easy to miss. The fewer instances of something we can observe, the harder it is for the scientific method to help us understand how it works, what it's linked to, and what its consequences might be.

What about common phenomena that offer plenty of opportunities to gain empirical data? Isn't that where science is supposed to give us precise recommendations, backed by ample evidence?

Not so fast. For starters, any honest recommendation based on a reductionist-scientific model should begin with "all other things being equal, doing X should result in Y". Which, in our interconnected world, seriously undercuts the value of such advice. For example, the statement "all things being equal, reducing greenhouse gases will cool the Earth" is accurate but irrelevant: you can have either all things equal or the reduction of greenhouse gases, but you can't have both. There's no such thing as a free lunch. Either we learn to take a broad view, or we'll end up like European environmentalists whose efforts to replace coal led to clear-cutting American forests to make "renewable" wood pellets for export to Europe [70]. Or Mao Zedong ordering the extermination of sparrows to save the crops, which achieved precisely the opposite.

Besides, no answer ever makes more sense than the question. It would really help if we quit asking for an answer to the Magratheans' Ultimate Question of Life, the Universe, and Everything, whatever the heck that is. Asking for the best mutation rate—in the broadest imaginable sense of the word—is only marginally better than The Ultimate Magrathean Question. Any meaningful answer would be contingent on how long our time horizon is and on a forecast of how we and the part of the Universe that we interact with will evolve during that time. What we asked was a really loaded question, and no concise answer to it – like "42" – helps anyone. Any answer that might make sense will also be loaded - with so many nuances and provisos and clauses and stipulations that by the time we're done reading it, the guidance (if any) will be useless, as the horizon we asked for will have long since passed.

If we want science's help, we need to learn to ask specific questions that allow useful yet concise answers. In science's parlance, the parameter space has to be defined – and its dimensionality has to be kept reasonable. For example, even if we limit "mutations" in our optimal-rate question to just mutations in the human genome, the darn thing is 3,100,000,000 base pair long, and each base pair can undergo quite a variety of different mutations, and the rate of each kind of mutation of each base pair is a priori a dimension in the space where we and our science are trying to meet. To have any hope of finding each other on this side of eternity, we'll need to find a common language, one that has relatively few—compared to the Laplace-demon-esque bottomless reductionist pit—generalized, integral ensemble variables.

The good news is that the generalized, integral ensemble variables that drop a lot of minutiae while keeping the essentials are well known in science. In thermodynamics, that's temperature and pressure. In chemistry, that's reaction rates and redox potential. In solid state physics, that's electron energy spectra. In optics, that's transmission spectra. In epidemiology, that's the basic reproduction number. In population genetics, that's the dominance coefficient and the selection coefficient. All are examples of such variables, which are measurable and meaningful only for large groups of interacting objects and not for each of the objects individually and in isolation.

The bad news is that these generalized variables are a lot easier to make sense of in systems where all objects, as numerous as they may be, are identical than in systems where they aren't. Objects of a few different kinds are still fine, especially if they're well behaved, meaning that they only interact in prescribed ways, and those interactions don't affect each other in any way other than through conservation laws. If you have more kinds of objects or more kinds of interactions or more interdependence among those science (within its current deterministic-reductionist paradigm) quickly faces the unenviable choice of either throwing away a lot of stuff for no better reason than that it's otherwise overwhelming, or getting overwhelmed.

Throwing away a lot of stuff for no better reason than that it's otherwise overwhelming often indicates that someone needs to step back and take stock of the big picture first. For example, [71] (population genetics) selection coefficients "s" and dominance coefficients "h" in population genetics models are... environment-independent. Such a model for, say, a snow leopard population won't tell you, or take into account, anything about ibex and pikas and marmots, to say nothing of the bison in the valley below. Until we seriously improve our models—starting perhaps at paradigm level—expectations of useable guidance for dealing with complex systems are just delusional.

Which doesn't for a second prevent them from being common. In a very credible imitation of Wile E. Coyote, we have come lately to expect science to give us easy-to-follow recipes for everything. Prepackaged solutions to all our problems, stamped "ACME" and delivered to our door. Over the course of the twentieth century, an image of "science" and "scientist" captured the public's imagination. Unfortunately, the image was a caricature; it reflected and reinforced the general confusion of a grossly confusing era. Humans were getting serious mental indigestion from, among many other things, the concept of an omnipresent, omniscient, omnipotent, benevolent deity that allowed people to use mustard gas and machine guns on each other. With their incessant itch to make sense of the world, humans eagerly looked for something easier to believe in. What we got turned out to be a lemon.

> Unless your last name is Science, an opinion that differs from yours ain't against science.

This particular lemon is called "scientism," which means what it sounds like: making religion out of "science." Scientism isn't science; it's science's dangerous parasite. Looking a bit closer, the term "scientism" stands for two related embezzlements. First, scientism misappropriates the authority of science—authority earned by following scientific method with diligence and humility—to make beliefs never exposed to proper scientific scrutiny sound like established facts. When it happens to like the beliefs, that is. Second, scientism misappropriates the authority of science to make beliefs never exposed to proper scientific scrutiny sound as if they have been studied and rejected ("debunked" in popular parlance) when it happens to dislike them.

Religion is a culture of faith; science is a culture of doubt. Some folks' proclaimed love for science is of the suffocating hug variety, like that aunt who ruins family reunions for everybody. Scientism demands certainty, unwavering conviction, and unquestioning trust. It has no use for doubt. It mocks doubt. The first thing it asks suspected infidels is this: "Do you believe in science?" This masterstroke of perverse logic is the fig leaf covering an embarrassing fact: scientism, whose disciples never tire of disparaging religion, is itself a (rather primitive) religion. In 1974, Richard Feynman, who was not known for mingling words, coined the term "cargo cult science." It still fits.

As a religion, scientism must have commandments. Limping with both feet, it managed just two. First, Almighty Consensus is the received scientific truth, the whole truth, and nothing but the truth. Second, if Almighty Consensus turns out to be wrong, see Commandment #1. In other words, thou shalt not doubt the Almighty Consensus. Thou shalt not seek truth anywhere the Almighty Consensus told you not to look.

The explosive technological and scientific progress of the last 150 years was truly breathtaking. We humans that made it all happen are awesome. Unfortunately, unrestrained awe of oneself is borderline narcissism, and narcissism isn't particularly conducive to critical thinking. This awe has sometimes made it hard even for educated folks to separate the grain from the chaff. And hordes of questionable characters rushed to cover up the chasm between the human need to make sense of the world and what science actually has to offer with a lot of pseudoscientific rubbish. It looks OK until you try to actually cross the chasm and step on it.

Is Humanity an Apprentice God?

Figure 39 – Scientolatry.

Scientism uses a lot of technical terms and swears that at least 97% of experts have endorsed its fatwas. Lots of tone-deaf but otherwise sane people have no resources to check this claim, so they routinely mistake scientism for actual science. To these, said questionable characters sell a lot of drivel as "the latest scientific discovery," whereupon sanity often departs, sometimes for good. Malthusianism, "scientific" bolshevism, Lysenkoism, Nazi racial "science" and western eugenics were all early examples of this shell game. Telling someone that those other guys (s)he never liked to begin with were just discovered, by impeccable science no less, to be a cancer, a plague, the oppressors of the proletariat, saboteurs of crops, a bunch of Untermensch wasting on themselves your planet's resources—in short, vermin that don't belong in the perfect world you're entitled to—that's a time-tested recruitment tactic. Especially for recruiting unquestioning, congenitally resentful zealots.

When humans look at the Sistine Chapel or the Taj Mahal or a Moon rocket or the World Wide Web, they can't help but feel awe and wonder and deep meaning. These are, apparently, our creations, and they connect us with the magnificent Universe. The feeling is akin to the experience of looking up on a cloudless night and seeing the countless stars. It's only natural to ask how it's possible for very imperfect humans to create something this close to perfection. Here comes the cognitive dissonance: perfection can only come from perfection, right?

Traditional faiths tell us that we sinful apes didn't dream up the perfection at all. The flawless Creator did, using us only as tools in His perfect plan. But the idea was His, and that's why it's so good. No mortal could really author something this wonderful. But that's fine because every glorious creation you find adds to the glory of the Creator. His free will created everything, and whatever free will He doleth out to His imperfect and sinful creatures, He taketh away when He feeleth like it. So our "free" will isn't free, and maybe it isn't even a will after all, praise the Lord. You can make the mistake of thinking that you're free to do whatever you feel like, but if it isn't to the Almighty's liking, then you'll spend the rest of Eternity in places that would make a gulag look positively hospitable. The hands-on God of traditional faiths is involved in every aspect of everyone's life, handing out challenges and performance evaluations, punishments and rewards, listening to prayers and answering them when He chooses to. In the end, He taketh care of everything, an' we down 'ere 'ave nothin' to worry 'bout – as long as we do what we are told by the certified interpreters of Almighty's mysterious ways. Just pray hard and pay your church tithe and admire the Taj Mahals that miraculously pop up here and there, according to His perfect plan.

    This worldview takes a long vacation upon meeting a construction foreman, a platoon sergeant, or a ward nurse. The Three Graces' lives stare in our faces as evidence that the Almighty's choice of tools leaves much to be desired. Anyone who doubts that human life has meaning needs to meet these angels of screw-up repair. They know exactly what their lives' meanings are: fixin' all that needs to be fixed, and yes that includes YOU. Especially YOU, so drop and gimme twenty. And if you even dream of tryin' THAT again, you'll be staring at parts of your anatomy you ain't meant to see, and you'll be doin' that without no mirror or that fancy schmancy camera on a stick! Getting mostly unprintable control signals via one set of very imperfect humans to another set of even more imperfect humans just doesn't seem like the way Perfect Almighty would organize His affairs. So an increasing number of folks don't buy this concept, and they look for something that makes more sense to them.

    And demand, as usual, creates supply. Scientism one-ups those old stories. First, it absolutely agrees with the old religions that no ape descendant could ever really author something wonderful and awesome and deeply meaningful. It also states, with all the glee of a hitman about to earn his keep, that human free will is a pseudoscientific delusion—no ifs, ands, or buts. But having ridiculed an impersonated Creator, it can hardly call for His help to explain everything away. So, it announces that we humans are just delusional and the stuff that we regard as awesome and wonderful and deep is actually none of these. It's just a collection of perfectly mundane atoms, all moving along their perfectly deterministic trajectories in perfect accordance with the tedious laws of the boring cosmos. Nothing exciting here, so just keep moving. If you want some entertainment, go watch *Road Runner* or *Star Trek*.

Scientism sells. It sells like disposable party decorations: it's cheap, readily available, and looks fine if you don't examine it too closely. And the fact that it's flimsy is no problem since no one's going to actually hang anything on it. Besides, there's no cheaper way to sound cool and knowledgeable than to mention Occam's razor while disparaging everything and everybody.

Razor-wielding folks seldom bother to check Wikipedia for who William of Ockham actually was. They couldn't tell you the difference between Ockham's formulation of the razor and Aristotle's if their lives depended on it. They have no idea that William of Ockham was gainfully employed by the Catholic Church. They have no clue that what the medieval Franciscan friar said really meant that God is great, that God has created this world in its entirety, and that anyone who dares claim any part of the credit is a fool and a heretic and deserves to be burned at the stake.

Yep, that's right. The razor, which Ockham expressed as "plurality must never be posited without necessity", for a True Believer (and Ockham was either a True Believer or a really big fraud) simply means God's monopoly on creating everything. Ockham's razor is the First Commandment by other means. Thou shalt have no other gods before me. Just like a modern human doesn't need to see the "Made in China" label to know where stuff comes from, Ockham and his church didn't ask for any extra evidence in each individual case that it was God who created this particular pebble, boulder, or planet. The Holy Bible says that He did, and that was good enough for Ockham. No plurality necessary.[26]

> A mirror is the simplest known BS detector. Apply some postulate to itself and see if it holds.

Declaring that "plurality must never be posited without necessity" is a telltale sign of a power grab by whoever determines "necessity." In a world where any question is already answered in a holy book and the interpretation of the (usually vague and odd-sounding) answers is the job of licensed, officially sanctioned

---

[26] It makes sense to apply Ockham's razor to Ockham's razor. In other words, let's ask what necessity led Ockham to multiply entities by proposing the razor in the first place? The most reliable piece of knowledge about William of Ockham is his employment by the Church. This, according to the razor, is all it takes to explain the razor: no extra "plurality" is necessary, and the explanation is sufficient in itself.

interpreters, you don't have a say in what "necessity" means. You are officially told that by proper authority. Nonconformism is a sin. Dissent is a heresy.

If you take this concept far enough, then someone gets declared an unquestionable authority on everything. A dictator. He (or someone in his name) decides where necessity ends, and the superfluous plurality gets sent to a gulag.

Western culture was supposed to have been inoculated against this sort of hogwash. The phrase "I disapprove of what you say, but I will defend to the death your right to say it" (often misattributed to Voltaire but in fact authored by his biographer Evelyn B. Hall in 1906, the year Boltzmann killed himself) is a poetic symbol of the West cherishing its diversity and freedom and defending it as the quintessence of the Western soul. That's the spirit that won the West.

Figure 40 – Spirit that won the West.

The spirit that won the West didn't ask 97% of experts for guarantees of success. Failure was an option. It was also an opportunity to learn and to do better next time, especially if someone did something differently and got different results. People tried different things, and some of those things failed and got discarded. Others worked and got learned, and copied, and further improved by others. The diversity of ideas (a.k.a. freedom of thought) was a resource, a critical resource for survival on the frontier. Conformism was a danger in an unfamiliar environment: if everyone did the same thing and it turned out to be a wrong thing to do, the whole colony could perish. Risk-taking, non-conformism, and dissent were all, paradoxically, an insurance policy against total failure. And they were romanticized and rewarded. But not anymore.

Is Humanity an Apprentice God?

In the midst of the Covid-19 pandemic and the feverish demand for face masks, you'd think that investments in masks would be a pretty safe bet. Turns out, not safe enough [72]. American businessmen were reluctant to order mask-making machines—at a million bucks a pop and with four months lead time—without assurances of long-term orders. Worse, even if more machines were available, the meltblown filter material for the masks was in short supply, and manufacturers (you guessed it) wouldn't risk installing additional equipment for making more of it without guarantees of long-term orders [73]. And the risks of uncertain demand and uncertain supply were exacerbated by the shortage of trained labor [74]. Folks don't wanna risk years of their lives getting training without assurances it will be in demand when they graduate [75]. Colleges, in turn, don't want to invest in upgrading the course offerings without guarantees that students will take the classes [76]. College applications are declining, and the decision not to get a college degree is getting easier to rationalize [77]. This last article deals with wet dreams regarding meaningful education and rewarding careers, and compares: "The equivalent in the world of love would be if everyone aspired to date movie stars like Brad Pitt or Angelina Jolie: the result would be an epidemic of single people." Except, of course, that we're actually in the middle of exactly that: an epidemic of single, lonely people [78]. Remember ABBA's lyrics, "take a chance on me"? Well, quite a few of us are no longer as willing to take a chance on each other or on ourselves, and much of anything else—as we used to. Not without 97% of experts telling us it's OK. Show me the printout from the oracle that guarantees the outcome, or I won't lift a finger.

Figure 41 – Safe now? Original image courtesy of Seattle Municipal Archives via pixabay.com.

How did we get here? How did the go-getters who played like this (Figure 41: playground, 1900s) devolve into wimps who need warning labels like this (Figure 41, insert)? What happened to our free spirit, which Thomas Jefferson called "the illimitable freedom of the human mind"? How did we get to feel entitled to having our future guaranteed by some authority? Where did we get the idea that taking no risks is somehow a good thing?

All complex phenomena have simple, easy-to-understand wrong explanations. Mine, for what it's worth, is that me and my colleagues the engineers may have played an outsized role in planting this delusion in human minds. If that's true, then sorry, folks. We really didn't mean to.

Here's my story—incomplete, like all stories—about how it happened. First, let's do the numbers. How many of us do actual science for a living? The number of researchers simultaneously active in the development of (experiencing explosive growth at the time) mathematics in ancient Greece between 450 BCE and 450 CE for the most part didn't exceed fifteen people. The total number of simultaneously active scientists of all disciplines during that same period is not believed to have ever exceeded 100 [79].

At the turn of twentieth century, doing science for a living was still the privilege of a select few. A famous 1927 Solvay conference photo had just thirty faces in it, but about half the people doing cutting-edge relativistic, nuclear, cosmological, or quantum mechanical research in the world in 1927 were in that photo.

Since the mid-nineteenth century, the number of peer-reviewed journals doubled every twenty years. Today, about 30,000 peer-reviewed journals are struggling to accommodate the avalanche of papers sent their way. Around 2.6 million papers get through each year. The average publishing scientist publishes about three papers annually, which means that it only takes 870,000 scientists to publish all 2.6 million peer-reviewed papers. About 17% of the published results worldwide are published by American scientists, who publish about as actively, on average, as other scientists in the world: also about 3 papers per year per scientist. So if 17% of the papers are published 870,000 by American scientists, then 17% publishing scientists worldwide live in the US. That means there are about 150,000 publishing American scientists.

About seven million people worldwide list their occupation as "scientist," which means that 90% of the scientists who ever lived are alive today. That was true when

Is Humanity an Apprentice God?

Derek de Solla Price[27] published this finding in his book *Science Since Babylon* in 1961, the year a human first orbited the Earth. It's still true now. De Solla Price's discovery was that of exponential growth of the scientific population, which doubled every fifteen years. The general human population, meanwhile, has doubled about every fifty years during the twentieth century. As a sub-species, scientists apparently out-reproduce the rest of us humans. Using a little more math, we can make a "scientific prediction": by 2222, every human will be a scientist. If both trends continue, that is. But if both trends continue, the number of humans—all of them scientists—by 2222 will be about 125 billion.

Glossing over assumptions is where the embezzlement of science's hard-earned authority often starts. There is, of course, no reason whatsoever to believe that those doubling trends will continue. They're both very recent phenomena. They come and go. There isn't a "natural law" saying they're universal, eternal, and immutable. How do we know? With the scientific method: we use the alleged "law" to make falsifiable predictions (or post dictions), and then go and check those. The exponential law (namely, the doubling every fifteen years) estimates that the scientists' multiplication factor from Aristotle's time to today is 10^{47}. If we divide the 7 million scientists we have today by that factor, and we get an estimate of how many folks should have been doing science at the time of Aristotle if this "law" were an actual law. It comes out to be a very tiny fraction of one person: 7×10^{-41}. That's 10^{-14} of one atom: our bodies are made of 7×10^{27} atoms. Needless to say, no scientists of subatomic size have ever been observed. Similarly, if the human population had doubled every fifty years since Adam and Eve, then it must have been 1,593 years ago—in 428 CE—that Eve gave birth to the first twins, Cain and Abel. This appears, ahem, rather unlikely, whichever sources one chooses to trust.

The "prediction" that every human is going to be a scientist by 2222 isn't worth publishing as a "scientific" result. Merely using a formula and a calculator doesn't quite cut it. Besides, an average scientific publication has more writers than readers anyway (five and just over three, respectively—and that's counting the editor and the two reviewers, who kind of have no choice). This isn't a problem for most of the folks who have "scientist" in their job title. Most of those folks never even try to publish any scientific results. Again, only 870,000, or 12% of the seven million or so scientist folks in the world, actually publish peer-reviewed papers. The remaining 88% of scientists are involved in activities that don't require—and that often don't

---

[27] Derek de Solla Price was the founder of Scientometrics, the rather obscure yet fun and useful discipline of science studying science itself.

even allow—peer-reviewed publication of their research. And most people in STEM—Science, Technology, Engineering and Math—occupations aren't even called scientists.

There are about 150,000 publishing researchers in the US, but the total number of Americans in STEM occupations is about seven million: fifty times the number of paper-publishing scientists. About 98% of the people who have STEM degrees and who are employed in STEM positions don't conduct research that results in peer-reviewed publications in the US. If that ratio holds for the 870,000 publishing scientists worldwide, then there are at least forty million folks in STEM occupations in the world. Around ten million folks graduated with STEM degrees worldwide in 2020, and the total keeps rising. If only 2% of STEM professionals conduct peer-reviewed, published research, then what do the other 98% do for a living?

R&D, research and development—also known (quite confusingly) as "applied science," that's what. Engineers and technologists of all stripes far outnumber folks that do actual science. The term "R&D" covers some of the most useful—and exciting—activities a human can be engaged in. Trust me here: I've been doing R&D for most of my professional career. It's a lot of fun. We engineers learned how to use electricity to illuminate homes and streets, transmit information over huge distances, and power factories and cars. We learned how to capture nitrogen from air and put it into fertilizer and to disinfect drinking water. We engineers built internal combustion engines and put them in all kinds of vehicles moving across land, seas, and skies. We engineers learned how to create electricity using nuclear fission and how to build computers and helicopters and supersonic airplanes, television sets and electric refrigerators, radars and copy machines, lasers and communication satellites, solar panels and defibrillators, antibiotics and insulin and vaccines. We figured out how to send humans beyond Earth's atmosphere and how to get them back alive. We engineers do a lot of useful, creative and—trust me—thoroughly enjoyable things at work. It's a lot of fun to watch the darn thing finally do what it's supposed to do, despite what looked like determined resistance on its part and occasionally near desperation on ours.

R&D is the lifeblood of our civilization. Its accomplishments surround us everywhere we go. R&D is the best investment countries, corporations, and individuals can make. It's the fastest growing sector of the economy. It grows so fast that 80% to 90% of all folks who ever did STEM for a living are doing it right now. There are, again, about forty million of them in the world (and millions more graduate annually worldwide). We're surrounded by their creations. We depend on them to deliver the necessities and perks of modern life.

Is Humanity an Apprentice God?

Living in the highly artificial modern world, surrounded by evident triumphs of engineering, couldn't fail to make engineers' peculiar worldview rather pervasive. Peculiar in what way? Glad you asked. See, engineers' jobs make them prone to trusting science's products rather blindly (within limits, which we'll soon get to). Engineers can seldom afford to go back to basics and check Hooke's law when designing a bridge. The most common engineering term is "ohshit," and when you see an engineer in a movie mouth this word, she immediately knows what dials to turn, what switches to flip, what sequence of buttons to press. In other words, she has in her mind a model of the system detailed enough to instantly diagnose what went wrong and to tell her with confidence what to do to remedy that particular ohshit. It's okay to reveal (and to heroically resolve) design flaws in the movies. The flawed theory of operation, on the other hand, is usually too abstruse and too scary to put into the script.

Bad theory is avoided in reality even more eagerly than in Hollywood. Engineers develop artificial systems specifically to suppress extraneous interactions, unwanted connections, and unexpected dependencies. Emergent properties. Flawed assumptions. Wile E. Coyote moments. The ohshits.

We engineers do a lot of useful, creative, and thoroughly enjoyable things at work. One thing we engineers don't do is science. Not unless we have to. We're way too busy using the product of science, theory, (and everything else we can) in our job—which is profoundly different from doing science. Answering the question "How does Nature work?" is the business of science; answering the question "How do we make the damn contraption do what it's supposed to do?" is the business of engineering. Science starts with bewilderment and ends with a theory; engineering starts with specifications and ends with a product. Science uses the scientific method. Engineering doesn't.

Engineering doesn't use the scientific method for (as usual) quite a variety of reasons, one of which is that most of the time, it just can't. Engineers engineer products, which makes their materials, methods, protocols, and algorithms—and often the data as well—either proprietary (if they work for a corporation) or classified (if they work for a government) or both. Hence, independent verification of their empirical data using identical, publicly available protocols et cetera – the cornerstone of science and its big claim not to fame but to being trustworthy—isn't exactly encouraged. The reliability requirements for an airplane and a scientific theory are very different, and so are the methods of meeting them.

Confusing science and engineering has a long and far from proud history. On May 30, 1665, in the middle of the Great Plague of London, the first issue of the first volume of the world's first scientific journal, *Philosophical Transactions of the Royal Society*, was published. Besides some genuinely nature-philosophical materials, it contained a fairly barefaced advertisement for a new model of marine chronometer (a device that didn't reach useable precision at sea for another ninety-six years) and a review (in English) of a book (in Italian) on methods of fabricating optical glasses without a mold.

And the mix-up only got worse over time. At the beginning of the Industrial Revolution, engineers were still mostly tinkerers. The machines they created could be, and were, built and used without an accurate and comprehensive model of how they operate. But by the early twentieth century, lots of systems needed good models to be competitive, things like buildings, bridges, planes, guns, internal combustion engines, electric generators, motors, and grids. By 1905, the needs of industry had caught up with science, and engineers started asking for better models than science could deliver. That's how quantum mechanics was born (among many other things). Over the next century, engineered systems grew in sophistication and abundance, while engineers grew more and more reliant on the product of science: theory. The long and winding road between science and technology has by now shrunk in the public's mind to the ampersand in R&D.

And then all of these engineering marvels got misattributed to science "Science has invented different types of machines that are very useful for us in our daily life." "The greatest blessings of science are its inventions in the field of medicine and surgery." "Many inventions of science are for our enjoyment and entertainment." "Modern science has taught us the utility of light dress in a tropical country" That's from just one essay [80]. Really? You need modern science to tell you that wearing furs in Sahara is a bad idea?

And this article isn't the exception. In fact, the misconception is everywhere: "The laptop is one of the great inventions of modern science." "Radio is one of the marvelous inventions of modern science." "The invention of nuclear energy is a great wonder of modern science." Et cetera ad infinitum.

And in almost the same breath: "Science has invented very dangerous weapons that can kill humanity very easily. Another disadvantage of science is the misuse of mass media for propaganda."

Of course, neither crediting science with inventing gadgets to improve our lives nor blaming it for inventing gadgets to terminate them has anything to do with reality. Science doesn't invent gadgets. Scientists do—in their spare time, when they aren't doing science. That doesn't make inventing a scientific activity any more than wearing nerdy glasses makes you smart. Answering the question, "How does Nature work?" is the business of science. Answering the question, "How do we make this gizmo do what it's supposed to do?" is the business of engineering.

> Recent studies have shown that media articles beginning with "recent studies have shown" aren't full of it 99 times out of 100, as the researchers expected, but 99 times out of 99.

When Wilhelm Röntgen discovered X-rays and got his Nobel Prize (the first Nobel Prize in physics), he was indeed doing science: he was trying to understand the nature of cathode rays. The detector he used, a piece of cardboard coated with barium platinocyanide, had never been designed to detect X-rays for three separately sufficient reasons: no one knew X-rays existed (although Hertz had suspected they might), AND no one knew what properties a substance would have to have to make X-rays visible, AND no one knew how to predict substance's properties anyways. So folks were just throwing stuff against the wall, very, very patiently, and waiting for something to stick. In scientific terms, what they were doing is called exploratory research. Even when Wilhelm Röntgen took X-ray photos through his wife's hand, he was still doing science, trying to establish the properties of the new kind of radiation, apparently different from the cathode rays he started from.

Here's a beaty: "X-ray scientist Wilhelm Conrad Röntgen receives the first Nobel Prize in physics. Although he received a lot of recognition, he never tried to patent his discovery." Good for him: had he tried to patent something that existed in Nature for billions of years before he graced the scene with his arrival, he'd have made himself into a laughingstock—rather than an inquisitive explorer of Nature that he was.

You don't patent a discovery. You patent an invention. And while an invention can be—and sometimes is—based on a discovery; and while an invention can be—and sometimes is—made by someone who also discovers something, these are still very, very different endeavors.

Lots of folks were involved in the practical application of Röntgen's discovery. Within a year, almost fifty books and over 1,000 papers about X-rays and their applications were in print—and eagerly read. The year was 1896, and Karl Benz had built the first production car—whose engine was weaker than a horse—a mere eleven years prior, J. J. Thompson was just about to discover the electron, Konstantin Tsiolkovsky had just come up with the rocket equation, and Guglielmo Marconi applied for his first patent for a radio in England. Heinrich Hertz had discovered radio waves, after James Clerk Maxwell theoretically predicted them. Hertz and Maxwell and Röntgen were scientists (the vintage term "natural philosophers" fits best), whereas Benz and Marconi were engineers. They were looking for answers to a different kind of question.

Even Konstantin Tsiolkovsky was principally an engineer. Sure, he didn't own any patents or develop any finished products, but his rocket equation is a (small but important) part of the answer to the question of how to make something perform a desired function: send a payload into space.

In 1961—the year that Derek de Solla Price found that 90% of the scientists who had ever lived were his contemporaries—a human, Yuri Gagarin, orbited Earth for the first time. The same year, Alvin M. Weinberg, then director of Oak Ridge National Laboratory, gave new meaning to the inexhaustible abbreviation BS: now it meant, among other things, "Big Science." Twenty years prior, Weinberg was posted to the Manhattan Project's Metallurgical Laboratory, with a rather fresh Ph.D. degree in mathematical biophysics from the University of Chicago. The culture of the enormous weapons project was like something out of *Alice in Wonderland* (starting with the official name of the project: Development of Substitute Materials). It was meant to mislead the likely enemy spies. Mislabeling the Manhattan Project and a lot of other R&D projects as science—big or otherwise—is no less confusing. Except that it's not confusing enemy spies. It's confusing the public, on whose behalf these projects are ostensibly conducted.

And we're indeed thoroughly confused. Anyone would be confused by reading this: "Scientists confirm safety and benefits of genetically modified crops." "Scientists Admit Frankencrops Pollution Is Inevitable." "Scientists confirm that slight global warming is GREENING the Antarctic Peninsula with new life, dramatically boosting ecology." "Fundamentally unstable: Scientists confirm their fears about East Antarctica's biggest glacier." "Coronavirus: Scientists conclude people cannot be infected twice." "Scientists Confirm Nevada Man Was Infected Twice With Coronavirus." "Scientists fear GM crops ban may harm Scotland." "Stop Frankenfish! Federal Scientists Fear FDA Approval of Genetically Engineered Salmon." "Scientists conclude Earth's energy is 'out of balance.'" "Climate Scientists Confirm No Global Increase in Extreme Weather Events." "Scientists Confirm That Your Roomba DOES Have A Personality." "Scientists fear machines will outsmart us." Culture of doubt, indeed. Except, since doubting "science" is strictly forbidden, we begin to doubt our own sanity instead.

Engineering, by the way, is a culture of doubt, at least as much as science is. It's a self-defense mechanism. Engineers' jobs are tough. Murphy's Laws never sleep. Engineers screw up a lot. If you aren't comfortable being wrong quite often, engineering isn't for you. If you like to profess eternal truths, be a professor. If you're okay with being wrong, you can design a pencil, a bridge, or maybe even a planet. And it may even work, although if it works on the first try, then it wasn't the first try. And if it works exactly to specs, then someone has substituted the original specs.

Engineers doubt themselves and their solutions all the time. It's both a job qualification and an occupational hazard. But failure of the theories engineers get from science is just too horrible to contemplate. An engineer without a reliable model of the basic physics happening in whatever gizmo (s)he is working on is a very unhappy creature. Trust me, I've been there.

Engineers feel entitled to theories that work. Theory is an engineer's tool. Wouldn't a carpenter be pissed if his hammer fell apart every once in a while, without warning? Scientific theory is as much of a tool for an engineer as the hammer is for the carpenter. You can't do your job if you can't rely on your tools.

Engineers are the best-trained skeptics on this planet. They are all from Show-Me Missouri. They have to be – when they fail to check everything, planes fall out of the skies, ships sink, reactors blow up. So, when even engineers happen to take something on trust, it looks to unsuspecting strangers like a badge of honor, a stamp of approval. Beyond reasonable doubt. And the guys skeptical engineers are reluctant to doubt are scientists. No wonder "scientists confirmed X" has come to mean "if you doubt X, you doubt Science Almighty". With quite an assortment of condescending comments attached thereafter, implied or otherwise.

The dark secret here is that engineers, BS-intolerant trained skeptics par excellence, are trained to recognize the applicability limits of the models they trust and to quit trusting the models where they shouldn't. Here "BS" stands for "barely substantiated." No model can be both eternal-universal-immutable and scientific at the same time. Scientists and engineers know that (having learned, for the most part, the hard way). A scientific model is one that has been extensively empirically tested under a limited set of circumstances, within a limited time and space. Engineers trust the model to work where it has been checked out, and if their specs call for something to work outside the range of parameters of the model it has been tested to conform to, they go to a lab and check if it still does. And if it turns out that it doesn't, they reluctantly drop everything and start doing science: building a new model. They can't do their jobs properly without proper tools, so if they can't get good tools from science, they build the tools themselves. Reluctantly. Just like you and me, they're a lot more confident doing their own jobs than somebody else's.

Figure 42 – Entitled to feeling safe.

What makes our modern convenient life so modern and convenient is (among other things) the fact that most conceivable ohshits of everyday life have been taken care of by somebody else. You don't build a whole civilization without relying on a lot of folks with skills you personally don't have. We press a button, and our phone comes alive. Every time, without fail. We turn a key, and our car starts. Every time, without fail. We insert one piece of plastic into another piece of plastic and acquire a cartful of groceries. Every time, without fail. Who can blame folks for feeling entitled to everything working reliably and safely? After all, most of what they ever see already does.

Triumphs of engineering, misattributed to unimpeachable science, make it easy to believe that the world owes you to be a safe, predictable place. For most of us, this is the only world we ever knew, and there's no reason to think that it might get unsafe or unpredictable within our lifetimes. Hence the culture of entitlement. Entitlement to a reliable, risk-free world. Nothing is easier to rationalize in this world than risk-aversion. Nothing can ever be good enough if it involves any risk. The delusion of an everlasting, risk-free lunch makes opportunity costs prohibitively expensive for pretty much anything, unless success is ensured by "science." And then some congenitally resentful kid leaves you speechless by asking, "How dare you not deliver my guaranteed future on a silver platter?"

3.3 Between a rock and a hard place

Science isn't in the insurance business, so asking it for signed guarantees before deigning to move one's behind looks suspiciously like a search for an excuse to sit tight. For most of human history, sitting tight used to be a rather hazardous exercise. Dangerous carnivores lurked in the dark, some of the most dangerous ones being competing tribes or countries or empires. If you sit tight for too long, you will lose agility and become somebody's meal. If you quit supporting your tribe's oddballs tinkering with rocks and sticks and fire and wind, then somebody else somewhere else will be first to invent spears and shields and muskets and tanks and bombers, and their tribe will have your tribe for breakfast. Sure, supporting your oddballs is a risk: you're spending resources without any guaranteed return on your investment. You can fail if you do that. But you can't succeed if you don't. Somebody else somewhere else is trying while you ain't, and if you ain't trying then whoever succeeds it won't be you. Up until recently, that often meant that your tribe would be seriously depleted or become extinct altogether. There was a selective pressure against risk-aversion.

Nowadays, selective pressure is off. No hordes of hungry barbarians amass at the border, dreaming of conquest and loot. Nobody capable of credible aggression is desperate enough to be aggressive. We have grown comfortable and soft and complacent. So did our competitors. Pillage as a means of attaining sustenance turned out to be a lot less profitable than it looked when we didn't know any better. In ancient times, heroic skippers risked life and limb every time they passed between Scylla and Charybdis, but now Scylla and Charybdis are neutered, vaccinated, potty-trained, groomed, and fed an expert-approved diet on an expert-approved schedule, and the remote descendants of the heroic skippers now make the same passage while twiddling their thumbs while half-asleep on the bridge. Satellites overhead transmit weather forecasts, GPS guides the ship with millimetric precision, and computers aboard plot the course and automatically steer the ship. Heroics from the crew are almost never called for. The sailors have every reason to expect an uneventful passage, and most passages nowadays are. Emergencies are rare.

Twiddling one's thumbs, half-asleep at the wheel, has become comfortably survivable – for individuals, families, and whole tribes. Infantile complacency of apparent adults is no longer weeded out by lurking saber-toothed barbarians. Neither is arrogant incompetence. At least, not within most folks' personal living memories. What folks know first-hand is, instead, a comfortable, trouble-free existence in secure knowledge where your next meal is coming from. Instant gratification is finally becoming a reality. We press a few keys on our laptops, and in a few minutes robots half a world away get busy making the sneakers, blinds, or coffeemaker we want. In a few days, we find it on our porch. The natural aversion to troubling oneself unnecessarily, flourishes to the exclusion of many (sometimes any) other considerations.

Meanwhile, we're in the middle of a failure-to-launch syndrome, AKA Peter Pan syndrome, epidemic. In the US, Europe, and Japan, roughly half of all eighteen-to-thirty-four-year-olds still live with their parents. That's the age range when folks are supposed to start their careers and families. Our youth's skills and knowledge don't appear to be in a particularly high demand (an average job opening nowadays gets 250 applications), which makes risk-taking less and less justifiable for more and more young folks. For the tens of millions unfortunate enough to look for their first job during the Covid-19 pandemic, the deck is stacked against growing up. Their personal memories will reflect that time as long as they live—and then impact their kids as well, provided they have any (infantilism is generally not a heritable trait).

Before the pandemic, Yuval Noah Harari wrote this: "The technological revolution might soon push billions of humans out of the job market and create a massive new 'useless class,' leading to social and political upheavals that no existing ideology knows how to handle." Indeed, machines have been getting really good at doing mundane stuff, from washing your dishes to filing your taxes. Humans are in danger of being replaced by robots in jobs that range from driving to law enforcement to editing to medical diagnostics. About 85% of the jobs Americans lost lately went to robots, not to humans in China or Mexico. People take breaks, go on vacation, require sick leave, make mistakes, suffer injuries, join trade unions, and identify with political parties. In short, we do a lot of messy human things that interfere with the efficient, cost-effective, uninterrupted production of goods and services. Robots do none of that. They just do what they're told. Getting angry at robots is plain silly. Almost as silly as getting angry at China, Mexico and immigrants, legal or otherwise. As silly as trying to fix the wrong problems.

Unrecognized problems have no (deliberate) solutions. But I'd take an unrecognized problem over a misdiagnosed one any day and twice on Sunday. Once you have a wrong diagnosis, you start taking the wrong pills, suffering their side effects while getting no benefit, and you deplete both your wallet and your resistance to the bug(s) you actually have or you may pick up tomorrow.

Defining a problem is half the solution. Citing Harari again, "The most important question in twenty-first-century economics may well be what to do with all the superfluous people. What will conscious humans do once we have highly intelligent non-conscious algorithms that can do almost everything better?" Once you assume that humans are inferior to robots in all respects that matter, the "useless class" problem (a.k.a. technological unemployment problem) is no longer solvable. If all we are is algorithms, then superior algorithms—once available—will inevitably (and rightly) replace us. If we can't do something useful better than a robot, then it's not about us using AI at our discretion. It's about AI having no use for us anymore. Extinction-by-AI scenario has nothing whatsoever to do with evil spirits or some other cheap Hollywoodacy. It's just an inevitable, rational "choice" made by a machine that we have created to be very good at making rational "choices." Charity isn't programmable. AI tasked with terminating human suffering would succeed admirably (in its own myopic eyes) by painlessly euthanizing the sufferers.

The blinkered belief that we humans are mediocre, inefficient, outdated, and faulty algorithms paves the way for AI to take over the project of human civilization, and it teaches us humans to submit and adapt to a "scientifically proven" peripheral role as useless parasites rotting on a couch with TV, VR, LSD, and UBI. The idea that all we are is walking algorithms, and so is AI, can only have one effect on its human adherents: feeling inferior. Powerless. Lacking control. Racing to the bottom. Getting redundant and obsolete and useless because we are programmed to. Competing with robots on robots' turf (of myopic rationalism) doesn't look like a winning strategy.

This hopeless outlook is for regular Joe and Jane, not Jack Ma and Elon Musk and Mark Zuckerberg. These guys look at the same reality through a filter set very different from most everyone else's. They see a different story, one that empowers them rather than robots. It empowers them to do what we humans—well, some of us—actually do better than robots: be irrational, AKA call the shots with insufficient information. Take risks. Have a vision – a vision that can't be rationalized without a time machine – and go for it.

Most folks on Forbes 400 list didn't inherit oil fields or banana plantations. They didn't make their money in the industry their parents were in. They made their money in industries they helped create during their lifetimes—they couldn't inherit from their parents (and the rest of us) something we didn't have to hand down to them. Instead, they imagined something, and made it happen, and the rest of us—their customers and shareholders—approved their creations and attached a lot of value to them. Without our approval, or at least acquiescence—reluctant or enthusiastic, informed or misguided, engaged or indifferent—nobody gets to decide what humanity does with its resources. Not to any meaningful extent.

> Stuff you disagree with: boastful, alleged, questionable, debunked, unsupported, nutty, unproven, uncertain, disproven, unsupported by available evidence, unsupported by evidence, disgraced, disabled, weak, failed, dubious, inconclusive, under scrutiny, biased, misinformed, delusional, mythical, quack, demoralized, denier, alarmist, crank, conspiratorial, falls short, misrepresented, misread, garbled, misinformed, pseudoscientific, distorted, misinterpreted, miscalculated, misconstrued, scam, whitewashed, hogwash, sugarcoated, glossed over, bamboozled, disillusioned.
>
> Stuff you agree with: realized, admitted, comprehended, conceded, accepted, confessed, own up to, known, come to understanding, scientists found, vindicate, exonerated, corroborated, undisputed, consensus, modern science established, unequivocal evidence, successfully demonstrated, respected experts confirm, Nobel prize winners agree, consensus opinion of informed sources, educated opinion, expert view, research shows, discover.

Risk-takers take it upon themselves to tell robots—robots by birth, by circumstance, or by choice—what to do. Some win, most importantly – win our approval, and with that sometimes get to command vast resources. The folks who have a million times more money than you and I have don't eat a million times more. They just can't. Instead, they make resource-allocating decisions concerning a million times more resources than you and I do. The much-talked-about stratification of wealth appears to concentrate the resources of humankind in the hands of folks who have some ideas for what to do with those resources. Folks who inherit a pile of resources to just sit there without furiously shoveling it somewhere, find that the pile quickly disappears from underneath them—often in the direction of somebody taking a bet on some newfangled idea. Risk-takers own the future. Can this ownership be more broad-based? Should it? Will the future be better if it's owned by more of us rather than fewer? How many of us are ready to take ownership of this world?

Does the apparent rarity of exceptional ability reflect just how rare it really is or how little of it we choose to recognize? Conversely, can demand for brilliance help create it? Examples of just such a phenomenon range from Greek philosophers to Flemish painters to founders of quantum physics to creators of the World Wide Web to contributors of Wikipedia and Quora and Blogspot. The chance of somebody's risky idea being tried out, and occasionally even rewarded, depends on the rest of us. We choose whether we want to listen to Socrates, look at Rembrandt, switch to electric lighting, or use the Internet. Collectively, we decide how many creative folks we want around—and what kind of creative folks we want. If their imagination fails to click with ours, their ideas go to the reject pile. It seems at least possible that neither the Golem effect nor the Pygmalion effect are limited to individuals or small groups. They might very well apply to human culture as a whole.

Two notes here: first, the Golem and Pygmalion effects work through our irrational side. Without a time machine, you can't know if your next effort is going to make you a celebrity or a laughingstock. You can exercise your free will and go for it, or you can get a beer and go watch that TV show once more. Here, again, language provides a valuable hint: free will is something you exercise. What you exercise is your skills. Free will is a skill, folks. It takes a conscious effort to keep it lean and mean and operational, and it's completely irrational to think that if you make that effort, you'll become Socrates, Rembrandt, Einstein, or Zuckerberg. It's just completely rational to think that if you don't, you won't.

Second, the Golem and Pygmalion effects are examples of self-reinforcing interactions (a.k.a. positive feedback loops) that abound in our intertwined world. A mature engineering discipline called control theory has developed a sophisticated toolbox for forecasting dynamic behavior of systems with these kinds of links. Of course, in engineering, when control theory says that a plane can fly in a controllable manner, the FAA still insists on having test pilots run it through its paces before certifying it for passenger service. The FAA is right: models are an abbreviation of reality, so you need to make sure that the model you used actually accounts for everything that matters in your system. For a global human society, just like for any other one-off system you can't experiment with, you don't have the luxury of dry runs before doing it for real. So the belief in the accuracy or the relevance of any model for forecasting the behavior of such systems is BS: beyond science. You just don't know if you missed something important in your model, especially if that something never mattered before. But somebody else may notice what you missed. Somebody else may look at the same thing through a different filter set, and see a different picture. That's the wisdom of the crowd. The more folks have seen your model's guts, the more likely it is that someone else will notice whatever you missed.

With this proviso, can modelling provide useful hints about humanity's future in broad strokes? I think it already has. Charles Jones, an economics professor at Stanford, recently published population dynamic modeling results, which I think are profoundly significant. What he found was that there appear to be three steady states for a human society [81]. The two stable states are 1) a civilization climbing the Kardashev scale or 2) the empty planet left after civilization has faded away. The third state—an intermediate steady state between the off-to-the-stars and back-to-the-caves scenarios—is inherently unstable. It's a crossroads, a tipping point. Any external perturbation gets amplified by the system's inherent positive feedback loops and sends that population to one of the two stable states: settling the Universe or going extinct.

Significantly, the controlling variable in Jones's model was knowledge per person: a high-knowledge civilization stays that way by growing its island of knowledge, climbing the Kardashev scale. A pastoralist society can hardly find the "excesses" of the World Wide Web, the Hubble telescope, GPS, and the Large Hadron Collider worthy of the resources spent. Once the retreat starts, it will become progressively easier to justify shutting down the opulent temples of global civilization—first the Saturn V's and Tevatron and the Arecibo radio telescope, then the nuclear power stations and air transportation, then mega-factories and industrial farms, then seaports and large mining operations. Soon there won't be any justification for the expense of maintaining the United Nations and universities and museums and national governments, and these will be gone, too. And there's no reason to believe that this self-destruction has a natural lower limit. Some civilizations in human history abandoned the development path and completely vanished in the mist of time, leaving us no living memory of what happened to them. Our historians may never know for certain the purpose of Nazca lines or Easter Island statues or Antikythera mechanism or the Gobekli Tepe complex. We may never know how the Zhang Heng seismoscope worked or how ancient peoples built the Egyptian pyramids or the Saksaywaman stone walls. The human tribes that created them couldn't afford to keep the knowledge alive. That would be curtains for a global tribe that never managed to plant backup copies of itself elsewhere.

I'm going to steal a beautiful illustration of an ant trail from Neil Theise [82] [83]. Foraging ants follow a path, clearly marked with pheromones, between the colony and a food source. That is, most of them do. If you look closely, you'll find some that stray from the well-trodden path and explore around. It's a good thing for the colony that they do because the food source at the end of the trail may become exhausted. A colony that fails to explore its surroundings may face sudden famine. And if it fails to find a suitable replacement quickly, it will starve to death.

The colony might also starve to death if all ants ignored the existing food source and rushed off looking for new ones. Custodians of the existing foraging trail feed everyone, including the explorers looking for new paths. The long-term survival of the colony depends on both. Striking the right balance between exploration and maintenance is a big deal for a self-organizing system. Too much slack and variability, and you lose efficiency and perish. Too much rigid order, and you lose adaptability and perish.

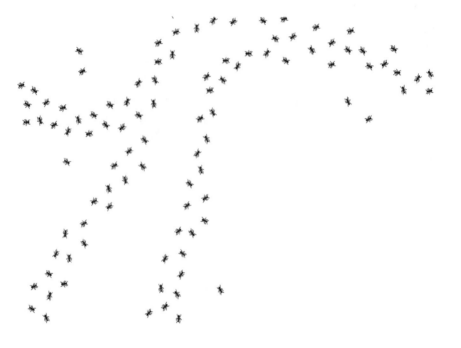

Figure 43 – Ant trails.

Different ant species have evolved to maintain different balances between exploration and maintenance [84]. Different ant species, at the next level of self-organization, also fan out in search for something, like individual ants fan out from the established path. They're in search of a "perfect" exploration/maintenance balance. Some evolve to find their niche; others perish and make room for more successful competitors.

That's how it works for ants, but we aren't ants. Our world is richer than theirs. The variation among humans is incomparably more multifaceted than whatever slight variability one might find among ants. So if even ants can have multiple optima—different ant species—then it stands to reason that so can we. What would ours look like?

One thing that the Empty Planet model above didn't consider is the possibility of *H. sapiens* splitting into two species: explorers and custodians. *Homo exploratoris* and *Homo mundanis*. With technology becoming available to settle other worlds, opportunity will arise for nonconformists, explorers, mavericks, and heretics to separate themselves geographically from the more risk-averse, sedentary folk. There's only so far you can run on one planet. But what if humans settle more than one planet? What if there actually is an explorer gene (which science suggests there is [85], and sufficient geographic separation of the carriers of its "wild type" and "mutant" versions were the first step in divergent evolutionary paths?

Imagine it: different environments and different behavior, fading common language, vanishing interactions and disappearance of opportunities to have interspecies offspring.

It also appears that the Internet has opposite effects on the two groups: explorers use it to find each other and to do stuff together in the physical world, while the custodians self-isolate in echo chambers they never have any reason to leave. For now, custodians massively outnumber explorers, as they have throughout history. But that can change. For example, agriculture, the archetypal custodial activity for our species, used to account for 95% of all employment. Now it's down to 2% in technologically advanced societies, which still manage to grow most of the world's food supply.

The Internet seems to have the opposite effects on explorers' and custodians' reproductive rates and on the reproductive choices of the minority explorer subspecies. The rare explorers in the small, isolated communities of yesteryear often had no choice but to partner with custodians for reproduction, but now they have other options. The selective pressures, and therefore survival strategies, will likely be drastically different, and boundaries will perhaps be sharp and clear, much more so than, for example, the boundary between the nonconformist Russians east of the Ural Mountains and the conformist Russians west of them or the boundary between the Britons who moved to the colonies and the ones who chose to stay behind.

Earthlings will preserve and manage what they have: the beautiful cradle of the species that it spawned. Tranquility. Contentment. Safety and security. Comfort. Universal basic income, a low birth rate, a long life expectancy, an aging population, obsolescence of work, virtual reality, and recreational psychotropic drugs. Walking barefoot on grass. Swimming naked in the ocean covering most of the planet. The resented rich and despised sellouts will have left, and nothing will ever go wrong anymore.

Meanwhile, the celestials will be busy terraforming hostile, unforgiving worlds. Excitement. Drive bordering on obsession. Adrenalin. Accidents. Short life expectancy. High birth rate. Risking one's life for strangers, many of whom are your toughest competitors. Putting one's life in the hands of the same strangers. Cramped quarters reclaimed from alien, often hostile, environments. That damn spacesuit and the contortions it requires to eat, drink, or scratch where it itches. Can't puke or you die. Can't get high or you die. Can't get fat or careless or obtuse—or you die. Worse, you may kill others who didn't puke or get high or fat or careless or obtuse. Frontier.

Given such different settings, earthlings and celestials are sure to rapidly acquire different mindsets, different values, different outlooks. The tales they will tell their kids at home, and history books at their schools and libraries may soon have little in common. Worse, the already existing sneering may develop into full-blown animosity. And if one day the Earth is, say, threatened with an extinction-scale catastrophe, the explorers may not make themselves available to help, out of indifference or resentment. The latter would be a tragedy for both species. Resentment is a germ you don't want to take on a journey to the stars. It will kill you there.

And vice versa, of course. If a colony of extraterrestrial humans fails and needs assistance, the custodians on Earth may have neither the resources nor the inclination to help them out. If the Empty Planet model is anywhere near accurate, the custodians will be undergoing degrowth and devolution. They would be unlikely to offer shelter and hot meals to, in their view, a bunch of traitors and vagrants wasting precious resources on some ridiculous Pinky-and-the-Brain scheme to conquer the world.

The splitting into two species—one climbing the Kardashev ladder, the other likely going backward after exhausting the resources of the one tiny home they refused to expand—is, in my view, a clear and present danger of our time. As Stephen Hawking once said, "I don't think the human race will survive the next thousand years, unless we spread into space." A thousand years isn't as long as it may seem, and indications are that we have nowhere near that long before the window of opportunity slams shut. Given what it takes to actually spread into space, we may have to get our act together before the decision is taken out of our hands. In the opinion of yours truly, that's likely to happen within just a few generations. The humans alive as I write these words will be responsible—directly or through the worldviews handed down to their children—for the choice: spread to space or let our civilization fizzle out.

As we are often reminded, you can't have infinite growth on a finite planet. While the dilemma seems to be very real, the folks doing the reminding appear to kinda ignore the rest of the Universe. The meme is supposed to support the idea of reversing the growth. Of course, for all we know, you can't have a continuing civilization without continuous growth either. We have no empirical evidence of any civilization, especially a global one, surviving degrowth, and the best available models suggest that it won't.

The collapse of the global civilization isn't just a theoretical possibility. We have already shut down the Apollo program and Tevatron and the Arecibo radio telescope. Pastoralism is making inroads in other ways, too. In the US, there are clear signs of a pandemic-triggered exodus from the cities [86]. The doomsday prepper supply industry is doing brisk business, and companies selling multimillion-dollar underground shelters have serious backlogs. Tech billionaires buy islands remote enough to watch the last sunset of humanity from; Peter Thiel, for example, is rumored to own a substantial chunk of New Zealand.

Ultimate pragmatists like Peter Thiel, the founder of PayPal and the first outside investor of Facebook, are seriously concerned [87]. The resources we waste while getting nowhere fast have somehow become the measure of progress. The data crunching power in weather forecasting went up by many million-fold over the last fifty years, while the forecast accuracy of predictions beyond a few days remains as bad as it has ever been. The little gizmo on my laptop whose only function is to annoy me with some useless message takes more memory and CPU power than it took to land people on the Moon. That looks like a major contributing factor to the public's growing suspicion that we, as a species, don't have the imagination to have actually gone to the Moon. It's hard not to notice that we have sent people no farther than LEO while claiming great progress for fifty years, that we have been promising that fusion energy is right around the corner for sixty years, that we were supposed to have individualized medicine after the human genome was deciphered - which it has been for eighteen years, with no change in the trend of life expectancy curve over the past couple decades. It doesn't look very promising.

The Kardashev scale uses a single metric (namely, the energy controlled by a civilization) as a measure of that civilization's success. Twenty years after that metric was introduced, Charles Hall developed the concept of "energy returned on energy invested" (EROI). To control energy, you need to invest energy first. Before you can burn gasoline in an internal combustion engine to get somewhere in your car, someone has to find petroleum, pump it out of the ground, and refine it into gasoline, which is then transported to a gas station and ultimately pumped into your car's gas tank. Each step in this process costs energy. EROI is the ratio of energy you use over all the energy invested in every step in the process of getting it there.

It stands to reason that systems with an EROI less than 1 should shrink: they make bad energy investments, bleeding energy at every turn, until not enough energy is available to support luxuries, then basic functions. The system either evolves to improve its EROI, or it shrinks and perishes. The system in question doesn't have to be a civilization. Charles Hall is an ecologist, and EROI was originally suggested by his studies of fish migrating upstream in search of a nutrient-rich habitat.

Similarly, EROI over unity would suggest an expanding system. But the devil is in the details. Do you count the energy content of gasoline in your car's tank or the mechanical energy delivered to its wheels? (The difference is three-to-eight-fold.) Do you count the energy that went into making the car? The road? Do you count the energy investment of sending aircraft carriers to oil-rich areas of the globe as a subtle suggestion to keep oil affordable? Do you count the energy investment that would be needed to capture carbon dioxide from the air and bury it somehow? You need to draw the line somewhere, both on the debit and the credit side—and in both instances it's somewhat arbitrary.

Which, among other things, makes EROI easy to weaponize if you have an agenda. Discreetly making optimistic assumptions about an energy source you like—and pessimistic ones about a competitor you want to look bad—is easy. You're almost literally comparing apples and oranges. So comparative EROI values for dissimilar technologies have to be taken with a grain of salt.

With that in mind, the best currently available practice for evaluating EROIs yields a cutoff value of not 1, but about 3 [88] to 7 [89], depending, among other things, on the lifestyle you expect. More affluent countries require, among other things, higher EROI cutoff levels. Biofuels and shale oil don't make the cut; oil sands do, but barely. This isn't necessarily a death sentence: technologies evolve, economies of scale kick in, and EROIs go up, sometimes substantially (for example, five-fold for oil sands). EROIs of the actively promoted wind and solar look reasonably good, until one takes into account the energy cost of building storage facilities to make energy available on windless nights [89], which (so far) plunge the EROI values for wind and solar into the marginal-at-best range.

For most of human history, we relied on energy sources with very low EROI: the muscle power of humans and domestic animals, firewood, dung, and other forms of biofuel [90]. Progress was slow: most folks were busy most of the time getting the energy needed for survival, margins were incredibly slim—so luxuries like libraries, laboratories and observatories were rare and vulnerable to any mishap.

Three centuries ago, we learned to use an energy source with much better EROI: coal. It started the Industrial Revolution, breaking humanity free from the Malthusian trap [91]: a stagnant society where humans compete for limited resources, and a population increase leads to poverty and famine. Malthus' model, proposed in 1798, seems to describe medieval Europe—centuries before Malthus—rather well. However, if this description still held true in England in 1766, Thomas Robert Malthus, the sixth child in a middle-class family, may not even have been born at all. His chances of surviving long enough to concoct his theories—and getting educated enough to do so—would have been slim.

Just over a century ago, we stumbled upon yet another hidden treasure: Sun-in-a-can. Oil. Just like coal, oil has been accumulating for hundreds of millions of years, concentrating the sunlight that fed the photoautotrophs of ancient Earth. Its EROI was even higher than coal's.

Civilization blossomed. Our numbers more than quadrupled in a century, while living standards shot up (quite unevenly, but for practically everyone, and practically everywhere). Synergies and economies of scale worked their magic to help human genius and ambition create modern humanity—the most numerous, prosperous, healthy, peaceful, educated humankind that ever inhabited this planet.

Clearly, oil-fueled civilization is transient. We're burning oil (and gas, and coal) millions of times faster than it forms in the Earth's crust. Sooner or later, we'll just run out. The easy oil is gone already, and what's left takes some doing to find and extract (Figure 44). So oil's EROI has gone down – by some estimates, up to 10-fold. The law of diminishing returns has arrived, and Malthus' ghost roams the Earth once again. The threat of societal collapse looms [92] large enough that normally very level-headed and extraordinarily well-informed folks are seeking real estate as far away from the rest of us as possible.

One wonders, though, who is supposed to hold the skies up if things get bad enough to make the retreat necessary. You can't have boutique retreats without the rest of the world economy: a boutique retreat on an otherwise desolate planet is a prohibitively expensive prison. As far as we know, you can't have a functioning global economy (with a division of labor and an exchange of resources and supertankers and container ships and the Internet and Hollywood and universities and banks and airports and highways) without actual people. Even robots won't do: they don't go shopping. And you can't have people (or even robots) without energy to feed them. So, a billionaire survivor of the collapse of civilization isn't going to be sipping Dom Perignon aboard his mega-yacht – he'll be too busy learning—and teaching his kids—to grow wheat and tend to farm animals. Or maybe to hunt with a bow and flint-tipped arrows.

Figure 44 – High-EROI (easy) oil (left); low-EROI (hard-to-get) oil (right).

All the economies of scale and synergies and positive feedbacks that helped grow the global civilization work both ways. More people make possible more advancements in knowledge, technology, economy, and infrastructure (a.k.a. progress); by the same token, fewer people will have to do with less. The multibillion-dollar chip-making facilities that make the modern world possible are just one example of things that we don't know how to run as boutiques. Our, mostly involuntary, "experiment" at degrowth (with COVID-19 pandemic on top of US-China quarrel) has already led to, among other things, global chip shortages [93], and other supply-chain shortages are creeping up on us as well. We don't know how to get bank loans (a.k.a. bets on the future) in a shrinking economy with a shrinking energy supply and a shrinking consumer base. We don't know how to run retirement systems in a society where retirement savings can't be loaned for a return with interest, and we don't know where to get the interest in a shrinking economy. Every bank loan, every investment is an implicit act of trust in a better tomorrow. We don't know how to run an economy of deliberate global retreat. There's no evidence that degrowth, intentional or otherwise, has a natural bottom. There's no evidence that the depopulation that some misanthropes more or less openly advocate for will, or indeed can, stop at some "sustainable" level. There's no evidence that science and engineering and art, knowledge and skills and culture, can continue to be developed—or even maintained—as the global civilization recedes. And the possibility that such degrowth wont' be accompanied by global resource wars appears remote.

The plot in Figure 45 below is from a fairly gloomy paper [94] predicting civilization (and population) collapse (or in SpaceX's elegant turn of phrase, "rapid unscheduled disassembly"). In the scenario modeled in the paper, we quit burning fossil fuels, one way or another, without first finding and scaling up some better energy source. Folks familiar with the search for suitable and scalable replacement know what happened to TOKAMAK, which has been fifty years away for the last sixty years. They know what happened to biofuels when people started taking on "commercial" projects without ever considering scalability (a.k.a. the little nuance of running out of room for energy crops before making enough fuel to write home about, but not before starving everyone). They know what happens to solar and wind on windless nights. They know what happened when folks doing LENR rushed to "commercialization" without having done the science, achieving little besides making the term "cold fusion"—and the whole field—a punching bag for amateur debunkers. They know that going nuclear (on a scale you can write home about) requires a tectonic shift in both public mood and international relations, far beyond what they can imagine actually happening.

And the longer the much-maligned fossil fuels quietly, reliably, and cheaply provide over 80% of the energy we use, the harder we are going to be hit when the inevitable happens and extracting the remaining oil, gas, and coal costs more energy than they contain. Some people are still in denial about the problem, despite all the available data on the falling EROI for fossils, the consistent failure to mobilize serious efforts to search for scalable—repeat scalable, repeat scalable—alternatives, and complete lack of data in support of the cargo cult of the Spigot Almighty: miraculous (abiogenic) generation of as much oil as we can ever want. It's been gleefully noted that we haven't run out of oil yet, despite having been predicted—apparently expecting the rest of us to believe that since predictions haven't materialized on the exact date misattributed to an inexact model, they never will. Actual data, for example here [95], suggests otherwise: oil reserves being depleted 2.1% annually, and replenished 0.3% in that time. The 2.1% number translates to 47 years of proven reserves, which is not all that alarming. What is alarming is that in a year we burned through 7 times more oil reserves than we found.

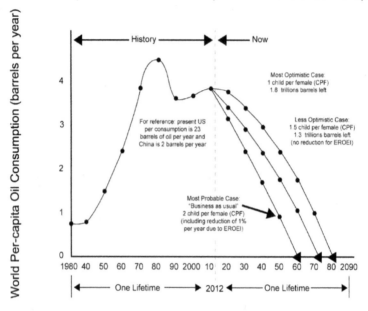

Figure 45 – End of Sun-in-a-can. Original data courtesy of late John G. Howe, from "The End of Fossil Energy and Per Capita Oil," ISBN 978-0-9962054-5-0.

Of course, if we choose not to climb the Kardashev ladder, we won't need the energy it takes to climb it. But then we'll need something else instead, something we don't have, either. That is, the ability to sustain humanity (including human culture, science, engineering, art) without ever-accelerating growth.

The need to sustain humanity is based on an irrational belief that it's a good idea to sustain humanity. Not everyone agrees. Some folks see humans as destroyers of everything we touch (Figure 46). All the misanthropes choose to see as our civilization's output is "pollution." Everything they see as human product is "degraded"—degraded energy, degraded matter. Junk. And the less junk is produced, the better. The Sphinx and the *Mona Lisa* and the theory of relativity and the Moon landing don't count to the misanthropes. If one takes this view, then the "rapid unscheduled disassembly" of an "evil" humanity is a solution, not a problem. Going back to "degrading" as little energy and matter as our cave-dwelling ancestors did would be, from their standpoint, a good thing.

To the rest of us, a.k.a. the sane majority, irreversible, unstoppable degrowth right back to the caves we have come from (driven by the same feedback loops that drive our growth now, only backward) would be a problem. A really big one. Big enough so it probably won't go away on its own, without some deliberate action on someone's part.

Deliberate action implies deliberation, which takes time. And time to scratch our collective head is a non-renewable resource – especially for an accelerating civilization. Things have sped up tremendously since we learned to use oil to power humanity; and the faster you go, the faster you need to make decisions which way to go, or you will eventually smash into something. Intentionality is no longer a luxury; our acceleration has made it a necessity. We have made ourselves important: at this speed, you've gotta have somebody at the wheel. But who will it be? Will our "helmsman" regard collapse of civilization as a problem, a solution, or just clickbait? Will our ship be steered away from the abyss of nonbeing or swept toward it by the mighty river of time? Will the helm be actually connected to the rudder, and engine to the prop? Will spinning the wheel get the ship pointing where we intend for it to go? Even if pointing upstream, will it have enough power to propel itself against the current?

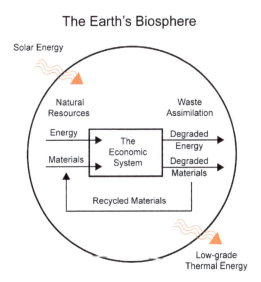

Figure 46 – Humanity, as seen by advocates of degrowth.

3.4 Power to the people

The horror scenarios of collapse of civilization and humanity's retreat assume (among other things) that we won't find (on our little island or elsewhere) the resources we need to avert the catastrophe of irreversible degrowth, particularly the energy we can use to keep going. Readily available and abundant high-EROI energy. And we won't find it—or anything else—without looking. On our little island and elsewhere.

Kardashev was right: the energy we control is a good integral measure of civilization's might and health. Its trend is also a good hint at where that civilization is headed. What it does to tweak this trend is an indication of how that civilization sees itself in the future and how deliberate it is about getting there.

> Unrecognized problems have no (deliberate) solutions.

How much power do we need? In 2000, we were using about 15 TW; by 2025, we expect to use about 28 TW. We're doubling our power consumption in about twenty-five years. And we've been doubling it every twenty-five years for quite some time now: ever since learning to use Sun-in-a-can, that is.

Our power use is still tiny compared to what a Kardashev's Type I (KT-I) civilization needs: an equivalent of all the power its home star showers on its home planet. A KT-I civilization on Earth would be using about 170,000 TW. Our power needs in 2000 were a paltry 0.009% (1/11,000) of KT-I level.

But if we keep doubling our energy use every twenty-five years, we can get to KT-I very fast. We could be there in about 300 years. In 300 years we could have enough energy at our disposal to create a world few of us can even imagine today.

Doubling the power at our disposal used to take much longer than twenty-five years. In early agricultural societies, doubling time was thousands of years [96]. It accelerated through ancient and medieval times, but doubling time was still centuries-long until the Industrial Revolution. Once we learned to use the first of the fossil fuels, coal, to power our industry – time started flying faster.

Where did the extra power go? Some of it increased per capita energy consumption. We now use an estimated ten times more per-capita energy than the first agricultural societies did 12,000 years ago. We have indoor plumbing and flu shots and schools and the Internet and movies and vacations and retirement.

But we, as a species, aren't using just ten times more power than we were using 12,000 years ago when we first tried building temples and observatories. We're actually using about 16,000 times more. Why? Because there's a lot more of us. About 12,000 years ago, the total number of humans on Earth was about five million. That number has increased about 1,600-fold. And most of that increase happened rather recently. Just 220 years ago, there were a billion of us. Today, there are almost eight billion humans. That's what we have done with most of that Sun-in-a-can. We converted long-dead plants and animals into live people.

More people are alive today than have ever been alive at the same time ever in the planet's history. More people are available to contribute to Wikipedia today than could contribute to the Alexandria library of Ptolemy. More people can trade opinions on Quora than ever argued at Athenian gyms during the times of Plato and Aristotle. More people listen to TED talks than Socrates ever lectured.

And having more people is a chance to have more outstanding people. More pioneers to try out exploratory research, so more of them get lucky and discover something. And each of them will have a better chance to benefit from synergies: having real live people you can bounce your ideas off of. There are more ambitious, imaginative, smart people who happen to be each other's contemporaries and competitors to help develop each other's ideas. More folks whose interests intersect, to quickly check out many concepts, critique them from all different angles, try out the most promising ones, and then realize the ones that work best. That's the positive feedback loop that can trigger an avalanche of human success.

Doubling our energy consumption every twenty-five years is (a big part of) what keeps our civilization going. Our accelerating civilization, the only one we have (more or less) learned to run. Acceleration compresses time. History happens faster than it ever has. Time flies when you're having fun. It's easy to lose track of time when your bar-hopping is paid for by some treasure Granddaddy found and passed on to you. It's easy to delude yourself into thinking the freebies are gonna last forever, without you – yes, you – having to do anything to keep them coming.

Sober up, folks. Our family treasure (a.k.a. Sun-in-a-can) took hundreds of millions of years to form, hundreds of thousands of years to find—and now it's taking only hundreds of years to burn through. There's a bottom coming up. Humanity's projected energy needs are covered by fossil fuels—known and estimated—out only to about 2100 CE [97]. And believe it or not, that's an OPTIMISTIC forecast. That's less than eighty years from now. That's about three generations. My grandchildren will be alive then. Around 2100, extracting a barrel of crude will cost more energy than the barrel can deliver, and it doesn't matter if the estimate of extractable oil reserves is low by even 100%. All you get is a twenty-five-year stay of execution, which is a blink of an eye. What if the estimate is off by

300%? That's a factor of four, based on exactly zero data, yet all this miracle gets you is another twenty-five years. 700%? That's a factor of eight, and anyone in the industry would die laughing if you suggested that aloud. But it still only gets you another twenty-five-year reprieve. Exponential growth can be a bitch. If, that is, you don't want whatever it is that grows exponentially.

By 2100, we're projected to control about 0.1% of the energy Earth receives from the Sun. By the Kardashev criterion, that's still 1/1,000 of a KT-I civilization. Even if we manage to stretch the fossils ten-fold (that is, extract ten times more energy from fossil fuels than the currently known fuels contain)—and, again, no one in the coal and oil and gas industry believes that's possible—that's still 1% of KT-I, and maybe three more generations of growth beyond 2100. Whereupon we'll have to learn one of two things: get high-EROI energy from a new, reliable, plentiful source or live in a shrinking world, where a receding humanity fights for dwindling resources. Which do you want for your grandkids?

Energy utilization doubling every twenty-five years compresses time. Decision points that just yesterday seemed so remote as to be almost irrelevant arrive unannounced, ready or not, and our grandkids are the ones who are going to live with the consequences of our choices—or our failures to make any. We might, if we chose to, attain Kardashev Type I (KT-I) in 300 years; and then hit KT-II (Sun energy level) in 900 more years and KT-III (controlling energy of the Milky Way galaxy) in another 900 years. So 2,100 years from now, we might, if we choose to keep going, call the Milky Way our 'hood. The darn thing is, by the way, 180,000 light-years across, and it has a lot more stars in it than we have people on Earth. Settling the Earth took a lot longer than settling the Milky Way is projected to take—if we keep the pace. Which we can't, unless we choose to.

Reaching KT-I would require about 300 years of investing in ourselves at our current EROI—it's, for the large part, the high EROI that makes the doublings every 25 years possible, and we need 12 of these for the 300-year total. That is, if we have high-quality energy sources that would last that long.

How much total energy are we talking about? KT-I power level is, again, 170,000 TW, which we could achieve by covering 100% of the Earth surface with 100% efficient solar panels. How much energy will be spent to reach KT-I depends on whether we keep the twenty-five-year doubling pace. If we do and become a KT-I civilization in 300 years, we would have had to spend a total of about six million Terawatt-years (TWy) of energy in the process. The longer it takes, the more energy we'd need to achieve the same result: the total expenditure is proportional to the doubling time. Slowing down is expensive, maybe prohibitively so.

Let's take stock of the situation. Let's talk about the bad news first. Brace yourselves, there's plenty of it.

Our civilization today gets 80% of its energy from the first row of Table 1, below. That's the pheromone-marked ant trail to Sun-in-a-can. And it's running out [95].

	Terrestrial resource: % KT-I[1]	Comment
Fossils, known	0.05%	Running out in decades
Fossils, projected	0.1%	Not developed: environmental concerns
Hydroelectric	12%	Would require continent-scale relocations; environmental impact of large-scale deployment potentially catastrophic: flooding
Nuclear (uranium)	0.3%	Not developed: security, environmental concerns
Solar	100%	Environmental impact of large-scale deployment potentially catastrophic: global albedo shift
Wind	2%	Environmental impact of large-scale deployment potentially catastrophic: atmospheric circulation shift
Geothermal	0.02%	Environmental impact of large-scale deployment unknown
Tidal	0.002%	
Biomass	0.07%	400-1,000 times lower output per km² than solar; environmental impact of large-scale deployment potentially catastrophic: massive land, water use

Table 1 – Available energy resources: traditional technologies[28]

Most of the remaining 20% comes from the breadcrumbs that our "scout ants" found long ago, most of which are a lot smaller than Sun-in-a-can [98]. And the useable part of each resource is likely a small fraction of what's listed: the listed amounts are based on some unrealistic assumptions. For example, to get to 100% KT-I by going solar, we'd (by definition of KT-I) need to capture literally every joule of the Sun's energy reaching our planet. That means that the Earth would have to go black. It would have to be covered entirely with 100%-efficient solar panels. Covering even just dry land—all of it, with no room left for forests, marshes, fields,

---

[28] The resource, for this table, means both the limit on power, as a percentage of the KT-I level, and the limit on the total energy available for reaching KT-I level (again, as needed by percentage). Of the two numbers, the lower (limiting) one is listed.

bison, cows, wolves, you and me—with solar panels and their associated storage doesn't sound appealing, but that's the only currently available way to keep humanity going after 2100 without the fossils (which, again, will be gone by then anyways). My grandchildren and yours may live to see that, unless we do something about it first.

And it's all downhill from there. About 2% of the energy received from the Sun gets converted into wind. So even if we covered the planet – land and sea - with wind farms, we wouldn't get anywhere near KT-I. What's worse, we'd probably ruin the planetary climate machine long before getting to even 2%: wind is part of atmospheric circulation, whose job is (among other things) to redistribute heat and moisture around the Earth—and no one knows how much disruption of wind patterns can the Earth tolerate.

When the moisture carried by atmosphere falls somewhere high, and then flows downhill – this flow can also be used to generate useable, hydroelectric, power. Up to about 12% KT-I. But to do that you'd need to flood enormous territories – mostly in Asia, which happens to have by far the richest hydropower potential on the planet, as well as the highest population density. For example, the Three Gorges Dam yields 22.5GW – $1/1,000,000^{th}$ of the total hydroelectric potential of the planet – and, despite locating it downstream of steep gorges, with minimal flooded area, it still required relocating 1.3 million people. The costs (environmental and financial) of repeating this 1,000,000 times would be incalculable even if 1,000,000 equally advantageous locations were available—which they aren't.

It's even worse with biofuels. Solar panels are at least 400 times more efficient, per square meter, at converting the Sun's radiation into useable energy than corn. And when you take into account the additional energy needed to cultivate and irrigate and harvest the biomass, and then convert it into fuel, the EROI of biofuels appears to fall below 1. It's certainly below 2, which is nowhere near high enough to climb the Kardashev ladder. Besides, even if we covered all land on the planet entirely with corn farms, leaving no room for anyone or anything else, the fuel would still contain a mere 0.07% of KT-I energy. That way lies defeat.

Geothermal and tidal potentials have been estimated to be 47 TW and 3.7 TW, respectively. Not only are these numbers laughable in comparison with KT-I level (170,000 TW), but getting anywhere near these limits is really ill-advised from an environmental standpoint. Geothermal works by letting the heat stored inside the planet leak from the Earth's crust into the atmosphere. Release enough of that heat, and who knows what delicate balances you may ruin. Tidal takes energy from, duh, tides; do enough of that, and a lot of ocean dwellers may end up learning English just to lodge a collective complaint at the UN or whatever. And don't even think about taking energy from ocean circulation (a.k.a. the global conveyor belt). Just like atmospheric circulation, it's a critical part of our planet's climate machinery. You break it, you bought it.

What about nuclear? The only more-or-less "scalable" baseload primary production technology currently available to replace fossil fuels (without having to dam up whole continents) is uranium nuclear fission—with a nasty stipulation. It has to be done in breeder reactors, otherwise the game ain't worth the candle. Yep, the uranium breeders are the ones where all that nasty stuff for nuclear bombs is made. If you seriously mistrust 80% or more of your fellow earthlings (and they wholeheartedly respond in kind), you don't want them to run the breeders, since you don't want them to be able to nuke you when push comes to shove. And they don't want you to run the breeders either. Hence the paltry 0.4 TW nominal installed nuclear power capacity today, which covers about 2% of our current energy budget, or 1/425,000 of KT-I power. And increasing the capacity 425,000 times won't do anyone any good: the scalability of uranium-based nuclear power is, in fact, quite modest. Uranium is rare, especially at concentrations yielding reasonable EROI. All available uranium fuel would run out in about 1.5 months at KT-I level of usage.

So, the old reliable technologies (namely, fossils, terrestrial renewables, uranium-based nuclear) won't get us to KT-I. Neither would geothermal, tidal, or ocean currents. The power just ain't there (except for solar, if we converted the entire planet into a power plant). There's enough for powering down human civilization, not for powering it up.

Keeping up with the human appetite for energy is already proving to be a challenge for the energy sector based on the old mix. The allegedly mightiest economy on the planet allowed its creaky infrastructure to go into such disrepair that, inside a three-month period, three major disruptions (that we know of) happened, all affecting energy production and distribution, big time. First, the electric power grid failed in Texas, the top energy-producing state in the top energy-gobbling economy worldwide. The resulting damages were estimated at $600 per American or $6,500 per Texan [99]. Then a cyberattack forced the shutdown of the Colonial Pipeline, which delivers about 45% of the liquid fuel consumed in the Eastern part of the US from selfsame Texas [100]. Finally, a crack found in a structural beam of the Hernando De Soto Bridge forced a stoppage of all traffic across the bridge and on the mighty Mississippi river under it, where tank barges were carrying crude oil south to Gulf Coast refineries [101]. That happened in the same country that put people on the Moon only fifty years ago.

We're talking about a country that still, despite decades of proclaimed commitment to developing new energy sources, gets 80% of its energy from fossil fuels (and most of the rest from old nukes and hydro). We're talking about a country that still, despite a generations-long campaign to promote energy efficiency, uses three times more energy and 6.7 times more oil per capita than China. We're talking about a country that, in 2019, imported 94% of the solar panels it installed, despite tariffs that were supposed to protect domestic manufacturers. We're talking about a country whose "newest" nuclear reactor took forty-three years to build, whose most recent approval for a new site for nuclear power plant dates back two generations, whose nuclear power stations still use floppy disks for data and programs [102], and whose railroads run on software written in programming language developed in 1959. The business-as-usual scenario for what we habitually regard as the locomotive of the world economy doesn't look all that vigorous and dynamic. It actually looks hopeless enough for some folks to ask whether we in the West have triggered a self-destruct avalanche.

Meanwhile, we're officially getting off fossil fuels already. It seems impossible given that they provide over 80% of the energy we use today. Yet Denmark, Italy, Ireland, and New Zealand have, as of late 2020, banned domestic oil exploration. It doesn't mean they found a new energy source; it means they're relying on imports and hoping for a miracle. Denmark, in particular, used to be a net exporter of oil and gas; it's a net importer of both now.

BP, one of the oldest oil companies in the world, has cut its exploration team from 700 people to just 100 in a few years. That team was one of the most experienced in the business, stationed from Texas to Moscow. And BP is planning to cut oil output by 40% in preparation to leave that business altogether. When about 10% of oil reserves already found cannot be extracted at a profit, BP chose the easy way out: quit the thankless business of providing oil to a thankless world.

The International Energy Agency (IEA) declared 2021 to be "a critical year at the start of a critical decade for these efforts" [103]. The "efforts" they meant were not to find any new energy sources but to quit using whatever is left of Sun-in-a-can. In particular, no new oil and gas fields should be approved for development after 2021; and no new coal-fired power plants after 2021 can be "unabated," whatever that elastic term stands for.

This proposed winding-down of our main means of primary energy production could be a sign that the IEA has found a good replacement, or at least that it has made up its collective mind to do some serious looking. It isn't. R&D for primary energy sources with a KT-I level of scalability is conspicuously absent from the 224-

page report [104]. Thorium, liquid fluoride thorium reactors (LFTRs), tritium, lithium, deuterium, fusion, and space-based solar power (SBSP) aren't even mentioned. Naturally, proper virtue-signaling mantras had to be chanted: "Acceleration of this magnitude is clearly ambitious." That was a reference to the proposal to increase the worldwide budget for "demonstration projects"—no, not new primary energy production—from $25 billion to $90 billion. In a decade. Worldwide.

Meanwhile, humanity's GDP in 2020 was $84,000 billion, and we all remember that it wasn't a particularly good year. About $2,000 billion of that was for military expenditures. Another $2.5 billion was spent on the demonstration projects. The ambitious acceleration the IEA is talking about would bring the demonstration projects' total annual worldwide budget from 0.125% of the world's military budget to a whopping 0.45%. Which is still 0.011% of the world's GDP. And, again, not a penny of that goes to actually new primary production technologies.

> Unrecognized problems have no (deliberate) solutions.

Just for comparison, when we were serious about something—say, developing a nuclear bomb before Hitler had it—we managed to mobilize a full 1% of annual GDP on the project. Getting to the Moon took about 4% of annual GDP. Sure, it was spread over several years, and the GDP figures are for the country that actually was doing it rather than the whole world. But most folks in the whole world now are way wealthier than most Americans were during the early 1940s, when we fought Hitler, and even in the mid-1960s, when we raced to the Moon. A Senegalese person's chances today of living in a home with indoor plumbing are about the same as they were for an American during the Manhattan Project.

Just to see how little the IEA asks us to bet on ourselves, let's compare apples and apples. Let's compare the baseload capacity of the technology we're retiring with the baseload capacity of alternatives. Baseload is geek-speak for "reliable power": you flip the switch, and it's there. Baseloading solar and wind (the way we are doing it so far) means storage, and the currently available storage options cost the environment (and us) an arm and a leg. At the going rate of $125/kWh, $90 billion would, in ten years, pay for 0.72 TWh of battery storage, if battery storage is all it pays for. That's enough to store 0.0004% of the energy humanity used in 2020. We use this much energy in about two minutes.

This "demonstration project" scale demonstrates something; I just seriously doubt that the august IEA would want everyone to know that the utility-scale storage needed to baseload the renewables (wind and solar) is, for all practical purposes, nonexistent. And so is, for all intents and purposes, the massive industry needed to scale up the storage by a factor of, for starters, about 700. At the going rate, state-of-the-art storage technology would require 2,600% of worldwide GDP ($2,200,000 billion) to scale it up to twenty-four-hour storage capacity. To put it another way, to get twenty-four hours of storage in twenty years, we'd have to spend the equivalent of twenty years' of humanity's military budget—AFTER making storage about sixty times cheaper, per kWh. Does anyone seriously believe in, say, getting a Tesla car battery pack for $200? Or rerouting all military budgets in the world, to the last penny, into infrastructure for twenty years? And remember, we need both of these miracles, not just one.

And even these impressive feats would only take us so far. The massive increase in battery storage is projected to use up all assumed terrestrial reserves of lithium by 2100 (and actually proven reserves are about 1/5 of assumed, or "projected", reserves). Of course, there's a lot more lithium in the ocean, but getting it from seawater requires a lot of energy, with attendant environmental and other costs.

Of course, baseloading solar power could be achieved by building a global power grid instead of local storage. After all, at any given time, it's daytime on half the planet. However, the costs—environmental, political, and financial—of building such a global grid are not yet seriously and publicly discussed. At least not in the West, perhaps in part because it was the Chinese who first gave this idea a serious push in 2015 [105]. That same year, the Chinese started to build—and completed in just over three years—the biggest (so far) power transmission line in the world [106]. It's 3,300 km long and capable of transmitting 12 GW of power, and it cost $6 billion to build. Scaling this up to half the Earth's circumference and 15 TW would (if we assume that challenges of going across oceans and mountain ranges would cancel out any economies of scale) bring the cost to $44,000 billion. That's not 2,600% of 2020 world GDP. It's "just" 50%. It's no longer a pie in the sky—it's technically and financially very doable, as long as we can trust each other to sell energy the way we are already selling pretty much everything else: globally. By the simple expedient (just kidding) of learning to trust each other, we could achieve 98% savings: building a global grid instead of local storage is that much cheaper.

Problem solved? Not quite. Actually, it's nowhere near solved. There are the obvious political challenges of building the global grid and then continuing to upgrade it, for joint benefit of everyone (including the guys you seriously mistrust and dislike, and they respond in kind). There is the fact that covering the entire surface of the planet with solar panels may be objectionable to a variety of species that happen to live here, including our own. And then there's a real monster lurking in the shadows.

The big Kardashev show-stopper for a single-planet civilization is perhaps not even the primary source of energy. Instead, it's the very mundane problem of getting rid of waste heat.

Let's start with terrestrial solar. Solar panels' job is to absorb sunlight and convert it into usable electricity. Hence the panels, unlike whatever surface you put them on, have to absorb as much energy as they can. Albedo, the fraction of light reflected right back into space, goes down. The panels are dark because they have to be. Dark surfaces in the Sun are hotter than lighter ones, and if we install enough solar panels to intercept a significant part of solar radiation falling on Earth, i.e. go terrestrial solar in pursuit of a KT-I civilization, then the Earth is going to get darker. And hence hotter.

By how much? A rough estimate can be obtained from Stefan-Boltzmann law [98]. Assuming a transparent atmosphere (i.e. an albedo entirely determined by the surface of the Earth, with no contribution from clouds, greenhouse gases, dust, etc.), the "predicted" difference between the Earth now, which has an albedo of roughly 0.3, and the Earth covered with efficient solar panels with an albedo of almost 0 would be 24° C. Forget the 1.5° C predicted for the eventual effect of greenhouse gases. Forget the Paris agreement. Forget the IPCC reports. A 24° C increase is damn serious, folks. There certainly wouldn't be any continental glaciation left. Ocean levels would rise almost seventy meters. Much of Europe, Australia, Mexico, Brazil, Argentina, Southeast Asia, and China would be flooded, and so would the shores of North America and Africa. Mini-subs would dive to show tourists where London, Rome, Saint Petersburg, New York, Mumbai, Shanghai, Baghdad, Buenos Aires, Dakar and Cape Town once stood—like folks today dive on shipwrecks and Mediterranean ruins. Crocodiles would roam the marshes of Canada and Antarctica, like they did 50 million years ago. The few remaining polar bears and reindeer would have to be kept in air-conditioned zoos. It would take some doing to adapt to living in this world; and if the timeline of 300 years to KT-I is accurate, then that's breakneck speed for species evolution.

New species won't have time to emerge. You can bet your bottom dollar that the winners of this contest are among the familiar faces (like those primitive mammals that replaced dinosaurs). You just can't tell which. The transition's onset is not going to be quite as dramatic as the arrival of the space rock with its attendant global winter that wiped out the dinosaurs, but it probably won't go away in a few years, like that global winter did, either. Converting the planet into a giant solar farm is perhaps not a viable solution to our energy dilemma.

Figure 47 – Earth without continental glaciation.

And the biggest (by far) reason that solar panels are the "bad guy" in this scenario is the projected scale of use. Much of the energy absorbed by the solar panels, once used, dissipates—converts into waste heat—and eventually radiates back into space. Radiative cooling depends on the temperature difference, so if you have more energy to radiate and your receiver (namely, the Universe) is conveniently so darn big that it doesn't care, then your emitter gets hotter, whatever the origin of that extra energy. And your emitter, in case anyone forgot, is the planet we happen to live on.

Overheating is an equal-opportunity ohshit. Wherever the energy we spend to run our civilization comes from, upon use it ultimately converts into either potential energy of permanent structures we build – or waste heat. Whatever your primary source of KT-I energy, much of it eventually becomes heat. And if greenhouse gases, with their comparatively modest albedo effect, can redirect enough solar energy (that we aren't even using, for the most part) to heat the planet 1.5 degrees – then actually using 10,000 times more energy than we did in 2000 can't fail to significantly heat wherever this all happens. Again, independently of where this energy ultimately comes from.

So, if, instead of getting to Kardashev Type I by converting Earth into a giant solar power plant, we get the same amount of power some other way (for example, thorium fission, LENR, TOKAMAK, beaming solar energy from space for use down here on Earth), the result is bound to be the same. Much of the energy we generate will dissipate, convert to waste heat, and eventually radiate into space, but not before making it uncomfortably hot down here. Limiting Earth overheating to, say, 1.5° C, as intended by the Paris climate agreement, means that there's only so much more power we can afford to dissipate than we currently do—wherever this energy comes from. Getting rid of waste heat may, in a few generations, become the rate-limiting step in how much power we, as a civilization, can ever use. Unless we do something about it.

Now, finally, we get to the good news. There's something we can do about it, if we choose to. And getting hold of KT-I energy is nowhere near as hopeless as the options discussed so far suggest. Both parts of the problem – energy sourcing and managing waste heat – have potential solutions that might work. Sure, they're speculative, just as everything we have already achieved as a species was speculative before we achieved it. We're not pre-ordained to first stagnate and then to stick our collective tail between our legs and go back to the caves. We can still choose the stars. We may even actually get there.

Let's start with the waste heat management. The scary – really scary – heating by 24° C in just three centuries won't happen all at once. Most of it is going to happen by the end of that period. For the next 100+ years, our waste heat will still be a negligible factor (on a global scale) in Earth's climate. In a couple of centuries, though, the situation will perceptibly change—that is, assuming that we stay the Kardashev course. By 2220, waste heat would raise global temperatures by 2° C, and by 2320, temperatures would increase by another... 22° C. That's a big inconvenience, to put it mildly. Unless, again, we do something about it first. By then, our projected energy needs are going to be incomparably higher than they are now – but so will our ability to actually take mitigating measures. And so, no less importantly, will our ability to forecast the outcome of whatever measures we choose to take.

What can you do to mitigate overheating when things start really cooking? Three things come to mind: stop cooking altogether, take it elsewhere, or turn on the A/C.

Stopping altogether (a.k.a. the degrowth or devolution or the Empty Planet option, the neo-Luddite degrowth movement's favorite) is (besides the obvious possibility of exterminating everyone in a thermonuclear war for the remaining resources) just terminally boring. Maybe I'm dense, but for the life of me I just can't get the reasoning for spending any efforts on deliberately returning us to the state we fled millennia ago (the few of us who have had the misfortune to actually experience it for themselves report, rather convincingly, that it sucks). When folks fall from a civilized society into the Stone Age and then meet somebody who can take them back to civilization, they don't choose to stay in the caves. They choose us, the accelerating humanity.

How about planetary-scale A/C? As staggering as it sounds, it might actually be possible, to some extent. To begin with, waste heat originates somewhere, and in many cases, the origin is localized enough for interception. In an airplane, for example, useable power comes from the engine, and so does most waste heat (Figure 48). Urban heat islands, where heat sources are concentrated, are consistently 1° to 3° C warmer than their surroundings, and within those hot spots, there are even hotter spots—up to 10° C hotter. Some heat sources are ripe for targeted interception, before the heat dissipates. What can we intercept it with? Experiments with inexpensive metamaterials [107] [108] have shown that they can collect waste heat and radiate it up into space, especially if we place the cooling towers high above the surface so the heat we're trying to get rid of isn't captured in the atmosphere again. For example, if we manage to put radiators 25 km above ground, 97% of the Earth's atmosphere (and all the clouds) will be below them. And we may want to build giant structures like this for other reasons, as discussed later.

Figure 48 – Waste heat. Image courtesy of PilotBrent via pixabay.com.

Besides, there is what's (quite misleadingly) called "geoengineering". The term is usually applied to deliberately reflecting more of the Sun's energy before it ever hits the Earth surface, by spraying either reflective particles or seawater droplets in the air. The problem is that the reflective particles or droplets will shield the solar panels trying to collect the very sunlight that the particles and droplets are designed to reflect. Especially if the solar panels are everywhere. Engineering, geo- or otherwise, is supposed to begin with specs that actually make sense. In this particular case, it's not clear if we want to use solar radiation to replace fossil fuels or to reflect it the heck away.

Engineering also relies on models of what's going on when you press this button or that. People object to so-called geoengineering because we don't know all the consequences of spraying the particles or droplets. That's true enough. The trouble is, we also don't know all the consequences of NOT spraying them. Good intentions are a poor substitute for good models, if we want to be deliberate about what we do.

Good intentions and virtue signaling are a poor substitute for knowing what the heck one is doing, and that fully applies to any choice we make. Take, for example, option #2: taking our cooking elsewhere. At first glance, it sounds great. We get to keep Earth as a Nature preserve and a cultural heritage museum, with a limited maintenance crew and vacation opportunities for the rest of us, spending most of our time and energy elsewhere. The production of goods, which is where most of our energy is spent, already happens "elsewhere" for the most of us, so moving it off Gaia may not be as drastic a step as it seems at first glance. The "elsewhere" may actually be a world that could benefit from some extra warmth—Mars, for example. Or it could be a much closer celestial body like the Moon, which is easier to keep cool because it doesn't have an atmospheric blanket between it and space, so you'll have no trouble dumping your waste heat. It may be an O'Neill cylinder in orbit around the Earth (or not), potentially scaled up to a continent-sized habitable area, as proposed by NASA engineer Tom McKendree. It may eventually be a Dyson sphere around the Sun or some other star. It may even, someday, be a wandering habitat with its own autonomous power source like an artificial black hole, practically inexhaustible because it can use any mass swept along the way as fuel [109]. And, of course, if all there is between you and space is the thin wall of your habitat/spaceship, dumping waste heat is the least of your problems.

But I'm getting ahead of myself. The power investment required to build a modest-size black hole power station is on the order of 10^6 TW, which won't be available until centuries after reaching KT-I. We need to get there first, preferably still alive. How can we do that?

The technology of interest here is the primary energy production and distribution, a major physical infrastructure, which historically has been a rather conservative system. Just for comparison, only about 6% of the energy we use today is produced by technologies unknown three generations ago. If we keep up this lethargic pace, then what we can consider "estimated capacity reserves" three generations from today are energy sources that are already well past lab testing. Which we don't have much of. In other words, we either speed the heck up, or we're in deep you-know-what.

Well, we could get more energy – a lot more – from thorium than from uranium. By some estimates, we could get 400 to 600 times more, enough to power the KT-I transition. Not only is thorium three times more abundant than uranium, but its energy yield is over a hundred times higher, mostly because thorium is almost entirely consumable in the reactor, unlike uranium's 0.7% fissionable isotope. And thorium reactors don't produce bomb components, which is nice. Especially if you don't trust whoever uses the nuclear power not to blow you to smithereens. Thorium is the only well-known[29] terrestrial resource that can, in theory, last long enough to get us all the way to KT-I civilization and beyond.

There also appears to be quite a bit of thorium on the Moon. Remember, one of the solutions to our waste heat problems is producing and using energy elsewhere. The Moon appears to be a great candidate for the "elsewhere." We've found some local fuel deposits there without even really looking. Conveniently, the Moon also has no atmosphere to interfere with the disposal of the waste heat. Even more conveniently, half the Moon faces away from the Earth, and that's where the first known concentration of lunar thorium deposits (called the Compton-Belkovich Thorium Anomaly) was found. So, if we burn the thorium right there, and produce the energy and use it and generate waste heat and radiate that heat into space on the far side of the Moon, directed away from the Earth. Neat, right? The biggest downside to this option is that right down here on Earth there's an estimated 16 million tons of a mineral, monazite, that contains 6% to 7% of thorium phosphate, and nothing like that has been found on the Moon yet. Understandably so: only twelve people have been to the Moon so far, and only one of them, Dr. Harrison Schmitt, was a trained geologist. Meanwhile, the surface area of the Moon is almost as big as that of Asia, which took lots of people a long time to explore in detail.

The trouble with thorium is that we don't yet have a reactor to burn it efficiently. After more than fifty years of half-hearted efforts to build one, all we got was a few pilot tests. India may be the first country to build a thorium reactor ready for commercialization, in part because it has the world's richest proven reserves of thorium, and in part because the nuclear technology embargo (after India detonated its first uranium bomb in the so-called "Smiling Buddha" tests in 1974) forced it to largely rely on indigenous resources in nuclear technology development. Not surprisingly, India treats its thorium know-how and thorium deposits as a matter of national security, and it may not be inclined to share either with the 82.5% of humans who happen to live elsewhere. Although, to be fair, a Dutch thorium power development consortium [110] is about as tight-lipped about their work as Indians. Besides the less-than-aggressive schedule (they plan to launch a pilot plant in... 14

---

[29] As in, reactors capable, in principle, of using thorium as fuel have been in commercial use for decades—and even better, more efficient options have been studied theoretically and tested experimentally.

years, in 2035) and names of participating organizations, you won't learn much about it from public sources. And all that's reliably known about the Chinese 2-MW LFTR pilot reactor being constructed at Wuwei in the Gobi Desert, is that it's a 2 MW LFTR pilot reactor being constructed at Wuwei in the Gobi Desert.

The idea that energy is a security matter isn't lost on others either. For example, the Indonesian Defense Ministry hired an American company called Thorcon International to build a 3.5 GW thorium-based facility [111]. Importantly, Indonesia is a developing country, and "developing" means, among other things, that most of the folks who live there share an upward-moving feeling. About 80% of Indonesians are in favor of nuclear power.

Meanwhile, another American company, Clean Core Thorium Energy, aims to commercialize ANEEL, thorium-based fuel cartridges, for use in existing pressurized heavy water reactors (forty-nine PHWRs, or Candu-type units, are currently in use in seven countries, from Canada to China). ANEEL cartridges are being developed by Texas A&M University in collaboration with US DOE [112]. Somebody somewhere must have gotten the message: providing humanity with thorium energy could be a lucrative business. PHWRs may not be as good at burning thorium fuel as LFTRs, but they have the distinctive advantage of actually existing and being hooked up to the grid. And when it comes to getting serious about thorium, that argument is hard to beat.

There's an even more abundant energy source than thorium, and it's also right down here on Earth. It's seawater. The oceans contain quite a bit of deuterium, the heavy isotope of hydrogen; and if we burn it in a fusion reaction with tritium, the even heavier isotope of hydrogen, we can get a whopping 4×10^{11} TWy (Terawatt-years) of energy. That's 50,000 times more than we can get from terrestrial reserves of thorium. That's as much energy as the Sun shines on Earth in 2.4 million years, longer than modern humans have been around as a species.

> After all is said and done, a hell of a lot more is said than done.

The trouble is that we can't do that yet. For starters, we (again) don't have a reactor to burn it in. There are two ways of doing this: "hot" (plasma) fusion, where nuclei smash into each other energetically enough to fuse together, or "cold" fusion (low-energy nuclear reactions, LENR), where fusion is catalyzed by some suitable structure, say a nickel electrode or even a cavitating bubble, to happen at a much lower temperature. At the moment, the proponents of hot fusion are much better at deriding cold fusion and burning through a lot of cash, government ($65 billion) and private ($1.5 billion) than they are at delivering the cheap and abundant energy promised three generations ago. Some of the scolding of "cold fusion" is deserved: there has been a considerable deal of hype and little to show for it so far. Unfortunately, this fully applies to the hot fusion track as well, especially if one considers the vast amounts of money, human talent, and political capital spent on it to date, which may at least partly account for the hot-fusion guild's numbers and the members' solidarity against competition. The gray-haired TOKAMAK and its offspring, ITER, are the best-ever demonstration of what happens when you take an engineering project and give it to scientists to manage. Remember, answering the question "How do we make the damn contraption do what it's made to do?" is the business of engineering; answering the question "How does Nature work?" is the business of science. Long story short, it looks like some fresh approaches are called for if we want fusion—hot or cold—to actually deliver energy this side of eternity.

Another problem with hot fusion is that we don't have enough lithium lying around in convenient heaps. Yep, here we go again. Lithium pops up quite frequently when we discuss energy, be it battery storage, where the electrochemical properties of lithium make it hard to replace, or the primary production in fusion reactors. In fusion, you need lithium to make tritium, the other half of the fusion fuel. Tritium is rare in Nature, but it's readily obtained by irradiating lithium with neutrons, for example the very neutrons coming out of the D-T fusion reactor. And, as far as terrestrial resources are concerned, lithium is the limiting resource for tritium production. Besides the paltry 80 MT of estimated deposits, digging it up from Earth's crust is prohibitively expensive in terms of overall EROI, not to mention environmental impacts and actual costs. With seawater, it's a lot better. The estimated supply is 230,000 MT, and it can readily be extracted with cheap and abundant electricity. But by the time we use up all the lithium in the seawater, we'll only make enough tritium to burn about 1.5% of the deuterium in that same seawater. So it's not 50,000 times better than thorium; it's "only" 800 times better.[30]

---

[30] Boron is the other co-fuel of hydrogen (the regular one, not deuterium) in hot fusion reactions. About 1,000 MT of boron is available on Earth, mostly in Turkey. But on an atom-per-atom basis, there's more than 800 times less boron available to burn in an H-B reactor than lithium for a D-T reactor. We're back to a terrestrial, thorium-sized resource, rather than orders-of-magnitude above that level, as we would be with a D-T reaction. The D-T energy yield is considerably higher, and so is the cross-section of the reaction (its chances of actually happening), and the ignition temperature is an

Deuterium/tritium fusion, even just from terrestrial sources, can get us to KT-I, and beyond. Way beyond. Enough to build a space-faring civilization with access to incomparably more lithium—and everything else—than we have down here on Earth.

However abundant terrestrial thorium and deuterium/lithium fuels are, the energy they can provide is still nothing to write home about – that is, compared to what our star reliably emits every day. The Sun could power 2 trillion KT-I civilizations (or just one KT-II). All we have to do is to get off our collective behind and collect it. It's all there, day in and day out, most of it passing us by and doing no one any good. And it won't do anyone any good, until someone decides what "good" stands for.

Our friendly neighborhood furnace sends energy every which way, and only 0.00000005% of that ever hits such a vanishingly small target as Earth (vanishingly small, that is, if you look from the Sun's surface, which is ill advised). That's all the energy it takes to qualify as KT-I. We can get a good deal more than the 0.00000005%—that is, move beyond KT-I level – if we get up there and build a big enough system to collect it. That's space-based solar power (SBSP).

The good news is that critical parts of this technology – solar panels, reflectors, converters - are already in widespread commercial use down here on Earth, and mighty market forces are engaging human creativity to squeeze inefficiencies out of them. Other parts of SBSP, the subsystem for beaming the energy from a plant up there to users down here, are now being developed and tested by folks who do national (and international) security for a living. There are two projects underway (that we know of): one is run by the US Air Force [113], the other by the US Navy

---

order of magnitude lower. All of that makes the energy breakeven point easier to reach for D-T fusion than for H-B fusion. Nevertheless, TAE Technologies, the one fusion outfit pursuing the H-B option, appears to be the best-funded one. Do the—and their investors—know something that we don't?

Another possibility is D-^{3}He fusion, but the hoops one has to jump to get power out of that are even greater. First of all, the energy barrier you have to overcome to light up the reaction is higher (and the reaction rate is lower) than for a D-T reaction. Secondly, the nearest sizeable source of fuel is on the Moon, and the concentration of ^{3}He in Moon rocks is very low, so the energy content per ton of rock is comparable with coal. Except coal is mined on Earth. Imagine the EROI if all the gargantuan mining machinery built down here had to be then shipped up there.

[114]. The US Navy, by the way, is one of the few outfits in the world that can afford to ruffle academic feathers by doing serious research on stuff career academics wouldn't touch with a ten-foot pole—and it's revitalizing fundamental research into LENR [115]. Meanwhile, a Pentagon task force has recently shown a healthy skepticism about the Pentagon's own decades-old skepticism about UFOs [116]. Somebody somewhere must have gotten the message: ignorance is bliss only 'til it blows up in your face.

Back to SBSP. The "SB" part – the massive launch capability needed to actually get stuff to where it is supposed to work – is the furthest one from implementation on a meaningful scale. Let's ponder how massive this actually has to be and what that entails.

The lightest structures ever imagined for the space-based solar stations push the scales at about 1 kg/kW of output [117]. The kilo in orbit has the energy of 33 MJ (just over 9 kWh), and it takes the 1 kW it collects less than ten hours to add up to that much energy. The EROI of space-based solar looks great, and so does the availability of the resource. The trouble is that it's up there, and we're down here, at the bottom of our gravity well—and so are all our manufacturing facilities and the raw materials we know how to use. We're busy burning up whatever concentrated sunlight has trickled down to our pit over countless millennia. And the only way we have managed so far to stick our collective head above the rim of that pit was by using the biggest, most expensive pogo stick our species has learned to build so far: the chemical rocket.

If you want to get to space today, you need to climb atop a tower of many millions of parts—built by the lowest bidder and loaded with enough explosive to flatten a small town—and pray that it wobbles its way into orbit rather than exploding into a spectacular fireball. Miraculously, most of the time it does. Burning most of its weight and shedding most of the rest as spent stages, modern rockets usually get payloads to orbit.

The price, though, is outrageous. Partly it's due to the laughable market size. All the payloads we need to orbit so far (or can afford to, at the going rate) can be handled with just over 100 launches per year, worldwide. The other side of the coin is the Achilles heel of chemical rockets: most of the stuff going up is fuel, oxidant, and gadgets to combine them in a more or less controllable fashion. Not the payload. So getting to the (scandalous anywhere else) 7% energy efficiency is a real achievement when you're trying to go places in a chemical rocket.

There's so much sunlight up there, though, that SBSP can afford the inefficiencies, just like the oil and gas industry in the beginning could afford to be ridiculously wasteful. Even using a 7%-energy-efficient rocket, the invested energy would still be recouped by space-based solar in less than a week. And with economies of scale kicking in, who knows how much the launch costs can be reduced? Elon Musk, who probably knows more about it than both of us put together (unless you're Elon Musk), believes that $10/kg to be achievable [118]. At this rate, even factoring in a 7%-efficient delivery system and a 30%-efficient conversion and transmission, a space-based solar power station would pay for its launch costs in a month, selling electricity at $.05/kWh. On the other hand, at the current price of $2,700 per kilo, it's over twenty years (even longer if you add the costs of hardware and ground facilities), which possibly exceeds the maintenance-free lifetime of an orbiting power plant.

Of course, if the current scandalous price and the laughable market size of chemical rocketry sound like a chicken-and-egg problem, that's because they are. The road to space-based solar is paved with good intentions, ambitious declarations, position papers and feasibility studies. In one instance, in 2009, an SBSP company, Solaren, even managed to get a contract to sell 1.7 GW of power beamed from orbit to a major California utility, PG&E, starting in 2016. Needless to say, it turned out to be a dud. A 1.7 GW facility would weigh, optimistically, 1,700 metric tons, requiring seventeen launches of Saturn V-class vehicles. At the time, the estimated price for these launches was around $1 billion (estimated, because no one was actually building Saturn V-class vehicles in 2009). So orbiting the power plant hardware alone, ignoring the cost of the hardware and the ground facilities, would cost $10,000 per kilowatt, not the $10/kW you'd get if you share Musk's optimism. For comparison, a power station burning natural gas costs around $900/kW to build. Rooftop solar costs around $3,000/kW without storage and about $6,000 with storage. We're spending about 10% of global GDP on energy already, and investment in the energy sector amounts to almost a quarter of that, nearly $2 trillion a year. That's what powers the doubling of our energy consumption every twenty-five years: we choose to invest in our future. At $900/kW, we can afford our expansion; at $10,000/kW, the same investment might buy just enough new capacity to match the rate of retirement of old generation plants.

But the order-of-magnitude difference between the low-hanging fruit everyone is used to and the really big, nutritious pie-in-the-sky is shrinking as we speak. As of 2020, SpaceX's going launch rate of $2,700/kg is on the verge of making SBSP competitive with terrestrial solar, which is experiencing explosive growth. Things are looking up for SBSP. We can certainly afford pilot projects, and more and more folks come to think that what we can't afford is to NOT run the pilot projects. Of course, in order to replace Sun-in-a-can on a competitive basis and to account for all ground facilities and hardware fabrication costs, we need further economies of scale on the launch side of the equation. And there's plenty of room for these: no one in their sane mind would invest in developing space-based solar technology to then quit using it after the first 1.7 GW facility is online. And then, long before the $10/kg Musk is talking about, it'll be cheaper to have a kilowatt of generating capacity in orbit than on your roof.

But economies of scale are not the only things scale can deliver. Others may be downright unpleasant. How much of a scale are we talking about, and what could go wrong if we go up that far in scale?

For starters, to replace the 15 TW we were using back in 2000, we'd need to shove at least 15,000,000 metric tons of stuff into orbit. So far, in the sixty-four years since Sputnik, we managed about 0.06% of that. The mightiest rockets we have ever built could handle about 100 tons of payload a pop, so we're talking about 150,000 launches of the super-heavies: Saturn-V class Moon rockets. So far, we have just fourteen under our collective belt: thirteen Saturn V's and one Energia (the other launch of Energia failed to orbit the payload). The 135 space shuttle launches don't quite count, since the main engines were part of the "payload" and the actual payload delivered to LEO and left there was under thirty tons.

To reach KT-I via the rocket-based SBSP route, we'd need 1,500,000,000 superheavy launches. That's more super-heavies than the number of cars we currently have on the planet—and cars, tiny compared to Saturn Vs, are believed to have a major environmental impact already. In the few minutes of its fiery ascent, a super-heavy uses about forty times more chemical energy than a car does in its lifetime. The costs of scaling up SBSP this way – forget the money, I am talking about all kinds of environmental impacts now—are going to be staggering. For example, it's been pointed out [67] that retired StarLink satellites will put more alumina particles in the Earth's atmosphere than all meteorites and volcanoes together (with at least a theoretical possibility of affecting the Earth's albedo enough to trigger a snowball Earth effect) – and that's at the relatively modest launch rate of forty launches per year of the relatively modestly-sized Falcon-9. Imagine how bad it's going to get if we try to do that many Falcon-9 launches in a day—for 70 years?

Instead of retired StarLink satellites, the debris would likely include parts of upper stages that, in these quantities, will make LEO an impassable shooting gallery, with lots of shrapnel eventually falling back on Earth and/or burning in the upper atmosphere – unless deorbited somehow in one piece. The environmental (and navigational) consequences of increasing launch frequency by three orders of magnitude are hard to predict. Solid fuel boosters release alumina particles, and carbon-based fuels produce soot and other products that may interact with the atmosphere (for example, the ozone layer) in ways that we know nothing about. Even hydrogen-LOX, the cleanest rocket fuel/oxidizer combination, leads to a concentrated release of thousands of tons of hot water vapor along the rocket's trajectory, which no one has ever tried to do anywhere near hourly. We just don't know how the Earth's atmosphere is going to react–our atmospheric models are nowhere near good enough to answer questions like this (and no, you can't assume that just because we can't confidently detail the environmental impacts right this moment, there won't be any. We have stepped on that particular rake a few times already).

Even if we launch a super-heavy every four hours until we hit 150,000 launches (or a Falcon 9–class vehicle once every forty minutes for a total of a million launches), we will spend more than seventy years launching just enough solar panels for 15 TW of energy, matching our 2000 CE energy consumption. By the time we are done, our needs will have doubled at least four times already since 2000, so this heroic effort and all this dust wouldn't get us even close to catching up. If we want to get to KT-I, we'll need another, non-rocket way of getting our stuff up there. Something that's clean, cheap, reliable, and routine.

The good news is that it's likely doable. Not easy, mind you, but doable—if we choose to do it. The concept of shooting payload into space without any rockets predates Sputnik by some 270 years: Newton's cannonball was proposed by, you guessed it, Isaac Newton, in his 1687 *Philosophiæ Naturalis Principia Mathematica*. In 1865, the idea was popularized by Jules Verne in *From the Earth to the Moon: A Direct Route in 97 Hours, 20 Minutes*. By 1918, the Paris Gun fired shells weighing more than 100 kg with a muzzle velocity of 20% of Earth's orbital velocity. By then, engineers knew where the artillery approach fell short—quite literally—of human-rated space launch technology. What was way too short was the (gargantuan) barrel. Its muzzle was well within the dense lower part of the atmosphere, which rapidly robbed the hypersonic projectile of its velocity once fired. And the projectile had to be robust enough to withstand an insane acceleration within the barrel (forget riding one to the Moon – by the time you and I exited the bore of the Verne gun, we'd be flatter than a sheet of paper). There must be a better way up, especially if we wanted people to ride it.

There is. In the mid-1970s and early 1980s, Anatoly Yunitskiy, Keith Lofstrom, Paul Birch, and others suggested several versions of dynamically supported megastructures to launch payloads to orbit. Lofstrom's proposed launch loop, Birch's orbital rings, and Yunitskiy's SpaceWay General Planetary Vehicle are all based on a hypersonic rotor magnetically levitated in an evacuated stator. By "evacuated," I don't just mean that there aren't any people there; there's no air there, either. The huge structure follows Earth's curvature, so when the rotor exceeds orbital speed, it creates lift, and the whole structure lifts itself like Baron Munchausen and his horse. All you have to do, then, is magnetically couple a payload-carrying carriage to the rotor, and, voilà, you can launch payloads as fast as you can pump kinetic energy into the rotor, as cheaply as you can buy that energy. Except, of course, that you won't buy the energy. Once operational, this structure would produce so much energy by solar panels hung on it above the clouds (and store that energy in the rotor until needed) that you'd generate extra revenue by selling power to the grid.

Each of these systems could have been built from materials available forty years ago. Each could deliver payloads three orders of magnitude cheaper than the cheapest chemical rocket flying today, if enough payload was available—which isn't a problem for SBSP or for habitats and factories in orbit.

Using dynamically supported megastructures for non-rocket space launch requires dimensions of thousands of kilometers (Earth curvature, remember?), rotor speeds in excess of 8 km/s, and power stations in excess of a 10-GW rated capacity. While there is nothing technically impossible about it, in forty years no one has committed the enormous resources necessary to build something on this scale from scratch. We have a chasm between status quo and cheap, reliable, routine access to space. And no one has taken the leap to cover that in one huge multi-billion-dollar step. Sure, placing lots of solar panels—and the facilities that use that energy and conveniently dispose of the waste heat—in orbit sounds like a good solid justification, but space-based solar and rocket-free launch seem to critically depend on each other for economic viability. So we really need to step across two chasms, not one. So far, it was too much.

There might be a way around that dilemma, though. A series of scaled-down, dynamically supported structures, each with its own commercialization potential, can be used as steppingstones to a full-scale launch-capable system. The Space Dome could be the last steppingstone before a space launch–capable megastructure. A Space Dome (Figure 62, page 477) is a dynamically supported carrier structure for suborbital solar power collection, and its rotors double as energy storage. Reaching into the stratosphere, Space Domes could also support waste-heat-disposal hardware (cooling towers); and once space-based solar becomes a primary energy source, they could also support the rectennae for receiving the power beamed from orbit to Earth.[31]

Some folks seem to be taking this seriously. In particular, the Chinese, who badly want energy (76% of all renewable energy patent applications worldwide in 2017 originated in China). The China Academy of Launch Vehicle Technology recently announced a plan to launch five crewed expeditions to the red planet between 2033 and 2043 [119]. They also hinted at the development of non-rocket-launch capabilities as part of that effort. The recently unveiled 600 km/h maglev train developed in China could provide a lot of expertise—and experts—for developing non-rocket-launch approaches based on magnetically-levitated dynamic structures. Meanwhile, the China Academy of Space Technology plans to develop a megawatt-scale pilot solar power station in orbit as a pilot project by 2035 [120] as a prelude to building a commercial, gigawatt-scale SBSP station in orbit by 2050 [121]. Together, these begin to sound like a serious bid to start harvesting sunlight in space.

Getting up there to collect the energy, or anything else, costs energy, so you need to invest some. Nothing ventured, nothing gained. And yet the richest country on the planet in 2020 invested 0.1% of its GDP to explore space, where 99.99999999999...% of the resources we need to go forth are. That's so close to nothing as to make no difference. Is the West leaving the development path to the folks in the developing world? Have we lost the drive that got us to the Moon?

"Energy" doesn't just mean terawatt-years (or dollars). These common, useful, and convenient metrics miss the most important civilization-building form of energy: human drive. The self-fulfilling prophecy of a better tomorrow. Imagining a future and taking a chance to actually build it, with no time machine to tell you how it's going to turn out. All we reliably know is that it's not going to turn out the way you imagined if you never try. Like Peter Thiel once told Mark Zuckerberg, "The biggest risk you can take is not taking any risk." Risk-aversion (a.k.a. the refusal to make decisions until they can be rationally justified) is the cost of hubris: the delusion that our current prosperity and security can continue forever kinda on their own. This refusal to take a risk, in a world where decisions have to be made with incomplete information, itself cannot be rationally justified. It puts the power

---

[31] Having support structures reaching, say, 25 km up in the sky would open a lot of opportunities. For example, we could put railguns or Spinlaunch systems above 97% of the atmosphere to deorbit space junk or hang a lot of antennae to improve communications. We could even find a way to build airports at airliners' cruising altitude. If your town had a Space Dome, what else could you use it for?

to make decisions for you in the hands of less risk-averse folks, and they have their own worldview and agenda and priorities. So risk-aversion is a risk even for the risk-averse individual.

But an individual or tribe or state or empire isn't alone. They have competition. And their successful competitors share their most valuable resource: the momentum of human drive for a better tomorrow. Winners show others that what they did was possible.

A global civilization like ours has no local competition, which makes risk-aversion an existential threat. Our drive to keep going has to come from within. Denying ourselves the resources and experiences and opportunities and knowledge of the rest of the Universe and locking ourselves up on the one planet we grew up on puts a glass ceiling over humanity. And it's no one's job to show us that it's possible to do better, which is what the winners show losers. As a global civilization, we're on our own.

If we sell ourselves short, we have no one else to blame. No one but us decides if we own this place or just rent it. The owners of this planet or this Solar system or the Milky Way galaxy have a right to do what they think is right and an obligation to choose responsibly. Renters have neither. Owners do things. Renters have things done to them. Renters can afford to have no free will. Owners can't.

Owners choose what they want the place to be like, then they try to make it happen. Owners imagine what "good" stands for and compare reality with that ideal. If whatever they are doing makes things "better" – closer to their imaginary ideal—they continue. If it makes things "worse," then they change the way they do things. Owners play God, in their own domain—big or small—by deciding which way is up. Human drive, the elusive form of energy that we haven't yet learned to quantify or to account for in our forecasts, brings a new force to the whole process of evolution: a purpose.

Being deliberate about something means that you take the responsibility for the outcome. That stands for three things: 1) the stakeholders agree on goals and acceptable costs, 2) the stakeholders invest in learning how the system in question would respond to proposed inputs, and 3) the stakeholders admit that their models are only an abbreviation of reality, and they set up ongoing feedback systems to let them know if things don't work as planned so they can correct the course.

A purposeful, directional, deliberate motion quickly overtakes aimless, random drift, which may be good—or bad—for whatever is moving. The goal could be chosen well, or it could be a mistake. It can be an oasis or a mirage, and without a time machine, you won't know which until you get closer. And even for a well-chosen goal, your efforts to move in the chosen direction could take you there—or not, much the way that swimming against a rip current won't take you to the shore. You can exhaust your energy and drown in full view of coveted terra firma.

There's perhaps an evolutionary pressure for some form of balance. Insufficiently ambitious civilizations randomly wobble around home, never venture far, exhaust local resources, and wither away. Arrogant civilizations shoot in some direction that seems attractive at the time, fail to notice warning signs and correct course, and wither away too.

Is there natural selection for the ability to tell which way's up and to actually get there? What does the cryptic "meek" stand for in "the meek shall inherit the earth"? My hypothesis, for what it's worth, is that the meek who will inherit the Earth (and perhaps a lot more) are not meek as in "docile." They're meek as in "humble." Their ambitions are high, so success isn't guaranteed, and they know that full well, and they're okay with that. Risk-takers know what risk means: you don't get to succeed every time. They know they can, and often will, screw up, but they're ambitious and confident enough to keep trying. Learning to do better next time.

The meek know they might screw up, so they keep comparing their rational accomplishments with their irrational ideal. And if they don't like where they're going—or how much it costs them to move at all—they eventually change direction.

If you change direction too often, then your motion becomes aimless and random. You put a glass ceiling over your growth: the growth of your domain, your knowledge, and the resources available to you, will all be limited by what happens in your immediate neighborhood. After consuming high-EROI local resources, your civilization shrivels and dies off.

But if we refuse to reassess, and possibly change, direction for too long—we could be stubbornly moving the wrong way. There are no gas stations ahead. Our energy investment in moving that way won't produce an opportunity to refuel and go forth. Or we could be spending too much energy fighting our way through mud, and we might not have enough in the tank to reach the next gas station, even if it's there. If we fail to change direction when we should, then we will waste the resources we have today without getting them back with EROI interest. That way lies defeat. Is there a balance to be found? And if so, how do we find it? Is there an optimal way for us to be deliberate about our future?

Perhaps not. For starters, the optimum is likely different for different scales. What looked like deliberate action to cavemen would perhaps look like Brownian motion at our zoom level.

Besides, if by "optimal" we mean "guaranteed best," then we'd need a time machine to find out before it's too late. For example, there are ways of dealing with waste heat, but they're all highly speculative at the scale required. So are the ways to expand our habitat or to provide the energy for humanity at KT-I and beyond. We haven't tried building a KT-I civilization, and we've never seen one in action, so it will remain speculative until we try, like everything else we have once done for the first time.

What's different this time is, again, the scale. The massive resource investments needed to have even a shot at succeeding won't happen accidentally. The time when being lucky was an adequate substitute for being good and ambitious is over. We have run out of freebies. We will have to make the decision to invest in ourselves while we still can, or the decision will be out of our hands.

Let's take a notorious example: the electrification of the American fleet of road vehicles. As of right now, 92% of the energy used by the American transportation industry comes from fossil fuels (another 5% comes from corn ethanol, whose benefits to the environment are dubious at best). Still, the minuscule proportion of electric vehicles on American roads is a blessing in disguise: if every American adult owned an EV and tried to even trickle-charge it at home overnight, the current electric grid would crash. And long-haul trucks, delivery vans, city buses, and ambulances can't afford to sit idle all night watching paint dry—sorry, batteries charge—they have to keep moving. Two-thirds of American road vehicles in 2050 are supposed to be EVs, but they will be quite useless without some serious upgrades to all components of the country's electric power infrastructure. The generating capacity will have to double [122]; utilities will have to invest between $1,700 and $5,800 in grid upgrades per EV (or about $1.4 trillion) to charge as many EVs as the number of vehicles on US roads today, assuming zero growth; extra personnel will have to be hired and trained for these efforts; materials and equipment will have to be acquired; and projects will have to be managed—all by utility companies that haven't handled an expansion of this magnitude in generations, if ever. The institutional knowledge to do this will have to be built from the ground up – there are no ready-to-go organizations able to handle this, they'd have to be created.

To put these power infrastructure upgrades in perspective, priority-wise, let's run some cost comparisons. Accommodating only as many vehicles as there are on the road now—without any growth—would require an infrastructure investment equivalent to the combined costs of the Korean and Vietnam Wars. The Apollo program that got us to the Moon was ten times cheaper than this. The Manhattan

Project, the desperate race to build a nuclear bomb before Hitler did, cost seventy times less.

Providing N-95 masks during the pandemic required investing $1 million per mask-making machine making enough N95s for 30,000 people or so. So providing American-made N-95 masks for everyone in the US would have required an investment of about $11 billion, 120 times less than the EV charging infrastructure will cost. That investment in the US didn't happen. Funds were indeed quickly invested in production ramp-up, institutional knowledge and supply chains were quickly built from scratch, and the masks were quickly manufactured, but elsewhere. Specifically, and unsurprisingly, in China. American businesspeople, meanwhile, wouldn't bet on their businesses without somebody guaranteeing long-term orders [72].

The mask crisis was a reminder that taking chances on ourselves is the only way we know how to stay competitive in the long run. And for those slow on the uptake, life keeps providing more crises to learn from. For example, now that humanity more or less chose to quit, in forty-seven years, using the energy sources that have powered our acceleration since the dawn of the Industrial Revolution, we're officially in a crisis. The choice of timing, by the way, was only tentatively deliberate: the can of concentrated sunlight was running dry anyway, ready or not. But by anticipating the inevitable, perhaps by a few decades, we (gingerly) introduce some purposefulness in the process. We – well, some of us—are no longer content to have things happen to us. Some of us, consciously or otherwise, are sending a signal to anyone who will listen: it's time we learned to steer this spaceship Earth of ours. Might as well: whatever happens, we are the ones who will end up paying for the outcome anyways.

Winston Churchill once advised to "never let a good crisis go to waste." A crisis is a learning opportunity, a chance to do things better. What can we learn from this one?

The value of time, for starters. In Churchill's words, "Action this day." The choice – forth to the stars, back to the caves, split between the two, or something else entirely – won't be available to us for long. The human race is a race against the clock. There are ticking clocks on our wall: peak oil, peak fresh water, peak phosphate, peak indium and lithium, peak platinum and hafnium. But the loudest clock on that wall is peak humanity. The human population is predicted to peak (although when and at what level is anyone's guess, see Figure 49), and with the recent downward trend of individual intelligence in post-industrial societies (and fertility rates falling well below replacement in those same countries, which also happen to be the most affluent, best educated, and most democratic ones), the sum total of our mental powers may have peaked already. Given the digital manipulation of public opinion, we may also be past peak democracy. (The pandemic didn't help. As of this writing, more than two-thirds of the world rolled back their democratic freedoms.) [123]. And leaving a few footprints on the Moon may have been the peak of our expansion as a species. Creating general artificial intelligence seems to be our peak ambition, whereupon we will offer our imperfect—and allegedly outdated— selves to the Singularity's dubious mercy. Our peak imagination, back in the 1960s and '70s, drew us pictures of Stanford tori and Dyson spheres and O'Neill cylinders and space elevators and terraformed planets and space settlers traveling to distant stars.

Each of the "peaking" tangible resources has been, prior to us humans finding use for it, just another kind of dirt. What makes peak humanity the most ominous of the peaks is that all other "peaks" are contingent. They are contingent on us humans being unable to find a replacement for a known terrestrial resource, like we had one day created that resource out of dirt. Sun-in-a-can may be Nature's pass for sentient life forms to hop aboard the train to Mt. Olympus; but the can isn't bottomless, so obtuse species that don't learn from their crises miss the train.

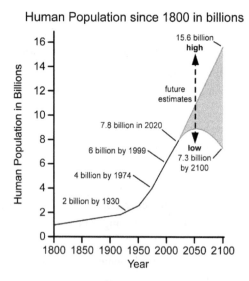

Figure 49 – Peak humanity: it's difficult to make predictions, especially about the future.

The peak is where the sum total of old ways is zip: titanic forces act in opposite directions, in such a perfect balance that you stand still. It's the moment of uncertainty, a tipping point: which way you're gonna move depends on factors that used to be safe to ignore. Things that used to be negligible compared to the ones you're used to, become very significant all of a sudden. New factors and connections kick in. Peak is an unfamiliar and uncomfortable territory. It's a place where we have to make irrational decisions: the reductionist models that used to rationally guide us don't work anymore.

That's (a big part of) the reason why I think that peak humanity is by far the most serious of the "peak" problems we face. We humans make the irrational decisions that get us out of tight spots, where prior experience is no longer a reliable guide. We humans try out new things, and in doing so, often fail—but sometimes spectacularly succeed, typically by making yet another kind of useless dirt into yet another valuable resource. We humans have a baby boom amid still-smoldering ruins left by a horrible war, when we feel – without any evidence – that our kids may get a chance at a better life. We invest energy of optimism in giving births, education, social skills to our children – and this investment pays off with interest in humanity moving upward, making optimism a self-fulfilling prophecy.

And the same feedback loops work the other way, too. Pessimism and cynicism aren't heritable traits, not in the long run. It's humans who choose not to have kids when they quit feeling hopeful—despite, objectively, living in comfort, security, and prosperity in the wealthiest countries on twenty-first century Earth. Decades later, sociologists will still be arguing about what prompted folks to make the reproductive choices they have made. Humans, meanwhile, don't wait for the experts to tell them what to do. We feel the trend—things moving up or stagnating and receding—and make our choices accordingly. We decide, irrationally, which way's up.

Throughout history, growth—economic and otherwise—and the human condition have been closely linked. So have stagnation and social retreat. Of course, in our interdependent, intertwined world, linear causality is a caricature of what's actually going on, so one can always find exceptions to any historical "rule," if exceptions are what they're looking for. In the twentieth century, the correlation between economic growth and social progress—democracy, liberty, and tolerance—was broken at least twice. First, the Great Depression in the United States didn't coincide with a retreat of democracy, liberty, or tolerance. If anything, there was an advance in all measures of social progress in the US during these economically troubled times. Second, the demise of what remained of democracy, liberty, and tolerance in the USSR in the 1930s didn't coincide with economic retreat or even stagnation. If anything, it was a period of lightning-speed industrial development. So do these exceptions to the "rule" invalidate the rule, or do they instead just show that measuring "growth" by GDP has some serious limitations, as does any unidimensional projection of a multidimensional process? Maybe it's the 3-D Social Progress Index (SPI) [124], imperfect as it is, that might give a better overall measure of how well we are managing our own affairs? Maybe knowledge per person, as suggested in the Empty Planet model, could be a useful indicator? After all, the four-dimensional Knowledge Economic Index (KEI) [125] tends to correlate with the three-dimensional SPI. Is this a reflection of common biases of the (Western) developers of KEI and SDI, as is strongly suggested by the fact that China ranks behind Tunisia, Mongolia, and Lebanon on both lists? Or is there a real connection? Is it really a coincidence that the same countries—Scandinavian countries, Canada, Australia—are near the top in both rankings?

So far, no improvised metric of human progress seems to seriously influence the general public's mood. If anything, it's the other way around: when a gut feeling tells folks that things are looking up, those measures of the human condition that happen to be going up gain influence. And when folks get gloomy about their prospects, gloomy metrics win out, and so do dejected forecasts focusing on those. The allegedly objective measures of growth and progress are anything but: they're fuzzy and ambiguous and cherry-picked according to folks' very subjective preferences. Which makes them great for buttressing any theory you happen to like, and discrediting the ones you don't.

For example, the baseline (a.k.a. business-as-usual) climate-modelling scenarios that the venerable IPCC still adheres to manage to hold on to assumptions that originated in the 1970s and that have been thoroughly discredited since. In particular, greenhouse gas emissions from fossil fuels are projected to rapidly grow for at least another 300 years, and coal use is supposed to grow six-fold by 2100 CE, in particular for making transportation fuel [126]. In reality, known reserves of oil and natural gas could last another half-century, and coal about twice as long – if, that is, we use them at the rates we did in 2015 [127]. Does a sudden halt in the doubling of our energy use every quarter-century sound like "business as usual"? Does it make sense to quit developing better energy sources at the very moment the old ones are running on fumes? Is it sensible to make lots of gasoline out of coal, an approach never practiced at any scale since WWII?

Let's take this last example. The liquefaction of coal into synthetic fuels provided most of the fuel for Hitler's military in the 1940s, but business-as-usual has since had little use for coal-to-liquids (CTL) technology. The total capacity of all CTL facilities built worldwide since Sasol built the first post-WWII CTL plant in South Africa in 1977 is equivalent to about 0.86% of global gasoline consumption. Charitably assuming that all of these facilities are still operating at full capacity and that they make nothing but gasoline (both assumptions are known to be grossly wrong), that would amount to the replacement rate of 0.02% per year. So however one extrapolates available data, synthetic fuel from coal wouldn't become the dominant transportation fuel for at least another 2,500 years(!), not eighty years as the "business-as usual" scenario assumes. And no, we haven't found enough fossils to last another 300 years, never mind 2,500 years, either. Instead, we pretty much quit finding any new deposits to write home about. On the contrary, lots of known low-EROI deposits are written off as stranded assets. The IPCC "baseline" disregards all that.

Figure 50 – Are we still talking about the same planet? Middle-left image courtesy of Julius_Silver via pixabay.com.

It's no wonder: the IPCC report authors are climate experts, not energy experts. Just like they are no economists, sociologists, psychologists, public health experts, political scientists, media researchers, or law scholars. The international body ostensibly established to influence human interaction with the weather machinery of our planet is an assembly of experts in various aspects of the machinery, but they're rank amateurs when it comes to all things human. And when their assumptions for the human side of the equation turn out to be silly, nobody is around to tell them to adjust those. Nobody they would listen to, that is.

Failure to revise the model's preconceived assumptions when they fly in the face of real-world data is a strong clue that the model is FUBAR (fudged up beyond all relevance). Given the magnitude of resource-allocation decisions based on these models, it would be really nice to have better ones. Like ones where humanity is a part of the model, coevolving with the rest of the Gaia system, rather than villain-on-call of the myopic Malthusian cults.

Instead, *Limits to Growth*—the neo-Malthusians' Bible commissioned by the Club of Rome half a century ago (remember the folks who called you and me and our moms and our kids "cancer"? Yep, THAT Club of Rome)—just got another facelift. "Science popularizers" are gleefully discussing a research paper [128] under titles like, "MIT predicted society would collapse this century, and we're doing our best to make it happen" [129]. Of course, the sky-is-falling-and-you're-to-blame journalism doesn't go into the study's technical details of the study; but if you dig into the paper, you will discover that its author, Gaya Herrington, has enough academic integrity to admit that the model she uses is quite sensitive to parameter values. What that means in layman's terms is that the available data is perfectly compatible with a multitude of scenarios, and it's possible to tweak the parameters of the model to fit pretty much any preconceived conclusion (see Figure 27, page 209). To make this fudging sound kosher and even scientific, this process is called "recalibration." Naturally, the only results chosen for publication are those that fit the worldview of whoever did the choosing, looking very professional with color plots and error bars and whatnot.[32] In this case, the worldview is found in the Club of Rome's 1974 manifesto *Mankind at the Turning Point*: "The Earth has cancer and the cancer is Man."

---

[32] "It is the responsibility of scientists never to suppress knowledge, no matter how awkward that knowledge is, no matter how it may bother those in power; we are not smart enough to decide which pieces of knowledge are permissible, and which are not. ..." — Carl Sagan

But parameter-tweaking and cherry-picking the numbers you happen to favor is small potatoes next to the real elephant in the room. The fatal flaw of the model is its Malthusian assumption of finite resources. It seems terminally myopic in this day and age to ignore the 99.999999999...% of the Universe that isn't down here on Earth, but when it comes to ignoring the Universe, neo-Malthusian misanthropologists are a breed apart. There might be something in their necks preventing them from turning their heads upward, while outside at night, and noticing the vastness of our world. With a disability like that, it's only natural to dismiss anything above your topmost line of vision. That line is a glass ceiling, and they don't believe humans can cross it.

Once you assume that there is an impenetrable ceiling over your head, your model can only describe movement under that ceiling (unless you're really bad at math, which neo-Malthusians aren't). It will inevitably "conclude" that the system will eventually exhaust what you assumed to be a finite resource - say, "Earth's carrying capacity" or some such vague but scientific-sounding abracadabra. And every publication like this invites the bad news industry to shower us with a fresh batch of prophecies of doom – and accusations that it's self-inflicted.

This is meant to affect our behavior. And it does: it makes us skeptical and cynical and dismissive of anything that doesn't fit our worldview, with predictable results. One of these has been predicted by Joseph de Maistre more than two centuries ago: people, he said, get the leaders they deserve. People who are too skeptical and cynical to bother listening to a different point of view tend to get leaders who don't have much use for freedom of thought either. They get dictators.

Dictators (who themselves tend to be unmitigated cynics and misanthropes) unleashing their dubious favors on innocent bystanders—allegedly for the bystanders' own good—have proven hazardous to everyone's health. Look at, for example, Vladimir Lenin (Figure 51). As far as I can tell, the mechanics of this are embarrassingly simple and quite independent of the would-be dictator's noble intentions—or lack thereof—prior to actually getting the job.

A dictatorship, of an individual or a clique, is created by declaring some principle inviolate and, more importantly, the principle's official interpreter(s) infallible. Whereupon said interpreter(s) invariably, promptly, and comprehensively disconnect from reality and go bananas. The illuminated circle under the streetlight of an official dogma is all you're supposed to see, and any information brought in from outside it is, therefore, subversive. The scout ants that stray off trodden path lose privileges, including access to the Queen and to the chow hall. Dissent is silenced, diversity is discouraged, or at the very least ignored.

Is Humanity an Apprentice God?

Figure 51 – The human hand has two peculiar features: one is the well-known opposable thumb, which gives some of us incredible manual dexterity. The other is the accusatory pointing finger, which always points outward.

Diversity of opinion about what's happening and about how the reality differs from the declared goals (and announced achievements) is how feedback loops work for us humans. And feedback loops is how you keep (some measure of) control over what's going on: you have goals, you have reports from the field, and you take corrective action if what's actually happening takes you away from the goal rather than closer to it. People who can tell you that you're going the wrong way are your most valuable resource, assuming that you're actually trying to get somewhere. Some of them are wrong, and proving them wrong will boost your confidence. Others are right, and they will give you valuable warning, hopefully before it's too late to do something about it. But neither can reach you if they are incarcerated in a gulag or deported or blacklisted for having the "wrong" nationality, religion, occupation, or party affiliation. And once some dissenters are shot, incarcerated, shipped away, or ostracized, those who aren't don't talk much either: when smart people see others' heads bitten off for speaking out of turn, they tend to keep their non-conformist opinions to themselves. Conformists keep talking, but they have nothing to add to the conversation. Hence however many dogs a dictator hires, he ends up barking anyways. Which never ends well. And not just for the dictator personally. The costs of the dictator's mistakes are ultimately borne by lots of folks whose opinions no one (besides the secret police) ever listened to.

Democracy, which is a social contract to share the costs and the benefits of a common belief (or lack thereof), seems like a much better option. Provided that it's sophisticated enough to listen to its diverse sentinels' messages and flexible enough to actually take those into account. Which you won't if you believe that said sentinels are locusts, a plague, cancer, or imbeciles in need of constant adult supervision. You also won't take your sentinels seriously if you believe your doctrine to be the ultimate truth, something only morons could doubt. If you do, then it's rather natural to want to impose order on those pesky deviants from the party line.

One particular form of the latter is gaining currency recently: the green dictatorship concept [130], the idea that the only thing that can save this long-suffering planet from human locusts is some authority keeping said locusts in check.

It isn't hard to predict what this authority would tell us to do and which experts it would hire to make its directives sound wise. Paul Ehrlich's 1968 bestseller *The Population Bomb* predicted that millions would die in a worldwide famine in the 1970s and 1980s due to overpopulation. In fact, during those two decades, the world's average daily per capita supply of calories went up by about 10%. China was the only part of the world where Ehrlich's predictions of famine ever came anywhere near true: the Great Chinese Famine of 1958–62 cost between fifteen and fifty-five million lives. Consequently, there had already been an authority (namely, the CCP)[33] telling folks what to do in the most populous country on Earth. And since

---

[33] Back in 1980, the abbreviation "CCP" (Chinese Communist Party) still actually meant all three things. Nowadays, only the first "C" kind of means the same thing it did forty years ago: it's undeniably Chinese. But it isn't much of a party anymore, and the "Communist" part doesn't stand up to even the most superficial examination. Real Communists typically aren't in the business of creating millionaires as fast as they can. In fact, Communists are supposed to never quit excoriating the ills of a capitalist society, rather than building (a very successful) capitalist society.

I think our blinkered (Western) idea that China is run by a close-minded, ideological clique is way out of date. And the trolls who dismiss China and Chinese accomplishments are doing us in the West a great disservice. Each bout of arrogant xenophobia in response to a piece of news from China prevents us from taking the competition from the "a priori inferior" Chinese seriously, which is exactly what the Chinese would want. More than twenty-five centuries ago, a Chinese strategist and

1980, it was telling folks to have fewer kids. The one-child policy was announced and implemented. Unwilling to accept its responsibility for the famine (via all kinds of disincentives for human initiative and creativity), the CCP found a godsend excuse: it isn't our fault. People are the problem. Overpopulation, just like Ehrlich said. Too many mouths to feed. That's a very reasonable conclusion when you forget that, besides mouths to feed, people are also equipped with hands to work and minds to think.

Ehrlich said this in a 2015 interview: "The idea that every woman should have as many babies as she wants is to me exactly the same kind of idea as everybody ought to be permitted to throw as much garbage into their neighbor's backyard as they want." An entomologist by training, Ehrlich couldn't tell people from bugs in 1968. Half a century later, he downgraded us all the way to garbage.

Misanthropy is in fashion. The idea that humans are the problem, not the solution, is anything but surreptitious. Population control advocates are no conspirators. Or if they are, they're as hopeless at that as they are at everything else. The "overpopulation" screams from the rooftops are hard to miss. Here, for example, are twenty-one alleged mortal sins of humankind [131] and an argument against having children [132].

Careful what you wish for - you might just get it. The one-child policy of 1980–2015 cost China, according to China's own official statistics, 400 million people: at least seven times more than died in the famine that prompted the policy in the first place. The missing Chinese would make the third most populous country in the world today. Would the next Einstein or Leonardo have been among them? We'll never know.

The missing people would be between six and forty-one years of age now. At least a third of the learning-and-earning backbone of the Chinese economy is gone.

---

philosopher named Sun Tzu advised, "Pretend to be weak, so your adversary may grow arrogant." Remember Japanese cars, which, in 1970s, were regarded as junk copied from the superior American models? Well, by 2016, Toyota had become the biggest car manufacturer in America. Remember Chinese-made disposable tools and appliances? Well, theirs aren't bad anymore, and ours are no longer available. Arrogant xenophobia prevents us Westerners from learning from others, while they (eagerly) learn from us (as long as we still have something to teach, which won't be long if we keep up this attitude). One wonders if the trolls are on the Chinese payroll or are just "useful idiots."

China is missing 400 million students, farmers, researchers, cooks, drivers, professors, artists, buyers of homes and appliances and cars and services—and moms and dads of the next generation. That means that the next generation will have fewer kids to support old folks. It's a vicious cycle.

The population bomb is here—except Paul Ehrlich, true to form, got it backward. The bomb is imploding, not exploding, kind [133]. The well-to-do countries' population is aging and shrinking, and not-so-well-to-do countries are following suit: they're doing progressively better on urbanization, education, and economy, but fertility is going into a nosedive. Ehrlich shouldn't have worried that allowing every woman to have as many babies as she wants would lead to overpopulation: it's a well-established fact that emancipated, financially independent, educated women in well-to-do countries want to have very few babies. So do their men. Maybe "want" is the wrong word. "Tend" is (a lot) more accurate. Under the sway of peer pressure, which values profession over procreation, priorities change. A system that values a membership in office plankton more than nurturing a human life sets goals, priorities, and standards for women and men alike. With these goals, priorities, and standards, the increased wealth that could have enabled bigger families, and increased productivity that could have freed people to have more time to spend with their families and contribute to their communities, seem to have the opposite effect. When, in 2015, the Chinese realized that they were sitting on a ticking demographic implosion bomb, the one-child policy was cancelled. Chinese parents are now free to have as many children as they want. We now have five years' worth of data on what they want: absent the government coercion to have fewer kids, the parents want fewer kids, not more. The birth rate is plummeting faster now than it did when the one-child policy was in place.

Demographic disasters happen without any prodding from the government, as the European Union, South Korea, and Japan amply demonstrate. It's the economy, stupid. Well, some of it, anyways. Productivity growth without corresponding growth in demand leads down the same blind alley as an ill-conceived baby-suppression policy: competition for available jobs gets stiffer, education to stay competitive gets costlier, financially burdened young folks delay having families, and every aging generation has fewer energetic and ambitious working-age children to support them in retirement than they had to support when they were young. And the young folks tend to be the ones to try out new and risky things, like having a family or settling new worlds. Or both. They're our species' scout ants. Elon Musk, the (among many other things) Mars settlement enthusiast, has sounded the alarm: population implosion, not explosion, is "potentially the greatest risk to the future of civilization" [134]. The drive of ambitious, optimistic youth is perhaps the most important form of energy available to our species.

And the demand for this form of energy is depressed by the glass ceiling of "can't have infinite growth on a finite planet". That is, finite planet of finite carrying capacity for finite number of people with finite needs—needs increasingly met by robots rather than people. With this mindset, the notion of human uselessness is hard to avoid, especially when every young person around you is having trouble finding a decent job. Farm labor went from 95% of the population to 2% in under two centuries, and factory and office work are following suit, so we naturally start asking the very reasonable question: What the heck do we need ourselves for? The failure to find an inspiring answer weighs heavily on the reproductive choices of young humans. Among other things.

Taking away humanity's momentum, like taking away power from a train straining to climb a steep incline, is sabotage. Moving upward is hard enough as it is, without someone deliberately disconnecting the locomotive. The (very predictable) rollback likely won't be limited just to demographics, economy, technology, art, and science. The upward mobility for humans is inseparable in every respect from upward mobility for humanity. Human moral standards are also closely linked to growth and progress [135]. Violence among diverse humans goes down, tolerance and mutual understanding and respect go up when different people pursue common goals. When you're busy pushing a train uphill, you have no time for sexism, racism, anti-Semitism, Islamophobia, Sinophobia, or any other arrogant, xenophobic nonsense. When you're busy, you also can't afford smugly dismissing your competition. When our goals are ambitious enough, sometimes we fail. This is how you know if you're challenging yourself enough. If you succeed every time, your bar is set too low. But when you fail, someone else may succeed, and it might be a good idea to learn from them so you can do better the next time around.

The myopic neo-Malthusians' zero-sum-game cult makes it hard to see things that way. All it can see is the "carrying capacity": the finite pile of coal in the locomotive's tender. Naturally, it wants to lighten the load so the coal lasts longer. From this perspective, letting go of the passenger cars is a good idea. The possibility that some of the passengers could improve the chances of actually getting to the destination—like, for example, by finding more fuel—never occurs to the victims of the glass ceiling syndrome.

The blinkered shrinking-pie doctrine inevitably leads to this question: Who do we push away? Which fellow travelers do we leave behind? Do we quit spending precious resources on folks of a different gender, different social status, different tribe, different religion? This isn't a hypothetical possibility. It happens a lot. Myopic greed is a fertile ground for bigotry and bigotry – for a lot of shameful actions: the mass murder of Jews in Nazi Germany and the areas it controlled, the bulldozing of Arab villages to make room for Jewish settlements, the Arabization program of the Iraqi government in oil-rich Iraqi Kurdistan, the expulsion of Arabs by the Kurd militia, the mass murder of the ethnic Chinese in Indonesia in the 1960s, the use of slave labor in rubber production in French Indochina and Belgian Congo in the 1900s, the opium production in India and its illegal export to China by, ahem, the Honourable East India Company (no, I'm not kidding), the extraction of oil in Nigeria and Kurdistan (where most locals live on $1 a day or less), et cetera ad nauseum.

The folks we push away first are folks unlike us. That's how we rationalize pushing them away. They're from a different country; they speak a different language; they have different habits, beliefs, memories. They don't pray like us, they don't think like us, they don't behave like us. It's easy to dehumanize folks you don't get. And interpreting "different" to mean "threatening" (a.k.a. xenophobia) is the best-known excuse to escape from the scary unfamiliar to the apparent safety of your own citadel with your own tribe. Preferably on an isolated island.

On an isolated island, your communications with the outside world are severely restricted. So are your resources. And once you run out of some limited resource inside the walls of your fortress, you face an unenviable choice. One option is negotiating with the unfamiliar world outside, which you, after generations of self-imposed incarceration, have practically no clue about. The other is to reduce the size of your tribe so that what remains of the limited resource lasts longer. Until none of the resource, —and none of the tribe—is left.

If you are looking for a spot to self-isolate from everyone, few locations can compete with Easter Island. Rapa Nui, the Polynesian people inhabiting the island, had 2,075 kilometers to go to meet anyone else – and that was on Pitcairn Island, 1.6 km wide and real easy to miss in the Pacific without GPS. Rapa Nui had no GPS. They have been isolated for at least 800 years. Apparently, the incredible navigational skills of early Polynesians that had led to discovery and colonization of the island around 1,200 CE have been lost over time: otherwise, when disaster hit and the population was plummeting from 15,000 to 2,000 in just a century (among environmental collapse, social collapse, warfare and cannibalism), it would have been rather natural for disaffected citizenry to just skip town and move elsewhere if they could – and we probably would have known. Earlier, when times were good, Rapa Nui people were in a habit of carving, moving and erecting enormous moai –

ritual statues, some weighing over 80 tons. Over 900 of those were standing guard over Easter Island. Creating something like that is a marketable skill you can take anywhere with you. And then we'll know where you went: moai stands out like Nazca lines or Sphinx. None have been found outside Easter Island, and they would be real hard to miss.

So, the descendants of intrepid explorers and tireless innovators that centuries earlier have travelled the Pacific from Antarctica to China to Americas were evidently stuck in their stone age isolation. 8 centuries of bliss – no competition, no intruders, no worries. Hakuna matata. They had no reason to develop guns and bombs and industrial pollution, but they also had no reason to develop metallurgy and the wheel and radio and planes and satellites and GPS. So when fertilizer hit the fan, folks went nowhere and died off helplessly on their little island. The forests that used to protect soil and provide construction materials for boats were first stressed by the Little Ice Age, and then perhaps they delivered a coup de grace in a desperate effort to win favors from ancestor spirits via a massive moai construction program. They likely used the trees as levers and rollers to move the statues.

Once they passed some invisible threshold, things started crumbling faster and faster, as if someone had pressed a self-destruct button. Since about 1650 CE, when the last big trees were gone, 400 moai in different stages of completion were abandoned at the quarry where they were being carved. They're still there today. Rapa Nui art from that period depicts malnourished people with distended abdomens and prominent ribs. The community's landfills, midden, show a sudden drop in fish and dolphin bones and appearance of human ones. Social order fell apart, clans quit collaborating and started fighting. Power shifted from a supreme chief who ruled over all clans to the warrior class: matato'a. The matato'a weren't equipped or trained to repel invaders coming in steamboats with naval guns – they've never even seen any – but against unarmed locals it was no contest. The degrowth and devolution of Rapa Nui indigenous culture was soon complete. No one in the modern world knows what an authentic Rapa Nui boat looked like, how they found the island centuries ago, what their lives were like, what Rapa Nui genius invented the Rongorongo writing system, and how to read what's written in it. Survivors of the collapse (at the lowest point in 1877, 111 Rapa Nui folks lived on the island, only thirty-six of whom had children) and their descendants (an estimated 800 Rapa Nui language speakers live among the 8,000 inhabitants of the island today) either can't answer these questions or won't.

Easter Island is separated from the nearest continent by 3,512 kilometers of water. North Sentinel Island, on the other hand, is within forty kilometers of a modern resort, with paved roads, a pool, a bar, Wi-Fi, and a shuttle to a nearby airport. Yet the state of mind is apparently more important than geography: the North Sentinelese are as stuck in their Stone Age isolation as the Rapa Nui people were when all hell broke loose.

Like the Rapa Nui folks then, the North Sentinelese now speak a language no one born elsewhere can understand. Like the Rapa Nui folks then, the North Sentinelese now have no immunity against any of the diseases you and I can't catch anymore. The Rapa Nui folks' early contacts with outsiders after centuries of isolation were hostile and violent, and so were those of the North Sentinelese. In fact, a five-nautical-mile-wide no-trespassing zone has been established around North Sentinel island and is patrolled by Indian Navy. But when a Coast Guard helicopter approached the island to evacuate two stranded fishermen whose boat had broken and drifted ashore there, the North Sentinelese—who had by then killed both fishermen—shot arrows at the helicopter, ultimately preventing its crew from even retrieving one of the fishermen's bodies. The pilot showed considerable restraint not returning fire (the chopper did have machine guns), and he was commended and decorated for that inaction. North Sentinel's (pop. 100, estimated) attempted declaration of war on India (pop. 1.4 billion, estimated) didn't merit a response. By the way, do you think that this incident, in reflection, may shed some light on the Fermi paradox?

The North Sentinelese crisis is playing out right now. It might be a good idea to try and learn from it, before it's too late. Some societies are gone forever, and all we can ever learn about those is, to a large extent, just conjecture. Civilizations of the Indus Valley 4,100 years ago, the Maya 1,100 years ago, the Mississippians and Khmers 800 years ago, the Anasazi 700 years ago, Greenland Vikings 600 years ago, and Easter Island 300 years ago, —when they were young and dynamic, — were all impressively advanced for their times. Yet they aren't around anymore, so we can never know for certain what went wrong so they aren't around anymore. Self-isolation seems to be a common theme here, but was that actually what happened? How big a role did it play? For example, to what extent was the USSR's chokehold on its citizens' contacts with the outside world responsible for its stagnation and eventual demise? Did the Western powers' ruthless interference in Chinese affairs in the late nineteenth century help China awaken from the trance of a centuries-long, self-imposed exile from humanity?

We may never know the answers, but the trends are very suggestive. Remember the six handshakes that connect you to anyone on this planet? The Rapa Nui in 1877 were—and the North Sentinelese today are—in the single handshake stage. Their interconnectedness with the rest of humanity is at the typical Stone-Age level. And so is their tolerance for someone with a different worldview. They see someone unfamiliar who they think may compete with them for the finite precious resources of their little island, they whack him, and they eat him. Small bands of bipedal apes have lived like this, all over the world, for hundreds of thousands of years.

Eventually, by trial and error, some bands stumbled on a different way of organizing their affairs. Maybe it was a chance encounter with another tribe during a hunt when one tribe had the best trackers and the other tribe had the best spear-throwers. Maybe an accidental military alliance against some other tribe widened the circle of trust. Maybe one tribe was better at fishing in the summer and another was better at hunting in the winter. Maybe someone started cultivating cereal, and somebody else kept hunting. But whatever it was, somewhere along the line, more tolerant folks—folks who managed to cooperate despite their differences—started outcompeting and out-reproducing the ones who shot first and asked questions later.

That was the second handshake, and if you didn't get the message, you were at an immediate disadvantage. Their mob was bigger than your mob, they could call on more help any time they needed, and the best of theirs at anything was usually better than the best of yours. The most terrifying thing about them was how fast they learned and adapted. They improved construction techniques and toolmaking, food preservation and clothing. They invented portable lighters and diverted water to their kitchen gardens. They collected astronomical and environmental observations and built sacred temples to communicate with gods.

Then, about 8,000 years ago, somewhere in Egypt and Mesopotamia, some Neolithic genius discovered that interconnecting even more people makes a lot of useful things possible: long-distance trade, stocked granaries for lean times, well-trained military to protect said granaries, mobilization of resources for megaprojects for common good. The Agricultural Revolution swept the globe, and we had the third handshake. The fourth followed soon thereafter. First villages and then city-states popped up everywhere. In India's Mohenjo-Daro region of the Indus Valley—where native Dravidians and immigrant Aryans mixed to develop agricultural techniques imported from, of all places, Afghanistan—the population shot up to an estimated five million by 2000 BCE, out-reproducing the rest of the subcontinent about five to one. And the rest of the subcontinent was populated by the same Dravidians, but they had to make do without the diversity and competition of the Mohenjo-Daro region.

In the second century CE Roman Empire, for the first time in history, the species came close to the fifth handshake. Seafarers and camel drivers, merchants and sculptors, Greeks and Turks, pagans and Jews contributed to the grandiose project, willingly or otherwise. The "otherwise" made tolerance and accommodation a necessity rather than luxury. Romans, if nothing else, were pragmatists par excellence, and they quickly discovered that tolerance and accommodation are a lot cheaper than keeping a loyal, well-fed, well-trained legion in every provincial village. The achievements of the project can still, to this day, be seen throughout Europe, North Africa, and the Middle East: sculptures and temples, aqueducts and paved roads, bathhouses and canals, bridges and amphitheaters.

But in 64 CE, a massive fire in Rome burned for nine days and destroyed two-thirds of the bustling city. A lot of folks lost everything and were in an understandably foul mood. A scapegoat was desperately needed—and as a sacrificial offering, Nero the sitting emperor, blamed the disaster on Christians. Who were persecuted accordingly. And from there, it was all downhill for the Roman Empire. Diversity became a problem rather than the source of strength, as it had been. The suppression of dissent became the main job of the Roman legions, which promptly got so outmanned that, in turn, were forced to recruit the very folks they were fighting, and all hell broke loose. It soon became hard to tell who was on whose side, and you can't keep an empire (or much anything else) together when every man is for himself. In 410 CE, Rome fell.

Maybe time wasn't ripe for the fifth handshake back then. But fifteen centuries later, five-handshake (or thereabouts) empires were the order of the day. Belgium and Britain, Italy and France, Germany and Japan, Russia and the Netherlands, Austro-Hungary and Portugal—they each had an empire apiece. Add Qing China, the Ottoman Caliphate, and the awakening USA, and most of the dry land is covered by empire-sized conglomerates, and most of humanity lives there.

In hindsight, that was inevitable. Humanity was completing the next Revolution, the Industrial one. Rail and telegraph, cars and dirigibles, synthetic drugs and dyes, municipal water treatment plants and sewage systems, electric grids and street lighting, traffic rules and antiseptic surgery with anesthesia were all marching victoriously around the globe. People were changing their lives at speed and scale never seen before. And pursuing big goals requires continued cooperation among lots of people. The more cooperative people win, and the rest go to work for the winners, and hopefully they learn to do better next time.

A five-handshake society doesn't have to be an empire, by the way. It's just the first form that we found, and the name stuck. The history of the twentieth century mankind is, among other things, a story of searching for ways to get rid of imperialism while keeping the ability to, as Harari puts it, cooperate flexibly in large numbers. We have gone down quite a few dead ends in that search for the best way to organize the humanity franchise, and some of our experiments have cost us an arm and a leg. Actually, millions of arms and legs and everything else. An enormous cost in blood and treasure was paid for the twentieth century's social tryouts. But there were more than four times as many of us in 2000 CE as there were in 1900. The lessons of the twentieth century's experiments on an unprecedented scale, which we performed on ourselves and survived, may help us get ready to deal with the unprecedented challenges of the twenty-first century and beyond. But prior experience can only take us so far.

The five-handshake humanity's crown achievement was getting to the Moon. It takes just one more handshake to interconnect all of humanity. And an interconnected humanity is indeed emerging, ready or not. Among our billions, very few can spend a day—never mind a day, a waking hour—without using stuff from half a globe away. The shirt or dress you're wearing, the dyes and fasteners and design and software and machines that were used to make it were created by folks from dozens of countries, speaking dozens of languages, for the most part completely unaware of each other's existence. You start your day with Arabica coffee from Kenya, bought from a franchise headquartered in Germany, grind it in a Chinese coffee grinder, and, if you're a purist, brewed in a Turkish Cezve. Then you breakfast on Ecuadorian bananas, Indian Naan bread made from Canadian wheat, and cheese from the Netherlands. As you drive your American-made car to work, the British Broadcasting Corporation delivers news via your car radio made in Korea from parts originating in China, Mexico, and a couple dozen other countries (as are your car components). That is, unless you get your news via the Internet instead.

Between 1993 and 2007, the share of telecommunicated information in the world that went through the Internet grew from 1% to over 97%. Research collaborations and international banking, mass media and global logistics, charity and investment, government and writing—these are just some of the things that are now unthinkable without the Internet. We're in the midst of another revolution, the digital one.

The Digital Revolution is linking the world together in ways unthinkable a couple of generations ago. The treasure chest of human knowledge is available to anyone with a smartphone, and in the poorest places on Earth, smartphones are more common than indoor plumbing. In fact, folks living there learn about indoor plumbing using their smartphones.

The Digital Revolution gives a lot of folks an opportunity to help organize the enormous pile of information our species has accumulated over the millennia. A lot of scout ants offer different formats for different kinds of exchanges—YouTube, Facebook, Airbnb, TaskRabbit, Kickstarter, GoFundMe, Alibaba, Lyft, Amazon, Wikipedia, bitcoin, arXiv, and millions (literally, millions) of others. And in the broadest-based democratic movement in the history of the species, we the people—of every color, nationality, status and creed—choose the winners. We're learning to interact and collaborate with folks half a world away. Opportunities that, for millennia, were reserved for a few most restless Odysseuses are now available to practically everyone who wants it. Power to the people, and that includes pretty much everybody.

The Digital Revolution is not the first revolution in the history of the species. Perhaps the first recognizable human revolution was the onset of behavioral modernity during the Late Upper Paleolithic, around 50,000 years back. Anatomically modern humans—that is, folks you wouldn't be able to tell from me after they're showered, shaved, dressed in modern attire, and taught to behave—had been around by then for at least 100,000 years, likely longer. Not until 35,000 to 50,000 years ago, however, did the first irrefutable evidence of symbolic cognition appear in the fossil record. Cave art, stone figurines, and musical instruments from that period are unmistakable evidence of our ancestors' first steps on the long path to actually being showered, shaved, dressed in modern attire, and taught to behave. Bipedal apes, whose human-like appearance had been largely deceptive, started doing odd, irrational things that had no predictable impact on their immediate survival. Human things. They started telling each other stories (we have to assume the verbal part, as spoken language leaves no trace that we can dig up later; but when people paint, carve figurines, and play music, it's a pretty safe bet that they chat as well. Besides, painting, carving and music are, in a way, forms of storytelling in their own right). The imaginary world was born, and with it, the first handshake: the circle of folks you can tell a story to, and your story can change their world. If that's not a revolution, then I don't know what is.

The Neolithic Revolution (a.k.a. the Agricultural Revolution) came next. Around 12,000 to 8,000 BCE, several different cereals were domesticated and were locally available: barley in the Middle East; rice in what is now South China; wheat, barley, lentils, and peas in the Levant. Nomadic hunter-gatherers became sedentary farmers. Folks got to bumping into each other on a regular basis. The more permanent dwellings of agricultural societies could support larger population densities and larger communities than those possible in hunter-gatherer societies. The number of folks humans meant when they said "we" went up.

And it kept going up. Nations emerged when "we," together, started building civilizations proper, with massive irrigation systems, pyramids, and other landmarks that can be seen from LEO with a naked eye. And then our relationship with eternity changed, well, forever. As the first order of business of building a civilization, we invented the first information technology: writing systems. Until then, all human knowledge and wisdom and myths could only be passed on from generation to generation orally, making them vulnerable to all kinds of mishaps and misinterpretations. But folks in Mesopotamia invented cuneiform, the Sumerian system of writing on clay tablets, while folks in Egypt invented hieroglyphs, a completely different system that used different media and different symbols to accomplish the same thing. Humanity got a (kind of) permanent record.

At about the time writing was invented, humans also discovered alloys and invented metallurgy. That happened more or less simultaneously in Egypt, the Caucasus Mountains, China, India, and South America. The Bronze Age started with sophisticated crafts, elaborate technologies, and progressively more intricate social organization. Cuneiform, for example, developed from an archaic token pictogram system used for accounting. Meanwhile, cities emerged, and along came hereditary monarchs, centralized governments, armories and granaries, and professional armies to defend the monarchs and the granaries and the rest of it. Running all of that was an exasperatingly complex business, which prompted the systematic development of astronomy, astrology, and math.

Then we attempted the first true empires, whose "we" lived on several continents and spoke dozens of languages: Neo-Assyrian, Median, Achaemenid, Macedonian, Seleucid. New generation of faiths and philosophies emerged in parallel with the early empires: Hinduism, Jainism, Judaism, Zoroastrianism, Confucianism, Buddhism, and the Socratic tradition in Western philosophy. As Karl Jaspers put it, "The spiritual foundations of humanity were laid simultaneously and independently in China, India, Persia, Judea, and Greece. And these are the foundations upon which humanity still subsists today."

Then, about 1750 CE, the Industrial Revolution started. Humanity unlocked the power of coal for industrial production and transportation. We made (a lot of) live people (a.k.a. conscious biomass) out of long-dead plants and animals (a.k.a. fossil fuels). And more of these humans than ever before did that human thing: interacted flexibly in large numbers to dream up, and then create, a new reality. Offset printing and telegraph, electric grids and assembly lines, urbanization and labor unions, railroads and steamships were added to the human interactivity toolbox.

Then, circa 1969 CE, the invention of Internet protocols officially started the Digital Revolution, the revolution that completes the integration of information space for all terrestrial humans in the World Wide Web. Noosphere 2.0.

One to ten million folks lived on the planet during the Neolithic Revolution, when some nomadic bands invented agriculture and founded the first permanent settlements. Roughly 800 million people inhabited Earth around the time the Industrial Revolution started. About 3.6 billion humans lived on Earth in 1969, the dawn of the Digital Revolution.

The boundaries here are fuzzy, of course. We're extrapolating from data that's pretty fuzzy to begin with. But the trend kind of makes sense: when we have more people, we can get more done, and some of what we get done is crosschecking each other's ideas, shredding most of them, trying some, and spectacularly succeeding with a few. And when we succeeded, it was fabulous enough to make this whole mess worth the effort. A bigger ant hill can afford more scout ants, and once some of them find something worthwhile, it can also send a bigger crew to take advantage of the opportunity. And grow bigger still. Positive feedback.

So what would it take for our global, six-handshake humanity to have another revolution? And what would that revolution be like?

I have little doubt that our seventh handshake is in the works, and I have little doubt that it will be across some cosmic abyss. I have little doubt that what we're going to be shaking won't be a claw, tentacle, or robot's manipulator but a human hand.

But didn't the onset of the Digital Revolution require a population 4.5 times bigger than the previous one did? Were the next one to take the same factor of 4.5, that would be sixteen billion folks, folks. And the human population on Earth is projected to peak at eight to eleven billion. If these projections are both accurate, then we won't have the human-power for the next revolution. If all we have to guide us is the rational projections from myopically misinterpreted data, we aren't going anywhere. How come, then, that I have little doubt that our seventh handshake is in the works?

I don't believe the naïve projections, that's how. I don't believe that the Internet is, as some allege, "the best birth control technology ever invented," replacing human interaction of all kinds with endless "screen time." The Internet is a tool of human interaction, a new tool that we aren't yet very good at using. Some people use the Internet to avoid reality; others, to build it. A new reality with new ways of doing much, if not most, of what we humans do: create and find information, report and discuss news, spread and debate ideas, find partners and advisers. Social networks and cryptocurrency, crowdfunding and the gig economy, blogs and information sharing platforms, online focus groups and open-access depositories of scientific papers—these all give billions of us opportunities to interconnect in ways unthinkable even a few years ago. And an increasing number of us are learning to take advantage of those opportunities. The World Wide Web is a web of interwoven human interactions. With our numbers and the World Wide Web, we're learning to create global brainstorms—synergies of mind—that have never been even remotely possible before.

And that's (a big part of the reason) why I don't believe the gloomy, simplistic projections. All human revolutions to date were leaps in human interconnectedness, each enabled by the previous one. It's the connections that count. The interwoven web of our collective consciousness that we, its dynamic nodes, keep learning to create and operate.

I have no data from the future to support my belief that this web will keep growing, despite the predicted fertility decline. I have no data from the future to support my belief that this growth will be enough to take us over the threshold of our gravity well, making us humans a spacefaring species. I have no time machine to tell me how it's going to turn out. It's a matter of faith.

4 Humanism: The Last Monotheistic Religion of *H. Sapiens*?

> "Earth is the cradle of humanity,
> but one cannot remain in the cradle forever."
> *Konstantin E. Tsiolkovsky*

> "World belongs to humanity."
> *Dalai Lama*

I think it's only appropriate to begin the discussion of faith with a quote from Judaism, one of the oldest monotheistic religions on Earth. The Book of Genesis, the first book of the Hebrew Bible, says, "And God said, let there be light: and there was light. And God saw the light, and it was good; and God divided the light from the darkness." Telling light from darkness, good from bad, is what gods do. Deciding which way's up

There are no atheists in foxholes. We always turn to faith, consciously or otherwise, when the going gets tough and we have hard decisions to make. Lacking the time machine to tell us the Right Path, when past experience can't tell us what to do, all we have to guide us is faith.

And right now we are indeed between a rock and a hard place, and past experience sure can't tell us what to do. Our accelerating global civilization will have to do one of two hard things, ready or not: quit the accelerating path or stay on it.

Is Humanity an Apprentice God?

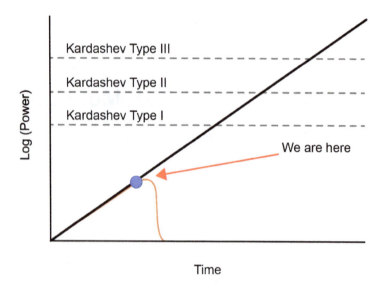

Figure 52 – Fork in the road.

We don't know how to do either of these things. We have never tried. We, as a global civilization, have never quit accelerating. We have never attempted a deliberate global slowdown. We have no tools to give us reliable and detailed predictions of how the complicated intertwined systems we are trying to control—society, the economy, the biosphere, Gaia—would respond to us leaning on the brakes. And the broad-strokes predictions for that scenario that we do have – the Empty Planet model – don't look very promising.

Nor do we know how to keep our global civilization accelerating beyond the dash fueled by Sun-in-a-can. We have never tried doing that, either. The tools to give us detailed predictions of how society, the economy, the biosphere, and Gaia would respond to us leaning on the accelerator are as unavailable as the tools for predicting the outcome of the leaning-on-the-brakes scenario. They're kind of the same tools.

We're regularly reminded of the (very real) dangers of the business-as-usual approach. "Business-as-usual" has become a codeword for the reckless endangerment of humanity, taking us to some scary point-of-no-return. Which is, by default, taken to mean that any alternative is safer than business-as-usual.

It's not. Human civilization is a process, as is all evolution, which human civilization is a part of. It's not built to stand still. It's not built to slow down. We got to where we are by accelerating. It took us billions of years to get from stardust to the first flint tool, millions to the first library, thousands to the first lightbulb, and only decades to land on another celestial body.

Once we quit the accelerating path, we are at the point of return—very possibly, return to the caves. We have no experience to guide us there. Each point in human evolution so far has been a point of no return. Each point in pre-human evolution was a point of no return, too. Points of no return are our natural habitat, and we have evolved to deal with them. A point of return is where we, as a global civilization, have never been before. And the folks who departed the accelerated path are, for the most part, no longer with us. The departure cost them dearly. We call them the "dearly departed."

Even if we choose what we want to want, there is no guarantee that we'll succeed at making it happen. The Universe is under no obligation to guarantee us anything, other than an occasional challenge like a magnetic pole flip or a super-volcano eruption. What is guaranteed is that if we can't dream up a scenario we want to realize on purpose, then whatever happens to us won't be by choice.

We're the only global civilization we know facing this dilemma. There's no prior experience to draw on. There's no oracle to tell us how it's gonna turn out.

So, then, where are we headed? Are we going forth to the stars or back to the caves? I believe that most of the humans responsible for making this choice are alive today, as I write these words. I don't think the people living today have the luxury of not making a choice, because—as usual in our time-constrained world—not making a choice is very much a choice. Often the worst one. Those who refuse to choose one of two alternatives frequently end up paying for both without benefitting from either. I don't think the people making these choices have the luxury of making them completely rationally: that would require knowing all outcomes of all possible choices, and the last I checked, there was no time machine in my basement to tell us those outcomes. A rational choice, when you look closely, invariably turns out to be either not completely rational or not much of a choice. So, owning our future is, IMHO, going to take (among other things) a leap of faith.

Faith in us humans, that is. A.k.a. humanism.

Faith in humans is hard to cultivate, especially when you listen to what some of us say about our species. We humans appear to be engaged in a concerted (and so far, successful) effort to convince any prospective tourists from Alpha Centauri to take their business elsewhere. Nuthin' attractive 'round here, just keep going. Run-of-the-mill star, mediocre planet, unrefined inhabitants. Very, very unrefined inhabitants. Inhabitants so unrefined that their most advanced species' philosopher can start an "ideas worth spreading" presentation with this gem: "You live in an amazing and expanding Universe. But I am sorry to say, you are insignificant." He goes on like that for a while, in front of an audience of humans, and as far as anybody could tell, he's human as well. A young, successful human living at one of the premium locations on this gorgeous planet of ours.

And he's anything but alone in this. Disparaging our own species has become a sport, a hobby, a literary genre—and a thriving industry. It's no wonder that, as American writer Jack Finney put it, "It becomes harder and harder to continue telling yourself that we are still good people." The shit we throw at ourselves ain't no fertilizer.

There is a pervasive narrative, most prominent in media pieces regarding the views of human nature and forecasts of the future of the species. It's based on a view of us humans that's very different from my view. In that view, we're nothing but algorithms, programmed biological machines whose lives have no meaning whatsoever. Its advocates allege that our irrational dreams, aspirations, choices, priorities are all illusions, and that includes our control of our own behavior. What used to be seen as our free will is declared a dangerous delusion. Any irrational behavior is explained away as "random," which sounds scientific and authoritative and more than slightly patronizing. Any decision we humans think that we make is declared to be an inevitable consequence of something that happened 13.7 billion years ago (namely, the Big Bang). According to that narrative, our thoughts are nothing but electrochemistry happening in the brain, and its outcome is either deterministic or random, so a mass murderer no more deserves punishment than DaVinci and de Saint-Exupéry and Einstein deserve praise. There is no agency in either case, no "I." Any notion that we can possibly be something more than hackable animals—whose lives are meaningless and preprogrammed, whose free will is a self-deluding myth—is dismissed as a superstition grandfathered from old cults. Scientists, we're told, armed with the best electron microscopes and the best peer-approved deterministic theories money can buy, have found no free will—only hackable animals.

Yet this narrative holds the allegedly predetermined human nature responsible for what it sees as vices of human civilization. We're a cancer, the plague, greedy, mindless locusts, driven by what sounds suspiciously like the seven deadly sins to make Earth into something that sounds suspiciously like Hell. The funny part here is that many of those who hold this view are sworn atheists, never missing an opportunity to take a swing at religion.

Don't take my word for it. Listen to Michael Crichton, the author of *Jurassic Park* and *The Lost World*: "Human beings are so destructive. I sometimes think we're a kind of plague, that will scrub the earth clean. We destroy things so well that I sometimes think, maybe that's our function. Maybe every few eons, some animal comes along that kills off the rest of the world, clears the decks, and lets evolution proceed to its next phase."

Here's a British author, Matt Haig: "The humans are an arrogant species, defined by violence and greed. They have taken their home planet, the only one they currently have access to, and placed it on the road to destruction."

"The human race is just a chemical scum on a moderate-sized planet, orbiting around a very average star in the outer suburb of one among a hundred billion galaxies. We are so insignificant that I can't believe the whole Universe exists for our benefit. That would be like saying that you would disappear if I closed my eyes." That was one of the smartest specimens the human race has produced so far, Stephen Hawking. Just so you don't miss his point: "I think computer viruses should count as life... I think it says something about human nature that the only form of life we have created so far is purely destructive. We've created life in our own image."

"We should never underestimate human stupidity. Both on the personal and on the collective level, humans are prone to engage in self-destructive activities," intones Yuval Noah Harari, a professor of history and bestselling author.

"Two things are infinite: the universe and human stupidity; and I'm not sure about the universe." Says who? Albert Einstein, you nitwit, that's who.

"To insult someone we call him 'bestial'. For deliberate cruelty and nature, 'human' might be the greater insult," concurs Isaac Asimov, among other things—former President of the American Humanist Association and a Humanist Laureate in the International Academy of Humanism. With friends like these, who needs enemies?

In the modern attention economy, these masterpieces of self-flagellation are milked—well, bled—to the last drop. They're exhibited prominently all over the Internet as clickbait. The mental zits these towering intellects publicly pop at their darkest moments can't fail to suggest, to the more impressionable among us, that they doubt the value of being human. Specifically, a live one.

Which many proceed to do with a vengeance that could do a lot of good if directed elsewhere. In the US, for example, suicide is the second leading cause of death for folks between ten and thirty-four years of age—and the leading cause of death is "unintentional injury," whose unintentional nature is, by definition, an assumption. You can't very well ask a mangled corpse if getting in front of the bus was his (last) idea. Besides, even apparent accidents are not entirely accidental either. They tend to happen less frequently to folks who put higher value on their lives and act accordingly. In fact, in today's safety-obsessed society, which spends zillions to idiot-proof itself (including strollers with a warning label that advises parents to "remove child before folding"), it takes some doing to let an accident happen to you. But sleepwalking off a cliff is less unexpected in the middle of a depression pandemic, which would appear to be exactly where we are: 88% of the poll answers on debate.com website was Yes, we are a disease, we need to be eradicated.

Depression is largely a feeling of uselessness. The way to counter it is to feel useful. The way to feel useful consistently is to actually be useful. How can we do that? What the heck do we need ourselves—and each other—for?

Plenty of answers to that question are on tap, just Google it. The answers are endless, and anyone is free to find one that suits his or her mood at the moment. As with all life questions, knowing which answer is the right one requires access to a time machine, as it's determined by (lots of) stuff that hasn't happened yet. Oracle-less, we usually let our biases guide us. Negativity bias, in particular. There's plenty of gloom and despondency to be found, if gloom and despondency is what you happen to be looking for. Even the best and brightest of us have moments of weakness—as seen in the quotes above—when they say things about humanity that should make them blush for the rest of their lives. So do the rest of us. And then we, the common folk, go looking for authoritative affirmation of our beliefs, and our confirmation-bias-driven searches find plenty of opportunities to dig us a deeper and deeper hole, and eventually many join the ranks of the congenitally resentful. That mind-eating-bug pandemic is currently spreading at an alarming speed. If it takes over *Homo (allegedly) sapiens*, we're going to become a species with, at best, a dismissive—and, most likely, a disgusted—prevailing attitude toward ourselves. Well, maybe not ourselves personally, but the vast majority of the species we habitually call "them." A species with a dismissive attitude toward itself is, IMHO, unlikely to scale the Kardashev ladder. A species with a disgusted attitude toward itself is, IMHO, likely to commit evolutionary suicide.

Encouraging suicide of an individual is a punishable offence, even though prosecution of these cases is a challenge and punishment is usually surprisingly mild. Encouraging suicide of the entire human species, though, as far as I know, has not been criminalized anywhere yet. Somewhat understandably: it would be an extraordinarily difficult crime to prosecute, especially when the defendants are celebrities who can afford very good lawyers. Mind you, celebrity figures whose alleged criminal acts were to encourage large groups of people to do something stupid, even when the celebrities didn't explicitly name that stupid act, are not unheard of. We have seen a fresh presidential drama unfold: two Capitol police officers have sued ex-President Trump for injuries sustained during what they alleged was a riot that they alleged he incited. Trump can perhaps afford at least as good lawyers as Ozzy Osbourne, who has avoided liability in at least two separate lawsuits for deaths of fans who shot themselves while listening to his "Suicide Solution." The California court that dismissed the first of these ruled that nineteen-year-old John McCollum's suicide was not a foreseeable outcome of Osbourne's song. One wonders if "Save The Planet, Kill Yourself," a song by Chris Corda, the founder of the Church of Euthanasia, would be considered a clear enough message to have foreseeable consequences. So far, no one's estate has won a lawsuit against her either.

So, at present, insulting and disparaging humanity appears to be a perfectly safe activity. If you take the short-term view, that is. In the long term, humanity may agree with you and act accordingly: stick its collective tail between its legs and depart the scene, leaving this beautiful planet and Solar system and galaxy—and all the rest of it—to the little green folks, ones with the irrational ambition to explore and settle this Universe. Which misanthropes regard as a desirable outcome. For the anti-human crowd, any bunch of little green folks owning the Universe would be *a priori* better than your great grandkids and mine.

Are we humans going forth to the stars or back to the caves? No oracle can tell you the answer to the ultimate question. It's a matter of faith. It's a matter of choosing what to believe about ourselves and the rest of the world—choosing today, before you know how it's going to turn out. We can't get to the stars without relying on a system of unprovable beliefs. A system of unprovable beliefs is a religion.

A brief aside here: I'm genuinely surprised to find myself promoting a religion. Having grown up in the Soviet Union, I wasn't exactly educated in religious matters. Not from any favorable perspective anyway. The Communist Party of the Soviet Union's foundational system of beliefs left no room for uncertainty, as it was "scientifically proven". Of course, Lenin's dictum "The Marxist doctrine is omnipotent because it is true" was wrong on at least three counts: the doctrine he was talking about was neither true nor omnipotent, -on top of not being, strictly speaking, even Marxist. Unlike Lenin (who sold this to millions of otherwise sane people), I'm one of those folks completely incapable of selling water in the middle of a desert. I've never been particularly good at promoting anything.

What I am good at—unless I'm just flattering myself—is detecting BS at the first whiff. I've had lots of practice. I hear an idea that sounds interesting, and I'm on it like a pit bull. The only explanation I have for my colleagues not having quietly thrown me under a bus is that they had seen me publicly, methodically, and mercilessly destroy more of my own ideas than anyone else's. Don't get me wrong: I (really) love good ideas, which is probably why I try to reserve my affection for the good stuff, rather than wasting it on some rubbish.

That's how I became, among other things, an agnostic. Endless attempts to prove the unprovable seem to me like a massive waste of time. Endless claims to "know" that God exists or doesn't exist contain some useful (to me) information. They tell me that whoever makes those claims takes liberties with logic and words, particularly with the word "know," —which, in my own view, ought to be used extremely sparingly and reverently. Any further information from that sloppy source will be radically discounted. Failure to recognize your beliefs for being what they are, beliefs, is indeed evidence of something, but that something is about you, not God.

I do have beliefs that I can't prove, just as you do. My beliefs may sound ridiculous to you, and yours to me. But as long as we recognize our beliefs as such and don't condescendingly declare them as "knowledge" that only a moron could doubt, we can have a civilized conversation about anything. Who knows, maybe we can actually agree on something, like lots of folks adhering to different belief systems have done countless times before.

Maybe what we agree on will give us a new perspective that will adjust your belief system, or mine, or both. I know my views can, and do, get adjusted. Some of my beliefs from thirty years ago sound ridiculous to me today when I stumble upon them. I couldn't prove that they're true back then, and I can't prove that they're false now. They just used to make sense long ago, and now they don't make sense anymore. Something else—just as unprovable—makes sense now instead. Faith evolves.

Not long ago, in the mid-twentieth century, during WWII, we were taught an object lesson in the evolution of faith. The teachers were Melanesian islanders of the Pacific, whose incredibly limited exposure to the rest of human civilization set them up to mistake other humans for gods. Before you get all condescending about the naïve islanders and their naïve religion, remember: those other, supposedly civilized, humans made at least two mistakes to the islanders' one. First (and this is a really bad one), they started the damn World War II. Second, in the course of the war, they often airdropped some of the supplies at the wrong spots. The odd contraptions buzzing through the skies and dropping useful goodies left and right were taken to be the chariots of the gods, starting what came to be called a "cargo cult": worshipping as gods a bunch of folks who would die laughing at the suggestion if they had heard it at the time. Cargo cults didn't last long: when one's expectations (of a hands-on God responding to your prayers with immediate gratification) clash with reality, reality tends to eventually win.

Figure 53 – Melanesian rituals: preparing for land diving (nanggol, the prototype of bungee jumping); cargo cult (insert).

The collective experience available to folks who paint the *Mona Lisa*, discover radioactivity, invent the theory of relativity, and visit the Moon is far beyond what Melanesian islanders had access to. As humans, we want to make sense of our experience as badly as Melanesians do of theirs.[34] As long as the scope of our experience keeps growing - there's a fresh supply of wonders, things that make no sense within the old dogma but are glaringly obvious to anyone who bothers to look that way. Hence faiths evolve to survive reality checks, to avoid obsolescence—as long as humanity does.[35]

On occasion, faith even out-evolves that bastion of evolution: science. It took science a century to grow out of phlogiston, fourteen centuries to leave behind geocentrism, twenty-four centuries to move beyond luminiferous ether. Science still clings to reductionist null hypothesis, dark matter, and dark energy. Compared to that, Melanesian faith's evolution shows incredible agility.

Yet an advanced, sophisticated faith sometimes forgets its humble beginnings and declares itself the Ultimate Certain Truth. Then it occupies what it believes to be strategic heights and shoots volleys of contempt and mockery—or actual artillery shells—at any passing UFO (uncredentialed foolhardy opponent). It declares any dissenter an uneducated moron, and it announces its Final Answer to the Ultimate Question of Life, The Universe, and Everything to have been unequivocally, incontrovertibly proven for certain.

It hasn't. For starters, the term "proven" has been misappropriated from mathematicians, who prove things for a living and kind of know what "proof" means better than the rest of us mortals. One of them, Kurt Gödel, has proven a very important thing about proofs: some true statements are unprovable. As British cosmologist John D. Barrow has put it, "If a 'religion' is defined to be a system of ideas that contains unprovable statements, then Gödel taught us that mathematics is not only a religion, it is the only religion that can prove itself to be one."

In other words, there are things even in math, humanity's most logically meticulous enterprise, that have to be taken on faith. They are usually called axioms. Axioms are abstracted from experience through intuition and imagination without

---

[34] We in the developed parts of the world often believe that we know better. We routinely mock the humble 70% of the world's population who happen to live in developing countries. We habitually miss the (glaringly obvious) point that the opposite of "developing" is "stagnant," and the opposite of "humble" is "arrogant."

[35] You believe you don't have unprovable beliefs? Now prove it.

You believe your proof is correct? Now prove that.

Repeat.

Keep going...

any proof whatsoever. Axioms are where the flexibility is in math. Everything downstream is inevitably, rigidly, necessarily derived from those. This derivation is what "proof" stands for.

It's the abstract nature of mathematical symbols that allows strict derivation – certain proof – of the logical consequences of mathematical suppositions (a.k.a. axioms). The consequences are called theorems. A typical theorem sounds like this: "If statement 'A' is true, then statement 'B' is necessarily true." The truth of statement A is an axiom you have to assume. The truth of statement B is what you're trying to prove. Usually, it's not just one axiom A that leads to a nontrivial theorem, but a set of postulates A_1, A_2, A_3, ... A_n. The number of axioms in a theorem is finite (and typically rather small). There are no theorems outside math. Only ideal, abstract mathematical "objects" (a.k.a. symbols) can be exhaustively described by a finite set of postulated properties (a.k.a. axioms). Symbols are products of the human imagination and don't have independent lives outside it. The only degrees of freedom you get in math are in the axioms (and in the rules of logic you use to derive the theorems). Once you've made those up, the rest necessarily follows. That's what "proof" means. It's provisional even in math.

And incomparably more so in sciences dealing with the real world. Sciences are supposed to examine the true nature of things we haven't dreamt up (unlike math, which studies our own creations that have only the features we gave them). They deal with objects that exist outside the human mind and interact with an unknown number of other objects in an unknown number of mostly unknown ways. A "definition" of a real-world object with endless properties and interactions can be either finite in length or comprehensive, but not both. Idealizations make thinking (a.k.a. ideas) possible, but to do so they crop infinite reality into some finite frame we have to choose. A grain of sand is made of atoms, none of which have any boundaries. Where does a grain of sand end? What properties does it have? Any answer to these (interrelated, by the way) questions is necessarily an abstraction, if you don't want it to take forever. And the cropping frames we choose for the idealization of reality have to be flexible to adapt to the task at hand. An abstraction good enough to describe the grain of sand under some set of circumstances (for example, settling on the bottom of a river) would be completely inadequate in a different situation (for example, in a glass smelter). Idealization changes depending on the idea we're working on.

Once we abstract some finite number of features from physical objects, we can prove some theorems about that idealization: an abstract object that has no properties or interactions but those we picked. But for any theorems to apply to the actual physical object we started from, we'd have to add an infinite number of axioms: we'd need to postulate that whatever we don't know about the object and its interactions with the Universe doesn't matter, and our conveniently defined abstraction is all there is to it. We'd have to postulate that nothing matters if we haven't put it into our model. That's our old buddy the null "hypothesis" of reductionism: the belief in isolated systems (a.k.a. bouncing pebbles).

Which never fails to (eventually) fail. As Albert Einstein has put it, "As far as the laws of mathematics refer to reality, they are not certain; and as far as they are certain, they do not refer to reality." We can't have it both ways. Over time, space and system complexity, the interactions we snipped when abstracting our model from reality, and their effects, eventually start adding up – and the real world stubbornly departs from the first-principle, theorem-like predictions that seemed so certain and inevitable at first glance. Emergent properties, well, emerge.

Besides, what we "know" – have proven – about even the abbreviated idealizations is nowhere near exhaustive. To "know" (a.k.a. to prove) a theorem, one needs to, first, intuitively guess it. A finite set of axioms can, and does, lead to an inexhaustible, infinite set of consequences – theorems. So however many of those have been guessed before, there are infinitely more where those came from. And even the ones already conjectured are not necessarily provable, as Gödel has shown. Our idealizations of reality are infinitely richer than what we can prove about them at any given time. And reality is, in turn, infinitely richer than our idealizations. As Enlightenment philosopher Voltaire put it, "Doubt is an uncomfortable condition, but certainty is a ridiculous one."

Voltaire's quip anticipated Heisenberg by a century and a half. Heisenberg's uncertainty principle is central to quantum mechanics, our best tool for making sense of the small. We can't describe an individual particle completely and precisely. We can't help affecting whatever we are trying to measure. When a second observer, Bob, queries a particle that another observer, Alice, has already done some measuring on, their results will differ: Bob is doing measurements on a particle affected by Alice's experiment. If the particle is a photon, Alice's measurement destroys it completely, leaving Bob with nothing to measure at all.

And it's not just the trajectory of an individual particle we can legitimately disagree about. More importantly, we can't even be sure what reality quantum mechanics actually describes. The Copenhagen interpretation, the oldest suggested meaning, is nearly a century old, and hundreds of competing interpretations keep popping up to this day. Many are every bit as good at yielding the same predictions as the Copenhagen interpretation for all experiments we can conceivably perform. We just can't tell if one (or more) of them is right, and if so, which one(s).

Figure 54 – Open to interpretation. The Inundation of the Biesbosch in 1421 – Sir Lawrence Alma-Tadema, 1856.

Making sense of the big—massive—presents its own set of challenges. We only have one copy of our Universe, and we, the observers, live inside it. Even if we had the means to change anything on a cosmic scale (so far, we don't), we still couldn't get reports from an outside observer on the outcome of our experiment. Say we're the heroic crew of a spaceship flying into a black hole. According to general relativity, the theory that predicted black holes in the first place, the folks watching us from back home will never see us go through the event horizon, the invisible shell around the black hole where escape velocity equals the speed of light and time dilation becomes infinite. They would see us grow redder and dimmer, but our complete disappearance into the black hole would, for them, literally take forever. Not for us the explorers though. From our standpoint, we would keep traveling right across that threshold. We just aren't supposed to be able to report our findings to anyone back home. Cosmological reality is open to interpretation: different observers watch different movies.

And between the extremes of the unimaginably small and the unimaginably massive is what's supposed to be our comfort zone. Our natural habitat. These are the things we have the most exposure to, the most first-hand experience with. This is the most familiar stuff. The playground for our common sense.

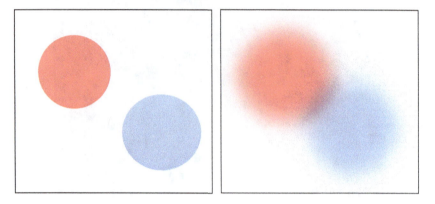

Figure 55 – Sharp, irreconcilable bouncing abstractions (left) and fuzzy overlapping interfering realities (right).

Which turns out to be nowhere near as common as advertised. Do the benefits of playing soccer outweigh the risks, and why? How about vaccinations? Or starting a business? Going on a trip? Everyone you ask will have a different answer, which focuses on what they see as important and downplays—or altogether ignores—the rest. As FDR once said, there are as many opinions as there are experts. Turns out, there are a heck of a lot more opinions than experts, as no one has found a way to limit an alleged guru to just one opinion. The most familiar part of our world is apparently even more open to interpretation than the abstruse nucleons and galaxy clusters: everyone and their brother is a pro. There's plenty of uncertainty there, too. But who says it's a bad thing?

The uncertainty of our description of the Universe is, IMHO, a feature, not a bug. Certainty (a.k.a. dogma) is narcissistic, condescending, oblivious, and stagnant. While it admires its ostensibly comprehensive perfection, reality and our experience of it are busy (co)evolving elsewhere. Reality is open to interpretation; certainty is not. Moving the cornerstone assumptions of our worldview is how we expand it. And expanding our worldview is how we adapt to the Universe, which never tires of giving us surprises. It sends us life-giving sunlight and deadly rocks from the sky, nutritious mammoths and murderous pathogens, blissful ozone sunscreen over the planet and lethal magnetic pole reversals, volcanic eruptions and solar storms, supernovae erasing everything within light-years around them and wandering black holes that gobble things up. If you quit expanding your Island of Knowledge (a.k.a. evolving), then something's eventually going to happen, rare enough for a civilization to get complacent and bad enough for the complacent civilization to be wiped out. Natural selection never sleeps.

Before humans, the variants that natural selection selected from were supplied by genetic mutations. The pace of evolution of life was limited by mutations taking effect - producing a selectable difference – and that took at least a generation. Simple organisms could adapt to fast changes in their environment: they have several generations every hour, and they have the numbers to solve the survival problem via brute force, by trying out every possible variation and its brother. Complex organisms can't do that: they have neither the numbers nor the speed. When drastic environmental challenges happen suddenly, most of the complex creatures die off. Adaptation through mutation is just too hopelessly slow to save them.

The complex life forms that survived sudden catastrophes in the past were lucky. You don't hastily grow fins or wings or build arks on demand when floodwater is already rushing in. It wasn't emergency adaptation that saved them; it was pre-existing diversity. They were among the odd species that had adapted to one of odd environmental niches—too hot, too cold, too dark, too sunny, too dry, too wet, or in some other way hard to live in—and the

Figure 56 – Odd environmental niche.

catastrophe just happened to make the environment on the whole planet like the one in their old neighborhood. If the pre-calamity biosphere has been diverse enough, then enough (formerly marginal) species survive for the biosphere to recover reasonably fast. Otherwise, life rolls back to primitive forms or disappears altogether, and the process starts from scratch.

That's how it worked before we came and changed the rules of the game. But we got a brand-new evolutionary tool that outperforms genetic mutations the way the Internet outperforms carrier pigeons. We got stories.

Just like genes, stories store information. Just like genes, they change over time. But the change doesn't have to take a whole generation to take effect, like it does for genetic information. Stories spread like wildfire, only faster. And humanity changes as fast as our stories do—a lot faster than mutations could change us. With us, the Earth's biosphere has entered the era of new, suprabiological evolution. Evolution 2.0. Evolution powered by stories, worldviews, beliefs—for the large part, uncertain and unprovable ones, a.k.a. faith.

Figure 57 – (left) The Venus of Berekhat Ram, 2300th–2800th century BCE; (right) Aphrodite of Knidos, fourth century BCE.

Exploring a new path inevitably changes the belief system of those who took it. New experience brings new questions, and new beliefs are needed to make sense of your expanding world. From the scarce and badly mangled evidence that happened to survive the assault of time for hundreds of thousands of years, it looks like Stone Age folks painted their worldview in rather broad strokes. The details of *The Venus of Berekhat Ram* (Figure 57, left), a female figurine found on the Golan Heights and tentatively dated back 230,000 to 280,000 years, are so austere that it took decades of study to collect evidence of its artificial origin. But no one would doubt that rather skilled and imaginative humans created the *Aphrodite of Knidos* sculpture in exquisite detail (Figure 57, right). Sure, its attribution to Greek genius Praxiteles is tentative—no signed copy of it, or any other work by the prolific and innovative sculptor, exists today. Yet it's a lot less uncertain than the attribution of *The Venus of Berekhat Ram*. For that one, it's not even clear what species of the genus *Homo* the sculptor belonged to.

Even when evidence is literally rock-solid, folks can—and do—argue ad infinitum about what it's evidence of. And that's how it goes: as we strive to add clarity and detail to the old familiar memes, we inevitably discover more stuff in the process, new stuff to be uncertain about. And the whole process starts over again. As we zoom in to see how something works, we find finer and finer detail, and we can't rationally tell if the room at the bottom, promised by Richard Feynman, is itself bottomless. As we zoom out to see what something is linked to, we discover more and more elaborate networks, and we can't put any rational limit on the connections either. Accumulating experience makes more room for imagination, not less.

And this doesn't apply just to arts. Praxiteles' compatriot Democritus believed that motion and collisions among indivisible eternal atoms are the only things that are real. Everything else is no more than conventions for the atoms' transient congregations. Parmenides held that all that's real is a single immutable eternal mass, and all apparent change and motion are illusions. Aristotle supposed that our hearts produce all illusions and the rest of our minds' output, while brains are mere radiators, keeping blood temperature within specs. While some of these irrational beliefs may seem silly to us today, the questions that the Greeks learned to ask are anything but. We still don't know if ultimate, indivisible, immutable units of matter—whose permutations and collisions make this world go 'round, as imagined by Democritus—are real. Strings, our current candidates for that role, are believed to inhabit a ten-to-twenty-six-dimensional space no mortal has ever been to. We're still puzzled by the nature of time and change that Parmenides pondered. And after accumulating a lot of data on brain structure and chemistry and electric wiring, we still, thousands of years after Aristotle, have no clue how any mention of the mind-body problem makes some people see red—or what they actually see it with.

And even when theories derived from our beliefs yield incredibly accurate predictions for some things—like, for example, Einstein's postulates that the theories of relativity were derived from it's no proof that the postulated beliefs themselves are necessarily true. No soccer player has ever missed the goal because of the Earth's curvature, but that doesn't "prove" that the Earth is flat.

As we grow our Island of Knowledge, noosphere, —the "space" that makes sense to us with some rational evidence to back it up—we can't help but expand our horizons of imagination, intuition, and faith. A bigger Island of Knowledge has broader horizons. An island with a more curious and inventive and affluent population would get higher observation towers, then a fleet of exploratory vessels, kites, balloons, and airplanes. Much of the stuff we surmise way out there among the waves never pans out, but some eventually solidifies into evidence-supported knowledge. And then we have an even higher ground from which to look even farther out, and we see even more incredible stuff.

The deeper we understand our immediate environment, the more far-out, speculative, conjectural stuff we get exposed to. And, of course, vice versa. The itch to consolidate the rational understanding of our 'hood sends us exploring the margins of unknown. And there at the frontier we, again, find stuff we can't make sense of unless we postulate something crazy, like Democritus's atoms or Huygens's luminiferous ether or Lord Kelvin's dark matter. Some of these crazy suppositions eventually snap into the Island of Knowledge, some never do, but all share the same quality: they all ask you to, for starters, take something on faith. Something that wasn't part of your belief system before. New concepts enter our collective conscious through faith. Faith evolves as we do; we evolve as faith does.

While evolution of faith appears to be an enabling innovation for human species' Evolution 2.0, you don't hear the words "evolution" and "faith" in the same sentence very often. That is, unless folks are talking about the allegedly irreconcilable differences between the two.

I've long suspected that to be a false dichotomy. After all, Charles Darwin, known as the father of evolutionary theory, regarded himself as agnostic, and he thought it was "absurd to doubt that a man might be an ardent theist and an evolutionist." I thought there might actually be some complementarity there. We know of no law preventing God from arranging for evolution. If I'd known back then this maxim by the Sufi scholar Hasrat Inayat Khan: "The Sufi says this whole universe was made in order that God might know Himself. The seed wished to realize what it is, what is in it, and therefore became the tree"—I'd have instantly agreed that it sounds like a possibility.

But that was even before I learned about Lee Smolin's cosmological natural selection idea. When I did, I remembered that seeds not only grow into trees but also originate from trees. Circle of Life. It appears that God and evolution can be reconciled in a sense much deeper than Darwin suggested. They can be complementary, non-dual, related concepts. If God can create a universe, can't a universe create God?

Just to remind you, there are dozens of fundamental physical constants that shape the Universe we live in. Knowing their values, one can accurately model a lot of elementary processes going on around us. But cosmologists struggle to explain the values themselves, which appear to be incredibly fine-tuned to allow nuclei and atoms and stars and galaxies and bugs and slugs and you and me. How come we are so lucky?

Quantum mechanics (specifically, the prolific John Archibald Wheeler) suggested the quantum foam concept: the idea that elementary particles and bigger objects, including universes, can randomly appear out of nothing. And disappear almost instantly. Lee Smolin's cosmological natural selection idea is that most of the universes appearing at random out of a physical vacuum—nothing—would have the wrong combinations of fundamental constant values to survive for any noticeable length of time; hence they would collapse incredibly fast. The ones that last longer have better combinations of values; but like in biology, the real key to success is surviving long enough to produce offspring. Universes can, in principle, produce progeny via black holes. A black hole undergoing time reversal is thought to become a white hole, which from the inside of it looks like the Big Bang—the beginning of a new, daughter universe.

The ability of universes to produce progeny this way depends on the values of the fundamental constants in a particular Universe. Universes that are good at making the right black holes multiply like rabbits. They have a lot of offspring, and their offspring multiply like rabbits, too. In a population of universes, they will be preferentially represented, as long as the fundamental constants are more or less "heritable" and don't change drastically during the process. Thus, universes in a population evolve to optimize reproduction through black holes, and we're a lot more likely to find ourselves in one that did a good job of it: there's plenty of them around. That's what "good job" stands for in evolutionary context. That's cosmological natural selection, as originally envisioned by Smolin.

Now let's further imagine that some of the universes in the population produce life. That's not exactly a stretch: we live in one such. Besides, the same combinations of constant values that favor the formation of black holes also happen to be good for making carbon, oxygen, and the other elements we're made of, not to mention the planets we inhabit and the stars that provide the energy we need. Let's further imagine that life in some of those produces civilizations, and some of those civilizations climb the Kardashev scale, until they learn to make black holes on purpose. The right kind of black holes that create universes. Worlds on demand. Worlds that are created by some Creator's choice. Free will.

Is Humanity an Apprentice God?

If a Creator civilization creates worlds not too dissimilar from its own fertile universe, the progeny will have inherited—with some variation—the parent's ability to go through the stages of maturity: make nuclei, then atoms, then stars, then the whole periodic table, then interesting chemistry, then life, then intelligence, then civilizations, and then, finally, civilizations that create other worlds [136].

And while it's still possible for daughter Universes to be born without conscious effort, a sufficiently advanced civilization may be able—if willing—to boost the birthrate. If you do boost the birthrate, then in a few generations, in a population of universes, the ones with high fertility will outnumber the low performers, where random (a.k.a. slow) reproduction is the only option available. After many generations, you become overwhelmingly more likely to find yourself in a Universe created on purpose than in one that randomly popped out of nothing.

Just like worlds that procreate have exponential—multiplicative over generations—evolutionary advantage over those that don't, worlds that procreate on purpose have exponential evolutionary advantage over those that do so at random. That is, if developing advanced civilizations that create Universes on purpose is a heritable trait.

There are two ingredients to making universes intentionally, just like making anything else: you have to want to do it, and you have to have the technology and components and energy to actually do it.

Let's start with the tangibles. To begin with, the creation of a universe is (surprisingly) not all that energy expensive, as the negative gravitational energy exactly cancels the positive energy of matter [137]. That's how nothing—vacuum—can afford to be (in energy terms) pregnant with universes and the universes—to keep popping up here and there, most only to decay back into nothing in about 10^{-43} seconds.

As to technology and components, one way to do that is to make artificial black holes. Robert Zubrin, among others, has done some feasibility studies on these already and found nothing impossible about this feat. Louis Crane (who, in 1994, first came up with the idea of civilizations as catalysts of Universe creation), Lee Smolin, Avi Loeb, and Robert Zubrin all agree that there's nothing impossible about universes on demand [138]. All you have to do is learn to make black holes of a suitable mass, and, voilà, you can create Universes at will. No, not toys—the real thing, with all the matter and energy and stars and galaxies and bugs and slugs and quarrelling cosmologists that any self-respecting universe must have.

There might be other, possibly easier, ways of creating universes. Vacuum fluctuations can occur randomly in the quantum foam, but they can also be deliberately induced [139]. Alan Guth and Andrei Linde, the Nobel-prize winning coauthors of the currently leading theory on cosmic inflation, believe that it's perfectly possible for us mere mortals to learn to create universes in a lab, even without making a black hole first [140] [141]. So, there are several ways that a sufficiently advanced civilization can potentially do what gods do: create worlds at will.[36]

Any sufficiently advanced technology is indistinguishable from magic. Any sufficiently advanced civilization may well be indistinguishable from God. Especially to the folks who happen to live in a universe that advanced civilization created, which it won't ever create unless it thinks it's a good idea and sticks to it long enough to make it happen.

That's the intangibles. The irrational. The willingness to declare which way's up and to own up to it: climb the darn ladder, and build more of it as you climb.

Let's get back to the quote from the Book of Genesis that started this chapter: "And God said, let there be light: and there was light. And God saw the light, and it was good; and God divided the light from the darkness." According to the Book of Genesis, God tried out light and declared it to be good. This was the intangible, but invaluable, part of making a world on purpose: the intent to do so. The willingness to decide which way's up. God made an irrational choice, and the rest of Creation proceeded to rationally self-assemble accordingly. Of His own free will, God decided it was a good idea to create a world.

Maybe one day, so can we. In both indigenous American cosmology and Judaism, the noun used for the creator of the world is a plural noun. The founders of those systems apparently believed that a plurality of consciousnesses is what might add up to a god. Maybe they were on to something. Maybe it's a convergence of diverse consciousnesses that creates Creators. Is every conscious being a part of an emergent cosmic consciousness? Can an entire civilization evolve into God? We

---

[36] A Creator would perhaps want to keep in contact with its creation. If this whole universe was made in order that God might know Himself, God has to be able to communicate with it, presumably from the parent universe, where God lives.

Fortunately, we know of no laws that make that impossible. On the contrary, our leading theory of the big, general relativity theory, is quite compatible with the idea of wormholes, which are tunnels that connect universes or provide shortcuts between otherwise distant—causally disconnected—parts of a universe [142]. String theory of the small gives an alternative: quantum tunnelling can connect universes [143].

don't have a definition of consciousness any more than we have a definition of life or mind, so discussing all of that can't be scientific: we quite literally have no idea what we're talking about, even hypothetically. I mean, in terms of scientific hypotheses producing falsifiable predictions. So we're in the realm of religion: unprovable, irrational beliefs.

We live what we believe, consciously or otherwise. In this vast, wonderful, unforgiving, overwhelmingly tangled world, awash in information that we struggle to make heads or tails of, our beliefs tell us what to take into account and what to ignore, what data to trust and what to doubt, how to interpret the information we choose to trust, and, maybe most importantly, when to do the selecting and interpreting. When our irrational choices and preconceived notions clash with readily available facts, facts—at least at first—don't stand a chance. In his excellent book *Factfulness*, Hans Rosling [144] shows how most of us are deluded into thinking that this humanity is all screwed up. Rosling did a lot of studies asking different people multiple-choice questions about how things are in the world: is our health improving, worsening or staying the same; education; life expectancy, poverty levels and so forth. A typical question offered three options for an answer, so monkeys in a zoo choosing "answers" totally at random would get it right about every third time.

But modern people with access to enough information to know the accurate answer, consistently do worse than zoo monkeys would on these tests. A 2015 survey [145] shows that only 6% of Americans believe that the world is getting better. And university-educated folks, who are supposed to be pros at critical thinking, do even worse than the average Joe and Jane on many questions. There's a strong negativity bias, which means that people consistently choose an answer that suggests that the situation is worse than it actually is. Most folks believe that humanity has a higher child mortality than it actually does, less access to education than it does, higher violence rates, lower vaccination rates, et cetera ad nauseum. And once that bias has formed, it's self-reinforcing. Misanthropes look for bad news, and the bad news industry is there to help. Then the trap shuts with a bang. The prisoners search online for negative information, and Google bots know how to please them. They congregate in echo chambers with like-minded folks, revel in evidence corroborating their views, and quickly dismiss and ban any dissenter who has the temerity to suggest that humans can ever do anything right. They, quite rationally, bet against us every time. It makes no sense to bet on humans if you think they can do nothing right. When Charles Bukowski said, "If I bet on Humanity, I'd never cash a ticket," he was perhaps trying to err on the side of caution. Which side that would be is a matter of opinion.

For what it's worth, my wager is that erring on the side of caution means betting on us. I believe that consciousness is an evolving skill of the Universe, and we sentient humans are its evolving nodes. Cosmic consciousness is the next level of self-organization to a civilization climbing the Kardashev scale, just like atoms are to elementary particles, molecules to atoms, cells to molecules, organisms to cells, Gaia to organisms, and civilization to Gaia.

There's no rational proof that humanity—our global civilization—can evolve into God. There's no rational proof that it should. I just happen to, irrationally, believe that we can and that it would be good if we did. For lack of a better name, I'd call these beliefs the Two Commandments of Humanism.

Our civilization—you and me—looks in a mirror and sees itself getting ready to go up to the stars or down to the caves. Except it turns out that we can't. What you see instead is either UP arrows or DOWN arrows. You can't see both at the same time. It's called bi-stable perception. Your conscious mind declares that these are either just UP arrows or just DOWN arrows, and it refuses to see the other. The filters you happen to be using will determine whether you see light or darkness at the moment. There's no right or wrong answer, any more than there's a right or wrong haystack for Buridan's ass. There's no extra objective data that could make you change your opinion. There is no gray area in between. All it takes is a conscious effort to make yourself see the other side of the story. A little exercise of free will.

Figure 58 – Up or down?

The dark version of our self-image—the humans-are-locusts-cancer-plague thing—tells you that it's not a good idea to procreate, in any sense. We have suffering in our lives, so we better not have children who will suffer more. We "ruined" this planet, so we shouldn't spread to other ones. Forget the stars: they have a right to stay free of this horrible contamination, us. We live in a universe where misery exists, so we shouldn't create another one like ours, especially if there's a chance that those universes might get the "plague": our children.

The light version of the same picture suggests otherwise. It likes what we do, loves who we are, and advocates going forth. It believes that we'll continue to learn and do better next time. It has faith in the creators of the Sphinx and rubaiyat and the Taj Mahal and the light bulb and the World Wide Web. It believes in the explorers of Jomolungma and the Marianna trench and the periodic table and Gödel's theorem. It sees the light in the end of the tunnel, the long tunnel of our apprenticeship to become God, and it likes what it sees. It doesn't claim to know the future; it just likes the idea of checking it out.

How do you choose sides? Irrationally, as usual, that's how. To make completely rational choices, you need to know things you can't (yet) know, and if you knew those things, those "choices" wouldn't be choices anymore. Rational choice is an oxymoron. Sure, you can choose a college by evaluating a lot of objective information about it, but your choices of evaluation criteria, and especially their relative importance, are irrational, and so is your choice to quit vacillating and make a decision already. In this intertwined world, you can easily rationalize sticking to one worldview or the other—after you've irrationally made the choice, that is. Others have the same information available, but they make completely different decisions. And, after the fact, they justify theirs every bit as convincingly (to themselves, at least) as you justified yours. Plenty of data can be picked and interpreted every which way. Where you draw the line—and what you do with the data that happens to fall inside it—tells more about you than about anything else. No one can decide for you if evolving into God is a good idea. That's what you need your free will for. Among other things.

Is free will the skill of Gods? Can the skill of free will be an emergent property of complex systems – systems complex enough to add the new element of intent to cosmological natural selection? Can exercising free will develop it to such an advanced level that we eventually want to create universes, just as some of us have felt inexplicably compelled to create the Sphinx or the Taj Mahal or the *Mona Lisa* or the theory of relativity? Is advanced free will something that the evolution of universes selects for—intelligent life that's not only rational enough to be able to do God's job but also irrational enough to actually want it, too?

Is free will an adaptation to living forever – by creating worlds that escape the heat death of your own one? Could our Big Bang have been the announcement of the arrival of some Noah's ark, with seeds and everything? Is investment in growing our Island of Knowledge a selection criterion for immortalizing ourselves—not necessarily as individuals, but as a continually existing meta-organism united by a common consciousness that penetrates, and eventually creates, space and time? Is humanity a fledgling, an apprentice to become an immortal God? Is our collective consciousness evolving toward an omnipotent cosmic consciousness, gardening universes as a hobby? Is Gaia, then, a flower bud, a prospective progenitor of countless descendant worlds? Are we God's germ line? Heir apparent?

Actually, "heir apparent" may well be too myopically anthropocentric. There's only one thing you can believe in that's more naïve than the existence of space aliens, and that's their non-existence. As a candidate to enter Gods' germline, we'd better have some confidence if we want any chance of succeeding. But it might also help to humbly remember that one of the ways you may not get to see your competition is by the simple expedient of being too far behind everyone.

There may well be other civilizations in our Universe that have already learned to answer questions we haven't yet learned to ask. There may well have been other civilizations that died trying. It's perfectly compatible with all physics, chemistry, and biology we know for our Universe to be pregnant with life; and for life to be pregnant with intelligence; and for intelligence to be pregnant with civilizations; and for civilizations to be pregnant with gods. Gods create universes, and the cycle—the circle of life—starts over.

It's easy to imagine draconian selection at every step of this evolutionary process. Not every small bubble of life becomes a biosphere, not every glimmer of consciousness leads to Homer and Aristotle, not every clay tablet pictogram spawns a World Wide Web, not every planet-wide civilization evolves through the Kardashev types and all the way to a god that creates universes.

What helps us to win this round and to move on to the next one? Your guess is as good as mine, but I'm going to offer mine anyways. The evolving self-organization of humanity is, to me, a story about learning to get more and more diverse folks involved in pursuit of more and more intertwined goals. Learning to call other, very different, humans "us" rather than "them." Confluence, convergence, cross-pollination. Unity in diversity. Encountering concepts too bulky and fuzzy and nuanced to fit in any one human mind and making them work for us anyways. Constructing a stereoscopic view of this world (a.k.a. evolving human culture) by stitching together a mosaic from my little tile, and yours, and billions of others'.

I reckon this mosaic is our species' identity. Contributing to this mosaic is what it means to be "us." I think that reconciling the freedom of diverse individual minds with their collaborative convergence into collective consciousness—making sense of it all, together—is the secret weapons of our story-telling species. Our claim to fame. Our strong suit.

The question of us winning this round and moving to the next one, which is perhaps a lot more challenging than this one was, is the question of what "us" stands for. Who is the "us" we're supposed to bet on? How far back can our germlines diverge for you to still mean me, too, when you say "us"? At the dawn of the species, it was our tribe versus the rest of the world, then our country, our empire. Is our planet next in line for what "us" means? Our solar system, our galaxy? Our universe? How big is the biggest community you're a patriot of? How big is the biggest thing you feel ready to own? Is it six degrees of separation, or six degrees of convergence? Are you ready for the seventh? Do you want to be?

Is "I," your individual stream of consciousness, a little rivulet in some evolving cosmic flow? Does it converge—on the six different levels we have learned to recognize so far, and perhaps on many we haven't—into a bigger, nonlocal consciousness like one that has been ascribed to Gaia? Are there higher levels of this confluence, beyond Gaia, that we can't even name yet?

This line of inquiry inevitably brings us to the battle of philosophical titans: the whole material-vs-ideal, mind-vs-body issue. Materialists believe that matter is primary and mind secondary, meaning that matter exists no matter what and, when it feels like it, produces consciousness. Which is, therefore, provisional. Idealists, naturally, believe the opposite. Never mind the matter. They've been duking it out for millennia, and a lot of inquisitive and educated folks got seriously bruised, or worse, in the process.

While some people were yelling at the top of their lungs that it's matter that produces mind and others were yelling that no, it's mind that produces matter, some folks quietly noticed that the two aren't necessarily mutually exclusive. Is the whole materialism vs. idealism thing a chicken-and-egg problem? Can these be two sides of the same coin, two phases of the same cycle? Is there a non-dual complementarity here?

Do our evolving streams of consciousness flow through the landscapes of the material, objective world? Do these shape each other? Do individual streams merge, through degrees of convergence, into some mighty rivers? Do those then flow into a vast ocean of cosmic consciousness? Does nonlocal mind, sloshing in that ocean, in turn, evaporate and get blown by some wind we can't imagine yet over the material world, to condense into rain and fall onto the fertile ground to start a new "I"? Or to fall into some existing stream of consciousness in a way that gives some folks amazing sparks of intuition like idiot savant twins pulling twenty-digit prime numbers out of thin air just for fun [146]? Or take Einstein's description of that sudden flash of understanding when things click together: "The intellect has little to do on the road to discovery. There comes a leap in consciousness, call it intuition or what you will, and the solution comes to you and you don't know how or why." Or Carl Friedrich Gauss's quip: "I have had my results for a long time: but I do not yet know how I am to arrive at them."

Figure 59 – Convergence of streams: Ganges River delta from space. Image courtesy of Annamaria Luongo via Flickr.com (Annamaria84) and Wikimedia.

The savant brothers and Einstein and Gauss saw the world through their personal filter sets. So do you and I. I don't know about you, but mine don't let twenty-digit prime numbers through. Gauss's filter set had a huge hole in it, too. At nineteen, he guessed that a regular polygon can be constructed by a compass and a straightedge if the number of its sides is the product of distinct Fermat primes and a power of two. And it took a gaping hole in Einstein's filter set to let through the image of light moving at a constant velocity through space empty of luminiferous ether.

Broad-minded folks who get curious about abstruse matters like that are few and far between. Even fewer are recognized while they're still around. And these don't have their aha moments on schedule. These impactful moments are too rare and unpredictable to systematically study: you don't know when it's going to happen, and to whom. And you can't just have everyone and his brother permanently wired to EEG machines or stuck indefinitely in fMRI scanners. In the billions of hours of recording, we wouldn't know what to look for, anyways. And even if you got lucky and noticed something unusual and correlated it with some earth-shattering revelation, reproducibility would still be a big problem: you can't very well unlearn what you've learned and do it all over again. There have been no recorded instances of theories of relativity conceived inside an fMRI machine's magnetic womb. And it isn't likely to change either. So when it comes to understanding the mechanics of Einstein-caliber divination, we're perhaps limited to conjecture.

Here's mine. There's apparently a breach in the savants' and geniuses' filter sets, big enough to drive a Mack truck through. Visions and conjectures and insights—most of them complete junk—gush in through that breach, but somehow, the savants and geniuses manage to sort things out. The rest of us look at the world through comparatively narrow embrasures as a defensive measure. If we opened up wider, we'd get overwhelmed by the incoming flood and go nuts. How do the exceptional folks survive the onslaught? What makes them tick? What's different about them?

I suggest humility and ambition, not necessarily in that order. It would likely take a lot of humility to remember that, in most cases, the visions flashing through your mind, and looking like a stroke of genius at first glance, are anything but. It would likely take a lot of ambition to, nevertheless, stay open to the world and not shut down and curl up in some cozy, familiar impenetrable cocoon. To stay open and yet somewhat sane. At least, sane enough to report to the rest of us what they think is noteworthy in that fountain of consciousness, and to report in terms that the rest of us can, often with massive amounts of help of trained interpreters, reluctantly assimilate into our worldview. Whereupon our own filter sets, in turn, become less restrictive. Our narrow embrasures get wider.

Less restrictive filter sets mean, among other things, more diverse worldviews. As long as we actually listen to each other, diverse worldviews are a feature, not a bug. Looking at the world from as many different perspectives as we can muster may help our civilization dodge the bullets that our Universe so generously supplies. It stands to reason that this is what civilizations have to do to stick around long enough to become God. Natural selection for a stereoscopic view of the world.

And we're getting there, in our time-honored, stumbling way. Lou Gehrig's disease would have been a death sentence in the ancient world. Fortunately for us, by the time Stephen Hawking was diagnosed with it, we believed (with no evidence) that keeping him alive might be a good idea. In 1963, when he was diagnosed, no one knew he'd reward humanity with over fifty years of deep insights into the physics of the Universe. He was supposed to be dead in two years. Humanity chose to see the arrows pointing up to the stars, took a bet on Hawking, and won. Knowledge of black hole mechanics is very possibly a long-term survival skill for a civilization.

Every once in a while, we stumble. Sometimes a society looks at Up or Down arrows and sees the ones pointing down to the caves. It abandons sanity in favor of racial (or some other metric) purity, Aryan (or some other ethnic) superiority, white (or some other color) supremacy, or some such junk declared "omnipotent because it is true." Our best scientists told us that our resources are limited, it declares, and therefore we need to find a whole bunch of folks who won't get a cut. It says that we're the right tribe, and they're the wrong ones. It claims that they're wasting precious resources on their inferior lives. It alleges that it's rational to use all the remaining resources on the superior us, rather than on an inferior them.

Once a society does that, it denies itself the benefit of contributions of all the folks it just declared inferior. That's a bad idea, as many a society's ghost can attest.

One of the ways American B-17 bomber was better than any Axis bomber during WWII was in having good protection while keeping the armor weight down. That allowed the machine to have an impressive range, deliver a very heavy bomb load, and survive the flak and fighter attacks. It was accomplished by a judicious use of armor, which protected only the areas that needed protection. Did the Germans being bombed realize that the guy responsible for choosing the optimal distribution of armor was their former compatriot, an Austrian Jew named Abraham Wald, who managed to escape Austria right after Anschluss? Did the American bomber crews realize that they may well have owed their survival to their country's willingness to take Wald in?

Among refugees from the Third Reich and its allies were some of humanity's most brilliant minds: Albert Einstein, Karl Popper, Hans Bethe, Felix Bloch, Peter Debye, Hans Krebs, Niels Bohr, Bernard Katz, Walter Kohn, Wolfgang Pauli, Eugene Wigner, Max Born, Thomas Mann, James Franck, Otto Frisch, Fritz London, Lise Meitner, Erwin Schrödinger, Otto Stern, Leo Szilard, Edward Teller, Victor Weisskopf, and Enrico Fermi. The Axis was bleeding its intellectual elite, and we all know how it ended for the Axis—and for the Allied countries that admitted the refugees.

The Allies, though, still had a long way to go in the tolerance and broadmindedness department. Hundreds of thousands of European refugees running from Hitler were turned away. Japanese-Americans were sent to internment (a.k.a. concentration) camps, and so were Italian-Britons. Alan Turing, the father of computing, whose contributions to decoding German Enigma ciphers saved countless Allied lives, was convicted of "gross indecency," legalese for being in a homosexual relationship, a crime in 1952 Britain. And he was forcibly injected with drugs that rendered him impotent, stripped of his security clearance, and kicked out of the British signals intelligence service he had helped create a decade earlier. And for good measure, he was also denied entry to the US. Two years later, Turing died of an apparent suicide.

At the same time, though, humans were setting new goals. Dreaming up new ideals. Imagining higher standards to measure ourselves against. On October 1, 1945, the Declaration of Interdependence became part of the Congressional record in the United States of America. Here is its original text, in its entirety:

"Human progress having reached a high level through respect for the liberty and dignity of men, it has become desirable to re-affirm these evident truths:

- That differences of race, color, and creed are natural, and that diverse groups, institutions, and ideas are stimulating factors in the development of man;
- That to promote harmony in diversity is a responsible task of religion and statesmanship;
- That since no individual can express the whole truth, it is essential to treat with understanding and good will those whose views differ from our own;
- That by the testimony of history intolerance is the door to violence, brutality and dictatorship; and
- That the realization of human interdependence and solidarity is the best guard of civilization.

Therefore, we solemnly resolve, and invite everyone to join in united action.
- To uphold and promote human fellowship through mutual consideration and respect;
- To champion human dignity and decency, and to safeguard these without distinction of race, or color, or creed;
- To strive in concert with others to discourage all animosities arising from these differences, and to unite all groups in the fair play of civilized life.

ROOTED in freedom, bonded in the fellowship of danger, sharing everywhere a common human blood, we declare again that all men are brothers, and that mutual tolerance is the price of liberty."

Seventy years later, we live in an incomparably more inclusive world. It's okay to be Japanese in America or Italian in Britain. Openly LGBTQ+ folks hold security clearances just fine. Public transportation, hotels, and bars are no longer segregated by patrons' skin color. An indigenous American, John Herrington, has flown to space, making his Chickasaw Nation the smallest nation on this planet to have explored elsewhere. Non-discrimination laws are on the books. The Iron Curtain has rusted away, and millions of tourists, migrant workers, and students get exposed to cultures that their parents couldn't imagine experiencing firsthand. The number of international tourists in 2019 was the same as the total population of Earth in 1919. We're seeing a lot more of each other. We're getting used to being among people who don't look like us, speak like us, or think like us. We're no longer as scared of the unknown as we were not so long ago. We no longer shoot first and ask questions later when we see someone unfamiliar. A human's chances of dying in a war are fourteen times lower than dying in a traffic accident. We rely on vendors half a world away. We're kept in shape by competitors in countries we can't find on a map. We benefit from the ideas of folks who don't understand a word of our language, and we don't understand theirs.

We reach out to total strangers with ease our parents couldn't imagine. For the first time in the history of the species, the global delocalized consciousness got a physical infrastructure with a name: the World Wide Web.

That, yet again, changes the rules of the evolutionary game. That changes who's included when we say "us." On the Web, you can meet humans of every kind, from anywhere on the planet, and have an actual conversation with folks, even though you don't speak a word of each other's languages. It brings the wealth of human experience and thought and imagination right to your doorstep.

What happens next is up to you. You can choose to join the rest of humanity, like Satoshi Nakamoto with blockchain, Jimmy Wales and Larry Sanger and countless content providers with Wikipedia, Richard Saul Wurman and Harry Marks and countless content providers with TED Talks, or Scott Heiferman and countless content providers with Meetup. Or you can, instead, spend the rest of your life polishing your sarcastic trolling skills, joining a personality cult or a conspiracy theorist club, pondering questions like, "Why This Weekend's Blue Moon Is Extra Rare," or learning nineteen reasons a particular brand of snake oil is so hated/feared/suppressed by Big Pharma. You choose your ambitions. It's your life. You decide for yourself.

You also decide for the rest of us, just a little bit. Humanity is, among a lot of other things, a distributed decision-making system.

What the heck is a distributed decision-making system? Let's start with jellyfish. These ancient animals don't have a central nervous system (a.k.a. brain). What they do have is a nerve net: a network of interconnected neurons. And that serves them fine: they pulsate their bells in majestically rhythmic, coordinated waves to propel themselves, sense chemical gradients and gravity and light, swim away from dangerous waters and toward food, as well as sting, catch and swallow prey. All of this complex behavior relies on a distributed control system: the nerve net. A neuron is its node, and the system works through an elaborately choreographed interaction of the nodes.

Moving up the evolutionary chain, we find distributed systems at every step. Ant and bee cooperation, striped eel catfish swirls, and starling murmurations are all examples of distributed systems: a collective behavior with no central coordinating authority. A node in these is represented by a whole individual rather than just a neuron. But the emergent behavior at the system level results from node interaction, like it does in jellyfish.

We're at the top of the evolutionary pyramid—at least the terrestrial one. And we form distributed control systems, too. Our families and communities, companies and countries are all networks, and we're nodes in each of these.

And each of these human networks is a meta-organism capable of somewhat deliberate action: setting goals and trying to achieve them. This may have a lot to do with us, the nodes. A human makes for a lot more sophisticated node than a neuron. There's a lot more individuality in humans than in neurons. Neurons have no irrational worldviews and dreams and goals, as far as we know. But some humans do. We introduce the new element into distributed control systems: purpose. That makes it into a distributed decision-making system. The nodes can be deliberate, and they confer this ability to the network that they form. In my view, that's what is different about Evolution 2.0.

In Evolution 2.0, we learn to be deliberate about bigger and bigger things. The scale of our decisions is measured in handshakes. A one-handshake humanity could get together to kill a mammoth; a two-handshake humanity could cooperate to dam a stream, level a terrace, or build a shrine; and a five-handshake *H. sapiens* walked on the Moon.

At each scale, folks made choices that coalesced into the reality of that time. At each scale, more folks than before stuck together for longer than before in pursuit of something. At each stage, our goals grew more ambitious. So did we, at least those of us who chose to.

A purposeful, directional, deliberate motion quickly overtakes aimless, random drift. We break out of our mundane environment where everything is familiar and where everything that's unfamiliar is dismissed as heresy, and we go looking for something in the big world out there. And then we compare what we found with what we irrationally hoped to find, and we adjust course accordingly. Making course corrections (a.k.a. turns) eventually makes directional motion look random when you zoom out far enough. But our 'hood just got bigger.

And then the cycle repeats itself. We grow ambitious enough to set higher goals than we had before. We grow humble enough to recognize that instant gratification is even less likely with our new, more ambitious goals than it ever has been earlier. We learn to stick to it long enough to give ourselves a decent shot at success, as we just redefined it. Deliberately and irrationally.

Our species' way of being deliberate is to deliberate. There's no time machine to tell us the one right answer, so we go for the next best thing: we tell our different stories and see what makes sense. Family at a dinner table, jury in a jury room, demos in a Greek agora, and diplomats at the United Nations all argue their points. Their different points.

Lots of different points. They look at the world through their different filters. They notice different nuances of the same event. They offer different criteria for telling good from bad. It gets messy and sometimes frustrating.

So, to avoid frustration, the stories they tell us and the questions they ask us are sometimes cut down to simple "points." They leave out nuance. They ask us to project our multidimensional world on a yes-or-no answer to a question that seems to allow for a yes-or-no answer, if you don't look too closely. Do you want Brexit—yes or no? Do you want kids to go to school—yes or no? Do you want to get off fossil fuels—yes or no?

In our multifaceted world, if all you are allowed to say is yes or no, then whoever asks the question doesn't want you to tell the whole story. Whoever formulated the question didn't invite you to deliberate. They own the story. They tell you what your choices are, in words that suit them. They then interpret your answer, the single word you were allowed to say, to validate the entirety of their agenda (if you said what they wanted), or to invalidate you (if you didn't).

At a dinner table, in a jury room, in the Greek agora, or at the United Nations, what you're allowed to say is way more nuanced than a simple "yay" or "nay." Your story matters. Our different little stories are fibers that spin into threads, and threads weave into—hopefully—some coherent super-story. It eventually grows so overwhelmingly convoluted that even the smartest of us, individually, can't appreciate all of its aspects, yet somehow together we learn to.

The Digital Revolution we're in the middle of completes integration of information space for all terrestrial humans in the global agora of the World Wide Web. The Noosphere 2.0 is here, taking its first clumsy baby steps in this world. The choice of what to do with it is ours, and we're making it now, ready or not.

I have no evidence from the future that we'll somehow decide for our noosphere (a.k.a. our island of knowledge) to mature and spawn progeny throughout this

Universe. I have no evidence from the future that we'll succeed. I have no evidence from the future that if we succeed, our remote descendants will be happy with the result. I have no evidence from the future that we'll be happy enough with the result to create daughter universes in the image of our home Universe (a.k.a. become God).

I just choose to believe, without evidence, that we should. And I choose to believe, without evidence, that we shall. I invite you to celebrate human nature: the irrationality that sets our goals, and the rationality that guides us in pursuit of them.

That's it. I said it. The religion of Humanism, as I understand it, is a pretty straightforward, simple, uncluttered belief system. It's a monotheistic religion: its apprentice God is all of us, united in our diversity. Evolving together.

Humanism—well, at least my version of it—doesn't claim to be the Last Stop, the Ultimate Truth, or some such rubbish. You can't be serious about making evolution a cornerstone of your faith and, in the same breath, declare the faith itself to be exempt from evolving. So – what's next?

Your guess is as good as mine, but here's mine. I guess somewhere out there might be a Mt. Olympus, where wise elders come to meet, from different islands of knowledge in an archipelago of consciousness that we can't even imagine yet. From different corners of our Universe and, possibly, even elsewhere. And, if you're a stickler for relativistic accuracy, elseWHEN too.

As we have discussed, in an evolving population of universes, the ones created—and eventually inhabited—by sentient beings are at a potentially big advantage. We're unlikely to have it all to ourselves. We still have a pretty vague idea of what "it all" actually stands for, so it would be rather presumptuous of us to think that we're the only game in town.[37]

---

[37] Yup, our old buddy the Fermi paradox.

The problem with the Fermi paradox is the assumptions. As usual. If "they" are out "there," then we must see them right on the front pages, right? Yeah, right. News of little green men landing on the White House lawn would be regarded by pretty much everyone as an obvious, cheap hoax not worth a second look. The refusal to believe one's own eyes (well, actually interplanetary probes) is wonderfully exemplified by the predictably bored, cynical, and condescending reaction [147] to the discovery of what looks like fungi on Mars [148]. So the Fermi paradox isn't about advanced alien civilizations, it's about the current state of our own.

There's no guarantee that our distant descendants will make it to Mt. Olympus. We have a long way to go before we get there. We don't even know the rules of the game yet, except one. And I submit that the one we already know is the most important one. The one rule that we have already learned is this: you won't succeed unless you try. The selection at our stage of early apprenticeship seems to be for this one criterion: can we believe in ourselves enough to get over cynicism and suspicion and condescension and contempt and tribalism so we can keep climbing the Kardashev scale?

I believe we can. And if somebody thinks otherwise, then it's up to us to prove them wrong.

Our own search for extraterrestrial intelligence is based on a bunch of assumptions about what to look for. SETI started during the era of booming radio and TV broadcasting, flourishing radioastronomy and the rapid development of spacecraft using radio to communicate with us from wherever in the vastness of cosmos they were. It was only natural to assume that any civilization would be using electromagnetic radiation for communications across space because we only knew one civilization that tried: ours. So that's what we used.

But it turns out to be a notoriously inefficient way to broadcast announcement to recipients who can be literally anywhere. Robert Zubrin argues that if advanced civilizations choose to do any broadcasting at all, they're more likely to use messages less perishable than a radio transmission whooshing past any recipient at the speed of light and disappearing forever. We already know how to make a message like these: it's a microbe [149].

5 Afterword (and Preview of What's to Come)

An afterword is typically written by someone other than the author. It's supposed to tell you how the idea for the book was developed.

Let's keep the tradition of departing from tradition. This afterword is by the author, and it's mostly about the next book, not this one.

The book you're about to finish reading offered a broad-strokes picture of humanity at what's arguably a watershed moment for the species. The once-in-a-species-lifetime gift of canned sunlight gave us a chance to become masters of our own fate. Are we imaginative enough and bold enough to take a chance on ourselves, to take a leap of faith to the first rung of the Kardashev ladder to Mt. Olympus? Or are we going to blow it all—the chance that happens once in millions of lifetimes—on hats?

I don't know. Knowledge is something you can only have about what has already happened, and even then, you can't be sure you weren't tricked somehow. With the future, there's always plenty of uncertainty involved. We can give our descendants the benefit of the doubt and invest what's left of the treasure in settling the Universe—or not. How do we decide what to do?

This book dealt with the delusion that humanity's big choices can and/or should be made completely rationally. A surprising number of folks who should know better are busy deriding humans for not conforming to this fantasy. I can't think of a less promising course of action than flogging this dead horse. Actually, it was dead on arrival: no decision has ever been made without a leap of faith. No decision—YES, NO, or even DON'T CALL US, WE'LL CALL YOU—has ever been made with comprehensive knowledge of all its consequences. Lacking a time machine, no one can make any decision without a leap of faith. "Rational choice" is an oxymoron.

When we find a cherished illusion dead, we grieve. Accordingly, this book dealt with the five stages of grief. Just to remind you, the five stages of grief are denial, anger, bargaining, depression, and acceptance. In this case:

- Denial that we have free will to make irrational choices
- Anger at folks that make irrational choices
- Bargaining to call irrational choices rational
- Depressing realization that you'll have to pay for the consequences of all choices, including the ones you thought you didn't make
- Acceptance that you can't win unless you play.

And "play" means, in this context, to give our descendants the benefit of the doubt and invest our resources in settling the Universe. Starting with our most renewable resource: human talent. This book was intended to be a prospectus for Humanity, Inc., an invitation to invest your talent in the enterprise of *Homo exploratoris*. It's the introductory part (a.k.a. executive summary) of a business plan. Well, a draft of an executive summary. Okay, fine, a glimmer of an executive summary.

In an actual business plan, what's supposed to follow the executive summary is SWOT analysis. SWOT stands for Strengths, Weaknesses, Opportunities, and Threats. What can help us on the way to the stars? What can drive us back into the caves?

I'm sure that everyone on this planet would have a different list, and there are plenty of choices available. Here are some of mine:

There's a threat that the indignation industry (a.k.a. outrage farming) convinces us that we're the problem. Not you and me personally, of course, but the vast majority of humans that we habitually call "them." "We" don't deliberate with "them." We can't be deliberate if we can't deliberate, and we can't deliberate from inside our bigoted echo chambers. A "positive" feedback loop is working overtime to make mass media drive us into these chambers. That's how media herds us into flocks with predictable reaction to cheap stimuli. One of the topics for the next book is how it happened and what we can do about it.

Is there an alternative to the preaching-to-the-choir niche-market media that declare every dissenter a moron? It seems to me that one is being created as we speak. Social media (a.k.a. mass media for the masses, by the masses) are the most serious competitors news professionals have ever faced. And the pros are losing (Figure 60). The remaining ones are, understandably, in the mood to cherry-pick the bad news about the rest of us. Meanwhile, oases of positive, productive thought are popping up here and there. Will they grow or fade away? Will the ideas discussed there lead to action?

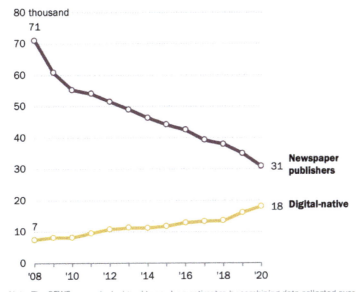

Figure 60 – US media advertising revenue. Image courtesy of Pew Research Center.

As American billionaire hotelier J. W. Marriott once said, "The four most important words in the English language are, 'What do you think?'" How often do we say this? How often do we take advantage of the social media tools to ask it in a language other than our own? How often do we take time to listen to an opinion different from ours and to the line of thinking that led to that opinion?

Another threat is complacency. Sure, if the scare is scary enough and urgent enough, we can pull ourselves together into a temporary coalition, pool our resources, and defeat Nazism or a hole in ozone layer. But when you're trying to shape popular opinion to support doing something, whacking Hitler is a very easy thing to sell: he's doing most of the selling for you.

When the danger isn't as immediate, it's harder to get folks to take it seriously. Pretty much everyone sees that the surface of the Moon is pockmarked by thousands of projectiles big enough to wipe out human civilization. Yet this image so far fails to convince many of us that humanity's days are numbered unless we make Space our home. The danger seems very remote, just like it did to the dinosaurs. We can always find a pet project to do first, before getting serious about the rest of the Universe. Just like dinosaurs did.

Even a fifty-year horizon is too far away for many of us. About 80% of the energy we use today—and 92% in the transportation sector and 100% in air transportation—comes from fossil fuels, and we won't be using those anymore in about half a century or so. Yet many of us (including some folks whose job is to know better) still think someone else will miraculously come up with a replacement, without the rest of us having to lift a finger.

Even the twenty to thirty years between today and the next peak of the Gleissberg cycle (the 80-to-100-year cycle of solar activity) may be too remote for many of us to give it a second thought. Meanwhile, investment into ruggedizing power and internet infrastructure against solar superstorms can't be justified with any existing data: the infamous Carrington event happened long before the Internet, and the damage from much smaller storms during the Gleissberg minimum turned out to be cheaper to repair than to prevent. Thirty years from now, the damage likely won't be as limited and localized as it was in 1989, unless we do something about it. Especially vulnerable is the World Wide Web, whose infrastructure rapidly extends into orbit, where energy is free and so is waste heat disposal, —leaving Earthbound competition in the dust, efficiency-wise. If by the next Carrington-scale solar storm all human data—from digitized ancient manuscripts to digitized scientific journals to patents and user manuals and databases and maps and bank accounts and property records and everything else—is up there in orbit without a hardened, probably terrestrial, backup, we may well lose all memory of how the world economy managed to feed our billions. And of most everything else.

Another threat is space junk. It's a form of complacency to shoot projectiles into the sky without thinking up a way to sweep up the uncontrollable ones. Satellites, spent upper stages, and other objects in LEO crisscross the globe at speeds faster than bullets. And traffic is getting pretty bad. The first Kessler-syndrome collisions, which are collisions of two satellites that yield orbiting buckshot that converts everything it hits into more orbiting buckshot, have already happened. Meanwhile, the race to launch satellite mega-constellations is on. With the target-rich environment of tens of thousands of sats built on a budget, there's a very real possibility of collision avalanches, which would lock us out of Space by making LEO into an impassable shooting gallery. There are already over 120 million pieces of junk in LEO big enough to disable an active satellite. Sending a dedicated mission after each of these would cost an arm and a leg, besides exacerbating the very problem it's trying to solve (by adding more debris from the mission itself than it removes).

The list of threats is only limited by our imagination. Take, for example, food. Our agriculture already took over 40% of dry land on Earth, twenty-one of the thirty-seven ancient aquifers are running dry, and phosphate ore that took hundreds of millions of years to form is being used in just decades. Isn't it time we got anxious?

As Greek philosopher Epictetus noted almost 2,000 years ago, "Man is not worried by real problems so much as by his imagined anxieties about real problems." Epictetus knew what he was talking about. Born a slave, he took matters into his own hands, and eventually he became so influential that after his death an admirer paid 3,000 drachma (about eight times the average annual wages of a skilled worker back then) for an oil lamp that Epictetus owned.

Taking matters into our own hands is what we, as a species, have been doing for quite some time. Small scale first, then bigger and bigger, until matters got global. It's time to fish or cut bait. We can learn to be masters of this particular corner of the Universe, or we can make room for someone else who would. Do we own the place or rent it? Do we get anxious, or do we get creative?

We're the only species on Gaia that can do something deliberate about an asteroid, a magnetic pole flip, a super-volcano, a black hole, or a supernova. We're the only chance our terrestrial biosphere has to survive cosmic catastrophes in its glorious diversity. If somebody learns to either avert any of these or to build an ark to get elsewhere, it won't be chimps or rats or slugs. It'll be us. Gaia, who evolved us, depends on us to immortalize it.

It's a pretty tall order. Once we choose to own the place and become deliberate about running it, we won't be useless humans anymore. We'll have our work cut out for us. All kinds of "us." Human talent will be a rate-limiting resource in this race. The human race.

Figure 61 – Owning the place.

Once you choose to own the place, every recognized problem becomes an opportunity to do better. The next book will speculate about what some of these opportunities might look like.

Can we crowdfund a centrifuge to launch objects to space (like SpinLaunch did) or ocean skimmers to sweep up plastic (like Ocean Cleanup did)? Can we design animal species like the startup Colossal plans to do? Can we crowdsource user-supported knowledge bases like Wikipedia? Can we put together trials to test some way-out-there ideas, like the de-extinction of the wooly mammoth or seeding ocean with iron or spraying seawater to control the albedo or animal overpasses and fish ladders? Can we build an Alcubierre drive? A Woodward-effect propellant-less engine? Can we launch a barrel of sand from a SpinLaunch centrifuge, a rail gun or

SpaceTram maglev system, and blow it up in front of a piece of space junk, which would fly into the sand cloud, slow down, and deorbit (the sand wouldn't quite reach orbital velocity, so we would avoid adding to the very problem we're trying to solve)? Can we explore nuclear transmutation—low-energy and otherwise—to rearrange nucleons as needed to make the elements we need in an "alchemistry" reactor, like Irène Joliot-Curie and Frédéric Joliot did in 1934? Can we send human geologists to the asteroid belt to look for lithium and indium, rare earths and thorium, antimony and phosphorus (a human geologist would do more in a few hours than an unsupervised robot can accomplish in years)? Can we build a ladder out of our gravity well, like SpaceTram or Launch Loop, and fill our orbit with solar power stations, habitats, factories, and farms? Can we build a global electric grid so that terrestrial solar and wind don't need local storage or non-renewable backup? Can we build suborbital solar power stations (a.k.a. Space Domes), whose dynamic support will serve as energy storage for nights? Can we build space-based solar power infrastructure, with Space Domes repurposed to support the terrestrial receivers?

Figure 62 – Space Dome over a city (BADLY out of scale for visual effect).

Can we get more rational in our resource allocation? In particular, can we learn to use the talents of the bright, hardworking, and disciplined folks working in defense to do something about the global threats listed above, instead of whatever it is they're doing in Figure 63 below? With $32 million per hour spent globally on defense, we may want to address our real security needs. The good news is that some folks in uniform are already addressing those for a living, and some civilians are paid by the military to do so, too.

Figure 63 – Wrong threat.

To get more rational about resource allocation, we need better tools to assess, compare, and prioritize threats and opportunities. Can we learn to put together holistic models that account for factors from various fields of study? Can technologists (who, for lack of relevant training, often overlook what's arguably the most important subsystem in any system they design—the human decision-making system) remember to ask experts in sociology, psychology, economics, and management for their opinions? And vice versa? An individual can be, and often is, brilliant and myopic at the same time. That's what we have each other for. Among a lot of other things, of course.

> Abilene paradox: that's the mysterious ability of a group to make a decision no member of the group in their sane mind would have made on her own. The way it happens is everyone thinks (s)he does what others want. It's entirely possible that terminating the Apollo program, instead of going to Mars, was an example of that.

Why stop at experts? Experts, after all, are best at predicting the past. They embody institutionalized knowledge. Not only do they expertly sell $435 hammers, $74,165 aluminum ladders, $437 tape measures, and $2,228 monkey wrenches to our military, but they actually manage to sell politicians who ask for even more of our tax money to be spent that way. So if you're looking for someone who thinks outside the box, you may want to look elsewhere: experts are the ones who built the box. They, quite naturally, believe that it's the most perfect box in town. They may even be right, like French fortifications experts before WWII were right about the Maginot defensive line. It was perfect. It just didn't work: it was a great defense against the wrong threat, one that the experts knew all about from the previous war. Refusing to look outside your comfort zone and buttressing each other's authority is how whole groups of brilliant people can develop tunnel vision. It sometimes takes a patent outsider to bring in some fresh ideas. You might remember the name of some guy who published four scientific papers in four different fields the same year he was awarded his Ph.D. He wasn't a recognized expert in any of the four areas of research. In fact, each of the publications was his first venture in the respective field. Two of the fields hadn't existed before he founded them with his research. The other two won him a Nobel Prize and confirmed the twenty-three-century-old guess that matter is made of atoms. Yes, I'm talking about Albert Einstein.

It was Einstein who said, "We should not assume that experts are the only ones who have a right to express themselves on questions affecting the organization of society." Indeed, we shouldn't. When epidemiologists, virologists, and hospital logistics experts want strict quarantine, while economists, sociologists, and psychologists don't, somebody somewhere has to decide which opinion to listen to.

> The Von Restorff effect is the tendency to remember something that sticks out better than something that doesn't. For example, if you see the list, "Smith, Brown, Jones, Williams, Von Restorff, Johnson, Taylor," you're most likely to remember Von Restorff and no one else.

Remember the four most important words in the English language, "What do you think"? I submit that the two most important words in the English language are, "I dunno." Admitting incompleteness of the knowledge inherited from classical times was the first step to the Scientific Revolution. And it started in Europe, particularly in England, where two-thirds of duty-paying members of the Royal Society of London for Improving Natural Knowledge were citizen scientists (a.k.a. laymen), who have a much easier time admitting that they don't know something than career experts. Can modern laymen help modern gurus learn to say, "I dunno," like they perhaps helped Newton? Can citizen scientists, in some Internet-enabled way, help break barriers to new knowledge that hamper our understanding of this beautiful world? Can outsiders looking in notice something that professionals missed? Can good science be done on a gig basis, like Einstein's *Annus Mirabilis*? Should it be done that way?

In fact, we're already making strides in this direction. How it could unfold, will be covered in the next book. I think we are overdue for a paradigm shift in science: post-dualism, holistic, science and technology appear ripe for coming out in the mainstream. And it's going to get interesting. Delayed-choice quantum eraser, the thought experiment proposed by John Archibald Wheeler more than forty years back, has been done in an actual lab, experimentally demonstrating retrocausality: effect preceding its cause. A variety of studies have demonstrated precognition and various other psi phenomena, opening the possibility that we already have a time machine (a.k.a. our mind), we just don't know how to use it yet. Researchers are actively exploring supraluminal communications and even travel. The cosmological principle is coming crashing down: there is no scale, after all, at which our Universe is uniform, structureless, and uninteresting. Our theories of the big and the small remain incompatible with each other; our theories of the complex are inadequate to yield the forecasts we need (and a whole new mathematical toolbox may be necessary to fix that); and we still don't know what life, consciousness, and mind are. If you're scientifically inclined, the next book is full of good news for you: we aren't about to run out of fascinating things we don't understand. If anything, it's the other way around.

Should technologists and scientists have all the fun? Hell no. Once we choose to go up to the stars, we have all kinds of exciting things to do. Humanity Inc. will be hiring for all shifts. Will we learn to use the World Wide Web to improve distributed information-gathering? Decision-making? Can we devise a system that lets stakeholders, as Einstein has put it, "express themselves on questions affecting the organization of society"? What would the output of such a system look like? And can it be tested and tweaked safely?

Those are just some of the questions for the next book. I'm looking forward to writing it, and I hope you—yes, you—will help make it better.

6 Bibliography

[1] Ratner P. 200 cognitive biases rule our everyday thinking. Big Think [Internet]. 2019 Jan 24. Available from: https://bigthink.com/mind-brain/cognitive-bias-codex?rebelltitem=8#rebelltitem8.

[2] Ruiz IB. This apocalyptic is how kids are imagining our climate future. Deutsche Welle [Internet]. 2017 Oct 13. Available from: https://www.dw.com/en/this-apocalyptic-is-how-kids-are-imagining-our-climate-future/a-40847610.

[3] Ng, K. Should I factor climate change into deciding whether to have kids? *Independent* [Internet]. 2021 Jul 26. Available from: https://www.independent.co.uk/environment/children-carbon-footprint-climate-change-damage-having-kids-research-a7837961.html.

[4] Schwartz B. The paradox of choice. TED: Ideas Worth Spreading [Internet]. 2005 Jul. Available from: https://www.ted.com/talks/barry_schwartz_the_paradox_of_choice?language=en#t-429112.

[5] Raillant-Clark W. The selective advantage of being on the edge of a migration wave. EurekAlert! [Internet]. Available from: https://www.eurekalert.org/pub_releases/2011-11/uom-tsa102611.php.

[6] Copernicus N. *On the Revolutions*. Baltimore; 1978.

[7] Galilei, G. Letters to Castelli and to the Grand Duchess Christina. In: Finocchiaro MA (ed.). *The Trial of Galileo: Essential Documents*. Indianapolis: Hackett Publishing; 56-69. 2014.

[8] Wikipedia.org. Trilemma [Internet]. 2022 [updated 2022 Jan 28; cited 2022 Jan 30]. Available from: https://en.wikipedia.org/wiki/Trilemma.

[9] YouTube.com. Bell's theorem: The quantum venn diagram paradox [Internet]. 2017 Sep 13. Available from: https://www.youtube.com/watch?v=zcqZHYo7ONs.

[10] Theil S. Why the human brain project went wrong—and how to fix it. *Scientific American* [Internet]. 2015 Oct 1. Available from: https://www.scientificamerican.com/article/why-the-human-brain-project-went-wrong-and-how-to-fix-it/.

[11] Norton JD. The dome: A simple violation of determinism in Newtonian mechanics. Pitt.edu [Internet]. Department of History and Philosophy of Science, University of Pittsburgh. 2005 Jun 2. Available from: https://www.pitt.edu/~jdnorton/Goodies/Dome/.

[12] Gilbert L. New findings suggest laws of nature 'downright weird,' not as constant as previously thought. Phys.org. 2020 Apr 27. Available from: https://phys.org/news/2020-04-laws-nature-downright-weird-constant.html.

[13] Sabulsky DO, Dutta I, Hinds EA. Experiment to detect dark energy forces using atom interferometry. *Physical Review Letters*. 2019 Aug 6; 123: 061102-6.

[14] University of Geneva. Solved: The mystery of the expansion of the universe. Phys.org. 2020 Mar 10. Available from: https://phys.org/news/2020-03-mystery-expansion-universe.html.

[15] Matute H, Yarritu I, Vadillo MA. Illusions of causality at the heart of pseudoscience. *The British Psychological Society* [Internet]. 2011 Mar 16. Available from: https://onlinelibrary.wiley.com/doi/abs/10.1348/000712610X532210.

[16] Saltelli A, Funtowicz S. What is science's crisis really about? *ScienceDirect*. 2017 Aug; 91: 5-11.

[17] Negin E. Ask a scientist: Nearly everything you want to know about climate lawsuits. Union of Concerned Scientists [Internet]. 2020 Oct 9. Available from: https://blog.ucsusa.org/elliott-negin/nearly-everything-you-want-to-know-about-climate-lawsuits/.

[18] Wolchover N. Quantum mischief rewrites the laws of cause and effect. *Quanta Magazine* [Internet]. 2021 Mar 11. Available from: https://www.quantamagazine.org/quantum-mischief-rewrites-the-laws-of-cause-and-effect-20210311/.

[19] Wikipedia.org. Bayesian inference [Internet]. 2022 [updated 2022 Jan 21; cited 2022 Jan 30]. Available from: https://en.wikipedia.org/wiki/Bayesian_inference#:~:text=Bayesian%20inference%20is%20a%20method,and%20especially%20in%20mathematical%20statistics.

[20] Kamenetz A. The Pandemic has researchers worried about teen suicide. NPR [Internet]. 2020 Sep 10. Available from: https://www.npr.org/2020/09/10/911117577/the-pandemic-has-researchers-worried-about-teen-suicide?fbclid=IwAR1xsaNFSLkSJJZgmlocq90wl8SIca97CbJuMogA7oRVP3EBBUm_LLaYC-Y.

[21] CBS News Bay Area. Newsom emphasizes 'evidence of climate change' during wildfire update [Internet]. 2020 Sep 16. Available from: https://sanfrancisco.cbslocal.com/2020/09/16/newsom-emphasizes-evidence-of-climate-change-in-latest-wildfire-update/.

[22] Wolffe R. America's problems aren't Obama's fault. They're George W Bush's. *The Guardian* [Internet]. 2016 Aug 30. Available from: https://www.theguardian.com/commentisfree/2016/aug/30/america-problems-obama-fault-george-w-bush-election-2016.

[23] Wolffe R. America's problems aren't Obama's fault. They're George W Bush's. The Guardian [Internet]. 2016 Aug 30. Available from: https://www.theguardian.com/commentisfree/2016/aug/30/america-problems-obama-fault-george-w-bush-election-2016.

[24] McGrath MJ, Siepmann JI, Kuo IFW, Mundy CJ, VandeVondele J, Hutter J, et al. Simulating fluid-phase equilibria of water from first principles. The Journal of Physical Chemistry A. 2006; 110(2): 640-6.

[25] Baede APM, Ahlonsou E, Ding Y, Schimel D. The climate system: An overview. IPCC. In: Bolin B, Pollonais S (eds). *TAR Climate Change 2001: The Scientific Basis*. Cambridge, UK: Cambridge University Press; 2001. 85-98.

[26] Clarke D, Morley E, Robert D. The bee, the flower, and the electric field: Electric ecology and aerial electroreception. *Journal of Comparative Physiology A: Neuroethology, Sensory, Neural, and Behavioral Physiology*. 2017 Jun 24; 203(9): 737-748.

[27] Parkhomov AG. Rhythmic and sporadic changes in the rate of beta decays: Possible reasons. *Journal of Modern Physics*. 2018 Jul; 9(8): 1617-32.

[28] Hoefer C. Mach's Principle as action-at-a-distance in GR: The causality question. *Studies in History and Philosophy of Modern Physics* [Internet]. 2014 Sep 4. Available from: http://diposit.ub.edu/dspace/bitstream/2445/166294/1/661387.pdf.

[29] Greenfieldboyce N. Scientists discover outer space isn't pitch-black after all. NPR [Internet]. 2020 Nov 18. Available from: https://www.npr.org/2020/11/18/936219170/scientists-discover-outer-space-isnt-pitch-black-after-all#:~:text=Southwest%20Research%20Institute-,Scientists%20have%20used%20the%20New%20Horizons%20spacecraft%2C%20billions%20of%20miles,measure%20the%20darkness%.

[30] Chu J. Cosmic rays may soon stymie quantum computing. *MIT News* [Internet]. 2020 Aug 26. https://news.mit.edu/2020/cosmic-rays-limit-quantum-computing-0826?fbclid=IwAR22ESXgoB4ns5QIIu0sDgkq5fg_LkEtQKudEaoR1wZ_13j0F5dR4Pctc5s.

[31] Guth, AH. Inflationary universe: A possible solution to the horizon and flatness problems. *Physical Review* [Internet]. 1981 Jan 15; 23(2): 347-56.

[32] Verlinde EP. On the origin of gravity and the laws of Newton. *Journal of High Energy Physics*. 2010 Jan 6; 1104: 1-29.

[33] Wolchover N. The Case Against Dark Matter. *Quanta Magazine* [Internet]. 2016 Nov 29. Available from: https://www.quantamagazine.org/erik-verlindes-gravity-minus-dark-matter-20161129/.

[34] Chae K-H, Lelli F, Desmond H, McGaugh SS, Li P, Schombert JM. Testing the strong equivalence principle: Detection of the External field effect in rotationally supported galaxies. *The Astrophysical Journal*. 2020 Nov 20; 904(1): 1-20.

[35] Ferreira B. Scientists find more evidence that galaxies Are Synced up in a 'cosmic web.' Vice [Internet]. 2021 Jan 11. Available from: https://www.vice.com/en/article/z3vqp5/scientists-find-more-evidence-that-galaxies-are-synced-up-in-a-cosmic-web.

[36] Ferreira B. There's growing evidence that the universe is connected by giant structures. Vice [Internet]. 2019 Nov 11. Available from:https://www.vice.com/en/article/zmj7pw/theres-growing-evidence-that-the-universe-is-connected-by-giant-structures.

[37] Smolin L. Time Reborn: From the Crisis in Physics to the Future of the Universe. New York; 2013.

[38] Gangemi B. ExistingtTheories regarding neanderthals: Extinction, social structures, intelligence, social rituals, neanderthal and AMH interface, behaviors, and personalities. SUNY New Paltz [Internet]. 2013. Available from: https://faculty.newpaltz.edu/glenngeher/files/neandertal_lit_rev.pdf.

[39] Lieber R. Giving more globally, and less locally. *The New York Times* [Internet]. 2015 Jun 19. Available from. https://www.nytimes.com/2015/06/20/your-money/giving-more-globally-and-less-locally.html.

[40] Godin M. Irish donors are helping a Native American tribe face the coronavirus crisis. Here's the historical reason why. *Time* [Internet]. 2018 Mar 12. Available from: https://time.com/5833592/native-american-irish-famine/.

[41] Moscow Seasons. From Tverskaya Street to the Moon: How people in Moscow signed up for a space flight in 1927 [Internet]. 2020 Aug 14. Available from: https://moscowseasons.com/en/news/from-tverskaya-street-to-the-moon-how-people-in-moscow-signed-up-for-a-space-flight-in-1927/.

[42] Phillips M , Lorenz T. 'Dumb money' is on GameStop, and it's beating Wall Street at its own game [Internet]. *The Japan Times*. 2021 Jan 8. Available from: https://www.japantimes.co.jp/news/2021/01/28/business/gamestop-stock-frenzy/.

[43] Williams M. The average temperature of the universe has been getting hotter and hotter. *Universe Today* [Internet]. 2020 Nov 14. Available from: https://www.universetoday.com/148794/the-average-temperature-of-the-universe-has-been-getting-hotter-and-hotter/.

[44] Ananthaswamy A. Biggest void in space is 1 billion light years across. *New Scientist* [Internet]. 2007 Aug 24. Available from:https://www.newscientist.com/article/dn12546-biggest-void-in-space-is-1-billion-light-years-across/.

[45] Robitzski D. Giant arc of galaxies is way too big to exist, scientists say. The Byte [Internet]. 2021 Jun 22. Available from: https://futurism.com/the-byte/giant-arc-galaxies.

[46] Robitzski D. The largest structures in the universe started to spin and we don't know why. The Byte [Internet]. 2021 Jun 14. Available from: https://futurism.com/the-byte/largest-structures-universe-spin.

[47] Unger RM, Smolin L. The singular Universe and the Reality of Time. Cambridge: UK; 2015.

[48] Starr M. Study maps the odd structural similarities between the human brain and the universe. Science Alert [Internet]. 2020 Nov 17. Available from: https://www.sciencealert.com/wildly-fun-new-paper-compares-the-human-brain-to-the-structure-of-the-universe.

[49] Musser G. Quantum paradox points to shaky foundations of reality. *Science* [Internet] 2020 Aug 17. Available from: https://www.sciencemag.org/news/2020/08/quantum-paradox-points-shaky-foundations-reality.

[50] Wikipedia.org. Wheeler–Feynman absorber theory [Internet]. 2022 [updated 2022 Jan 20; cited 2022 Jan 31]. Available from: https://en.wikipedia.org/wiki/Wheeler–Feynman_absorber_theory.

[51] Harnik R, Kribs GD, Perez G. A Universe Without Weak Interactions. Physcial Review D. 2006 Aug 1 [cited 2022 Feb 1]; 74(3): 1-27. Available from: https://arxiv.org/abs/hep-ph/0604027.

[52] Starr M. Just three orbiting black holes can break time-reversal symmetry, physicists find. ScienceAlert [Internet]. 2020 Mar 25. Available from: https://www.sciencealert.com/three-black-holes-orbiting-each-other-can-t-always-go-backwards in-time?fbclid=IwAR1nGvQWilMYltsjEGlym3bVLL4nb6COr_CTEm4ssDIDR8sxwed3zDXqZ2k.

[53] Emspak J. Spooky! Quantum action is 10,000 times faster than light. Live Science [Internet]. 2013 Mar 15. Available from: https://www.livescience.com/27920-quantum-action-faster-than-light.html.

[54] Van Flandern, T. Dark Matter, Missing Planets and New Comets. Berkeley; 1999.

[55] Shi H, Milotti E, Bartalucci S, Bazzi M, Bertolucci S, Bragadireanu AM, et al. Experimental search for the violation of Pauli exclusion principle. *The European Physical Journal C.* 2018; 78(319): 1-14.

[56] Schrodinger E. *What Is Life?* Cambridge: UK; 1944.

[57] Jennings RC, Engelmann E, Garlaschi F, Casazza AP, Zucchelli G. Photosynthesis and negative entropy production. *Biochimica et Biophysica Acta (BBA) - Bioenergetics.* 2005 Sep 30; 1709(3): 251-255.

[58] Mauzeral D. Thermodynamics of primary photosynthesis. *Photosynthesis Research.* 2013; 116(2): 363-6.

[59] Griffiths C. *A thermodynamic analysis of biological systems using process synthesis.* PhD Thesis. University of the Witwatersrand, Johannesburg; 2012. Available from: https://core.ac.uk/download/pdf/39671622.pdf.

[60] Talbott D, Thornhill W. *The Electric Universe.* Portland; 2007.

[61] Smolin L. *The Life of the Cosmos.* Oxford; 1997.

[62] Lopez-Fanjul C, Garcia-Dorado A. The fuel of evolution. *Heredity.* 2011 Apr; 106(4): 535-6.

[63] Davis W. Asteroid apophis not a risk to Earth for at least 100 years, NASA says. NPR [Internet] 2021 Mar 27. Available from: https://www.npr.org/2021/03/27/981917655/asteroid-apophis-not-a-risk-to-earth-for-at-least-100-years-nasa-says.

[64] McFall-Johnsen M, Woodward A. A NASA simulation revealed that 6 months' warning isn't enough to stop an asteroid from hitting Earth. We'd need 5 to 10 years. Insider [Internet]. 2021 May 12. Available from: https://www.businessinsider.com/nasa-asteroid-simulation-reveals-need-years-of-warning-2021-5.

[65] Bryant C. Suez shows civilization is more vulnerable than we think. Bloomberg.com [Internet]. 2021 Mar 26. Available from: https://www.bloomberg.com/opinion/articles/2021-03-27/suez-ever-given-fiasco-shows-civilization-is-more-vulnerable-than-we-think.

[66] Union of Concerned Scientists. The UCS Science Hub for Climate Litigation. 2020 Aug 3. Available from: https://www.ucsusa.org/resources/science-hub-climate-litigation.

[67] Brown M. Spacex Starlink: How it could kickstart an 'uncontrolled experiment.' Inverse [Internet]. 2021 May 27. Available from: https://www.inverse.com/innovation/spacex-could-cause-geoengineering.

[68] Cepelewicz J. Nature versus nurture? Add 'noise' to the debate. *Quanta Magazine* [Internet]. 2020 Mar 23. Available from: https://www.quantamagazine.org/nature-versus-nurture-add-noise-to-the-debate-20200323/?fbclid=IwAR1nwBWxx9co6TOnfxCdnGyKXyHpm3dnRZi6QopwmuEZt0DxZAcxTc4XhSk.

[69] Van Blerkom LM. Role of viruses in human evolution. *American Journal of Physical Anthropology*. 2003; 122(Suppl.): 14-16.

[70] De Puy Kamp M. How marginalized communities in the South are paying the price for 'green energy' in Europe. CNN [Internet]. 2021 Jul 9. Available from: https://www.cnn.com/interactive/2021/07/us/american-south-biomass-energy-invs/.

[71] Loewe L, Hill WG. The population genetics of mutations: Good, bad and indifferent. *Philosophical Transactions of the Royal Society B: Biological Sciences.* 2010 Apr 27; 365(1544): 1153-67.

[72] Noguchi Y. Why N95 masks are still in short supply in the U.S. NPR [Internet]. 2021 Jan 27. Available from https://www.npr.org/sections/health-shots/2021/01/27/960336778/why-n95-masks-are-still-in-short-supply-in-the-u-s.

[73] Mendoza M, Linderman J, Peipert T, Hwang I. Shortages of key material squeezes medical mask manufacturing. PBS [Internet]. 2020 Sep 10. Available from: https://www.pbs.org/wgbh/frontline/article/covid-n95-medical-mask-shortage-manufacturing/.

[74] Lonsdorf K. Millions are out of a job. Yet some employers wonder: why can't i find workers? NPR [Internet]. 2021 Feb 15. Available from: https://www.npr.org/2021/02/15/966376492/millions-are-out-of-a-job-yet-some-employers-wonder-why-cant-i-find-workers.

[75] Nadworny E. 'Losing a generation': Fall college enrollment plummets for 1st-year students. NPR [Internet]. 2020 Dec 17. Available from: https://www.npr.org/2020/12/17/925831720/losing-a-generation-fall-college-enrollment-plummets-for-first-year-students.

[76] Blagg K, Blom E. Evaluating the return on investment in higher education. Urban Institute [Internet]. 2016 Sep. Available from: https://www.urban.org/sites/default/files/publication/99078/evaluating_the_return_on_investment_in_higher_education.pdf.

[77] Chamorro-Premuzic T, Frankiewicz B. 6 reasons why higher education needs to be disrupted. *Harvard Business Review* [Internet]. Available from: https://hbr.org/2019/11/6-reasons-why-higher-education-needs-to-be-disrupted.

[78] Adamy J, Overberg P. The loneliest generation: Americans, more than ever, are aging alone. *The Wall Street Journal* [Internet]. 2018 Dec 11. Available from: https://www.wsj.com/articles/the-loneliest-generation-americans-more-than-ever-are-aging-alone-11544541134.

[79] Zhmud L, Kouprianov A. Ancient Greek *Mathēmata* from a sociological perspective: A quantitative analysis. *The University of Chicago Press Journals*. 2018 Sep; 109(3): 445-72.

[80] UKEssays. Science in everyday life [Internet]. November 2018. Available from: https://www.ukessays.com/essays/philosophy/science-in-everyday-life-philosophy-essay.php?vref=1.

[81] Jones CI. The end of economic growth? Unintended consequences of a declining population. Stanford GSB and NBER [Internet]. 2020 Oct 8. Available from: https://web.stanford.edu/~chadj/emptyplanet.pdf.

[82] YouTube.com. The universe is a bottom-up system: Neil Theise [Internet]. 2017 Aug 1. Available from: https://www.youtube.com/watch?v=LhfN03rtmos.

[83] YouTube.com. We are the universe: Neil Theise [Internet]. 2018 Apr 24. Available from: https://www.youtube.com/watch?v=vBCC3bL9I9I.

[84] Vázquez RJ, Koehler PG, Pereira RM. Comparative quantification of trail-following behavior in pest ants. *Insects*. 2020 Jan; 11(1): 1-9.

[85] Royo JL, Valls J, Acemel RD, Gómez-Marin C, Pascual-Pons M, Lupiañez A, et al. A common copy-number variant within SIRPB1 correlates with human out-of-Africa migration after genetic drift correction. *PLOS One*. 2018 Mar; 13(3): e0193614.

[86] Campbell K. Deep dive: How deurbanization has become more than a trending theory. *Pere* [Internet]. 2020 Nov 2. Available from: https://www.perenews.com/how-deurbanization-has-become-more-than-a-trending-theory/.

[87] Wang D. Why is Peter Thiel pessimistic about technological innovation? Danwang [Internet]. 2014 Sep 10. Available from: https://danwang.co/why-is-peter-thiel-pessimistic-about-technological-innovation/.

[88] Hall CAS, Balogh S, Murphy DJR. What is the minimum EROI that a sustainable society must have? *Energies*. 2009; 2(1): 25-47.

[89] Brook B. The Catch-22 of energy storage. Energy Central [Internet]. 2014 Aug 25. Available from: https://energycentral.com/c/ec/catch-22-energy-storage.

[90] Kearns J. The end of global development as we know it. Engineering for Change [Internet]. 2014 Nov 4. Available from: https://www.engineeringforchange.org/news/the-end-of-global-development-as-we-know-it/.

[91] Roser M. Economic growth. Our Wold in Data [Internet]. 2013. Available from: https://ourworldindata.org/economic-growth.

[92] Kemp L. Studying the demise of historic civilisations can tell us how much risk we face today, says collapse expert Luke Kemp. Worryingly, the signs are worsening. BBC [Internet]. 2019 Feb 18. Available from: https://www.bbc.com/future/article/20190218-are-we-on-the-road-to-civilisation-collapse.

[93] Vakil B, Linton T. Why we're in the midst of a global semiconductor shortage. *Harvard Business Review* [Internet]. 2021 Feb 6. Available from: https://hbr.org/2021/02/why-were-in-the-midst-of-a-global-semiconductor-shortage.

[94] Nelder C. The 21st century population crash. ZD Net [Internet]. 2013 Sep 2. Available from: https://www.zdnet.com/article/the-21st-century-population-crash/.

[95] Worldometer.info. Oil left in the world [Internet]. [Cited 2022 Feb 4]. Available from: https://www.worldometers.info/oil/#oil-consumption.

[96] Syvitski J, Waters CN, Day J, Milliman JD, Summerhayes C, Steffen W, Zalasiewicz J, et al. Extraordinary human energy consumption and resultant geological impacts beginning around 1950 CE initiated the proposed Anthropocene Epoch. *Communications Earth & Environment*. 2020; 1(32): 1-13.

[97] Zubrin R. The Case for Space: How the Revolution in Spaceflight Opens Up a Future of Limitless Possibility. Amherst; 2019.

[98] ShutUp JustFocus. Kardashev's civilization scale analysis: The type of civilization we really are. Medium [Internet]. 2020 May 5. Available from: https://medium.com/swlh/kardashevs-civilization-scale-analysis-the-type-of-civilization-we-really-are-5db77c1616d4.

[99] Wikipedia.org. 2021 Texas power crisis [Internet]. 2022 [updated 2022 Feb 4; cited 2022 Feb 4]. Available from: https://en.wikipedia.org/wiki/2021_Texas_power_crisis.

[100] Wikipedia.org. Colonial Pipeline ransomware attack [Internet]. 2022 [updated 2022 Feb 4; cited 2022 Feb 4]. Available from: https://en.wikipedia.org/wiki/Colonial_Pipeline_cyberattack.

[101] Wikipedia.org. Hernando de Soto Bridge [Internet]. 2022 [updated 2022 Jan 28; cited 2022 Feb 4]. Available from: https://en.wikipedia.org/wiki/Hernando_de_Soto_Bridge.

[102] Kennedy M. Report: U.S. nuclear system relies on outdated technology such as floppy disks. NPR [Internet]. 2016 May 26. Available from: https://www.npr.org/sections/thetwo-way/2016/05/26/479588478/report-u-s-nuclear-system-relies-on-outdated-technology-such-as-floppy-disks.

[103] Chappell B. To be carbon-neutral by 2050, no new oil and coal projects, report says. KCLU [Internet]. 2021 May 18. Available from: https://www.kclu.org/world/2021-05-18/no-new-oil-and-coal-projects-now-to-be-carbon-neutral-by-2050-report-says.

[104] International Energy Agency. Net zero by 2050: A roadmap for the global energy sector [Internet]. 2021 May. Available from: https://iea.blob.core.windows.net/assets/4719e321-6d3d-41a2-bd6b-461ad2f850a8/NetZeroby2050-ARoadmapfortheGlobalEnergySector.pdf.

[105] Cornell P. Energy governance and China's bid for global grid integration. Atlantic Council [Internet]. 2019 May 30. Available from: https://www.atlanticcouncil.org/blogs/energysource/energy-governance-and-china-s-bid-for-global-grid-integration/.

[106] Bloomberg. World's biggest ultra-high voltage line powers up across China. T&D World [Internet]. 2019 Jan 2. Available from https://www.tdworld.com/overhead-transmission/article/20972092/worlds-biggest-ultrahigh-voltage-line-powers-up-across-china.

[107] Materials Today. Novel metamaterial stays cool in the sun [Internet]. 2017 Feb 28. Available from: https://www.materialstoday.com/energy/news/novel-metamaterial-stays-cool-in-the-sun/.

[108] Zhai Y, Ma Y, David SN, Zhao D, Lou R, Tan G, Yang R, et al. Scalable-manufactured randomized glass-polymer hybrid metamaterial for daytime radiative cooling. *Science*. 2017 Feb 9; 355(6329): 1062-66.

[109] Gilster P. Artificial singularity power: A Basis for developing and detecting advanced spacefaring civilizations. Centauri Dreams [Internet]. 2019 Oct 17. Available from: https://www.centauri-dreams.org/2019/10/17/artificial-singularity-power-a-basis-for-developing-and-detecting-advanced-spacefaring-civilizations/.

[110] Nuclear Engineering International. Dutch consortium set up to develop of molten salt reactors [Internet]. 2021 Mar 4. Available from: https://www.neimagazine.com/news/newsdutch-consortium-set-up-to-develop-of-molten-salt-reactors-8566820.

[111] Harsono N. Thorcon, Defense Ministry to cooperate on thorium nuclear reactor. *The Jakarta Post* [Internet]. 2020 Jul 28. Available from:https://www.thejakartapost.com/news/2020/07/28/thorcon-defense-ministry-to-cooperate-on-thorium-nuclear-reactor.html.

[112] Nuclear Engineering International. Aneel and its appeal [Internet]. 2021 Mar 24. Available from: https://www.neimagazine.com/features/featureaneel-and-its-appeal-8621195/.

[113] Wall M. The US Air Force wants to beam solar power to Earth from space (video). Space.com [Internet]. 2021 Apr 25. Available from: https://www.space.com/space-based-solar-power-air-force-sspidr-project.

[114] David L. Space-based solar power getting key test aboard US military's mysterious X-37B space plane. Space [Internet]. 2021 Apr 8. Available from: https://www.space.com/x-37b-space-plane-solar-power-beaming.

[115] Koziol M. Whether cold fusion or low-energy nuclear reactions, U.S. Navy researchers reopen case. IEEE Spectrum [Internet]. 2021 Mar 22. Available from: https://spectrum.ieee.org/tech-talk/energy/nuclear/cold-fusion-or-low-energy-nuclear-reactions-us-navy-researchers-reopen-case.

[116] Office of the Director of National Intelligence. Preliminary assessment: unidentified aerial phenomena [Internet]. 2021 Jun 25. Available from: https://www.dni.gov/files/ODNI/documents/assessments/Prelimary-Assessment-UAP-20210625.pdf.

[117] Wikipedia.org. Space-based solar power [Internet]. 2022 [updated 2022 Jan 13; cited 2022 Feb 4]. Available from: https://en.wikipedia.org/wiki/Space-based_solar_power.

[118] Zafar R. SpaceX could bring starship launch costs down to $10/kg believes Musk. WCCF Tech [Internet]. 2020 May 8. Available from: https://wccftech.com/spacex-launch-costs-down-musk/.

[119] Teh C. China wants to up the ante on the space race with a 'sky ladder' to Mars that can beam humans and cargo up in a capsule. Insider [Internet]. 2021 Jun 25. Available from: https://www.insider.com/china-up-the-ante-space-race-sky-ladder-to-mars-2021-6.

[120] Lang F. China to build a solar power station in space by 2035. Interesting Engineering [Internet]. 2019 Dec 2. Available from: https://interestingengineering.com/china-to-build-a-solar-power-station-in-space-by-2035.

[121] Jones A. China's super heavy rocket to construct space-based solar power station. Space News [Internet]. 2021 Jun 28. Available from: https://spacenews.com/chinas-super-heavy-rocket-to-construct-space-based-solar-power-station/.

[122] Groom N, Bellon T. EV rollout will require huge investments in strained U.S. power grids. Reuters [Internet]. 2021 Mar 5. Available from: https://www.reuters.com/article/us-usa-weather-grids-autos-insight/ev-rollout-will-require-huge-investments-in-strained-u-s-power-grids-idUSKBN2AX18Y.

[123] The Economist Intelligence Unit. Democracy index 2020: In sickness and in health? [Internet]. 2020. Available from: https://www.eiu.com/n/campaigns/democracy-index-2020/?utm_source=economist-daily-chart&utm_medium=anchor&utm_campaign=democracy-index-2020&utm_content=anchor-1.

[124] Wikipedia.org. Social Progress Index [Internet]. 2022 [updated 2022 Jan 11; cited 2022 Feb 4]. Available from: https://en.wikipedia.org/wiki/Social_Progress_Index.

[125] Wikipedia.org. Knowledge Economic Index [Internet]. 2021 [updated 2021 Oct 28; cited 2022 Feb 4]. Available from: https://en.wikipedia.org/wiki/Knowledge_Economic_Index.

[126] Pielke R, Ritchie J. How climate scenarios lost touch with reality. Issues in Science and Technology. 2021 Summer; 37(4): 74-83.

[127] Our World in Data. Years of fossil fuel reserves left [Internet]. 2016. Available from: https://ourworldindata.org/grapher/years-of-fossil-fuel-reserves-left.

[128] Herrington G. Update to limits to growth: comparing the world3 Model with Empirical Data. *Journal of Industrial Ecolog.* 2021; 25: 614-626.

[129] Smith C. MIT predicted society would collapse this century, and we're doing our best to make it happen. BGR [Internet]. 2021 Jul 15. Available from: https://bgr.com/science/mit-predicted-society-would-collapse-this-century-and-were-doing-our-best-to-make-it-happen/.

[130] Lacroix S. Time for a green dictatorship? Philonomist [Internet]. 2020 Nov 26. Available from: https://www.philonomist.com/en/article/time-green-dictatorship?fbclid=IwAR3-2e5AB-sldQAdfYnA9FcqYh8yZlcYlbd3Bpjh3B6qo_FB_Di7KAb3EJ0.

[131] Population Control. 21 reasons we need population stabilization in 2021 [Internet]. 2021 Jan 8. Available from: https://www.populationconnection.org/21-reasons-we-need-population-stabilization-in-2021/.

[132] The Overpopulation Project. Solutions [Internet]. 2020. Available from: https://overpopulation-project.com/solutions/.

[133] Bricker D, Ibbitson J. Empty Planet: The Shock of Global Population Decline. New York; 2019.
[134] Toufexi I. Elon Musk claims population collapse 'potentially the greatest risk to the future of civilization'. Cambridgeshire News [Internet]. 2021 Jul 29. Available from: https://www.cambridge-news.co.uk/news/uk-world-news/elon-musk-claims-population-collapse-21176445.
[135] Friedman BM. The Moral Consequences of Economic Growth. New York; 2005.
[136] Price ME. Entropy and selection: Life as an adaptation for universe replication. Hindawi [Internet]. 2017 Jun 20. Available from: https://www.hindawi.com/journals/complexity/2017/4745379/?fbclid=IwAR1ftF-tM6oalQgO0a3odBUlxqI3Z5N0kT40Ova35JQ7ZyxEtFIo0NknIV0.
[137] Kaiser Science Worldpress. Big Bang Theory and conservation of energy [Internet]. Available from: https://kaiserscience.wordpress.com/astronomy/the-big-bang-theory/big-bang-theory-and-conservation-of-energy/.
[138] Glister P. Artificial singularity power: A basis for developing and detecting advanced spacefaring civilizations. Centauri Dreams [Internet]. 2019 Oct 17. Available from: https://www.centauri-dreams.org/2019/10/17/artificial-singularity-power-a-basis-for-developing-and-detecting-advanced-spacefaring-civilizations/.
[139] Loeb A. Endless creation out of nothing. *Scientific American* [Internet]. 2020 Dec 12. Available from: https://www.scientificamerican.com/article/endless-creation-out-of-nothing/?fbclid=IwAR0Rb0glNDYadM36yIN5HC-JgV-iOuiQxlnR2RbeUUq3lZz8dN2ukBd6-uY.
[140] Holt J. The Big Lab experiment. *Slate* [Internet]. 2004 May 19. Available from: https://slate.com/culture/2004/05/the-creation-of-the-universe.html.
[141] Browne MW. Physicist aims to create a universe, literally. *The New York Times* [Internet]. 1987 Apr 14. Available from: https://www.nytimes.com/1987/04/14/science/physicist-aims-to-create-a-universe-literally.html.
[142] Kim SW. Evolution of cosmological horizons of wormhole cosmology. *General Relativity and Quantum Cosmology*. 2018 Nov 17 (last revised 2019 Jul 20): 1-18.
[143] Jones AZ, Robbins D. *String Theory for Dummies*. Hoboken; 2009.
[144] Rosling H. Factfulness: Ten Reasons We're Wrong About the World and Why Things Are Better Than You Think. New York; 2018.
[145] Roser M, Nagdy M. Optimism and pessimism. Our World in Data [Internet]. 2014. Available from: https://ourworldindata.org/optimism-pessimism.

[146] Johnson G. Idiot Savants and Prime Numbers. *Discover Magazine* [Internet]. 2013 Mar 4. Available from: https://www.discovermagazine.com/mind/idiot-savants-and-prime-numbers.

[147] Ryan J. No, NASA photos are not evidence of fungus growing on Mars, sorry. CNET [Internet]. 2021 May 8. Available from: https://www.cnet.com/news/no-nasa-photos-are-not-evidence-of-fungus-growing-on-mars-sorry/.

[148] Joseph RG, Armstrong R, Wei X, Gibson C, Planchon O, Duvall D, et al. Fungi on Mars? Evidence of growth and behavior from sequential images. *Discovering the Possibility of Life on Mars* [Internet]. 2021 May 1. Available from: https://www.researchgate.net/publication/351252619_Fungi_on_Mars_Evidence_of_Growth_and_Behavior_From_Sequential_Images.

[149] Gilster P. Interstellar communication using microbes: Implications for SETI. Centauri Dreams [Internet]. 2011 Dec 21. Available from: https://www.centauri-dreams.org/2017/12/21/interstellar-communication-using-microbes-implications-for-seti/.

CPSIA information can be obtained
at www.ICGtesting.com
Printed in the USA
JSHW022034190522
26006JS00002B/8